Challenges to the Welfare State

NEW HORIZONS IN SOCIAL POLICY

Series Editors: Patricia Kennett and Misa Izuhara, *University of Bristol, UK*

The New Horizons in Social Policy series captures contemporary issues and debates in social policy and encourages critical, innovative and thought-provoking approaches to understanding and explaining current trends and developments in the field. With its emphasis on original contributions from established and emerging researchers on a diverse range of topics, books in the series are essential reading for keeping up to date with the latest research and developments in the area.

Challenges to the Welfare State

Family and Pension Policies in the Baltic and Nordic Countries

Edited by

Jolanta Aidukaite

Chief Researcher, Institute of Sociology at the Lithuanian Centre for Social Sciences, Lithuania

Sven E. O. Hort

Formerly Professor of Sociology, Linnaeus University, Sweden and Professor of Social Welfare, Seoul National University, South Korea

Stein Kuhnle

Emeritus Professor of Comparative Politics, University of Bergen, Norway and Emeritus Professor, Hertie School, University of Governance, Berlin, Germany

NEW HORIZONS IN SOCIAL POLICY

EE Edward **Elgar**
PUBLISHING

Cheltenham, UK • Northampton, MA, USA

Published by
Edward Elgar Publishing Limited
The Lypiatts
15 Lansdown Road
Cheltenham
Glos GL50 2JA
UK

Edward Elgar Publishing, Inc.
William Pratt House
9 Dewey Court
Northampton
Massachusetts 01060
USA

A catalogue record for this book
is available from the British Library

Library of Congress Control Number: 2021947464

This book is available electronically in the **Elgar**online
Sociology, Social Policy and Education subject collection
http://dx.doi.org/10.4337/9781839106118

MIX
Paper from
responsible sources
FSC
www.fsc.org   FSC® C013604

ISBN 978 1 83910 610 1 (cased)
ISBN 978 1 83910 611 8 (eBook)

Printed and bound by CPI Group (UK) Ltd, Croydon, CR0 4YY

Contents

Contributors

Jolanta Aidukaite (PhD in Sociology from Stockholm University, Sweden) is Chief Researcher at the Institute of Sociology at the Lithuanian Centre for Social Sciences. She has published extensively on the topics of social policy, family policy, housing policy and community mobilisation. Her research has been published in the *Journal of European Social Policy*, *Social Inclusion*, the *Journal of Baltic Studies*, *Communist and Post-Communist Studies*, the *International Journal of Sociology and Social Policy*, *Social Policy & Administration* and *East European Politics*.

Mare Ainsaar (PhD in Social Sciences) is an associate professor and a senior research fellow in Sociology and Social Policy at the Institute of Social Studies, University of Tartu. Her main research interests are related to comparative social policy, comparative family policy, population processes (including migration) and local governments' activities for children and families. She has been project leader for numerous projects, including 'Children and Family Policy of Local Municipality Governments in Estonia', 'Analysis of the Work and Family Responsibilities by non-Estonians', 'Values as Guiding Forces in society', etc. She is also a coordinator of the European Social Survey in Estonia and an author of more than 300 academic publications.

Sunnee Billingsley is Associate Professor of Sociology at Stockholm University. Her current research interests comprise the effects of social stratification, social policy and social change on demographic patterns. Her research has involved both comparative and micro-level analyses of fertility and mortality trends. Her research has been published in *European Sociological Review*, the *Journal of Marriage and Family*, *Social Science & Medicine* and *Social Science Research*, amongst others.

Šarūnas Eirošius is a lecturer at Vilnius University, currently teaching Econometrics and Operational Research at the Faculty of Economics and Business Administration. He holds a PhD in Economics. His research interests and publications are in the field of pension policy, searching for a balance between pensions adequacy and sustainability. He has been involved in several national and international research projects for social security policies and energy sector projects.

Mia Hakovirta is Academy Research Fellow at the Department of Social Research and Senior Research Fellow at the INVEST Flagship Program, University of Turku. Her research has centred on family and child support policies, and the issue of the economic well-being of single-parent families. She has published on post-separation family policies, child support policies, shared care, post-separation fatherhood and child poverty, mostly from comparative perspectives.

Barbara Hobson is Professor Emerita of Sociology at Stockholm University, having held the chair in Sociology with an emphasis on gender. Her scholarship spans a range of research areas, including welfare regimes, citizenship, social movements and diversity. Over the last few years, she has sought to develop dynamic and agency-centred models elaborating Amartya Sen's capability framework and applying them to studies of women's employment and childbearing, work–life balance and marketisation of care/domestic services sustained by low wage-migrant workers. Her most recent work on the capability to aspire and alternative futures engages with the expanding field of the sociology of futures.

Sven E. O. Hort is an emeritus of Linnaeus University, Kalmar and Växjö, Sweden. He is Editor-in-Chief of *Asia Social Work and Policy Review*, published by Wiley. In 2015 he retired from Seoul National University, where he was a professor in Social Welfare at its College of Social Sciences. With two colleagues he is an editor of *Globalizing Welfare: An Evolving Asian–European Dialogue* (Edward Elgar 2019). He has twice been a Fulbright Scholar in the US. A third, enlarged edition of his work *Social Policy, Welfare State and Civil Society in Sweden* (in two volumes) is available (Arkiv 2014). He received his PhD in Sociology from Stockholm University and is an alumni of Lund University, Sweden.

Stein Kuhnle holds a Cand.polit degree (1973) from the University of Bergen. He is Emeritus Professor of Comparative Politics at the University of Bergen, and Emeritus Professor at the Hertie School of Governance, Berlin, where he taught Comparative Social Policy from 2006 until 2014. He directed the Department of Comparative Politics in Bergen for a total of 14 years after becoming a professor in 1982. He has published widely in many languages, including Chinese, within his main field of research on the historical, comparative study of social policy and welfare state development. Amongst his publications are: *Survival of the European Welfare State* (ed., 2000), *The Normative Foundations of the Welfare State: The Nordic Experience* (ed. with N. Kildal, 2005) and *Globalizing Welfare: An Evolving Asian-European Dialogue* (ed. with P. Selle and S. E. O. Hort, 2019).

Kati Kuitto is Senior Researcher at the Finnish Centre for Pensions. Her research focuses on comparative welfare state analysis and the nexus between employment, social policies throughout the life course and the adequacy of pensions. In addition, her current interests cover gender inequalities in employment and pensions. She holds a PhD in Political Science from the University of Greifswald and is one of the principal investigators of the Comparative Welfare Entitlements Dataset project (CWED2).

Susan Kuivalainen is Head of Research at the Finnish Centre for Pensions. She has worked as a research professor at the National Institute for Health and as a professor at the University of Turku. Her research focuses on social security schemes, comparative analyses of the welfare state, the adequacy of pensions and income poverty. She holds a PhD in Social Policy from the University of Turku and is a member of numerous working groups and advisory boards.

Teodoras Medaiskis is a professor at Vilnius University, currently teaching Social Protection Economics at the Faculty of Economics and Business Administration. He has published 25 research papers, mainly on social protection and pension economics issues. A Lithuanian partner in the European Union's TRESS (Training and Reporting on European Social Security) and ASISP (Analytical Support on the Socio-Economic Impact of Social Protection Reforms) initiatives and other projects, in the years 1991–94 he led the work groups on preparation of the first Lithuanian social protection and pension laws.

Gerda Neyer is a political scientist and demographer. She has been Senior Research Fellow at the Linnaeus Center on Social Policy and Family Dynamics in Europe (SPaDE) and Associate Professor at the Department of Sociology, Demography Unit, Stockholm University. Her research lies at the intersection of welfare states, family policies, gender and fertility.

Mikael Nygård, PhD, is Professor of Social Policy at the Åbo Akademi University, Finland. His research interests range from research on societal participation of various groups, such as older adults, youth and people with disabilities, to health-related research and comparative welfare state analysis, with a special focus on family policy reforms.

Livia Sz. Oláh is Associate Professor of Demography (PhD 2001, Stockholm University) at the Department of Sociology at Stockholm University with expertise also in law and political science, comparative welfare state research and gender studies. She has published widely on policy impacts on fertility and partnership dynamics, and the interplay of family patterns and societal and familial gender relations in European societies, in highly ranked international journals such as *Social Forces*, *Population Studies*, *Population and Development Review*, *Demographic Research* and the *Journal of Gender Studies*, and authored a number of book chapters and co-authored others for well-known publishers (Springer, Palgrave Macmillan, Berghahn Books).

Axel West Pedersen is a professor at NOVA (Norwegian Social Research) and the Department of Social Work, Child Welfare and Social Policy at Oslo Metropolitan University. He has a PhD in Political and Social Science from the European University Institute in Florence. His research interests include historical-comparative studies of the development of pension systems, studies of welfare opinion and studies of the consequences of welfare policies for income inequality and income poverty.

Magnus Piirits (PhD student of Economics at the University of Tartu) is an expert at the Foresight Centre at the Parliament of Estonia. He has worked as an analyst at the Praxis think tank, where his research mainly concerned social protection. More specifically, he focused on pension research both in Estonia and in Europe, using quantitative analysis methods. His doctoral paper examines the impact of pension system reforms in Estonia on inequality by applying the microsimulation method.

Olga Rajevska is a researcher at the Scientific Institute of Economics and Management, Faculty of Business, Management and Economics of the University of Latvia. She holds a PhD in Public Administration. Her research interests and publications are in the field of pension policy, social inclusion, social justice, combatting poverty and income inequality, where she has been involved in several national research projects.

Kristina Senkuviene is a PhD student of Sociology at the Lithuanian Centre of Social Sciences. She has written a PhD paper, *Support for Large Families in Lithuania: Challenges and Situation in the Context of the European Union*. Her areas of research, in addition to large families, are family policy and the welfare state.

Mona Sõukand is a master's student at the Institute of Social Studies, University of Tartu. Her academic work has been related to analyses of child-care in Estonia. She is studying media and communication and is an active member of the University of Tartu Students' Society.

Katharina Wesolowski has a PhD in Sociology (2015) and works as a lecturer at Örebro University. Her research interests are family policies and individuals' childbearing decisions, and especially how family policies that support a more gender-equal division of paid and unpaid work might influence the family-formation process of individuals. Her research has been published in

Population, Space and Place, Europe-Asia Studies, the *Journal of Family Issues*, and *Demographic Research*, amongst others.

Preface

This book is the result of long-term (more than ten years) formal and informal cooperation amongst Baltic and Nordic scholars. The idea of this book originated in the project 'Challenges to Welfare State Systems in Lithuania and Sweden', financed by the Research Council of Lithuania (grant no. S-MIP-17-130). The project was led by Jolanta Aidukaite at the Lithuanian Social Research Centre (2017–2020) (currently the Institute of Sociology at the Lithuanian Centre for Social Sciences) and carried out in cooperation with the Department of Sociology, Stockholm University (coordinated by Livia Sz. Oláh) and Linnaeus University (coordinated by Emeritus Professor Sven E. O. Hort).

However, this book is not only the outcome of the aforementioned project. More than half of its chapters were funded by other grants/projects and numerous Nordic and Baltic universities/institutions, thus demonstrating the strong interest in and support for Baltic–Nordic cooperation in social policy. Professor Emeritus Stein Kuhnle kindly accepted an invitation to co-edit the book.

The editors would like to warmly thank all the authors for their enthusiasm and willingness to contribute to the book, and for their time and efforts in developing their chapters.

Annotation of the book

The overarching aim of the book is to demonstrate the dynamics of welfare policies (family support and pension protection) in different socioeconomic settings. It challenges the conventional welfare state research by choosing to compare the most developed welfare states of the Nordic countries with the little-researched welfare states of the three 'young' market-oriented democracies of the Baltic area. By doing so, the book revives 'old' welfare state theories, welfare state models and family policy/gender regimes, and contributes to a better understanding of the complex inequalities that families and individuals are facing in the 21st century.

The comparative analyses of the Baltic and Nordic welfare state systems respond to a number of theoretical and empirical questions that are relevant to contemporary welfare state studies: what is – or should be – the role of private actors (non-profit organisations and commercial firms) in the welfare state? How should the pay-as-you-go principle be combined with the cumulative principle in reforming pension insurance? What kind of family policy measures can best ensure gender equality and a work–life balance and solve the problems of child poverty?

By addressing policy developments in the field of family support and pension protection in these two groups of welfare states, the book contributes to finding, and reflecting upon, innovative solutions to common or similar challenges in European welfare states.

This book is of great interest to social policy scholars, students and policy makers with an interest in the Baltic and Nordic countries, and in family policy and pension protection reforms, and to those with a general interest in the contemporary welfare state studies in Europe.

1. Introduction: Baltic and Nordic countries from a comparative perspective – family policies and pensions in the era of ageing

Jolanta Aidukaite, Sven E. O. Hort and Stein Kuhnle

THE AIM AND SCOPE OF THE BOOK

The aim of this book is to discuss challenges faced by the welfare state systems in contemporary Baltic and Nordic societies. Challenges concern implications of demographic change (due to ageing, migration, de-institutionalisation of the family) for the development and sustainability of comprehensive welfare states, and the challenge of work–life balance, which is also relevant for demographic development, gender equality and child poverty. This volume outlines a number of challenges that are not unique to the Nordic–Baltic area, but which for various reasons may find – or have resulted in – different policy solutions among the countries in the area, and different from other European countries.

The major focus of this volume is on public support for families and pension protection. These two policy domains belong to the core of the social protection systems in both the Nordic and Baltic countries. Moreover, these policy fields concentrate on the most vulnerable periods of the life-course, when dependencies on familial, state and/or market-related arrangements are highest. Family support and pension protection have experienced significant reforms in the Baltic states over the last thirty years, as have the Nordic countries, where ageing of the population, increasing immigration and technological change have led to policy reforms. Furthermore, the Baltic republics thoroughly redesigned their social policies following the transformation of their social order after new-won independence in the early 1990s, sometimes learning from the best practices in the Nordics and, perhaps most prevalent, more restricted European Union (EU) standards partly supported financially by European funds (Aidukaite 2014, 2019; Rajevska 2009; Trumm and

Ainsaar 2009). Now, after almost thirty years of reforms, the book asks the following questions: how do the Baltic and Nordic countries compare as to family
policy and pension protection designs and outcomes? What are the differences
and similarities and what can be learnt from their experience?

There are also historical reasons to focus on Baltic–Nordic/Scandinavian
comparisons (Rimlinger 1971). One rationale is that there were scientific and
political proposals to establish a Balto-Scandinavian federation or union in the
inter-war period, after the Baltic states gained their independence following
World War I (Anderson 1967; Lunden 2019). There was a vision to establish
a geographical-political union of the Baltic and Nordic states. But as a result
of the Hitler–Stalin pact (1939) and the experience of World War II, the Baltic
countries ended up as part of the Soviet Union until their liberation in 1990–91,
and thus the idea of a Baltic–Nordic/Scandinavian union was buried. However,
given the turbulent political history over the last 100 years, it is of interest to
see to what extent the Baltic countries today, as new democracies and market
economies – almost thirty years after secession from the Soviet Union – are
(again) looking towards the Nordic countries and 'the Nordic welfare model'
for inspiration to develop social policies, and also to assess the importance
of the legacy of the Soviet Union. Shortly after independence in 1990–91,
and 13 years before the Baltic states joined the EU, the Nordic–Baltic Eight
was formed, which is a framework within the Nordic Council for cooperation
among the five Nordic countries and the three Baltic states. Perhaps this is
a first step towards reviving the inter-war idea of a closer union. Given that the
Baltic countries are rarely part of comparative studies, and given their diverse
history over the last 100 years, we think that this Nordic–Baltic comparison is,
in any case, of significant academic and political interest.

The overarching aim of the book is to demonstrate the dynamics of welfare
policies (family support and pension protection) in different socioeconomic
settings. It challenges the conventional welfare state research by choosing to
compare the most developed welfare states of the Nordic countries with the
little-researched welfare states of the three 'young' market-oriented democracies of the Baltic area. By doing so, the book revives 'old' welfare state theories, welfare state models and family policy/gender regimes and contributes to
a better understanding of the complex inequalities that families and individuals
are facing in the 21st century. Do existing theoretical frameworks (varieties
of capitalism/welfare, family/gender models, the familialisation/de-familiali-
sation dichotomy, convergence and divergence in welfare state development)
provide appropriate analytical tools to understand the welfare state challenges
and the complex social risks that families and individuals encounter during
their life-course?

The Baltic and Nordic welfare systems encounter a number of challenges
that are typical of the majority of the EU countries: the ageing of the popula-

tion; family de-institutionalisation; increasing migration; a decline in demand for unskilled labour and the consequent rise in unemployment; and techno-logical change, which results in 'flexible work' and short-term contracts, requiring new forms of social security since the established system was based on long-term contracts and job security (Aidukaite et al. 2012; Brady and Young Lee 2014; Hudson and Kühner 2009). In addition, new challenges may come, such as global pandemics; for example, Covid-19 has emerged, which has posed unexpected demands for social policy. In Europe, on the background of these challenges, it has become customary to speak of the welfare state 'crisis'. To address the challenges of the welfare state, policy makers were forced to implement social policy reforms and adapt existing policy structures to the changing conditions. Politicians and social scientists increasingly pose the rhetorical question of whether the European welfare state model, based on the solidarity between generations and classes, is sustainable in this globalised and liberalised world (see, for example, Kvist 2004; Palier and Guillen 2004; Pascall and Manning 2000).

The challenges faced by the Baltic and Nordic welfare systems differ in 'qualitative' terms. The Nordic ones are among the most developed welfare states in the world, characterised by generous and universal pensions and family support systems, high de-commodification (but also by relatively high labour market participation by women) and increasing immigration (Esping-Andersen 1990; Hort 2014; Palme 2016). Meanwhile, the three Baltic states are among the leanest welfare states in Europe, at least when measuring their scope by the level of spending as a proportion of gross domestic product, the generosity of welfare state benefits, the high level of commodification and high rates of outward labour migration (Aidukaite 2019; Aidukaite et al. 2012; Genelyte 2019; Sipavičienė and Stankūnienė 2011). Still, there are important reasons to analyse the Baltic and Nordic welfare systems from a comparative perspective.

The family support systems (maternity, paternity, parental leave, childcare) in the Baltic states share many similarities with the Nordic model, not least as to their design, but also if benefit replacement rates, women's labour market participation rates and maternal employment rates are considered (see Javornik and Kurowska 2017; Chapters 2, 4, 5 in this volume). Therefore, it is important to investigate to what extent and how the similarities and differences in the family support systems of the Baltic and Nordic countries generate differ-ent results in terms of the degree of familialisation/de-familialisation, child poverty, and gender (in)equality. Elements of privatisation have increased in the Nordic countries in the two most recent decades; for example, an increase in private pension insurance (as a supplement to public pensions), the growth of private health insurance and private health services, and the outsourcing of public services to private providers (see Hort 2014; Svallfors and Tyllstrom

2019; Tunberger and Sigle-Rushton 2011). In the Baltic states, the privatisation elements in pension protection, health care, and child and elderly care
services are widespread. Therefore, it is important to investigate and assess
how privatisation of social protection will affect the level of inequality and
poverty in the Baltic and Nordic countries in the long run (see Chapters 10, 11,
12, 13 in this volume).

The comparative analyses of the Baltic and Nordic welfare state systems
respond to a number of theoretical and empirical questions that are relevant
to contemporary welfare state studies: what is – or should be – the role of
private actors in the welfare state (non-profit organisations and commercial
firms)? How should the pay-as-you-go principle be combined with the cumulative principle in reforming pension insurance? What kind of family policy
measures can best ensure gender equality and work–life balance and solve the
problems of child poverty?

By addressing policy developments in the field of family support and
pension protection in these two groups of welfare states, the book contributes
to finding, and reflecting upon, innovative solutions to common or similar
challenges in European welfare states.

The book contributes to the existing literature in two important ways: (1) it
documents the dynamics of family policies and pension protection systems in
two contrasting socioeconomic settings (Baltic and Nordic), and (2) it contributes in particular to a more informed understanding of welfare state policies of
the little-researched Baltic states. These new nation-states have been largely
ignored in broader comparative welfare state research.

STRUCTURE OF THE BOOK

The book is divided into two parts. Part I is devoted to family policy challenges
in the Baltic and Nordic countries. Chapter 2, written by Jolanta Aidukaite,
provides a rigorous comparative overview of the situation in the Baltic and
Nordic countries. Using a familialism/de-familialism dichotomy it shows that
the Nordic family policy model still adheres strongly to its principles of gender
equality and universalism and still produces positive results in this respect
if compared to the Baltic states. The Baltic family model is catching up, but
delivers inconsistent and ambiguous outcomes pointing to the gaps in the
complementarity of social policy. The paid leave policies (maternity, parental,
paternity) in the Baltics are not yet supported by widely available services.
Elderly care is a field that does not receive much attention from the state and
is prescribed by the constitution to be a family obligation. These features
strongly divide the Baltic and Nordic nations in their family policy domain.

In Chapter 3, Livia Sz. Oláh and Gerda Neyer delineate the challenges
faced by Europe's welfare states and the core features of the Swedish family

policies as a way to tackle new social risks. The authors claim that by pursuing a social investment strategy and aligned family policy measures that promote commodification, de-familialisation and the de-gendering of employment and care while also upholding old virtues of the Social Democratic welfare state, such as de-commodification, universalism and social equality, Sweden seems to have met the new challenges quite successfully. The chapter highlights important features of the Swedish example to tackle new social risks, as well as the main lessons regarding the policy challenges ahead.

Chapter 4 by Mia Hakovirta and Mikael Nygård shows that during the 2000s, the Nordic countries continued to invest in early childhood education and care while their parental leave systems became more gender-equal; for instance, through the enhancement of 'daddy quotas'. When it comes to protecting families economically, on the other hand, there has been an incremental erosion of universal child allowances, although some improvements have been made in selective transfers to the most economically vulnerable families. It shows that child poverty rates have climbed in conjunction with the 2008–2009 international financial crisis, most notably in single-parent and immigrant households. This development warrants a discussion of the future family-friendliness of the Nordic family policy model.

In Chapter 5, Katharina Wesolowski, Sunnee Billingsley and Gerda Neyer explore harmonised data on social policies over time to describe how policies support earner-carer and traditional family models in Lithuania and Sweden. The authors highlight areas of convergence and divergence in family policy in these two countries with very different histories.

Chapter 6 further develops the comparative discussion on family policy issues of Lithuania and Sweden. Jolanta Aidukaite and Kristina Senkuviene investigate the challenges that the public family support systems experience in the two countries, and evaluate subjective citizens' opinions and rating of different family policy schemes. It shows that in the 21st century, the family policies that address gender equality, such as parental leave policies, are highly appreciated by the population. However, policies have to be backed up by care services. The low ratings of elderly care and disabled children's support show that in the future, policy makers in both countries have to fulfil increasing demands for care services in order to maintain sustainable family support systems. In Lithuania, the emphasis on means-testing in the family support system does not prove to be a sustainable strategy. Despite the long-lasting tradition in supporting families according to the proven need, the majority of respondents view this as the least adequate policy of support provided by the state.

Chapter 7, written by Mare Ainsaar and Mona Sõukand, explores the evolution of day care in Estonia and the parents' day care fees. The authors use data from special surveys conducted by them in local municipalities in Estonia from

1999–2015. Results show that the contribution of parents varies essentially by different local municipalities and creates huge regional differences in treatment of families with children. It also increases regional inequality.

Part II focuses on pension protection issues in the ageing Baltic and Nordic societies. In Chapter 8, Jolanta Aidukaite, Sven E. O. Hort and Mare Ainsaar review the welfare policy arrangements developed in the Baltic and Nordic countries to address ageing problems. The chapter describes policies directed towards the elderly citizens in different socioeconomic and ideological welfare state settings, reveals older people's objective and subjective economic situation and attitudes towards the state role in ensuring safety. The findings show that after almost thirty years of social policy reforms in the Baltic countries, senior citizens remain in a precarious situation according to both objective and subjective indicators. The analyses show essential existential gaps among younger and older generations, if poverty, age discrimination and income security are considered. The situation, as expected, is more positive in the Nordic countries. However, Finland exhibits similarities with Estonia and Lithuania in terms of overall satisfaction of elderly people with their household income and preference for stronger support from the government. This is explained by the lower availability of long-term care services in Finland, and especially in the three Baltic states, and an emphasis on familial care.

In Chapter 9, Kati Kuitto and Susan Kuivalainen explore the case of Finland in more depth. They discuss how family-leave-related career breaks relate to gender inequalities in employment and pensions in Finland. While being considered as one of the most gender-equal countries in the world, the gender gap in earnings and pensions is still a considerable matter in Finland. Career breaks related to parenting are one of the reasons for the persisting gap: although the Finnish family leave scheme offers gender-neutral possibilities for both mothers and fathers to stay at home for child-rearing, in practice over 90 per cent of all parenting leave days are still taken by the mothers. The home care allowance, which is available until the child's third birthday, offers an incentive for long leaves from the labour market. This results in comparatively long career breaks, which, in turn, negatively affect women's earnings during the life-course and, eventually, their pension accumulation, too.

In Chapter 10, Axel West Pedersen compares the nature of minimum protection schemes for old-age pensioners in Denmark, Norway and Sweden. Variation and developments in the overall generosity of minimum protection provided through the pension system proper and other relevant instruments are assessed. The interaction between minimum protection and the earnings-related components of the respective systems are also assessed with a view to the implications for distributive outcomes and labour market incentives.

In Chapter 11, Olga Rajevska investigates the risk management of the pension systems in the three Baltic states. Pension systems are mechanisms of insurance against certain risks associated with old age: risk of longevity, risk of poverty and social exclusion, risk of low interest rates in funded schemes, risk of devaluation of savings, risk of a drop in living standards, risk of poor health, etc. Some of the risks are personal; others are public or corporate.

In Chapter 12, Teodoras Medaiskis and Šarūnas Eirošius compare the Lithuanian and Swedish pension systems from the point of view of their design and performance. The Swedish income, premium and guaranteed old-age pensions system is compared with the analogous Lithuanian system of the 'first' and 'second' pillars and 'social' pensions. The main features of the systems are discussed, and the performance of the systems, mainly from the point of view of adequacy, is compared. The differences in the systems' design and performance are identified, and the possible reasons for these differences are examined. Special attention is paid to the differences in financing and the approach to the definition of benefits. The Lithuanian pension points approach is compared to the Swedish Notional Defined Contribution (NDC) approach. Each system is analysed, and the relevance of transforming the Lithuanian first-pillar pensions into an NDC system is examined.

In Chapter 13, Magnus Piirits focuses on the case of Estonia. The chapter aims to assess the impact of pension reforms on retirees' income inequalities between 2017 and 2100. The proposed individual-level population microsimulation model is used to simulate pensions in all three pillars (pay-as-you-go, mandatory funded and voluntary funded schemes). Although all three pillars are linked to wages in a large scale, the results of the microsimulation model show that inequality of pensions rises slowly. The adopted pension reforms at the end of 2018 (linking retirement age to life expectancy, a decrease of the wage part in pay-as-you-go) do not change the inequality significantly, and rather increase it. The pension reforms are seen as needed from the sustainability point of view because without the reforms the pay-as-you-go scheme will be in deficit, at least until 2050.

In the last chapter, Barbara Hobson, using the metaphor of stretching the canvas, aims to take the conversation on comparative welfare states further by focusing on the conceptual and theoretical challenges that emerged from this book. In comparing Nordic and Baltic countries, she underscores both the hybrid features of these welfare states as well as the commonalities across them. Beyond revealing the shortcomings of typologies that assume coherence in policy frameworks and path dependencies, she argues for a dynamic agency-centred framework that allows conceptual space for welfare state changes and their effects on diverse groups.

EPILOGUE

In comparative terms, counter-posing Baltic and Nordic welfare states has never been done to such an extent before as in this volume. Analytically the book highlights two key welfare policy areas (family policy and pension insurance), and at a time when both the traditional Western and the post-socialist welfare states were undergoing tremendous transformations – in both cases towards more market conformity, 'new public management' and privatisation. What can we learn from the comparative analysis of the family policies and pension protection in the Baltic and Nordic countries? The answer is clear. The state remains the most important agent in providing financial security and empowerment services for families and individuals experiencing social risks. Familialisation and/or marketisation has not proven to guarantee the well-being of the most vulnerable groups of the population (Aidukaite et al. 2021, forthcoming; Kuhnle et al. 2019).

REFERENCES

Aidukaite, J. (2019), 'The welfare systems of the Baltic states following the recent financial crisis of 2008/2010: expansion or retrenchment?', *Journal of Baltic Studies*, 50 (1), 39–58.

Aidukaite, J. (2014), 'Transformation of the welfare state in Lithuania: towards globalization and Europeanization', *Communist and Post-Communist Studies*, 47 (1), 59–69.

Aidukaite, J., M. Ainsaar and S. E. O. Hort (2021, forthcoming), 'Current trends in social welfare policies towards the older people in the Baltic and Nordic countries: an exploratory study', *Journal of Baltic Studies*.

Aidukaite, J., N. Bogdanova and A. Guogis (2012), *Gerovės valstybės raida Lietuvoje: mitas ar realybė?* Vilnius: Lietuvos socialinių tyrimų centras.

Anderson, E. (1967), 'Toward the Baltic union, 1927–1934', *Lituanus: Lithuanian Quarterly Journal of Arts and Sciences*, 13(1), accessed at www.lituanus.org/1967/67_1_01Anderson.html.

Brady, D., and H. Young Lee (2014), 'The rise and fall of government spending in affluent democracies, 1971–2008', *Journal of European Social Policy*, 24 (1), 56–79.

Esping-Andersen, G. (1990), *The Three Worlds of Welfare Capitalism*, Cambridge: Polity Press.

Genelyte, I. (2019), '(In)equality of life: Lithuanian labor migration to Sweden during the economic crisis and its aftermath, 2008–2013', *Journal of Baltic Studies*, 50 (1), 79–104.

Hort, S. E. O. (2014), *Social Policy, Welfare State and Civil Society in Sweden*, Volume I and II, Lund: Arkiv.

Hudson, J., and S. Kühner (2009), 'Towards productive welfare? A comparative analysis of 23 countries', *Journal of European Social Policy*, 19 (1), 34–46.

Javornik, J., and A. Kurowska (2017), 'Work and care opportunities under different parental leave systems: gender and class inequalities in Northern Europe', *Social Policy Administration*, 51 (4), 617–637.

Kuhnle, S., P. Selle and S. E. O. Hort (eds) (2019), *Globalizing Welfare: An Evolving Asian–European Dialogue*, Cheltenham, UK and Northampton, MA, USA: Edward Elgar Publishing.

Kvist, J. (2004), 'Does EU enlargement start a race to the bottom? Strategic interaction among EU member states in social policy', *Journal of European Social Policy*, 14 (3), 301–318.

Lunden, T. (2019), 'The dream of a Balto-Scandian federation: Sweden and the independent Baltic states 1918–1940 in geography and politics', *Baltic Worlds*, 2, 20–28.

Palier, B., and A. M. Guillen (2004), 'Introduction: does Europe matter? Accession to EU and social policy developments in recent and new member states', *Journal of European Social Policy*, 14 (3), 203–211.

Palme, J. (2016), 'The Swedish welfare state system: with special reference to inequality and the redistribution paradox', in Christian Aspalter (ed.), *The Routledge International Handbook to Welfare State Systems*, London: Routledge, pp. 203–215.

Pascall, G., and N. Manning (2000), 'Gender and social policy: comparing welfare states in Central and Eastern Europe and the former Soviet Union', *Journal of European Social Policy*, 10 (3), 240–266.

Rajevska, F. (2009), 'The welfare system in Latvia after renewing independence', in K. Schubert, S. Hegelich and U. Bazant (eds), *The Handbook of European Welfare Systems*, London: Routledge, pp. 328–343.

Rimlinger, G. (1971), *Welfare Policy and Industrialization in Europe, America, and Russia*, New York, NY: Wiley.

Sipavičienė, A., and V. Stankūnienė (2011), 'Lietuvos gyventojų (e)migracijos dvidešimtmetis: tarp laisvės rinktis ir išgyvenimo strategijos', *Filosofija. Sociologija*, 22 (4), 323–333.

Svallfors, S., and A. Tyllstrom (2019), 'Resilient privatization: the puzzling case of for-profit welfare providers in Sweden', *Socio-Economic Review*, 17 (3), 745–765.

Trumm, A., and M. Ainsaar (2009), 'The welfare system of Estonia: past, present and future', in K. Schubert, S. Hegelich and U. Bazant (eds), *The Handbook of European Welfare Systems*, London: Routledge, pp. 153–171.

Tunberger, P., and W. Sigle-Rushton (2011), 'Continuity and change in Swedish family policy reforms', *Journal of European Social Policy*, 21 (3), 225–237.

PART I

Perspectives on family policy

2. Family support systems in the Baltic and Nordic countries: an explorative overview

Jolanta Aidukaite

INTRODUCTION

This chapter looks very closely at differences and similarities in family support arrangements among the Baltic and Nordic countries. This is important for at least two reasons: First, family support systems have experienced significant reforms in the Baltic states over the last 30 years (Aidukaite 2006; Ainsaar 2019), as well as in the Nordic countries (Grødem 2014, 2017), where ageing of the population, increasing migration and family deinstitutionalisation have led to policy reforms. Second, the Baltic states reformed their family support systems by copying and learning from the Nordic ones (Aidukaite 2004; Trumm and Ainsaar 2009). However, until today, after 30 years of reforms, there are very few studies that review how Baltic and Nordic countries compare to each other. A previous study (Javornik and Kurowska 2017) showed that there is a great variation within and between the Baltic and Nordic cluster in their parental leave policies and how they create opportunities for equal parental involvement and employment. This chapter seeks to further contribute to the debate on the Baltic and Nordic comparison. It aims to document public policies directed towards families in different socioeconomic and ideological welfare state settings.

The study is guided by two empirical questions: How do Baltic and Nordic countries compare to each other? What are the differences and similarities, and what could be learned from them? The focus is on support to families with children. Specifically, it looks into work–family reconciliation policies (parental leave policies, childcare services) and financial support policies (cash benefits, tax allowances). These policies are the most important for increasing female labour force participation, improving reconciliation in work–life balance, increasing gender equality in childcare and reducing child poverty (see Hobson 2018; Korpi 2000; Nieuwenhius et al. 2019; Yerkes and

Javornik 2018). Moreover, a few elements (expenses of long-term care and the state's constitutionally imposed familial obligations) of elderly support are reviewed too, as they are becoming increasingly important in the era of ageing. While systematically comparing family support policies among Nordic and Baltic countries, we look for similarities and differences not only between two clusters – Baltic and Nordic – but also within each cluster.

For this study, the latest comparative Organisation for Economic Co-operation and Development (OECD) data on family policies are being used. Additionally, the Eurostat data are occasionally employed when the OECD data are incomplete. To illustrate differences and similarities in family support systems, Saraceno's (2017) typology, based on the familialisation–defamilialisation dichotomy, is being applied in this study, though not systematically. It is used to illustrate major differences among Baltic and Nordic countries. Additionally, the outcome indicators are examined, such as maternal employment, child poverty, gender pay and employment gap to grasp a broader picture of family support system performance in the Baltic and Nordic countries from a comparative perspective.

This chapter is arranged as follows: First, a theoretical background is discussed, followed by an examination of major features of the Nordic and Baltic family policies. Then, the analysis of the family support systems is carried out based on policy analysis and statistical data. Finally, concluding remarks are offered.

THEORETICAL BACKGROUND: FAMILIALISATION–DEFAMILIALISATION CONTINUUM

Family policy is understood as a broad field of social policy; it refers to government provisions (benefits and services) that contribute to family wellbeing, including health care, education and housing policy (Hobson 2018; Wendt et al. 2011; Wennemo 1994). Provisions of care services and tax benefits and the transfer of benefits to families with children directly affect their immediate living conditions and possibilities, especially for mothers to take part in employment and social life. This study utilises the terms 'family support system' and 'support system for families with children'. By the latter we mean work–family reconciliation policies and financial support policies. It has been agreed in the scientific literature that reconciliation policies consist of policies facilitating parental employment and carer opportunities, usually for mothers, as well as gender equality within the family, as noted. These include maternity leave, parental leave, paternity leave policies and childcare services. Financial support policies for families with children consist of tax deductions and various benefits for such families (see Esping-Andersen 2009; Javornik 2014; Korpi 2000; Lohmann and Zagel 2016; Nieuwenhius et al. 2019; Yerkes and

Javornik 2018). By the family support system, we mean not only the support systems for families with children, but also elderly care services and other provisions reducing the family's burden to take care of its dependent elderly.

Over recent years, researchers have developed typologies of familialisation/defamilialisation to understand differences in family support systems across countries and/or to measure variations at the policy level, as both familialising and defamilialising policies can coexist in a single country (see Esping-Andersen 2009; Leitner 2003; Lohmann and Zagel 2016; Saraceno 2017; Yin-Nei Cho 2014). It has been widely agreed that well-developed and widely available public childcare services (or those provided by the market or voluntary sector), as well as generous paid maternity, parental and paternity leaves, with a strong attachment to the labour market, ensure defamilialisation. Flat-rate cash payments that support family care at home and underdeveloped childcare services have familialising effects. The paid paternity leave, reserved for the exclusive use of fathers, clearly has defamilialising effects as it promotes gender equality in child-caring responsibilities and equal division of unpaid work at home (Leitner 2003; Lohmann and Zagel 2016; Yin-Nei Cho 2014).

Concepts of familialisation and defamilialisation allow the capture of variations in familialism–defamilialism among different countries and also within a country in different family policy domains. As far as is known to the author, there have not been any previous studies that attempted to analyse the differences and similarities in family support systems in the Nordic and Baltic countries through the defamilialism–familialism dichotomy. There are many useful familialisation–defamilialisation typologies (see, for example, Leitner 2003; Lohmann and Zagel 2016; Yin-Nei Cho 2014). For this study, we stick to Saraceno's (2017) typology, as it synthesises many previous ones. It looks into the public provisions, and the state's and the market's roles in providing services, and also how, by law, the state prescribes the care and/or financial responsibilities along gender and intergenerational lines. In this chapter, the ambition is to not only look into family and care support provisions for families with small children, but also to look at how the constitutions of the Baltic and Nordic countries prescribe elderly care and financial responsibilities to families. Saraceno's (2017) typology is particularly useful in this respect, as it is designed to capture family support system arrangements, including elderly care. Saraceno delineated five types/patterns of familialism/defamilialism: familialism by default, prescribed familialism, supported familialism, supported defamilialisation through the market and defamilialisation through public provision.

According to Saraceno (2017), familialism by default, also defined as unsupported familialism, happens when there are no, or very limited, publicly provided services for family care (childcare and elderly care) and/or financial support for needy family members. Namely, it means that state support for families, whether it is services or financial provisions, is very limited. Familialism by default can translate into defamilialisation through the market when individuals and families use their own private resources to buy market care or other services. By 'other services', Saraceno means education services, and health and old age insurances that are not provided by public policies.

Prescribed familialism happens when civil law imposes care responsibilities and/or financial obligations within the family.

Supported familialism is found when the state supports families through direct or indirect (via taxation) financial transfers to help them uphold their financial and/or caring responsibilities.

There is a disagreement among social policy scholars whether defamilialisation occurs only via public provisions and/or via market-provided services too. For instance, Lohmann and Zagel (2016) claim that only public policies can be considered as defamilialising. Others (Esping-Andersen 2009; Korpi 2000; Leitner 2003) state that defamilialisation can occur either through public or market provisions. Saraceno (2017) joins the latter group, distinguishing between two types of defamilialisation: supported through the market and/or through public provision. However, in both cases the state plays a vital role in funding services.

Supported defamilialisation through the market occurs when the state provides income transfers (cash benefits or tax deductions) to families to help them buy services on the market, or when the state (or local government) outsources public money to fund the provision of services via the market instead of providing them directly (Saraceno 2017).

Defamilialisation through public provision appears when the state supports the individualisation of social rights offering generous and universal entitlements to public services, granting at least minimal protection in all social risks, and providing work–family reconciliation policies that decrease a family's burden of responsibilities and dependencies for care. The care services are widely available and publicly administered and financed by the state or local governments. In each country one can find a mix of these five types/patterns. However, some patterns may prevail over each other (Saraceno 2017).

For the purpose of this study, it is particularly useful to apply Saraceno's typology as it allows for the coexistence of familialism and defamilialism at the same time. This is especially helpful for analysing countries that are still in flux, such as the three Baltic states. Previous studies (Aidukaite 2006, 2016, 2019; Ainsaar 2019) revealed that family policies in Estonia, Latvia and Lithuania have undergone numerous reforms since the 1990s. Many changes were implemented over the 30-year period, and there were no coherent political views, at least in Lithuania, on how family policy should be reformed and which direction it should take.

It has to be stated that the familialisation/defamilialisation typologies are ideal types and do not exist in a pure form in real life. Their constellations can change over time, and the mix of different types can coexist within one country. Therefore, this study does not seek to systematically apply the typology, more so to better illustrate and understand differences and similarities among Baltic and Nordic countries.

Before moving into the analysis of family support policies in the Nordic and Baltic countries from a comparative perspective, major features of 'Nordic' and 'Baltic' family policy will be presented.

FAMILY POLICY FEATURES OF THE NORDIC AND BALTIC COUNTRIES

Family Policy Features of the 'Nordic Model'

Family policies in the Nordic countries have developed consistently over time, placing great importance on gender equality and individualism and putting emphasis on providing public services instead of cash benefits (Grødem 2017; Leitner 2003). The Nordic family policies, with some variations, are also characterised by universal child allowances, weak pronatalism, the relatively good economic position of single mothers, income equality among families with children and a high level of female income from paid work (Hiilamo 2002a, 2002b).

Hence, the Nordic model exhibits a high degree of defamilialism, with well-developed public services for children and the elderly. Gender equality has been a cornerstone of the family policy in the Nordic countries. In support of gender equality, the Nordic nations developed work–family reconciliation policies to facilitate female labour force participation and ensure gender equality within a family by incentivising fathers to take parental leave. However, recent literature (Grødem 2017; Tunberger and Sigle-Rushton 2011) suggests that Swedish (and also Norwegian) family policy models started to show signs of re-familialisation. Cash benefits for home care have become available, providing more choices for families to arrange their childcare responsibilities in a more nuanced way. However, they became predominantly used by migrant families. Other class and ethnic divisions began to appear in family policy. A recent study (Ma et al. 2019) showed that better-educated fathers, those living in metropolitan areas and surrounding suburbs, as well as Swedish-born fathers, were using parental leave more than young fathers, low-income earners and foreign-born fathers. In Sweden, recently introduced compensation for private childcare increased inequalities in childcare as the compensation was mainly used by higher-income families. Yet, the marketisation of childcare services increased divisions between Swedish- and foreign-born children, as private childcare services are predominantly used by Swedish-born parents. Immigrant parents have been less likely to have their children in private childcare arrangements (Sainsbury 2018). The evidence suggests that Nordic countries might be deviating from the 'defamiliarisation by public provisions' model, as marketisation of public services is increasing (Therborn 2017) and some forms of re-familiarisation have appeared (Estevez-Ave and Hobson 2015). This makes it even more interesting to explore family policy arrangements through the familialisation–defamilialisation dichotomy.

To sum up, the family policy model of the Nordic countries has been experiencing transformations; it is especially failing to integrate immigrants into established family policy practices and norms. The ageing of the population and lack of care workers are transforming elderly care services (see Kalliomaa-Puha and Kangas 2018; Kvist 2018; Schon and Heap 2018). Outsourcing of elderly care to private providers compromises the quality of care (Estevez-Ave and Hobson 2015). However, it is still the most defamilialising family policy model in the world. The most distinguished feature of the family support system is its emphasis on gender equality and commitment to providing services instead of cash benefits for child and elderly care.

Family Policy Features of the 'Baltic Model'

Family policies in the Baltic countries have undergone dramatic reconfigurations over the last 30 years, especially in the earliest part of the 1990s, right after the collapse of the communist regimes (Aidukaite 2006, 2019; Ainsaar 2000, 2019). The Baltic states have gone through many reforms that have been described by a number of studies (see, for example, Aidukaite 2006; Javornik 2014; Rajevska and Romanovska 2016; Stankūnienė 2001). Estonia and Latvia have been more consistent in the development of their family policies since the 1990s compared to Lithuania. They developed universal family support systems, providing benefits to every child irrespective of its social background, while at the same time benefiting those active in the labour market by providing earnings-related benefits. The Lithuanian family policy has been developed rather inconsistently. The means-tested benefits have been an important part of the financial support for families in Lithuania, together with earnings-related benefits. In all three Baltic states, the emphasis was placed on financial support, while services have not been so well developed (Aidukaite 2006, 2016). The general reforms' paths have been observed from defamilialism (the Soviet system supported maternal employment through well-developed childcare services) to familialism (the period from 1990 to 1996 saw a massive decline in childcare services); and from familialism to defamilialism again (the period from 1997 and onwards when emphasis was again placed on policies encouraging a mother's employment), with, however, some coexistence (or elements) of familialism at the same time (Aidukaite 2016).

Nevertheless, the three Baltic states have developed different types of familialism/defamilialism. Javornik (2014), focusing on parental leave and childcare policies (from birth to mandatory schooling age), attributed Lithuanian systems as supporting defamilialism as states seek to incentivise women's continuous employment and active fatherhood through parental and paternity leave policies and available public childcare. In Estonia, the state appeared to support explicit familialism, with emphasis on familial childcare and gendered parenting. The Latvian system was recognised as maintaining implicit familialism, as the state leaves parents without public support.

To sum up, family support systems in the Baltic states can be characterised by different types of familialism and defamilialism, and inconsistent development since 1990, at least in Lithuania. Services in all three Baltic states are less developed than income transfers.

ANALYSIS OF PUBLIC SPENDING ON FAMILY BENEFITS

Public spending on welfare programs is an important indicator of the state's commitment to ensure an adequate safety net for its population. Therefore, we start our analysis by reviewing public spending on family support. The OECD data offer the opportunity to review public spending on the family in three categories: child-related cash transfers to families with children, public spending on services for families with children, and financial support for families provided through the tax system. As expected, the Nordic countries spend remarkably more on support for families (see Figure 2.1). The OECD average is about 2.4 per cent of gross domestic product (GDP) being spent on family benefits, while the Nordic countries exceed 3 per cent, making them the highest spenders in the world.

However, if we examine spending according to three categories, the Nordic countries are not necessarily the leaders when it comes to spending on cash transfers. Estonia's spending on cash transfers for families with children (2.01 per cent of GDP) is not only higher than the OECD-33 (1.23 per cent GDP) average, but also higher than any other Nordic country (that ranges from 1.02 in Iceland to 1.41 per cent in Finland) when compared. Estonia is a small country with a population of only about 1.5 million. This shows the state's commitment in Estonia to support families with children. However, support directed to services in Estonia (0.8 per cent) is lower compared to the OECD-33 average (0.94 per cent) and negligible if compared to any other Nordic country. The situation in Lithuania is worse; it spends only 0.8 per cent of its GDP on cash and 0.95 per cent on services. Latvia is in the middle if

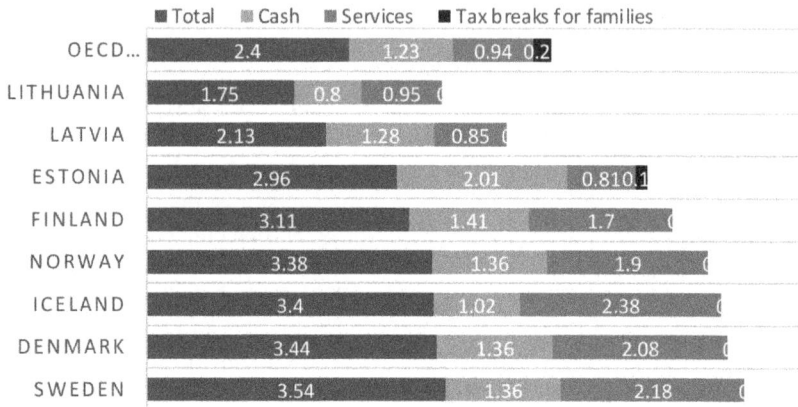

Source: OECD Family Database.

*Figure 2.1   Public spending on family benefits in cash, services and tax
measures, in per cent of GDP, 2015 and latest available*

compared to Estonia and Lithuania, with 1.28 per cent spending on cash and
0.85 per cent on services. Obviously, the three Baltic states spend more on cash
benefits than on services, especially Estonia and Latvia. In the Nordic countries, the opposite is true. The spending on services for families with children
is almost twice as large than on cash in Denmark (2.08 per cent), Iceland (2.38
per cent) and Sweden (2.18 per cent). Finland, however, displays more equal
spending on cash (1.4 per cent) and services (1.7 per cent). There is no support
provided to families with children via taxation in the Nordic countries. The
data for the three Baltic states are incomplete; however, all three Baltic states
provided support via taxation to families with children in 2015, for which the
latest OECD data are available. At present, Estonia's support for families with
children is via taxation (EU 2016a). The same is true for Latvia (for details,
see EU 2016b). Lithuania abolished support for families via taxation in 2018.
Thus, it became more like the Nordic model.

At first glance, it can be said that the Nordic welfare model still holds its
major features. One of the major features of the Nordic welfare model, as
indicated in the previous sections, is a heavy reliance on services. The public
spending patterns on family benefits strongly confirm it. If we try to place the
Nordic nations into Saraceno's typology, it is clear that supported defamilialisation through public provisions prevails in Sweden, Denmark, Iceland and
Norway. These countries spend heavily on services. The spending patterns
in Finland are more ambiguous, and we can claim that both defamilialisation
and familialisation might prevail at the same time. Estonia's spending patterns

allow us to claim that supported familialism can prevail as the state's spending is heavily concentrated on cash, and little on services. Latvian data suggest that two options can be either familialism by default or defamilialism via the market as the state provides relatively little support for families with children, or supported familialism as the government's support is concentrated on cash benefits. The Lithuanian situation is similar to the Latvian as spending on family benefits and services is relatively small. Thus, based only on spending information, we cannot draw a precise picture for Latvia and Lithuania. Further observations on family support design are needed, which we explore in the subsequent sections.

EVALUATION OF WORK–FAMILY RECONCILIATION POLICIES

In this section, we examine work–family reconciliation policies, which include parental insurance (maternity, parental, paternity leaves and home-care leave) and childcare services. These are policies for the youngest children, and they are most important for the Nordic welfare state and central for the analysis of the familialisation–defamilialisation dichotomy (Grødem 2014; Sainsbury 2018). The parental insurance will be analysed according to the generosity of entitlement, take-up and statutory replacement rate. The childcare services are assessed by the share of children attending them.

Parental Insurance

The OECD Family Database provides data on entitlements to paid maternity, parental and paternity leaves as well as home-care leave (which might not be paid, but is employment-protected) that can be used by the mother or father until the child is 2 or 3 years old. In all countries analysed, the duration and average replacement rates are quite generous. However, the three Baltic states offer a more generous paid maternity leave in length of weeks and average replacement than the Nordic countries, especially Estonia and Lithuania (see Table 2.1). The duration in Estonia is 20 weeks, in Lithuania 18 weeks, with the average replacement rate in both countries amounting to 100 per cent. The Nordic countries offer a shorter and less generous maternity leave. The shortest maternity leave is found in Iceland, Sweden and Norway – only 13 weeks. The highest average replacement is provided by Norway (94.2 per cent), the lowest by Denmark (53.6 per cent) and Iceland (68.2 per cent). In between, we find Sweden (77.6 per cent) and Finland (74.4 per cent).

On average across OECD countries, mothers are entitled to 18 weeks of paid maternity leave with about 77 per cent of previous earnings (see Table 2.1).

Table 2.1   *Generosity of maternity insurance, 2018*

	Generosity of entitlement (length in weeks)	Average payment rate (per cent)**	Full-rate equivalent (weeks)
Estonia	20	100	20
Latvia	16	80	12.8
Lithuania	18	100	18
Denmark	18	53.6	9.5
Iceland	13	68.2	6.9
Finland	17.5	74.4	13
Norway	13	94.2	12.2
Sweden	12.9	77.6	10
OECD average	18.1	76.8* (2016)	-
EU average	21.1	85* (2016)	-

Source: OECD data.
* Statutory replacement rate, 100 per cent of average earnings (per cent)
** The 'average payment rate' refers the proportion of previous earnings replaced by the benefit over the length of the paid leave entitlement for a person earning 100 per cent of average national (2015) earnings. If this covers more than one period of leave at two different payment rates, then a weighted average is calculated based on the length of each period. In most countries benefits are calculated on the basis of gross earnings, with the 'payment rates' shown reflecting the proportion of gross earnings replaced by the benefit.

Parental and home-care leave payment rates tend to be lower than those for maternity leave (OECD 2019). The eligibility and generosity of paid parental leave and home-care leave varies considerably across Baltic and Nordic countries (see Table 2.2). If we examine paid parental leave, Lithuania is closest to the ideal defamilialisation model, as it offers very generous (average replacement 100 per cent) parental leave for one year (44 weeks). The most familialising parental leave can be found in Finland and Estonia, as both countries offer very long leaves (143 and 146 weeks, respectively) at a low replacement rate (19.1 per cent and 44.1 per cent, respectively). The shortest parental leave is found in Iceland (13 weeks) with the replacement up to almost 60 per cent.

Slightly lower replacement rates can be found in Denmark (53 per cent) and Sweden (about 57 per cent), with the length of weeks 32 and 42.9 respectively. Norway and Latvia offer 78 weeks of parental leave at average replacement rates of about 40 per cent and about 50 per cent accordingly.

Father-specific leaves are usually better paid than parental leaves across OECD countries, especially if they are short. If father-specific leave lasts longer, the payment rate tends to fall (OECD 2019). The data on father-specific leaves are summarised in Table 2.3. By 'father-specific leave' we mean paternity leave (paid leave for employed fathers that can be taken simultaneously together with a mother who is on maternity or paternity leave) and/or paid

Table 2.2   *Paid parental and home-care leave available to mothers, 2018*

	Length (weeks)	Take-up: number of users/recipients per 100 live births, 2016		Average payment rate (per cent)**	Full-rate equivalent (weeks)	Male share of recipients (per cent), 2016
		Women	Men			
Estonia	146	204.3	18.6	44.1	64.4	8.4
Latvia	78			49.8	38.8	Not available
Lithuania	44	106.2	29.3	100	44	21.6
Denmark	32	134.4	49.3	53	17	26.8
Iceland	13	158.9	131	59.7	8.9	45.2
Finland	143.5	145.8	50.9	19.1	27.4	25.9
Norway	78	149.1	96.1	39.4	30.8	39.2
Sweden	42.9	380	314.1	57.4	24.6	45.3
OECD average	35.8	118.2	43.4	47.9* (2016)	43.7	18
EU average	43.7	-	-	49.1* (2016)	35.8	-

Source: OECD data.
* Statutory replacement rate, 100 per cent of average earnings (per cent)
** The 'average payment rate' refers the proportion of previous earnings replaced by the benefit over the length of the paid leave entitlement for a person earning 100 per cent of average national (2015) earnings.

parental leave reserved specifically for the father, which cannot be transferred to the mother or taken simultaneously with a mother who is on parental leave. Only two Nordic countries (Iceland and Norway) have no paternity leave. However, both have generous parental leave reserved for the father, which is longest in Iceland (13 weeks), paid at almost 68 per cent of the average payment rate. Norway has 10 weeks of father-specific parental leave, paid at almost a 94 per cent replacement rate. All other countries have paternity leave ranging from 1.4 weeks in Sweden and Latvia, to two weeks in Estonia and Denmark, to three weeks in Finland; the longest and most generous paternity leave is in Lithuania, lasting for four weeks. The most generous paternity leaves can be found in the Baltic states, paid at a 100 per cent average replacement rate in Lithuania and Estonia, and 80 per cent in Latvia. In the Nordic block, the generosity is a bit lower: from 53 per cent in Denmark and more than 75 per cent in Sweden.

The reserved parental leave for the father exists in Sweden, Finland, Iceland and Norway, as noted. In Finland, it is up to six weeks, paid at the 62.9 per cent

Table 2.3   *Generosity of father-specific leaves, 2018*

	Paternity leave (length in weeks)	Take-up: number of users/ recipients per 100 live births, 2016****	The average payment rate across paid paternity and father-specific leave for an individual on national average**	Paid parental and home-care leave reserved for father
Estonia	2	48.9	100	0
Latvia	1.4	-	80	0
Lithuania	4	53.2	100	0
Denmark	2	73.3	53	0
Iceland	0	-	68.2***	13
Finland	3	77.5	62.9***	6
Norway	0	-	94.2***	10
Sweden	1.4	75.3	75.7	12.9
OECD average	1.4	-	68.8* (2016)	6.7
EU average	1.7	-	72.0* (2016)	4.5

Source: OECD data.
* Statutory replacement rate, 100 per cent of average earnings (per cent)
**The 'average payment rate' refers the proportion of previous earnings replaced by the benefit over the length of the paid leave entitlement for a person earning 100 per cent of average national (2018) earnings
*** Average payment rate for the paid parental leave and/or home-care leave reserved for father
**** Recipients/users of publicly administered paternity leave benefits or publicly administered paid paternity leave per 100 live births, 2016

average replacement rate. In Sweden, it is up to almost 13 weeks, paid at 75.7 per cent replacement rate (see Table 2.3).

To sum up, the generosity (average payment rate) of the maternity and paternity insurance is higher in the Baltic states than in the Nordic countries. This means that the governments in the Baltic states provide greater incentives for mothers and fathers to use them, especially in Estonia and Lithuania. These policies also create an attachment to the labour market, which ensures defamilialism. Finland, Sweden and Norway have parental leave that is reserved exclusively for the father, and it is not transferable in Finland and Sweden. Sweden offers the higher replacement rate for the father's leave than in Finland, which might create more incentives to use it than in Finland. However, as noted, the replacement rate of maternity, parental and paternity insurance is generally higher in the Baltic than Nordic countries.

The OECD data permit us to look into the take-up rate of the paternity and parental insurance. As noted by a number of authors (Hobson 2018; Javornik and Kurowska 2017; Saraceno 2017), designed family policies do not always produce intended outcomes. This is especially common for the family policy, as it is most constrained by cultural norms and/or socioeconomic situations.

The use of statutory paternity leave is high in both the Nordic and Baltic countries. Paid paternity leave recipient rates are above 50 per 100 live births – in other words, there are more than 50 individuals claiming publicly administered paternity benefits or using publicly administered paternity leave for every 100 children born (see Table 2.3). In Finland, this rises to above 77 recipients per 100 live births, while in Sweden the rate is a little over 75 per 100 live births. Although the paternity leave is more generous in Lithuania and Estonia, there are many more fathers who took paternity leave (in 2016) in Finland, Sweden and Denmark than in Lithuania and Estonia. In Estonia, the recipient rate for paternity leave is less than 50 per 100 live births, in Lithuania 53 per 100 live births. Thus, despite a greater generosity of paternity leave in the Baltics, the Nordic fathers are more ready to accept father-specific leave than the Baltic fathers.

The analysis of the OECD's latest available data, for 2016, shows that countries that have parental leave reserved for the father (non-transferable) have a greater use rate of parental leave by the fathers, although mothers in all countries are still major users of parental leave. In Iceland, Sweden and Norway, fathers take up to about 40 per cent of parental leave compared to mothers, who take up the rest – 60 per cent. In Finland and Denmark, the gender distribution of users of parental leave is about 20–25 per cent taken by fathers and 75 per cent by the mothers. In Estonia, the share of fathers taking parental leave was slightly above 8 per cent in 2016. In Lithuania, the situation is different. The male share of recipients of parental leave was above 21 per cent; this is higher than the OECD average (18 per cent), but it is lower than in any other Nordic country.

Childcare Services

If we examine the enrolment rate of children from 3 to 5 years old, it is higher in the Baltic states, except for Lithuania, than the European Union (EU) average (about 87 per cent) (see Table 2.4). However, it is lower than in the Nordic countries (as expected), but not dramatically lower. In Latvia, slightly more than 93 per cent of all children from 3 to 5 years old attend childcare and pre-primary education. In Denmark, Iceland and Norway, it is more than 96 per cent. In Sweden, it is about 94 per cent. Finland shows the lowest rate of enrolment if all Baltic and Nordic countries are compared, amounting to more than 79 per cent. Lithuania is the second country (after Finland) if all Nordic and Baltic countries are compared, having the lowest enrolment (85 per cent) of children from 3 to 5 years old in pre-primary education.

Table 2.4   *Enrolment rates in early childhood education and care services, and proportion of children using informal childcare arrangements during a typical week, 2017 (per cent)*

	0- to 2-year-olds	3- to 5-year-olds	Average usual weekly hours in early childhood education and care services, 0- to 2-year-olds	Use of informal childcare, 0- to 2-year-olds	Use of informal childcare, 3- to 5-year-olds
Estonia	29.1	91.1	34.1	28.5	28.5
Latvia	31.3	93.3	37.7	10.3	17.0
Lithuania	24.8	85.0	-	23.1	25.3
Denmark	55.4	97.5	34.5	1.1	1.1
Iceland	59.7	97.4	37.2 (2015)	18.7	21.2
Finland	31.2	79.5	31.6	1.4	1.0
Norway	56.3	96.9	33.6	6.4	6.4
Sweden	46.6	94.1	31.8	0.3	0.3
OECD average	35.0	86.3	29.5	26.4	28.6
EU average	32.7	87.7	30.2	28.1	30.8

Source: OECD data.

The differences are much greater if the enrolment rates of children up to 2 years old are examined. In all three Baltic states the enrolment rates for 0 up to 2 years old are lower than the EU (almost 33 per cent) or OECD (35 per cent) averages. Lithuania has the lowest enrolment rate, 25 per cent, while in Latvia (31 per cent) and Estonia (29 per cent) it is slightly higher. The enrolments for children from 0 to 2 years are much higher in the Nordic countries, ranging from almost 60 per cent in Iceland to almost 31 per cent in Finland. If we examine changes in the enrolment rate over time (from 2005 to 2016), it is remarkable that for all three Baltic states for all age groups the enrolment has gradually increased, while for the majority of the Nordic countries it has stayed more or less stable, except for Norway, which also shows a steady increase in the enrolment rate over time. This tells us we might see an improvement in the future in the Baltic states.

In all three Baltic states the proportion of children using informal childcare (care provided by grandparents or other relatives, neighbours and friends for which the provider did not receive payment) is higher than in the Nordic countries. However, variations exist among the Baltic states. Latvia shows surprisingly low informal care use for all age groups. It is only 10 per cent for the 0- to 2-year age group, and only 17 per cent for the 3- to 5-year age group.

Estonia and Lithuania show more or less similar rates, which close to EU and OECD averages (25–30 per cent). Surprisingly, Iceland shows much higher informal care use than other Nordic countries, which is almost 19 per cent for 0- to 2-year-olds and 21 per cent for 3- to 5-year-olds. In this way, Iceland joins the Baltic cluster and exhibits the same or even higher informal care use for childcare. In the Nordic cluster, the informal care is either non-existent (in Sweden) or around 1 per cent (in Denmark and Finland), or comprises about 6 per cent in Norway.

CARE FOR THE FRAIL ELDERLY AND A SEARCH FOR PRESCRIBED FAMILIALISM

As stated by Saraceno (2017, p. 321) and also illustrated by the OECD (2018, 2019) data, on average 70–90 per cent of those who provide care for frail elderly people are family carers, yet the majority of them are women. Thus, highly gendered familialism appears to be the most prevalent approach to caring for the frail elderly in developed countries. Nevertheless, the variation exists among different welfare states.

The ageing of the population puts great pressure on the social protection systems of many European societies. Some countries, such as the Nordic ones, are well equipped to solve frail elderly care issues, while others, including the Baltic states, seem to have a way to go to adopt the increasing needs of the elderly. This is remarkable if we examine public spending as a percentage of GDP on long-term care (health and social components). In 2016, the Nordic countries were in a group of the highest OECD-30 spenders, while Estonia, Latvia and Lithuania were at the very bottom among the countries with very poor spending on long-term care. The Nordic countries spent about 2–3.2 per cent of their GDP on long-term care, while for Lithuania, Latvia and Estonia these expenses were much less than the OECD-30 average (1.3 per cent), approaching only 0.4 per cent in Latvia, 0.9 per cent in Estonia and 1.0 per cent in Lithuania (see Figure 2.2). The expenditures show that the states in the Baltic countries show little commitment to support their elderly via services. In this case it is worth looking for any traces of prescribed familialism while reviewing the constitutions of the Baltic countries.

Elderly care has been an important part of the family support system in the Nordic countries, while in the Baltic countries it is rarely debated as a family policy measure. In all three Baltic states, the constitutions enforce the family's obligations upon its members. In the Lithuanian constitution (1992), it is explicitly stated that it is the right and duty of parents to bring up their children and to support them until they come of age. The children have to respect their parents and to take care of them in their old age. In Estonia (1992), it is expressed not so explicitly, but clearly that a family has an important respon-

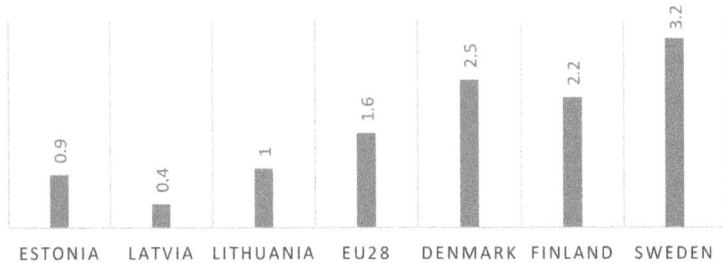

Bar chart showing values: ESTONIA 0.9, LATVIA 0.4, LITHUANIA 1, EU28 1.6, DENMARK 2.5, FINLAND 2.2, SWEDEN 3.2

Source: OECD (2018).

Figure 2.2   Public spending on long-term care as a percentage of GDP, 2016

sibility to raise its young and care for each other. It is stated in the Estonian constitution that parents have the right and the duty to raise their children and to provide for them. The family is required to provide for its members who are in need, and presumably its elderly too. The Latvian constitution (1922) is more difficult to interpret. However, it is obvious that the state's obligation is to protect the rights of parents and rights of the children. But support is granted only when family capacities are depleted (for example, children left without parental care) or to special families (with disabled children and so on). However, there were no statements that the state should protect its elderly. This becomes a great contract if compared to statements expressed in the constitutions of the Nordic countries. It was not possible to detect any traces of 'prescribed familialism' patterns by reviewing the constitutions of the Nordic countries. For instance, in Finland the state is responsible for ensuring the basic subsistence in the case of old age. The family is mentioned in Section 19 of the constitution, but only to impose the public authorities' obligations: 'the public authorities shall support families and others responsible for providing for children so that they have the ability to ensure the wellbeing and personal development of the children' (Constitution of Finland, 2019).

In the Danish (1953), Norwegian (1814), Icelandic (1944) and Swedish (2012) constitutions, the word 'family' is rarely used, but instead 'citizen', 'person', 'children', 'human dignity' and 'personal integrity' are used. There is no prescribed obligation for children to take care of their parents in old age.

To sum up, when it comes to long-term care expenditures, we find familialistic approaches prevalent in the Baltic states. It can be assumed that this situation is backed up by the 'prescribed familialism' pattern when, according to the constitutions, children are responsible for taking care of their parents in their old age. Nothing like this is prevalent in the Nordic countries.

OUTCOMES: MATERNAL EMPLOYMENT, CHILD POVERTY, GENDER PAY AND EMPLOYMENT GAP

One way to examine whether family support systems achieve their goals is to look into the share of maternal employment. Maternal employment is high in the Baltic states, higher than in the OECD (66 per cent) and the EU (68 per cent); averages for Latvia are 70 per cent and much higher for Lithuania (76 per cent). Estonia (65 per cent) shows slightly lower maternal employment rates than the OECD and the EU averages. In all Nordic countries, employment rates for women with at least one child are very high, ranging from 83 per cent in Sweden to almost 74 per cent in Finland. However, we should keep in mind that part-time employment is also widespread in the Nordic countries, which helps to increase female employment rates. Part-time jobs are not very popular in the Baltic countries. To illustrate this, we can turn to the latest available Eurostat data for 2017, as the OECD data do not offer complete statistics on part-time employment. In the Baltic states, female part-time employment ranges from 9 per cent (Lithuania) to 13 per cent (Estonia), while the EU-28 average is almost 32 per cent. In the Nordic countries, female part-time employment ranges from 34 per cent (Sweden) to almost 37 per cent (Norway). It is higher than the EU-28 average. Only Finland deviates from other Nordic countries, with only 20 per cent of female part-time employment.

Thus, the Nordic and Baltic countries stand first in line in Europe with their very high female full-time labour force participation rate. Even if we find many women working in the Baltic states, child poverty is higher than in the Nordic countries, especially in Lithuania (see Table 2.5). Child poverty in Estonia and Latvia amounts to about 12 per cent, while in Lithuania it is 19 per cent, which is higher that the OECD average (13 per cent). Lithuania is also the only country among the Baltic and Nordic countries in which child poverty is higher than the total population income poverty rate. This shows that family policy or social policy in a broader sense is not well equipped to mitigate poverty among children. In the Nordic countries, child poverty ranges from the lowest, 3 per cent (in Denmark), to the highest, 9 per cent (in Sweden). However, as illustrated by Table 2.5, fertility rates are quite similar in all Baltic and Nordic countries, ranging between 1.6 and 1.9. The gender gap in employment is also very low if compared to the OECD average (about 12 per cent). The highest gender employment gap is found in Estonia (almost 7 per cent) and Denmark (slightly above 5 per cent). The lowest is found in Lithuania (less than 2 per cent) and Sweden (3 per cent).

The examination of outcomes of social policy shows that different family policy regimes can produce similar results. The family support systems are clearly most effective in Nordic countries. However, the Baltic states have

Table 2.5   *Outcomes of performance, 2016 or latest available (per cent)*

	Child relative income poverty rate, 2015 or latest available year (0–17 years old)	Total population income poverty rate	Total fertility rates, 2017 or latest available	Employment rates (per cent) for women (15-to 64-year-olds) with at least one child aged 0–14, 2014 or latest available	Gender gap in employment rates (per cent), 2018	Gender gap in median earnings of full-time employees, 2016
Estonia	12.1	16.1	1.6	65.5	6.7	28.3
Latvia	12.2	16.2	1.7	70.1	3.5	21.1
Lithuania	19.1	16.5	1.6	75.8	1.7	12.5
Denmark	2.9	5.5	1.8	82.0	5.5	5.6
Iceland	7.2	6.5	1.7	-	4.8	9.9
Finland	3.7	6.3	1.5	73.6	3.1	16.5
Norway	7.3	8.1	1.6	-	4.3	7.1
Sweden	9.1	9.2	1.8	83.1	3	13.4
OECD average	13.4	11.8	1.5	66.2	11.1	13.5
EU average	-	-	1.6	68.2	-	12.1

Source: OECD data.

experienced similar results in terms of female labour force participation and fertility rates, but there are remarkable differences if child poverty is compared. Looking at child poverty we can clearly distinguish a line between Baltic and Nordic countries, while for other indicators there is no clear distinction. However, we can see a pattern for Estonia. It has the lowest rate of maternal employment among all Baltic and Nordic countries and also has the highest gender gap in employment and highest gender gap in median earnings of full-time employees.

DISCUSSION AND CONCLUSIONS

This chapter has reviewed similarities and differences in family support policy arrangements among Baltic and Nordic countries. It has sought the answer to the question: How do the Baltic and Nordic countries currently compare to each other in their family support systems?

The findings of this chapter show that the Nordic countries still maintain a very strong foothold in the 'defamilialisation through public provision' and/

or 'market provision' models. The data have not allowed to detect how much the state is outsourcing money to private providers; however, the pattern of defamilialisation is very strong. This is entrenched in the family support system design and in the positive outcomes of family policy. The state's expenses on family policy are the highest among the OECD countries, and the work–family reconciliation policies support female labour force attachment and gender equality in care. However, there exists a variation within the Nordic countries if we study programs and outcomes in more detail. Finland seems to show some signs of a supported familialism pattern as the state is less keen on providing services, putting more emphasis on cash benefits by offering long parental leave. Overall, if Baltic and Nordic countries are compared, the strong defamilialisation pattern prevails in the Nordics. This is entrenched by the state's commitment to ensuring personal integrity and independence through the constitutional rights.

In the Baltic states the situation is more complex. The findings show a strong pattern in Estonia of supported familialism as parental leave is long and fathers' involvement in childcare is low. Latvia falls somewhere in between familialism by default and defamilialisation through market provision as the state's support is minimal, enrolments in childcare for 3- to 5-year-olds are high and the use of informal childcare is low, signalling that families actively purchase the services in the private market. In many ways, Lithuania seems like it is following a pattern of defamilialisation through public provisions or through market provisions, as it has relatively generous paid childcare leave policies. The fathers' involvement in childcare is higher than in Estonia and is tending to increase. However, the use of informal care is also prevalent and the numbers of children from 0 to 2 years old attending care services are low. Yet Lithuania entrenches a prescribed familialism by law, as children are obliged to take care of their elderly parents according to the constitution. Thus, for Lithuania we see an unusual pattern of coexistence of defamilialism of public provision, prescribed familialism and familialism by default at the same time.

This chapter advances common knowledge in two important ways. It provides very detailed comparative analyses of Baltic and Nordic countries; very few studies provide such rigorous comparisons. It contributes to a better understanding of how Baltic and Nordic countries compare to each other according to family support programs. It also examines some patterns of prescribed familialism by looking into the constitutions of the Baltic and Nordic countries and expenses for long-term care.

Based on the analyses provided in this chapter, it is possible to claim that the Baltic and Nordic countries converge in their family policy arrangements. One distinctive feature of the family support system of the Baltic countries is the generosity of paid childcare leave policies such as maternity, paternity and parental leave. They are more generous than in the Nordic countries. However, the advanced paid leave policies (maternity, parental, paternity) in the Baltics are not yet backed up by widely available services.

The distinctive feature of the Nordic family model is emphasis on services and on the father's involvement in childcare. The Baltic states can still learn from the Nordic countries on how to better involve the father in childcare.

REFERENCES

Aidukaite, J. (2004), *The Emergence of the Post-Socialist Welfare State: The Case of the Baltic States – Lithuania, Latvia and Estonia*, Flemingsberg: Södertörn University College.

Aidukaite, J. (2006), 'The formation of social insurance institutions of the Baltic states in the post-socialist era', *Journal of European Social Policy*, 16 (3), 259–270.

Aidukaite, J. (2016), 'Support to families with children in the Baltic states: pathways of expansion and retrenchment from 2004 till 2016', paper presented at the workshop Baltic States after the Crisis? The Transformation of Welfare Systems and Social Problems, 25–26 December 2016, Vilnius University.

Aidukaite, J. (2019), 'The welfare systems of the Baltic states following the recent financial crisis of 2008/2010: expansion or retrenchment?', *Journal of Baltic Studies*, 50 (1), 39–58.

Ainsaar, M. (2000), 'The development of children and family policy in Estonia from 1945–2000', *Yearbook of Population Research in Finland*, XXXVII, 23–41.

Ainsaar, M. (2019), 'Economic crisis, families, and family policy in the Baltic states, 2009–2014', *Journal of Baltic Studies*, 50 (1), 59–79.

Constitution of Finland (2019), accessed on 15 March 2019 at www.refworld.org/docid/3ae6b53418.html.

Constitution of the Kingdom of Norway (1814), accessed on 11 May 2019 at www.stortinget.no/en/In-English/About-the-Storting/The-Constitution/.

Constitution of the Republic of Estonia (1992), accessed on 9 March 2019 at www.riigiteataja.ee/en/eli/530102013003/consolide.

Constitution of the Republic of Iceland (1944), accessed on 1 November 2019 at www.refworld.org/docid/3ae6b5627.html.

Constitution of the Republic of Latvia (1922), accessed on 11 March 2019 at https://likumi.lv/ta/en/en/id/57980.

Constitution of the Republic of Lithuania (1992), accessed on 15 March 2019 at www.lrs.lt/home/Konstitucija/Constitution.htm.

Constitution of Sweden (2012), accessed on 1 April 2019 at www.constituteproject.org/constitution/Sweden_2012.pdf?lang=en.

Constitutional Act of Denmark (1953), accessed on 6 March 2019 at www.stm.dk/_p_10992.html.

Esping-Andersen, G. (2009), *The Incomplete Revolution: Adapting to Women's New Roles*, Cambridge: Polity Press.

Estevez-Ave, M., and B. Hobson (2015), 'Outsourcing domestic (care) work: the politics, policy, and political economy', *Social Politics*, 22 (2), 133–146.

European Union (2016a), Estonia: increase in family benefits and focus on implementing evidence-based practices, accessed 2 October 2016 at http://europa.eu/epic/countries/estonia/index_en.htm.

European Union (2016b), Latvia: the economic crisis still reverberates on the wellbeing of families and children, accessed 1 October 2016 at http://europa.eu/epic/countries/latvia/index_en.htm.

Grødem, A. S. (2014), 'A review of family demographics and family policies in the Nordic countries', *Baltic Journal of Political Sciences*, 3, 50–66.

Grødem, A. S. (2017), 'Family-oriented policies in Scandinavia and the challenge of immigration', *Journal of European Social Policy*, 27 (1), 77–89.

Hiilamo, H. (2002a), 'Family policy changes at the micro-level in Sweden and Finland during the 1990s', Working Paper No. 291, Luxembourg Income Studies.

Hiilamo, H. (2002b), 'Family policy models and family policy outcomes: a Nordic perspective', Working Paper No. 290, Luxembourg Income Studies.

Hobson, B. (2018), 'Gendered dimensions and capabilities: opportunities, dilemmas and challenges', *Critical Sociology*, 44 (6), 883–898.

Javornik, J. (2014), 'Measuring state de-familialism: contesting post-socialist exceptionalism', *Journal of European Social Policy*, 24 (3), 240–257.

Javornik, J., and A. Kurowska (2017), 'Work and care opportunities under different parental leave systems: gender and class inequalities in Northern Europe', *Social Policy Administration*, 51 (4), 617–637.

Kalliomaa-Puha, L., and O. Kangas (2018), 'ESPN thematic report on challenges in long-term care: Finland', European Social Policy Network (ESPN), European Commission.

Korpi, W. (2000), 'Faces of inequality: gender, class, and patterns of inequalities in different types of welfare states', *Social Politics International Studies in Gender, State and Society*, 7 (2), 127–192.

Kvist, J. (2018), 'ESPN thematic report on challenges in long-term care: Denmark', European Social Policy Network (ESPN), European Commission.

Leitner, S. (2003), 'Varieties of familialism: the caring function of the family in comparative perspective', *European Societies*, 5 (4), 353–375.

Lohmann, H., and H. Zagel (2016), 'Family policy in comparative perspective: the concepts and measurement of familization and defamilization', *Journal of European Social Policy*, 26 (1), 48–65.

Ma, L., Andersson, G., Duvander, A. Z., and M. Evertsson (2019), 'Fathers' uptake of parental leave: forerunners and laggards in Sweden, 1993–2010', *Journal of Social Policy*, 49 (2), 361–381.

Nieuwenhuis, R., Need, A., and H. van der Kolk (2019), 'Family policy as an institutional context of economic inequality', *Acta Sociologica*, 62 (1), 64–80.

OECD (2018), Public spending on long-term care as a percentage of GDP, 2016 to 2070: Ageing Working Group reference scenario, accessed 2 May 2019 at https://doi.org/10.1787/health_glance_eur-2018-graph165-en.

OECD (2019), OECD Family Database, accessed 11 March 2019 at www.oecd.org/social/family/database.htm.

Rajevska, F., and L. Romanovska (2016), 'Latvia: both sides of the economic recovery success story', in K. Schubert, P. de Villota and J. Kuhlmann (eds), *Challenges to European Welfare Systems*, Cham: Springer, pp. 473–497.

Sainsbury, D. (2018), 'Policy constructions, immigrants' social rights and gender: the case of Swedish childcare policies', *Journal of European Social Policy*, 29 (2), 213–227.

Saraceno, C. (2017), 'Varieties of familialism: comparing four southern European and East Asian welfare regimes', *Journal of European Social Policy*, 26 (4), 314–326.

Schon, P., and J. Heap (2018), 'ESPN thematic report on challenges in long-term care: Sweden', European Social Policy Network (ESPN), European Commission.

Stankūnienė, V. (2001), 'Family policy of Lithuania: a changing strategy', paper presented at the European Population Conference 2001, Helsinki, Finland, 7–9 June 2001.

Therborn, G. (2017), 'The "People's home" is falling down, time to update your view on Sweden', *Sociologisk Forskning*, 54 (4), 275–278.

Trumm, A., and M. Ainsaar (2009), 'The welfare system of Estonia: past, present and future', in K. Schubert, S. Hegelich and U. Bazant (eds), *The Handbook of European Welfare Systems*, London: Routledge, pp. 153–71.

Tunberger, P., and W. Sigle-Rushton (2011), 'Continuity and change in Swedish family policy reforms', *Journal of European Social Policy*, 21 (3), 225–237.

Wendt, C., Mischke, M., and M. Pfeifer (2011), *Welfare States and Public Opinion: Perceptions of Healthcare Systems, Family Policy and Benefits for the Unemployed and Poor in Europe*, Cheltenham, UK and Northampton, MA, USA: Edward Elgar Publishing.

Wennemo, I. (1994), *Sharing the Costs of Children*, Stockholm: Swedish Institute for Social Research.

Yerkes, A. M., and J. Javornik (2018), 'Creating capabilities: childcare policies in comparative perspective', *Journal of European Social Policy*, 29 (4), 529–544.

Yin-Nei Cho, E. (2014), 'Defamilization typology re-examined: re-measuring the economic independence of women in welfare states', *Journal of European Social Policy*, 24 (5), 442–454.

3. Demographic challenges of Europe in the new millennium: Swedish family policies as an answer to them?

Livia Sz. Oláh and Gerda Neyer

INTRODUCTION

Welfare states have changed greatly in the past few decades, manifested in retrenchment, deregulations and reduced state engagement in traditional social protection, unlike the Golden Age of Welfare in the mid 1940s to mid 1970s (Palier 2010; Wincott 2013). Back then, based on the dominant family structure of the mid twentieth century, social policies targeted the male breadwinner with an industrial job. Indeed, the rationale of the post-war welfare state was to protect men as providers, and thus their families, against the risk of welfare losses when not being able to work for pay due to illness, unemployment or old age. Women could uphold a decent living standard in the face of these old social risks via stable marriage (and upon widowhood) as they were expected to 'de-commodify'; that is, to give up work when entering marriage or having the first child (Bonoli 2007; Orloff 1993). The implicit gender contracts of the 'housewife era' relegated women to unpaid work in the family, and made their welfare, social and economic status dependent on that of their husbands (Pateman 1988).

From the 1970s onwards, however, post-industrial transformations have increasingly come to characterise advanced societies. Deindustrialisation and tertiarisation of employment resulted in changing labour markets attracting large masses of women into the labour force. These developments coincided with increasing destandardisation of employment, career interruptions and deregularisation of full-time and standard work contracts, creating new social and economic risks for families (Bonoli 2007; Charles 2005). The Nordic and the English-speaking countries were among the first to enter the post-industrial stage of economic development. Continental and Southern European societies followed this path with a delay of two to three decades. In the 1990s and early 2000s, Central-Eastern Europe, including the Baltic countries, were to handle

challenges around the transformation of their socialist economies into a capi-
talist market-based system (Gros and Steinherr 2004), and this transition is still
ongoing in many of the region's countries.

The socioeconomic transformations brought along by post-industrialisation
altered not only the labour market, but also the gender division of labour in
families and, related to this, family patterns and structures. Women's labour
force participation, while reducing their dependence on the male breadwinner,
contributed to growing family instability, and accentuated the quest for solutions to combine paid work and domestic responsibilities. Lone parenthood and
diminished opportunities to reconcile an economically sustainable employment with family life emerged as new social risks, particularly for women and
children, who were inadequately covered by 'old' male-breadwinner-oriented
welfare states (Taylor-Gooby 2004). This gave rise to calls for a new welfare
state and new family policies with new gender contracts, new family forms and
equal opportunities for children (Esping-Andersen et al. 2002).

In this chapter we address the new social risks related to family changes and
the resulting changing demographics of Europe, relying on data from established databases such as Eurostat. We pay special attention to the interplay
with changing gender roles. Thereafter we present the family policy measures
enacted in Sweden, the poster country of the social investment strategy aimed
at tackling new social risks of new family biographies, with emphasis on
developments from the 1990s onwards. In the concluding thoughts we briefly
summarise the main lessons for the policy challenges ahead.

DEMOGRAPHIC CHALLENGES

The welfare provision in the post-war welfare state was structured around
the single male-earner model, assuming stable family and employment life
courses. However, since the 1970s new patterns of family and gender behaviour have emerged. Given that they qualitatively differ so much from earlier
post-war developments, the demographic literature has recognised them as
jointly constituting the Second Demographic Transition (Lesthaeghe 2010). In
this section, we highlight the main features of family changes in Europe, which
together impose what we call 'demographic challenges' on post-industrial
welfare states, and we compare them to the developments in Sweden.

Low Fertility and Population Ageing

A feature of the new demographic trends that received the most attention by
policy-makers is persistent low fertility (Macura et al. 2005). Throughout
human history, this is the first time that fertility levels have been below the
so-called replacement level of 2.1 children per woman on average in a large

number of (advanced) societies for decades, with severe consequences for the age structure of the population in the long run. The pace and the range of fertility decline have, however, varied substantially across countries in Europe. Despite national variations, some distinct country clusters have emerged since the 1970s (Figure 3.1). Demographers and welfare state researchers tend to relate this development to European welfare and family policy regimes and the social conditions they create for childbearing (see Esping-Andersen 1999; Thévenon 2011):

- Nordic countries (Denmark, Finland, Iceland, Norway and Sweden): the Social Democratic welfare regime with mainly universal social provisions, promoting the dual-earner family model and gender equality,
- Anglo-Saxon countries (the United Kingdom and Ireland): the Liberal welfare regime with usually means-tested support and the dominance of market-based solutions in welfare provision,
- Western Europe (Belgium, France, Luxembourg and the Netherlands): the Conservative welfare regime that supports men's primacy at the labour market but also provides possibilities via policy measures for women to combine paid work and family responsibilities,
- German-speaking countries (Austria, Germany and, given the welfare logic followed, Switzerland, its several official languages notwithstanding): also the Conservative welfare regime but less supportive of women's employment than the West European group,
- Southern Europe (Greece, Italy, Portugal and Spain): the Familistic welfare regime with extremely limited family support and pronounced gender-role differentiation (Lewis 2006), and
- Central-Eastern Europe (Bulgaria, Czech Republic, Estonia, Hungary, Latvia, Lithuania, Poland, Romania, Slovakia and Slovenia): the Transition Post-Socialist cluster with large variations in the range of state support to families and in facilitating the combination of paid work and family for women.

Fertility declined to less than two children per woman first in the German-speaking, the Western European and the Nordic countries in the early 1970s (Figure 3.1), but even earlier in some societies within these groups, most specifically in Sweden. Southern Europe entered the low-fertility path in the early 1980s, joined by the Anglo-Saxon countries and Central-Eastern Europe at the end of that decade. In German-speaking countries and the latter clusters, with the exception of Anglo-Saxon countries, fertility levels have lingered even below the so-called critical level of low fertility (1.5 children per woman on average), known to accelerate population ageing (McDonald 2006), from the early-mid 1990s onward. Fertility increased in the Nordic

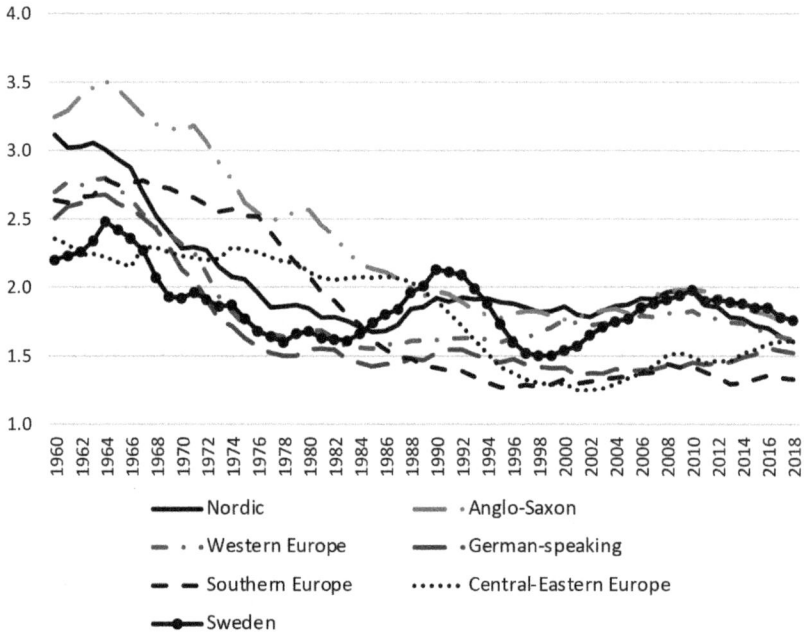

Notes: Unweighted data; means for each group. Countries are grouped as follows: *Nordic* – Denmark, Finland, Iceland and Norway; *Anglo-Saxon* – the United Kingdom and Ireland; *Western Europe* – Belgium, France, Luxembourg and the Netherlands; *German-speaking* – Austria, Germany (for the years 1960–1989, West Germany only) and Switzerland; *Southern Europe* – Greece, Italy, Portugal and Spain; *Central-Eastern Europe* – Bulgaria, Czech Republic, Estonia, Hungary, Latvia, Lithuania, Poland, Romania, Slovakia and Slovenia. Sweden is depicted separately.
Source: INED (2013) for the years 1960–2008; Eurostat (2020) for the years 2009–2018; own calculations.

Figure 3.1   Period total fertility rates (average number of children per woman) in Sweden and different country clusters in Europe, 1960–2018

countries from the late 1980s, and in Anglo-Saxon countries and Western Europe from the early 1990s, until the Great Recession brought along a new decline in the 2010s. Sweden displayed a rather unique pattern, reaching the replacement level in 1990, followed by a dramatic fertility decline at the end of the decade due to an economic crisis. In the 2000s, Sweden experienced a fertility recovery close to the replacement level, and a slow decline in recent years. At the end of the 2010s, with policy strategies in Europe more strongly geared towards austerity (Lennartz and Ronald 2017), fertility seems to converge across country groups at a low level but, with the exception of Southern Europe, above the critical margin.

Another trend that accompanies the fertility decline is the increasing mean age of entering parenthood. During the male-breadwinner era, women in Europe had their first child in their early or mid twenties on average. Since then, childbearing has been increasingly postponed, related to the rise of female employment levels and women's educational aspirations (Blossfeld 1995). In the early twenty-first century, women enter motherhood first in their late twenties or even early thirties, although somewhat earlier in Central-Eastern Europe and the Baltics. As the ability for reproduction declines from the late thirties, the ageing of fertility is likely to contribute to the 'fertility gap', an acknowledged policy concern referring to the difference between the intended number of children, which remains above the replacement level across Europe, and the much lower realised fertility levels (Beaujouan and Berghammer 2019).

The main policy concern with low fertility from a welfare system point of view relates to the diminishing stock of future taxpayers, as the labour force shrinks due to fewer young people entering it than old ones leaving for retirement. Long-term below-replacement fertility levels also contribute to the ageing of the population, as the proportion and numbers of elderly increase beyond the level that is considered fiscally sustainable, jeopardising the future of the welfare state (McDonald 2006). Indeed, a large share of elderly in the population undermines the intergenerational contract, central for the redistribution of incomes coordinated by the welfare state (Taylor-Gooby 2004). There should be enough young people to fill in the position of currently middle-aged in the future so when turning old they can expect levels of support similar to those they provide now (Komp and Van Tilburg 2010). Low fertility and population ageing thus challenge the intergenerational contract, and increase the burden to provide care for the elderly.

Family Instability and Implications for Household Structures

Another important challenge of the marriage-based provisions of welfare in post-war welfare states is the substantial weakening of the supremacy of marriage in the European family landscape from the late 1960s onwards (Sobotka and Toulemon 2008). This pattern again emerged first in Sweden and the Nordic countries, linked to an increasing prevalence of non-marital cohabitation, followed by Western Europe, the Anglo-Saxon and the German-speaking countries in the mid 1970s. High marriage rates prevailed in Central-Eastern Europe and the Baltics, but decreased rapidly after the fall of state socialism. In parallel, non-marital cohabitation increased with pronounced country variations (rare in Poland, but common in Estonia). In Southern Europe, marriage rates only started to decline rapidly in the early twenty-first century.

All over Europe, declining marriage propensities were paralleled by an increasing mean age of entering marriage, exceeding the mean age of first motherhood in many countries. Sweden has led the other European countries in this development since the early 1970s. The postponement has been interpreted as the materialisation of people refraining from long-term commitments, seen as a main feature of the Second Demographic Transition (Lesthaeghe 2010). Related to the rising prevalence of non-marital cohabitation, researchers also noted an upsurge of extramarital childbearing throughout Europe, starting in Sweden and other Nordic countries in the late 1960s, followed by other country clusters in the 1980s and Southern Europe in the early 2000s. In recent years, about one-third of births occurred out-of-wedlock in Southern Europe and the German-speaking countries, around 40 per cent in Anglo-Saxon countries and Central-Eastern Europe, and more than half of all births in Sweden and other Nordic countries and Western Europe (Eurostat 2020).

The changing partnership and childbearing patterns also have implications for family stability. Consensual unions are more fragile than marriages, given the partners' lesser commitment to each other and low, if any, legal barriers to break-up (Perelli-Harris and Sánchez Gassen 2012). Even among families with children, the risk for family dissolution is much higher in cohabiting relationships than in marriages (Booth and Crouter 2002). Nevertheless, divorce rates increased in all country clusters, with Sweden among the forerunners, beginning in the 1970s, but not before the late 1990s in Southern Europe. Also, family reconstitution, that is, re-partnering with children and possibly having children with a new partner, has become rather common in Europe. Many children live with a step-parent and often with a half-sibling within a few years after their parents' break-up. Such families are even more fragile than first partnerships, thus further strengthening the trend of family instability. In addition, a non-negligible proportion of children live with a lone parent. Break-ups becoming more common in the less educated segment of societies in recent decades (Matysiak et al. 2014) adds to the new social risks posing new challenges to welfare states.

Increasing Population Heterogeneity Due to Immigration

New social risks are not confined to family fluidity, but also include changes in the ethnic composition of populations in Europe. Between 1996 and 2010, the proportion foreign-born in Western Europe grew from around 8 to 14 per cent of the population, exceeding such a share in the USA (D'Amuri and Peri 2014). This proportion has increased even further since then. The majority of the new immigrants are of non-European origin, coming as labour migrants, their family members or as refugees. Their labour force participation rates vary across Europe. The Nordic countries, and Sweden especially, while listed at the top in terms of social rights covering immigrants and natives equally, have surprisingly large differences in native-immigrant labour force participation rates, and tend to be among the countries with the greatest negative employment disparities in the OECD (Brochmann and Hagelund 2011). Researchers argue that the reason for the large disparities are the high female employment rates and high public service provision in the Nordic countries reducing labour opportunities for the often low-skilled migrant labour (ibid.).

Given low fertility and population ageing in Europe, immigration has often been discussed from the viewpoint of 'replacement migration'; that is, that immigrants' labour force participation and fertility should compensate for below-replacement fertility levels and sustain the work force and the welfare state (for a review of this debate, see Wilson et al. 2013). Due to a shift of attitudes towards immigration, their often higher fertility compared to the natives has, however, become increasingly considered a sign of a lack of integration. The diversification of immigration has turned the attention towards whether globalisation and substantial migrant inflows lead to welfare state expansion or retrenchment. A recent analysis over the 1990s to 2010 shows that social welfare spending in relation to gross domestic product increased with little change in welfare generosity levels, in line with the growing needs for social protection (Fenwick 2019). Another aspect is changing public attitudes towards welfare redistribution. Support for the welfare state was argued to have become 'immigrationised'; that is, directly related to people's attitudes about immigration (Burgoon and Rooduijn 2020). Analyses revealed that the share of foreign-born people, the level of welfare spending and migrants' welfare dependency relative to the natives govern anti-immigration sentiments and develop into anti-solidarity effects undermining support for redistribution in general, posing another challenge for the welfare state (Burgoon and Rooduijn 2020; Finseraas 2008).

CHANGING GENDER ROLES

The changes in family patterns, often described as the individualisation of families, have been paralleled by evolving gender roles, known as the gender revolution (Goldscheider et al. 2015). Most of the changes relate to women's roles expanding to include economic provision to the family on (nearly) equal footing with men. In this respect, Central-Eastern Europe was a vanguard with high levels of female and maternal full-time employment in the socialist period, embodying the regime's perception of gender equality. When the institutional structure that supported the combination of paid work and family broke down in the transition period of the 1990s, women's economic activity declined substantially, and the process towards recovery has been slow ever since. For the rest of Europe, Sweden and other Nordic countries acted as a forerunner not only of new family trends but also regarding the increase of women's and mothers' labour force participation from the 1970s onwards, displaying the highest female employment rates even today (Oláh et al. 2018). Other country clusters joined the trend during the 1980s, Southern Europe lagging behind up until the 2010s. In recent years, the gender employment gap has greatly diminished across Europe, although with further pace for catching up for both Southern Europe and Central-Eastern Europe (Figure 3.2).

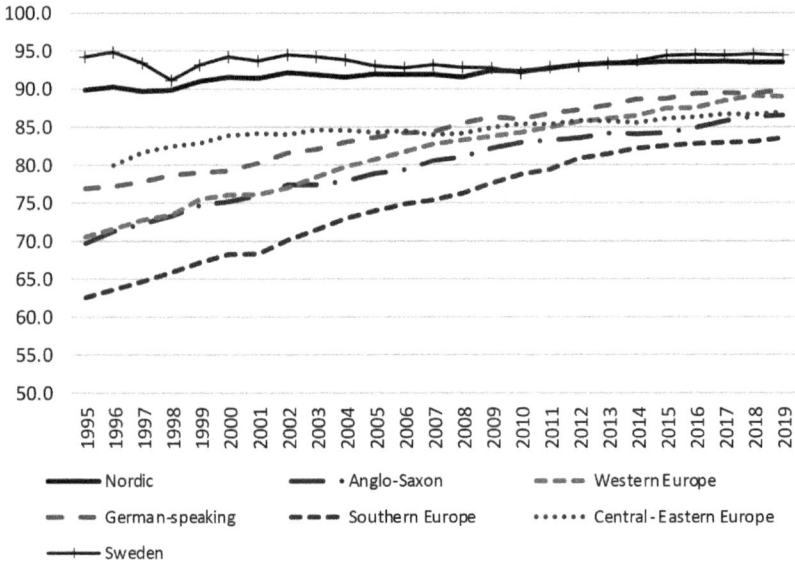

Notes: Unweighted data; means for each group. Countries are grouped as in Figure 3.1. Sweden is depicted separately.
Source: Eurostat (2020), own calculations.

Figure 3.2   *Gender differences in labour market activity (women's activity rate in proportion of men's rate) at ages 20–64 in Sweden and different country clusters in Europe, 1995–2019*

Economic theorists have seen women's increasing economic independence as the main driver of family changes, with respect to both the postponement of family formation and childbearing, and the erosion of family stability (Becker 1991). However, unlike among men, female labour force activities involve much part-time work in most country clusters, except for Southern Europe and Central-Eastern Europe, where labour market structures are quite rigid. Hence, despite the reduced gender gap in paid work, it is the one-and-a-half-earner model rather than the dual-earner family that has been firmly established across Europe (Daly 2011). To some extent, this is surprising, because women have gained educational advantage over men. From the 1990s onwards women's share among the highly educated exceeds that of men, with important implications for couple relationships. Homogamy – that is, equal educational attainment among partners – has become the dominant pattern, followed by hypogamy; that is, the woman's educational attainment exceeds that of her partner (Van Bavel et al. 2018). These educational pairings have basically replaced the old pattern with men's superior economic position in families all over Europe in recent decades.

However, women's gain in earning and bargaining power within the couple has not yet translated into gender-equal family and work–life arrangements. Time-use studies revealed that the carrying-out of unpaid care and housework in most families remains gendered. There have been some (smaller) changes in men's gender role, particularly in relation to their children, recognised in the literature in the concept of 'the new father' (Ranson 2001). The second phase of the gender revolution, namely men's engagement in care and housework on equal terms with women, has only just begun. Demographic theories regard the resulting dual burden on women as a reason for low fertility and the increasing instability of couple relationships (Goldscheider et al. 2015). For example, women's exclusive responsibility for the home sphere in Central-Eastern Europe and Southern Europe is considered to contribute to the very low fertility levels in these regions, while the higher fertility levels in Sweden and the Nordic countries are attributed to men's widespread engagement in childrearing.

Reconciling paid work and family life unequally has emerged as a new social risk for families and gender relationships. Increasingly, both women's and men's income are needed to provide for a family, but time and personal energy are limited resources. Men's engagement in care and household chores as well as state or market provisions to de-familialise (parts of) care and housework have become necessary components to achieve work–family balance and well-being (Bonoli 2007). In this respect, the Nordic countries, and Sweden in particular, are often seen as models to be followed by European welfare states. These countries have adjusted their welfare state policies to address the new social risks and are thus regarded as better equipped to meet the social, family and welfare state challenges that jeopardise the intergenerational contract and the welfare system's sustainability in the long run.

SWEDISH FAMILY POLICIES: CONTENT, ORIENTATION AND OUTCOMES

Changing structures of labour markets and social risks have elicited new welfare strategies. In many countries, the emphasis of social protection has shifted from simple social provision to social-investment-oriented policies, the latter most fully implemented in the Nordic countries from the 1990s onwards. The origin of the paradigm lies in the 1930s, in particular in Alva and Gunnar Myrdal's social and family policy suggestions to tackle that time's low-fertility crisis in Sweden. The Myrdals conceived social policies as an investment in individuals and the future of society by supporting women's employment and various family configurations alongside the male-breadwinner model. The emergence of new social risks has contributed to the recent revival of the approach (Morel et al. 2012).

The core features of a social investment welfare state are active labour market policies, human capital investment starting with early childhood education, publicly funded childcare and old-age services, family policies that promote employment irrespective of care obligations and gender equality in all aspects of public and private life (ibid.). This proactive approach combined with universal welfare provision is likely to impede the development of severe social problems. Therefore, we address key policy measures in Sweden, the pioneer of the social investment paradigm and of employment-oriented family policies. We focus on family policies since they are considered an essential response to the demographic challenges discussed above, namely low fertility, changing household structures and gender relationships, as they provide a means of social integration and equality.

Parental Leave Scheme: Flexible, Employment-Oriented and Care-Facilitating

In 1974, Sweden was the first country in the world to implement a gender-neutral parental leave program with an income-related benefit and job protection. The benefit level was originally 90 per cent of a parent's previous gross income. Like all social benefits, it was lowered during the economic crisis of the 1990s, first to 75 per cent of previous income in the mid 1990s, then raised to 80 per cent at the end of the decade. Currently (2020), it is 77.6 per cent up to a certain ceiling. However, collective agreements ensure extra payments to most employees to cover the loss of income, even beyond the ceiling. State employees, for example, receive 90 per cent of their total income as leave benefit, the ceiling notwithstanding (Duvander et al. 2017). Since its introduction, eligibility to income-related parental leave benefit has been based on a parent having worked for at least 240 days before the delivery or before using the leave. Parents who do not fulfil this requirement receive a low flat-rate benefit (currently 250 Swedish crowns, or about 25 euros, per day).

The main aim of introducing a gender-neutral, income-related parental leave scheme was originally to encourage women's labour force participation and to enable women to both be employed and have children. By facilitating parents' mutual engagement in the care for their children, the scheme sought to also promote gender equality (Oláh and Bernhardt 2008). Although the parental leave scheme was directed at both parents, mainly mothers used it, as no specific regulation enforced leave-sharing. To incentivise fathers' involvement, in 1995 one month's leave was reserved for each parent on a 'use it or lose it' basis, known as the 'father's quota'. At the same time, the leave was individualised, requiring (electronically) signed consent by a parent for the other parent to be able to use more than half of the total leave. This applied also to parents not living together but both having custody for a child, which included the vast majority of separated parents (Ferrarini and Duvander 2010). Except for one month in the first year after the birth, the so-called double days, parents cannot use the leave at the same time. The number of reserved months was increased to two in 2002 and to three in 2016, making the individualisation of parental leave more and more explicit.

Currently each parent can use 240 days with benefit per child (480 days in total), 90 days of which are non-transferable to the other parent. For 180 of these 240 days, a parent receives an income-related parental leave benefit, and for 90 days a flat-rate benefit of 180 Swedish crowns (about 18 euros) per day. In all, 384 days must be used in the first four years after the birth. The rest (96 days) can be used any time before the child turns 12. Leave of absence from work is allowed even if no leave benefit is used during the child's first 18 months (the use of such leave does not affect the number of leave days with benefit). Moreover, the Swedish parental leave scheme has a unique flexibility, allowing parents to take half-days, quarter-days or one-eighth of a day instead of full days. This flexibility, together with the options of paid and unpaid leave days, makes it possible for parents to combine employment and taking care of one's child at home as best fits, and it allows for the parental leave to be stretched out to facilitate everyday life puzzles beyond the immediate toddler years (Duvander and Viklund 2020). Parental leave is a parental right; employers cannot deny parents from taking time off for parental leave.

Beside parental leave, parents are also entitled to temporary parental leave to care for their sick children up to 120 working days per year and per child until the child is 12 years old, with the same flexibility and income-related benefit as for parental leave (although with a lower ceiling). Temporary parental leave may be granted for older children and/or for more than the 120 days in case of severe illness or extensive care needs. Part of the temporary parental leave may also be taken if the usual carer of the child is sick. The Swedish parental leave program is thus a true activation and social-investment-oriented measure of a post-industrial welfare state, as it offers a wide range of possibilities to take leave, while not distinguishing between mothers and fathers nor by partnership type. It is based on individual eligibility, and the rules of provision do not depend on the other parent's circumstances. The leave schemes are intended to facilitate employment for each parent while having a child and to promote gender-equal parenting, in line with the earner-carer orientation of Swedish family policy.

Public Childcare: From Promoting Parents' Employment to Equal Opportunities of Children

The public childcare system is the second main component of Swedish family policy, facilitating partial defamilialisation of care. Its foundations were laid in the late 1960s to promote mothers' employment retention. In 1975 municipalities became obliged to provide at least half-day care for all 6-year-old children free of charge. For younger children, day care was related to a fee to be paid. However, access was ensured only if the parents were employed or studying. Increasingly, the aim and focus of public childcare broadened from facilitating parental employment to providing equal early childhood education to all children. Based on the 1995 Act on childcare, children are guaranteed to have a place in public childcare within three to four months upon parents' requests. Regardless of the parents' activity, public childcare is provided on a full-day basis for all children aged 1 to 6. Since the early 2000s, even children whose parents are unemployed, on leave or in other ways outside the labour market have full rights to public childcare, but at reduced hours (Ferrarini and Duvander 2010), currently 15 hours per week.

Formal childcare is offered not only by municipalities, but since the 1990s also by private providers and cooperatives. All providers have to align with the rules of parental fees, are financed to the same extent by subsidies from the municipality and have to meet the same regulations and curriculum standards. In order to eliminate regional differences in costs, a system of maximum fees, the so-called *maxtaxa* that parents can be charged for, was introduced in 2002. The fee is proportional to the parents' income up to a certain ceiling and dependent on the number of children they have in day care. The amount paid may be maximally 3 per cent of the household's income for the first child, 2 per cent for the second, and 1 per cent for the third. There is no fee for any further children. Since 2004, children over 4 have a right to public childcare of 15 hours a week free of charge (ibid.). Public childcare is highly subsidised so that parental fees cover only about 10 per cent of the total costs, demonstrating the social-investment nature of the service.

From the start, public childcare was designed to ease challenges around the combination of child-raising and paid work, removing obstacles to employment for parents with preschool-aged children, especially mothers, hence promoting gender equality. The provision of childcare services enables both parents to support their family economically; it thus reduces the risk of poverty and contributes to the welfare of children. In addition to increasing mothers' employment, childcare was recognised early on to have a crucial role in the pursuit of social equality by mitigating differences in children's life chances, especially for those of disadvantaged backgrounds. Providing affordable, full-day, high-quality early childhood education based on a pedagogically informed curriculum and with educated staff ensures meeting this aspiration.

Child Home-Care Allowance and Gender-Equality Bonus: Failed Policy Attempts

Along with the successful policy measures discussed above, some relatively recent reforms turned out to be a failure. The strong gender-equality-based earner-carer orientation of Swedish family policy notwithstanding, coalition governments – not including the Social Democrats – attempted twice to introduce a child home-care allowance that opposed the basic endeavour of involving both parents in earning as well as caring activities. In favour of a traditional family–work arrangement but in modern packaging, the policy rhetoric around the first introduction in 1994 referred to it as aiming to increase freedom of choice with respect to the care for children, although it basically sought to strengthen re-familialisation of care. The timing was not a coincidence, as it accompanied the reform of the first reserved month to each parent in the gender-neutral parental leave scheme, in force from 1995. The latter reform sought to increase gender equality in care, incentivising fathers, while the home-care allowance could counteract such efforts, providing an untaxed flat-rate benefit for home care of children aged 1 to 3 and not using public childcare (Ferrarini and Duvander 2010). The low payment level made the measure unappealing to fathers, turning the home-care allowance into a tool also for re-gendering care. It was abolished after a few months upon a change of government.

The child home-care allowance was reintroduced in 2008, again with the alleged aim to increase freedom of choice for care. The amount was 340 euros per month, to be paid by municipalities to parents who had used at least 250 days of paid parental leave and wanted to care for their child at home thereafter. There was no previous work requirement, and parents could be employed, but not receive any other benefit, such as unemployment benefit or social assistance. The child home-care allowance never gained popularity in Sweden. Only about one-third of the municipalities introduced the option, and 4 per cent of all parents, mainly mothers with weak labour force attachment, including the foreign-born, used it (Duvander and Ellingsæter 2016). The measure was abolished in 2016.

To counter the potentially undermining effect on gender equality of the child home-care allowance, a gender-equality bonus was introduced simultaneously in 2008. It was a tax reduction paid for every day a father used parental leave beyond the days that were reserved for him. Parents who fully shared the leave could receive about 1,500 euros extra (Duvander and Ferrarini 2013). However, the regulations were too complex and confusing. Even after some simplification in 2012 of the administrative procedure linked to it, the gender-equality bonus remained rather ineffective and was abolished in 2017. Being a tax reduction, the measure implied a delay for the parents to benefit from it, and its failure also shows the importance of a reform being easily understandable for the target population. The fate of the child home-care allowance indicates instead that the social-investment orientation of family policies in Sweden has become a social norm that may prevent a return to more gender-segregating family policies.

Societal Outcomes

Swedish family policies do not contradict the social-investment orienta- tion of other social policies, strengthening the logic of the entire welfare system. Active labour market policies focus on maintaining and advancing human capital during unemployment, while high income-related benefit levels prevent a decline into poverty. The educational system allows individuals to upgrade, advance or change their education throughout their life course. Swedish family policies, aligned with active labour market and consistent gender-equality policies promoting full employment and the dual-earner model, are an acknowledged success in providing protection in face of new social risks (Bonoli 2007). The outcomes are internationally high levels of female labour force activity, including of mothers with young children; rela- tively high fertility and a balanced population age structure; high prevalence of new fatherhood, with men's active engagement in their children's care; and relatively low child poverty despite high levels of family instability (OECD 2020). Various features of family policy measures have contributed to these advantageous outcomes.

The gender-neutral parental leave scheme combined with income-related benefit of a high replacement level not discriminating between mothers and fathers, but incentivising them to engage both in earning and caring, was a key labour-activation measure for women, and it pushed men to become active fathers. The latter effect was increased mainly by the father's quota, as losing leave days if not taken by the father motivated mothers to involve the fathers in the care of children. Even vis-à-vis employers, this feature strengthened fathers' role as active parents, although the uptake is polarised by social group and income. The highest strata is the most likely to use father's leave, as the concept of gender-equal parenting is more fully embraced by those mothers and fathers (Duvander and Viklund 2020).

Fathers' parental leave uptake is also positively associated with second-birth propensities, keeping fertility at a reasonable level (Oláh and Bernhardt 2008). Moreover, the father's quota is shown to be quite effective in involving immigrant fathers in their children's care, strengthening societal integration (Mussino et al. 2018). Both immigrant mothers and immigrant fathers use less parental leave than Swedish mothers and fathers, related to their lower labour market integration. Their use of parental leave increases with the duration of their stay in Sweden. However, the most gender-equally used measure is the temporary parental benefit to care for sick children, with fathers taking 43 per cent of such leave days.

Parents', especially mothers', labour force participation has also been facilitated by high-quality public childcare, increasing options to ease social risks around the reconciliation of paid work and family life. Thus, poverty risks do not escalate despite high family instability and the variety of family structures children are brought up in (OECD 2020). Research has even shown that children in shared physical custody living alternately with either parent after their union dissolution, which is a rather common arrangement among separated parents in Sweden, experience lower levels of stress than children who live only or mostly with one parent, irrespective of parental income (Turunen 2017). Childcare provision also supports social equality by reducing the gap in children's life chances, no matter of any (dis)advantaged backgrounds. This is related to public childcare use being nearly universal in Sweden. In the 2010s, about half of the 1-year-olds were cared for by their parents using parental leave, while the rest attended public childcare, along with 90 per cent of the 2-year-olds and 94 per cent of children aged 3 to 5 (Skolverket 2020). The high rates of utilisation also demonstrate the high social acceptance of childcare services as part of the social investment paradigm and universal welfare provision Sweden is known for.

CONCLUDING THOUGHTS

Changing labour markets and a previously unprecedented diversity of family constellations annihilating the gender contract of the male-breadwinner era brought along new social risks to accompany old risks for post-industrial welfare systems to handle. The individualisation of families proved the earlier, marriage-based provision of welfare inadequate, putting reconciliation of paid work and family responsibilities in the forefront to reduce social and economic risks for adults and children alike. Moreover, changing demographics due to very low fertility and ageing populations as well as increasing population heterogeneity challenge the viability of the intergenerational contract and the legitimacy of redistribution, which are at the heart of the welfare state. Therefore, the Swedish example is especially valuable, since Sweden managed to keep fertility from plummeting and remaining at very low levels, preserving a rather stable population age structure and keeping new social risks at bay despite high levels of family instability in society. The social investment strategy followed from the 1990s onwards combined with employment-oriented family policy offers some valuable lessons for welfare systems in the post-industrial era.

An essential aspect is that Swedish family policies are not geared to support a specific family form, such as marriage, but are rather directed at the individual, independent of family structure. The main aim is to reduce socio-economic differences and gender differences in employment and the family, and ultimately to ensure social and gender equality for all. Hence, Swedish family policies are designed to support the employment of all adults and to enable women and men to reconcile paid work and care for their children, even in the case of separated parents. When gender-neutral policies prove largely ineffective to break old gender patterns of care, policy-makers do not shy away from gendered incentives to promote gender equality, such as the father's quota in the parental leave scheme, which can also function as a tool for migrants' social integration. Last but not least, service provision is better aligned with the principle of universalism in the (re)distribution of welfare than cash transfers; hence, offering all children high-quality early childhood education via the public childcare system is an investment benefiting the entire society in the long run.

ACKNOWLEDGEMENTS

We gratefully acknowledge financial support to Livia Sz. Oláh from Stockholm University via the research program Ageing Well – Individuals, Families and Households under Changing Demographic Regimes in Sweden (grant number 2016-07115) by the Swedish Research Council for Health, Working life and Welfare (FORTE), and to Gerda Neyer via the Project on Fertility Intentions, Fertility Considerations and Fertility Decline in Sweden (Dnr 2020-01976) by the Swedish Research Council.

REFERENCES

Beaujouan, Eva, and Caroline Berghammer (2019), 'The gap between lifetime fertility intentions and completed fertility in Europe and the United States: A cohort approach', *Population Research and Policy Review*, 38 (4), 507–535.
Becker, Gary S. (1991), *A Treatise on the Family* (enlarged ed.). Cambridge, MA: Harvard University Press.
Blossfeld, Hans-Peter (ed.) (1995), *The New Role of Women: Family Formation in Modern Societies*. Boulder, CO: Westview Press.

Bonoli, Giuliano (2007), 'Time matters: Postindustrialization, new social risks, and welfare state adaptation in advanced industrial democracies', *Comparative Political Studies*, 40 (5), 495–520.

Booth, Alan, and Ann C. Crouter (eds) (2002), *Just Living Together: Implications of Cohabitation on Families, Children and Social Policy*. London: Routledge.

Brochmann, Grete, and Anniken Hagelund (2011), 'Migrants in the Scandinavian welfare state: The emergence of a social policy problem', *Nordic Journal of Migration Research*, 1 (1), 13–24.

Burgoon, Brian, and Matthijs Rooduijn (2020), '"Immigrationization" of welfare politics? Anti-immigration and welfare attitudes in context', *West European Politics*. https://doi.org/10.1080/01402382.2019.1702297 (accessed August 1, 2020).

Charles, Maria (2005), 'National skill regimes, postindustrialism, and sex segregation', *Social Politics: International Studies in Gender, State & Society*, 12 (2), 289–316.

D'Amuri, Francesco, and Giovanni Peri (2014), 'Immigration, jobs, and employment protection: Evidence from Europe before and during the Great Recession', *Journal of the European Economic Association*, 12 (2), 432–464.

Daly, Mary (2011), 'What adult worker model? A critical look at recent social policy reform in Europe from a gender and family perspective', *Social Politics: International Studies in Gender, State & Society*, 18 (1), 1–23.

Duvander, Ann-Zofie, and Anne Lise Ellingsæter (2016), 'Cash for childcare schemes in the Nordic welfare states: Diverse paths, diverse outcomes', *European Societies*, 18 (1), 70–90.

Duvander, Ann-Zofie, and Tommy Ferrarini (2013), 'Sweden's family policy under change: Past, present and future', *Friedrich Ebert Stiftung International Policy Analysis*. https://library.fes.de/pdf-files/id/10232.pdf (accessed July 6, 2021).

Duvander, Ann-Zofie, Linda Haas and Philip Hwang (2017), 'Country notes: April 2017. Sweden', in Sonja Blum, Alison Koslowski and Peter Moss (eds), *13th International Review of Leave Policies and Research 2017*, pp. 392–400. www.leavenetwork.org/fileadmin/user_upload/k_leavenetwork/annual_reviews/2017_Leave_Review_2017_final2.pdf (accessed October 30, 2020).

Duvander, Ann-Zofie, and Ida Viklund (2020), 'How long is a parental leave and for whom? An analysis of methodological and policy dimensions of leave length and division in Sweden', *International Journal of Sociology and Social Policy*, 40 (5/6), 479–494.

Esping-Andersen, Gøsta (1999), *The Social Foundations of Post-Industrial Economies*. Oxford: Oxford University Press.

Esping-Andersen, Gøsta, Anton Hemerijck, Duncan Gallie and John Myles (2002), *Why We Need a New Welfare State*. Oxford: Oxford University Press.

Eurostat (2020), Database. http://ec.europa.eu/eurostat/data/database (accessed August 3, 2020).

Fenwick, Clare (2019), 'The political economy of immigration and welfare state effort: Evidence from Europe', *European Political Science Review*, 11, 357–375.

Ferrarini, Tommy, and Ann-Zofie Duvander (2010), 'Earner-carer model at the cross-roads: Reforms and outcomes of Sweden's family policy in comparative perspective', *International Journal of Health Services*, 40 (3), 373–398.

Finseraas, Henning (2008), 'Immigration and preferences for redistribution: An empirical analysis of European survey data', *Comparative European Politics*, 6, 407–431.

Goldscheider, Frances K., Eva Bernhardt and Trude Lappegård (2015), 'The gender revolution: A framework for understanding changing family and demographic behavior', *Population and Development Review*, 41 (2), 207–239.

Gros, Daniel, and Alfred Steinherr (2004), *Economic Transition in Central and Eastern Europe: Planting the Seeds*. Cambridge: Cambridge University Press.

INED (2013), Developed countries database. www.ined.fr/en/pop_figures/developed _countries_database/ (accessed July 3, 2013).

Komp, Kathrin, and Theo Van Tilburg (2010), 'Ageing societies and the welfare state: Where the inter-generational contract is not breached', *International Journal of Ageing and Later Life*, 5 (1), 7–11.

Lennartz, Christian, and Richard Ronald (2017), 'Asset-based welfare and social investment: Competing, compatible, or complementary social policy strategies for the new welfare state?', *Housing, Theory and Society*, 34 (2), 201–220.

Lesthaeghe, Ron (2010), 'The unfolding story of the Second Demographic Transition', *Population and Development Review*, 36 (2), 211–251.

Lewis, Jane (2006), 'Gender and welfare in modern Europe', *Past & Present*, 1 (Suppl 1), 39–54.

Macura, Miroslav, Alphonse L. MacDonald and Werner Haug (eds) (2005), *The New Demographic Regime: Population Challenges and Policy Responses*. New York, NY: United Nations.

Matysiak, Anna, Marta Styrc and Daniele Vignoli (2014), 'The educational gradient in marital disruption: A meta-analysis of European research findings', *Population Studies*, 68 (2), 197–215.

McDonald, Peter (2006), 'Low fertility and the state: The efficacy of policy', *Population and Development Review*, 32 (3), 485–510.

Morel, Nathalie, Bruno Palier and Joakim Palme (eds) (2012), *Towards a Social Investment Welfare State? Ideas, Policies and Challenges*. Bristol: Policy Press.

Mussino, Eleonora, Ann-Zofie Duvander and Li Ma (2018), 'Does time count? Immigrant fathers' use of parental leave for a first child in Sweden', *Population*, 73 (2), 363–382.

OECD (2020), 'Family database: Indicators'. www.oecd.org/social/family/database .htm (accessed September 6, 2020).

Oláh, Livia Sz., and Eva M. Bernhardt (2008), 'Sweden: Combining childbearing and gender equality', *Demographic Research*, 19 (28), 1105–1144.

Oláh, Livia Sz., Irena E. Kotowska and Rudolf Richter (2018), 'The new roles of men and women and implications for families and societies', in Gabriele Doblhammer and Jordi Gumà (eds), *A Demographic Perspective on Gender, Family, and Health in Europe*. Cham: Springer, pp. 41–64.

Orloff, Ann Shola (1993), 'Gender and the social rights of citizenship: The comparative analysis of gender relations and welfare states', *American Sociological Review*, 58 (3), 303–328.

Palier, Bruno (ed.) (2010), *A Long Goodbye to Bismarck? The Politics of Welfare Reform in Continental Europe*. Amsterdam: Amsterdam University Press.

Pateman, Carol (1988), *The Sexual Contract*. Stanford, CA: Stanford University Press.

Perelli-Harris, Brienna, and Nora Sánchez Gassen (2012), 'How similar are cohabitation and marriage? Legal approaches to cohabitation across Western Europe', *Population and Development Review*, 38 (3), 435–467.

Ranson, Gillian (2001), 'Men at work: Change or – no change? – in the era of the "New Father"', *Men and Masculinities*, 4 (1), 3–26.

Skolverket (2020), Statistik om förskola. www.skolverket.se/skolutveckling/statistik/ sok-statistik-om-forskola-skola-och-vuxenutbildning?sok=SokC&verkform=F%C3 %B6rskola&omrade=Barn%20och%20grupper&lasar=1998&run=1 (accessed September 1, 2020).

Sobotka, Tomáš, and Laurent Toulemon (2008), 'Overview Chapter 4: Changing family and partnership behavior – Common trends and persistent diversity across Europe', *Demographic Research*, 19 (6), 85–138.

Taylor-Gooby, Peter (2004), 'New risks and social change', in Peter Taylor-Gooby (ed.), *New Risks, New Welfare: The Transformation of the European Welfare State.* Oxford: Oxford University Press. https://oxford.universitypressscholarship.com/view/10.1093/019926726X.001.0001/acprof-9780199267262-chapter-1

Thévenon, Olivier (2011), 'Family policies in OECD countries: A comparative analysis', *Population and Development Review*, 37 (1), 57–87.

Turunen, Jani (2017), 'Shared physical custody and children's experience of stress', *Journal of Divorce & Remarriage*, 58 (5), 371–392.

Van Bavel, Jan, Christine R. Schwartz and Albert Esteve (2018), 'The reversal of the gender gap in education and its consequences for family life', *Annual Review of Sociology*, 44, 341–360.

Wilson, Chris, Tomáš Sobotka, Lee Williamson and Paul Boyle (2013), 'Migration and intergenerational replacement in Europe', *Population and Development Review*, 39 (1), 131–157.

Wincott, Daniel (2013), 'The "Golden Age" of the welfare state: Interrogating a conventional wisdom', *Public Administration*, 91 (4), 806–822.

4. Nordic family policy in the 2000s: from a 'transfer-based' towards a 'service-based' family policy?

Mia Hakovirta and Mikael Nygård

INTRODUCTION

The Nordic family policy model is often depicted as the most family-friendly and gender-equal model in the world. For example, in the 2019 UNICEF report on family friendliness, Sweden, Norway and Iceland were declared world leaders, with Denmark and Finland following closely behind (Chzhen et al. 2019). Not only have the Nordic states protected the vast majority of families from poverty and compensated them for the costs of children, but they have also invested in public services that emancipated women and created a dual-earner model (Korpi 2000). However, during the last three decades, deindustrialisation, new social risks, globalisation and migration, as well as economic crises, have put the welfare state under increasing pressure (see, for example, Hemerijck 2013), including in the Nordic welfare states. For instance, poverty and economic inequality is on the rise, partly because of higher capital incomes and increasing numbers of immigrants (Nygård et al. 2019; Søgaard 2018; Chzhen et al. 2017). The 2008–2009 international financial crisis led to a temporary slump in parental employment across the Nordic countries (OECD 2019a), and pushed public spending on family cash benefits downwards in Denmark and Iceland (Nygård et al. 2019; Farnsworth and Irving 2015). Some parents still find it difficult to balance work and care responsibilities. For example, nonstandard work schedules and long working hours are associated with increased time-based work–family conflict (Tammelin et al. 2017). Some households also encounter a relatively high risk of working poverty, especially those with many children, single-parent households and migrant households (Halleröd et al. 2015).

The aim of this chapter is to discuss these questions by examining the changes and outcomes relating to family-friendly and gender-equal policies in the five Nordic countries during the 2000s. More specifically, we want to know what the main traits of family policy change have been in these five countries during this time of economic turmoil and changing social needs, and second what the outcomes of family policy have been in terms of poverty and gender equality.

Family policy consists of different instruments and objectives. Using Kamerman and Kahn (1978) as a starting point, we distinguish between explicit policies that affect families directly, such as income transfers and services for families, and implicit policies that affect families indirectly, such as labour market policies, education, tax policies, and so on. As to objectives, Thévenon (2011) proposes the following list: (a) poverty reduction, (b) cost compensation of children, (c) employment promotion through work–family reconciliation, (d) gender equality through equal sharing of both paid and unpaid work between parents, (e) early childhood development and/or (f) societal reproduction through sufficiently high birth rates. When we speak about 'family friendliness' in this chapter we refer primarily to the first two of these objectives; that is, strategies to combat poverty and economic ine-quality through cash transfers, whereas for analytical reasons we treat gender quality and early childhood development as separate, albeit interrelated, policy ambitions. Also, employment promotion is seen as closely linked to gender equality.

We argue that during the 2000s policies advocating children's development as well as gender equality have become more accentuated in the Nordic coun-tries, while family-friendly income strategies have lost ground. This suggests a gradual shift in accentuation away from a 'transfer-based' income protection strategy towards a 'service-based' family policy that highlights parental labour market participation as the foremost remedy for poverty, and that focuses on the rights and development of children. Meanwhile, child poverty rates climbed after the 2008–2009 international financial crisis, most notably in single-parent, multi-child and immigrant households (see, for example, Povlsen et al. 2018; Galloway et al. 2015) – something that warrants a critical discussion about the future family friendliness of the Nordic family policy model. Thus, this chapter contributes to the literature on Nordic family policy in the 21st century, but also seeks to revisit some theoretical arguments about this model.

The structure of the chapter is the following. We first discuss some general policy traits and family spending patterns in the Nordic countries during the 2000s, and then go on with the outcomes of these policies, notably to assess their effects upon child and family poverty. Finally, we sum up our conclu-sions and discuss the future viability of the Nordic family policy model.

ADVOCATING GENDER EQUALITY AND CHILDREN'S RIGHTS: FAMILY REFORM PATTERNS IN THE 2000S

The Nordic countries already had a well-documented track record of gender-equal parental leave schemes and subsidised childcare services by the turn of the millennium (Leira 2006). Nevertheless, the trend since 2000 has been to further advance these policy areas. For instance, massive investments in care services, individualised social rights and tax schemes have made it easier for women and mothers to participate in the labour market, while fathers increasingly take part in their children's upbringing through paternal leaves and notably the 'daddy quotas' (Eydal et al. 2018). One of the most conspicuous trends during the 2000s has been to enhance gender equality and to strengthen children's life chances through parental leave and early childhood education and care (ECEC) reforms.

The Nordic parental leave systems belong to the most generous and flexible systems in the world and enable parents to stay at home with their toddlers and receive wage compensation. These rights also include elements of shared or partial leave aimed at facilitating work–family balance and enhancing gender equality (NOSOSCO 2017). Maternity leaves were introduced early, while dual parental leaves and paternity leaves were put in place incrementally from the 1970s. Sweden was the first country in the world to introduce paid leave for both parents in 1974, with a separate paternal leave in 1980. Norway and Finland gave their fathers paternal leave in 1977 and 1978, respectively, while Denmark and Iceland followed in 1984 and 1998. Norway was also the first country to legislate on earmarked 'daddy quotas' in 1993, followed by Sweden in 1994, and later on by the other Nordic countries (Eydal et al. 2015).

This trend has continued in the 2000s, since flexibility and notably 'daddy quotas' have generally been considered to be the most efficient way of inducing fathers to stay at home with their children. As an example, Iceland extended the right to parental leave from six to nine months in 2000, giving the mother and father three months each with a shareable extra three months. There was also a plan to extend the leave further to 12 months, but this was later dropped due to the recession of 2008–2009. It resurfaced in the 2010s, as the Icelandic government proposed an extension of the earmarked leaves until 2022 for both mothers and fathers (Eydal et al. 2018). In Finland, paternal leave was extended a couple of times during the 2000s, and since 2013 it has stretched to 54 weekdays with a three-week-long 'daddy quota' (Nyby et al. 2018; Salmi and Närvi 2014). A further reform has been on the agenda for some time, and in February 2021, the Finnish government finally announced a reform that will take effect in 2022 and introduce a 6.4-month-long leave quota for both the mother and the father together with a transferable period of 0–63 days. In Norway, the pioneer of paternal leave and 'daddy quotas', the right to this leave was made independent of the mother in 2005 at the same time as the length of the 'daddy quota' was extended to five weeks, and in 2006 to six weeks (Skevik and Hatland 2008). In 2009, after some political controversy, the quota was again extended, this time to ten weeks (Eydal and Rostgaard 2017), and in 2018 both the mother's and the father's quotas were stretched to 15 weeks each with a shareable 16-week leave (Government of Norway 2018). Sweden made similar improvements during the 2000s. In 2002 the daddy month, introduced in 1995, was extended to two months (Björnberg and Dahlgren 2008). In 2005 the social-democratic government's plan to increase it further was blocked. Instead a 'gender equality bonus' meant to encourage fathers to use a larger share of the parental leave was introduced in 2008, but this was phased out in the 2010s because of its meagre effects. On the other hand, the right to use parental leave was made more flexible in 2014, and in 2016 both the mother's and father's quotas were prolonged to three months each (Government of Sweden 2018). When it comes to Denmark, finally, the trend has been somewhat different, since the government abolished its 'daddy quotas' in 2011, arguing that this interfered with parents' freedom of choice (Rostgaard and Lausten 2015).

Along with parental insurance, child home care leave was also used for enabling the care of children in the home, and thus extended the leave periods. In Finland this option was introduced in 1985 as a way of easing the pressure on municipal childcare and providing a 'mothers' wage' (Hiilamo and Kangas 2009). Denmark followed in 1992, Sweden in 1994 and Norway in 1998. However, this leave has been controversial since it has been seen as counter-productive to gender equality. Consequently, it was abolished in Sweden by the Social Democrats in 1996. It was reintroduced in 2008 by the conservative government but again abolished in 2016 by the Social Democrats. Denmark also removed this option in 2002, whereas Norway has proposed a phasing out of the right (Eydal and Rostgaard 2017). It is still in use, though with a more flexible modus operandi since 2018 (Government of Norway 2018). Iceland is the only Nordic country that has not legislated in home care of children, but still local authorities can pay a home care allowance for parents caring for their children at home (NOSOSCO 2017).

When it comes to ECEC policies, the Nordic countries made important policy reforms in the 2000s. The underlying ambition behind these reforms was to enhance children's life prospects by strengthening their human capital in accordance with a social investment paradigm (see, for example, Hemerijck 2013; Morel et al. 2012), and to facilitate work–family reconciliation and get more mothers out in the labour market. In 2004 Denmark adopted a 'childcare guarantee' that provided 26-week-old children with publicly subsidised childcare until school age (which starts at the age of 6). In Finland this right was legislated in 1996, and in 2001 voluntary pre-school education was introduced. After a lengthy discussion about strengthening ECEC and children's rights, pre-schooling between 6 and 7 (the official school age) was made compulsory in 2015, and shortly after that the childcare legislation was reformed in a more child-oriented and pedagogical way (NOSOSCO 2017). Later that same year, the right to full-day ECEC was restricted to children with working parents (Lundkvist et al. 2017), but was reinstated by the newly appointed government (in office from 2019). In Iceland and Norway there was also an expansion of childcare services during the 2000s, although the Icelandic development was somewhat more modest than the Norwegian, where rapid expansion took place after a 2003 parliamentary cross-party agreement on kindergarten for all children (Karila 2012). In 2009 Norwegian children over one year of age became entitled to publicly subsidised childcare, making the Norwegian system the most comprehensive in this region (Eydal and Rostgaard 2017). In Sweden children aged 1–5 became entitled to public childcare in 2003 while 6-year-olds can claim pre-schooling until they reach school age (at 7). The Swedish childcare right initially covered only children of gainfully employed parents, but was later expanded to all children. A system of maximum fees lowered the childcare costs for most parents, while childcare became free to 4- to 5-year-olds, and from 2010 also for 3-year-olds (Björnberg 2016). During the 2010s, the Swedish government made further investments in ECEC quality and expanded private care options in order to ease the pressure on municipalities and to enhance freedom of choice (Duvander and Ellingsæter 2016).

When it comes to income transfers to families, finally we see a slightly different policy trait than in the case of gender-equal and child-investing policies. The Nordic states have protected the income of families with children through different income transfers, of which the child allowance (or family allowance) is of foremost importance.[1] These transfers were introduced shortly after the Second World War as a way of compensating for the costs of children (Wennemo 1994). They are paid to children under 18 (under 17 in Finland and 16 in Sweden) and are universal, except in Iceland, where they are means-tested. They are mostly progressive, meaning that the second and subsequent children receive higher allowances, and also come with a supplement for single parents (NOSOSCO 2017, p. 63).[2] Moreover, different forms of selective income transfers are used for preventing poverty, such as child maintenance assistance or single-parent supplements to last-resort social assistance. Together these benefits have constituted an important economic foundation for the family-friendly family policy model in the Nordic countries. However, during the 2000s the overall pattern to be discerned is an incremental erosion of the purchasing power of the child allowances, whereas selective income transfers have received a somewhat more prominent role.

In Denmark, as an example, child allowances became overshadowed by investments in childcare during the 1990s and early 2000s, although there was a continuous upgrading of their generosity from time to time (Abrahamson 2010). A major reform followed in 2011, when the universal right to child allowances was abolished for families with an annual income over a certain amount (in 2016 this line was approximately 90,600 euros) at the same time as the right was expanded to all children in the family, regardless of their number. The main ambition was to concentrate the allowances to the neediest families in an attempt to curb child poverty and prevent social exclusion, and to curb the increase in public spending (NOSOSCO 2017; Danish Government 2012). In Finland, there were a number of piecemeal improvements of the child allowance and the child home care allowance in 2004 and 2009 as a way of improving their purchase power after the cuts that were made during the economic crisis in the 1990s (Nyby et al. 2018). However, since the improvements were quite modest, they did not stop child poverty from almost tripling between 1995 and 2009 (Salmi and Närvi 2014). In 2014, the government cut the child allowance by approximately 8 per cent. Moreover, in 2012 it froze the indexation formula, and in 2015 abolished it altogether. A symbolic tax relief was introduced in 2014, together with several piecemeal improvements of single-parent supports during the 2010s, which suggests a selective turn in Finnish family policy during this period (Nyby et al. 2018). However, some of the cuts made by the previous governments were withdrawn by the government inaugurated in 2019, indicating a gradual shift back to a more universalistic family policy. In Iceland there was a resolution to improve income transfers to families in 1994, which led to a continuous upscaling of the child allowances and also other transfers between 1997 and 2007 (Ólafsson 2016). However, the Icelandic child allowances have generally been modest in Nordic comparison (NOSOSCO 2017), but on the other hand they have not been subjected to cuts in the same way as in Finland. However, when the financial crisis hit Iceland in 2008, the government was compelled to cut public expenditures including spending on child allowances, although the cuts were not dramatic (Ólafsson 2016).

In Norway child allowances remained more or less stable from 1990 to 2005. One exception is the reform in 2000 that made 17-year-olds entitled to these allowances. At the same time the sibling supplements were abolished in 2001. In the 2010s, the government in Norway improved selective family transfers, notably to low-income families, and also child home care allowances (Government of Norway 2018). On the whole this suggests an erosion of the purchasing power of child allowances in Norway over time. The fact that child allowances were not raised after 2000 did not cause much political controversy, since major improvements were simultaneously made in the area of childcare and ECEC (Sørvoll 2015; Skevik and Hatland 2008). However, in 2018 the Norwegian conservative coalition proposed a noticeable increase of the universal child allowance, something that was implemented in 2019. In Sweden the child allowances were not improved much during the 2000s. In the midst of the economic crisis in the 1990s the child allowances were cut, but the original levels were reinstated a couple of years later. A couple of further raises were made (2000, 2001 and 2005), together with some improvements of selective transfers in 2003 with the aim of curbing child poverty (Björnberg and Dahlgren 2008). After this, the general trend was to leave the child allowances untouched for almost a decade, which caused their purchasing power to drop over time. After the Social Democrats regained power in 2014, some improvements were made in selective transfers, such as the guaranteed child maintenance allowance (Duvander and Ellingsæter 2016). The child allowance was also raised in 2017 (for the third child) and again in 2018 (Försäkringskassan 2018).

The child maintenance, which in a post-separation situation obligates one parent to pay cash to the other parent in order to share the costs of raising their children, is an important income for single parents (Hakovirta and Jokela 2019). All Nordic countries, except Iceland, made changes in their child maintenance systems in the 2000s. In 2003 Norway overhauled its child maintenance policy by treating the care and incomes of both parents equally in the determination of child maintenance benefits. In 2009, Finland transferred the administration of the guaranteed child maintenance scheme and the responsibility for enforcement from local municipalities to the Social Insurance Institution (Kela). Also, Denmark centralised its child maintenance system in 2007. In Sweden, the child maintenance system was changed in 1997, and in the 2000s there were small technical changes (Skinner and Hakovirta 2020). There are some differences among the Nordic countries as to how their child maintenance policies work in terms of structure and outcomes. Norway, Sweden and Denmark are more gender-equal in their child maintenance policies as they lean more towards the dual-earner/dual-carer model, according to which both parents are responsible for providing children with cash and care in post-separation families. In Finland and Iceland, the dual-earner/dual-carer model has not yet received attention in child maintenance policies, as most support is provided to one parent who is classified as being responsible for the everyday care of the child, while a non-resident parent, typically the father, remains seen as a provider (Hakovirta and Eydal 2020).

To conclude, what we see here, then, is something of an incremental erosion of (universal) economic protection of families and a creeping selectivity. The trend seems to have been to let the purchasing power of child allowances lag behind inflation and real wages, whereas there are multiple examples of improvements of selective and means-tested transfers. At the same time, important reforms have been made in parental leave schemes and ECEC,

Table 4.1   Public expenditure on families in the Nordic countries during the 2000s

Expenditure type	Year	DEN	FIN	ICE	NOR	SWE	OECD
Total spending on families (% of gross domestic product, or GDP)	2000	3.4	2.9	2.1	3.0	2.8	1.8
	2007	3.6	2.7	3.4	2.7	3.2	1.9
	2012	3.7	3.2	3.5	3.0	3.6	2.1
	2015	3.4	3.1	3.4	3.3	3.5	2.0
Total spending on families (per capita)	2000	973	785	632	1,107	822	430
	2007	1,386	1,027	1,380	1,533	1,297	665
	2012	1,643	1,297	1,408	1,991	1,595	817
	2015	1,675	1,309	1,613	2,011	1,694	841
Spending on family cash benefits (% of GDP)	2000	1.5	1.7	1.0	1.8	1.4	1.1
	2007	1.5	1.4	1.3	1.3	1.4	1.2
	2012	1.4	1.5	1.1	1.3	1.4	1.2
	2015	1.4	1.4	1.0	1.4	1.4	1.1
Spending on family cash benefits (per capita)	2000	417	456	296	673	415	278
	2007	586	539	550	737	575	414
	2012	634	621	434	865	644	485
	2015	662	594	484	838	651	482
Spending on family in-kind benefits (% of GDP)	2000	1.9	1.2	1.1	1.2	1.4	0.6
	2007	2.1	1.3	2.0	1.4	1.8	0.7
	2012	2.3	1.7	2.4	1.7	2.1	0.9
	2015	2.1	1.7	2.4	1.9	2.2	0.9
Spending on family in-kind benefits (per capita)	2000	557	329	337	433	407	152
	2007	800	488	829	797	723	251
	2012	1,009	676	974	1,126	951	332
	2015	1,014	715	1,130	1,173	1,043	358

Notes: The data is from the OECD SOCX expenditure database (OECD 2019b). Spending per capita is reported in US dollars, current prices and current purchasing power parity.

which suggests a gradual shift away from a 'transfer-based' family policy to a 'service-based' strategy. This interpretation receives support from Table 4.1, which shows public spending on families over time in the five Nordic countries (OECD 2019b).

The OECD SOCX family spending data, which gives an indication on the spending pattern of a welfare state, indicates a gradual increase of total family spending during the 2000s, both in terms of their share of GDP and per head, with a slight boost during the 2008–2009 financial crisis and afterwards. It is important to remember, though, that public social spending data does not say anything about the more fine-grained policy changes behind changes in spending. It gives a rough pecuniary measure of 'welfare state effort' in different policy areas, which is not totally uninteresting since it can help to trace changes in policy preferences over time (Nygård et al. 2019). A closer look at Table 4.1 reveals that since 2012 the amount of family spending relative to GDP has decreased in four out of five countries, whereas per-head spending has continued to climb. This is hardly surprising given the fact that spending relative to GDP usually drops when economic growth sets in. What we can also see, and what is more interesting for our case, is that the in-kind spending, such as spending on childcare services and ECEC, has increased over time, whereas spending on cash benefits, such as the child allowance, has not grown in the same way. In some countries, such as Finland and Norway, spending on cash benefits per capita has dropped somewhat since 2012, while the opposite is true for spending on benefits in kind in all countries since 2012.

Also, Figure 4.1, which shows average public spending on ECEC and child allowances over time, suggests that the focus of Nordic family policy during the 2000s was on benefits in kind, notably ECEC services, rather than on improvements of child allowances.

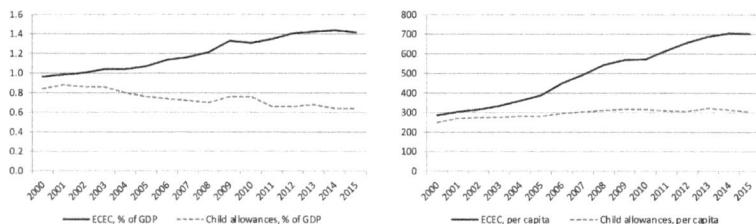

Source: OECD (2019b).

Figure 4.1   *Average public spending on ECEC and child allowances in the Nordic countries, 2000–2015, in per cent of GDP (upper) and per capita (lower)*

As we can see, public spending on ECEC has climbed steadily over the 2000s, both relative to GDP and per head, while spending on child allowances has dropped over time relative to GDP and remained more or less on the same level in terms of per-head spending. Perhaps this is not very surprising given the strong impact that EU imperatives on childcare enrolment or employment pro-

motion have had, as well as the increasing influence of so-called social investment ideas highlighting investments in children and employment-friendly
family policies (Morel et al. 2012; Esping-Andersen 2009). Although Nordic
countries have been forerunners in the field of social investments, it is clear
that this ambition has not lost its attraction during the 2000s, since there have
been numerous reforms to improve the quality of ECEC and widen the access
to formal childcare.

FAMILY POLICY OUTCOMES: TOWARDS CREEPING CHILD POVERTY?

What have the outcomes of this overall policy trend been? A glance at Table
4.2, which points out some changes in Nordic family policy during the 2000s,
suggests that some progress has been made when it comes to gender equality
and childcare enrolment. In all five countries the enrolment rate for 5-year-old
children has increased, although at different paces. In 2017 it was highest in
Iceland and lowest in Finland, which partly reflects the fact that many children under 3 are not in ECEC in Finland, but in home childcare. According
to a report from the Nordic Council of Ministers (NOSOSCO 2017), about
84 per cent of the Danish children participated in some kind of childcare in
2016. The corresponding rate for Finnish children was 45 per cent, but among
3- to 5-year-olds it was 81 per cent. In Iceland about 91 per cent of children
under 3 participated in childcare, while the share of children between 3 and
5 was almost 97 per cent. The same rates also apply for Norway and Sweden
(NOSOSCO 2017).

As to gender equality, we see that female employment has climbed during
the 2000s in all five countries, with a temporary slump after the financial crisis.
It has been highest in Iceland and lowest in Finland. Also, when it comes to
fathers' engagement in childcare we see an upward trend, which is perhaps
most conspicuous in Denmark, Finland and Sweden, whereas it seems to have
stagnated in Iceland and even gone down somewhat in Norway. On the whole,
however, these findings, although fragmented, suggest that the child-oriented
and gender-equal policies have been fruitful, at least to some extent.

What is more worrisome is the upper half of Table 4.2, which shows that
the poverty risk among children under 18 has increased in all five countries
during the 2000s. This can also be seen in Figure 4.2, which shows the change
in average poverty rates for children under 18 and 6 years old, respectively.

We see that both indicators of child poverty have climbed from 2004, the
first year of data availability, to 2008, with a somewhat more pronounced climb
during the 2008–2009 financial meltdown. The poverty curves even out after
the financial crisis, which is partly connected to higher growth rates and lower
unemployment, but also to the fact that some of the Nordic countries, such as

Table 4.2   Family policy outcomes in the Nordic countries during the 2000s

Indicator	Year(s)	DEN	FIN	ICE	NOR	SWE	EU
Poverty, children under 18 (%)	2003–4	9.4	9.8	11.5	8.5	12.1	..
	2007	9.6	10.9	11.9	11.0	12.0	20.1
	2012	10.4	11.1	10.0	8.3	17.7	20.5
	2018	11.0	11.1	..	13.2	19.3	19.9
Poverty, children under 6 (%)	2003–4	10.6	11.0	14.7	6.8	11.7	..
	2007	10.6	11.9	15.8	12.6	11.9	18.5
	2012	7.6	12.3	12.9	11.2	18.9	18.8
	2018	9.7	11.5	..	13.1	21.4	18.5
Poverty, children under 18 with foreign-born parents (%)	2003–4	25.4	23.4	14.5	17.6	24.6	..
	2007	25.8	22.6	10.9	19.7	25.2	30.4
	2012	26.9	23.9	12.6	19.7	33.7	32.0
	2018	25.4	19.7	..	24.8	38.0	32.3
Poverty, single parent with dependent children (%)	2000	12.0*	22.0	..	..	13.0*	..
	2007	16.0	21.9	23.3	24.8	25.0	33.4
	2012	18.7	22.0	24.5	20.5	29.4	33.2
	2018	27.2	24.4	..	28.6**	34.6	35.4
Poverty, two adults and one dependent child (%)	2000	3.0*	5.0	..	..	5.0*	..
	2007	4.3	6.0	6.3	4.6	5.8	4.7
	2012	4.2	5.7	4.9	6.6	10.8	12.9
	2018	4.5	4.8	..	5.6**	10.4	12.0
Poverty, two adults and two dependent children (%)	2000	3.0*	5.0	..	..	4.0*	..
	2007	4.2	5.3	7.3	5.0	5.6	13.7
	2012	4.3	5.5	5.6	2.5	9.1	15.0
	2018	2.8	4.9	..	3.5**	8.7	14.4
Poverty, two adults and three or more dependent children (%)	2000	13.0*	5.0	..	..	8.0*	..
	2007	14.6	12.5	12.1	8.1	13.6	26.1
	2012	9.8	14.3	6.5	7.4	26.2	26.0
	2018	12.4	12.0	..	13.1**	24.7	25.5
Share of 5-year-old children in ECEC (% of same age group)	2000	..	..	..	..	..	..

Indicator	Year(s)	DEN	FIN	ICE	NOR	SWE	EU
	2005	..	73.29	..	91.1	..	..
	2010	95.3	77.4	..	97.3	..	..
	2017	96.9	85.0	97.8	97.5	95.2	..
Female employment rate (%)	2000	71.6	61.2	..	73.7	..	..
	2007	73.2	68.5	80.8	74.0	71.8	58.0
	2012	70.0	68.2	77.9	73.8	71.8	58.2
	2018	72.7	70.6	82.5	72.7	76.0	62.0
Fathers' parental leave take-up rate (%)	2000	..	..	2.9	6.9	..	..
	2005	..	..	32.7	8.8	..	..
	2010	9.5	7.9	31.7	14.5	..	..
	2016	10.7	10.5	28.8	18.8	28.2	..

Notes: * indicates year 2001 and ** year 2017. Poverty rates (Eurostat 2019) report at-risk-of-poverty rates (cut-off point: 60 per cent of median equivalised income after social transfers). ECEC enrolment rates (OECD 2020) are calculated by dividing the number of students of a particular age group enrolled in ECEC by the size of the population of that age. The figures do not distinguish between full- and part-time enrolment. Data on female employment is from OECD (2019a). Data on fathers' parental leave take-up is from NOSOSCO (2017), and reports the share of men (in per cent) receiving daily cash benefits at childbirth and adoption during the year.

Denmark and Finland, made certain improvements to their child allowances and other selective family transfers during, or soon after, the financial crisis. After 2014, Sweden also followed this path. A closer look reveals that child poverty is much more of a problem in households with foreign-born parents, and that this kind of poverty has climbed markedly, especially in Sweden but also in Norway. This is not surprising when knowing that immigrant households are especially vulnerable in this sense, and that the annual number of immigrants since 2013 has been the highest in Sweden and Norway. Since this year the annual number of immigrants in Sweden has been over 100,000, and in Norway it has circled around 50,000–60,000 new immigrants per year (Eurostat 2018). Also, single-parent families, and families with two adults and three or more children, face a much higher poverty risk than other families with native parents (cf. Nygård et al. 2019; Chzhen et al. 2017). In the case of single-parent families we see a climbing trend over time, except for Iceland, whereas the poverty rate among multi-child families has been more stable over time, and even dropped somewhat during the 2010s in Finland and Sweden.

An overall comparison of the five Nordic countries in Table 4.2 shows that the rise in child poverty during the 2000s has been most accentuated in Norway and Sweden. In Norway, the child poverty rate for children under 18 years old was 11 per cent in 2007 and almost 12 per cent in Sweden. In 2012, it had dropped to 8.3 per cent in Norway, but climbed to almost 18 per

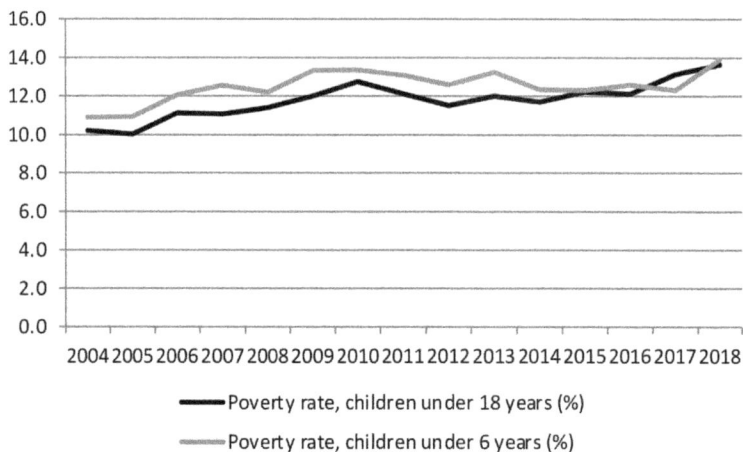

Note: The table shows the percentage of children under 18 and 6 years old, respectively, living in households with an equivalised disposable income below 60 percentage of the annual medium income.
Source: Eurostat (2019).

Figure 4.2   *Development of the child poverty rate in the Nordic countries, 2004–2018*

cent in Sweden. After 2013 the poverty rate in both countries climbed, and in 2018 it was around 13 per cent in Norway and over 19 per cent in Sweden. In Denmark, Finland and Iceland, the poverty rate stabilised after the financial crisis, but on a higher level than before the crisis. Taken together, though, the child poverty levels in the Nordic countries have remained below the European Union (EU) 28 average during the 2000s, except for Sweden, where the child poverty rate for children under 6 and children with foreign-born parents actually exceeded the EU average in 2018. This is perhaps somewhat surprising, knowing that the Swedish government made improvements in the family allowances and other selective transfers during the 2010s. However, the explanation probably lies in the fact that the purchasing power of the family benefits suffered from almost a decade of stagnation, and the fact that selective transfers were not raised sufficiently. The fact that Sweden has a large number of immigrant families with weak or no labour market affiliation also accounts for the finding. Finally, there has been a rapid growth of real wages together with an increase in the wage differential and a rise in top incomes, which has pushed the medium wage upwards and thus caused a rise in relative poverty risks (that are linked to the medium wage) (see Søgaard 2018).

As child poverty is a complex phenomenon that can be defined and measured in several ways, there is a need to also consider alternative ways of measuring it than just looking at relative incomes (Nygård et al. 2019). To date, child poverty in high-income countries is mostly measured in terms of children's 'theoretical' incomes based on their parents' or the household's disposable incomes, and by using a relative poverty threshold, such as the EU at-risk-of-poverty threshold. The main advantage of this procedure is that it facilitates international comparisons and is theoretically relevant since it relates poverty to the general standard of living in a particular country (Bäckman and Ferrarini 2010). However, as said, poverty is complex, which is why a growing literature stresses the importance of measuring child poverty multi-dimensionally. For instance, the UN Sustainable Development Goal 1 suggests that we should use different indices on child deprivation. It is also important to take into account the value of services or benefits in kind (such as free or subsidised ECEC) when comparing poverty levels across countries, since this may affect poverty estimates (see, for example, Aaberge et al. 2013). This does not, of course, mean that aggregated measurements of child poverty, based on relative income methods, are outdated, since they facilitate comparative analyses and – as in the case of this chapter – allow a closer inspection of country trends over time.

CONCLUSIONS AND DISCUSSION

This chapter set out to unravel the changes in family policy that took place in the five Nordic countries during the 2000s, and to discuss the outcomes in terms of poverty, gender equality and children's enrolment in ECEC. We focused on explicit family policies (Kamerman and Kahn 1978) and three specific objectives: 'family-friendly' income transfers aimed at combating poverty and economic inequality, policies fostering gender equality and child development. More specifically, we wanted to investigate whether the Nordic family policies shifted over time, what the outcomes were and whether the acclaimed family-friendly and gender-equal Nordic family policy model is still in place.

A number of conclusions can be drawn. First, we found that the main emphasis of Nordic family policies has shifted from a 'transfer-based' income strategy seeking primarily to combat poverty and economic inequality towards a 'service-based' family policy that emphasises higher gender equality in terms of higher female labour market participation and a higher degree of paternal involvement in childcare, as well as 'social investments' in child development. We reached this conclusion by reviewing the policy changes that were made in the five countries during the 2000s and by analysing patterns of aggregate public spending on families. These analyses reveal that not only have gender cquality and investments in child development been more highlighted in social politics than improvements of (universal) child allowances, but also that the public spending pattern shows a clear accentuation of the two first objectives. We also see a trend indicating that selective income transfers gained in importance over time – for example, in Finland – and that universal child allowances were made income-tested in Denmark. In Norway, the guaranteed child maintenance is income-tested and can be paid with three different rates depending on the income of the recipient. This would suggest a creeping selectivism, at least in some of the countries at the expense of universal income protection. If this is the case it may indicate a possible breach with the assumption of Nordic family policy as the stronghold of universalism.

Second, we can see that child poverty rates have climbed during the 2000s, and especially after the 2008–2009 international financial crisis, most notably in single-parent, multi-child and immigrant households. The rise in overall child poverty, as well as poverty among single-parent and immigrant households, seems to be ubiquitous, albeit with a more moderate rise in Finland in terms of overall child poverty. The reasons for the rise are not straightforward. More refined analyses are needed to unravel what drives rising child poverty. Still, the evidence presented here is highly suggestive, and it also aligns with previous research (for example, Nygård et al. 2019; Chzhen et al. 2017; Bäckman and Ferrarini 2010). Based on this, we can perhaps make some postulations as to potential drivers. One plausible reason is the increasing multitude of families, something that goes hand in hand with a growing number of divorces, increasing immigration and other new 'social risks' pertaining to families (cf. Esping-Andersen 2009; Esping-Andersen et al. 2002). Another potential reason is macroeconomic; that is, the economic crisis following in the wake of the 2008–2009 international financial meltdown that at least temporarily has undermined parental employment (cf. OECD 2019a; Chzhen et al. 2017). The third 'suspect' is higher wage differentials and increasing real wages that in combination with a stagnation of child allowances have lifted the medium wages while leaving low-income families behind – something that results in higher relative poverty (cf. Søgaard 2018).

Taken together, these developments suggest a shift of emphasis in the Nordic family that has given gender equality and spending on benefits in kind the upper hand over ambitions to curb poverty and economic inequality among families – at least from a short time perspective. This is also the case in post-separation child maintenance policies, which aim to provide equal opportunities for both parents to earn and care for their children (Hakovirta and Eydal 2020). This can perhaps be interpreted as a partial reformulation of the meaning of 'family friendliness' for the Nordic family policy model insofar as ambitions relating to poverty reduction and the levelling of economic differences in a 'here-and-now' sense are not considered central in the same way as before, while higher female employment and investments in children are viewed as central for gender equality and better future life prospects of children, but also indirectly for preventing poverty and inequality for families in the long run. If this is the case, it is hardly surprising knowing that one of the most important prerequisites for the future fiscal sustainability of the Nordic welfare state rests on higher employment levels. Also, the fact that traditional Social Democracy has lost most of its former predilection for equality in outcome (cf. Hemerijck 2013) offers an important clue as to why governments in the Nordic countries – both those led by Social Democrats and conservative–liberal governments – seem to have become less preoccupied with poverty reduction and problems of rising inequality as 'short-run' political objectives. In fact, the social investment paradigm, in its more critical interpretation, may have served as an ideological legitimisation of this trend, since it has advocated policies that aim to integrate as many as possible in the market instead of protecting them from market forces. Thus, gainful employment – that is, to be integrated in the labour market – has become depicted as the best recipe for social security and the most efficient antidote to poverty.

On the other hand, continuous improvements of child allowances, to make these keep pace with real wages and inflation, is becoming increasingly difficult in a world where fiscal austerity (Farnsworth and Irving 2015) and social investment ideas (Morel et al. 2012) for quite some time have encouraged politicians and state civil servants to focus on things other than rising poverty and inequality. Yet it should also be remembered that the Nordic countries still have lower poverty rates and levels of economic inequality than most other countries in the world. Still, poverty seems to be rising, which is problematic since it undermines the wellbeing of families and children. Child poverty is normally considered more problematic than poverty in general, since children do not have control over their life circumstances (Bäckman and Ferrarini, 2010). Furthermore, experiences of poverty in childhood may have important adult outcomes, potentially leading to an inter-generational transmission of disadvantages. For instance, children who have lived their first five years in a low-income family are more likely to drop out from school, to become teenage parents, to develop inferior cognitive capacities, or to demonstrate some kind of anti-social or criminal behaviour as they get older (see, for example, Esping-Andersen et al. 2002). If low levels of poverty and inequality are to be maintained as core values in the Nordic welfare states in a world of 'new social risks' and higher immigration, it is not sufficient to create a model where the dominant norm is for parents to work (and balance their work and family commitments) both pre- and post-separation. Instead, we need to maintain and develop policies of 'family friendliness' in a broad sense. One way forward is to continue to provide sufficient income protection through income transfers or tax relief.

NOTES

1. In the literature, the terms 'family allowance', 'child allowance' and 'child benefit' are used interchangeably. In this chapter we use the second term, since it is more in accordance with the Nordic practices (for example, the Finnish/Swedish term 'Lapsilisä'/'Barnbidrag' or the Norwegian term 'Barnetrygd'; cf. NOSOSCO 2017).
2. In Norway the amount is the same for all children, but with a supplemental allowance per child for children of single parents.

REFERENCES

Aaberge, Rolf, Langørgen, Audun, and Lindgren, Petter (2013), 'The distributional impact of public services in European countries', Discussion Paper No. 746, Oslo: Statistics Norway.

Abrahamson, Peter (2010), 'Continuity and consensus: governing families in Denmark', *Journal of European Social Policy*, 20 (5), 399–409.

Bäckman, Olof, and Ferrarini, Tommy (2010), 'Combating child poverty? A multilevel assessment of family policy institutions and child poverty in 21 old and new welfare states', *Journal of Social Policy*, 39 (2), 275–96.

Björnberg, Ulla (2016), 'Nordic family policies in a European context', *Sociology and Anthropology*, 4 (6), 508–16.

Björnberg, Ulla, and Dahlgren, Lillemor (2008), 'Family policy: the case of Sweden', in Ilona Ostner and Christoph Schmitt (eds), *Family Policies in the Context of Family Change: The Nordic Countries in Comparative Perspective*, Wiesbaden: VS Verlag, pp. 37–56.

Chzhen, Yekaterina, Gromada, Anna, and Rees, Gwyther (2019), *Are the World's Richest Countries Family Friendly? Policy in the OECD and EU*, Florence: UNICEF Office of Research.

Chzhen, Yekaterina, Nolan, Brian, Cantillon, Bea, and Handa, Sudhansu (2017), 'Impact of the economic crisis on children in rich countries', in Bea Cantillon, Yekaterina Chzhen, Sudhansu Handa and Brian Nolan (eds), *Children of Austerity: Impact of the Great Recession on Child Poverty in Rich Countries*, Oxford: Oxford University Press, pp. 8–29.

Danish Government (2012), *National Reform Programme 2012*, Copenhagen: Danish Government.

Duvander, Ann-Zofie, and Ellingsæter, Anne Lise (2016), 'Cash for childcare schemes in the Nordic welfare states: diverse paths, diverse outcomes', *European Societies*, 18 (1), 70–90.

Esping-Andersen, Gøsta (2009), *The Incomplete Revolution: Adapting to Women's New Roles*, Cambridge: Polity Press.

Esping-Andersen, Gøsta, Gallie, Duncan, Hemerijck, Anton, and Myles, John (2002), *Why We Need a New Welfare State*, Oxford: Oxford University Press.

Eurostat (2019), 'At-risk-of-poverty rates by age, family size and household type'. EU-SILC and ECHP surveys, accessed 22 November 2019 at https://ec.europa.eu/eurostat/data/database.

Eurostat (2018), 'Number of immigrants per year and sex', accessed 21 November 2019 at https://ec.europa.eu/eurostat/data/database.

Eydal, Guðný B., Gíslason, Ingolfur, Rostgaard, Tine, Brandth, Berit, Duvander, Ann-Zofie, and Lammi-Taskula, Johanna (2015), 'Trends in parental leave in the Nordic countries: has the forward march of gender equality halted?', *Community, Work & Family*, 18 (2), 167–81.

Eydal, Guðný B., and Rostgaard, Tine (2017), 'Variations in Nordic family policy over time: cash and care services in times of austerity', Paper to the 15th ESPAnet Conference, 14–16 September 2017, Lisbon, Portugal.

Eydal, Guðný B., Rostgaard, Tine, and Hiilamo Heikki (2018), 'Family policies in the Nordic countries: aiming at equality', in Guðný Eydal and Tine Rostgard (eds), *Handbook of Family Policy*, Cheltenham, UK and Northampton, MA, USA: Edward Elgar Publishing, pp. 195–208.

Farnsworth, Kevin, and Irving, Zoe (2015), 'Austerity: more than the sum of its parts', in Kevin Farnsworth and Zoe Irving (eds), *Social Policy in Times of Austerity*, Bristol: Policy Press, pp. 9–21.

Försäkringskassan (2018), *Barnhushållens ekonomi –resultatindikatorer för den ekonomiska familjepolitiken*, Sweden: Försäkringskassan.

Galloway, Taryn, Gustafsson, Björn A., Pedersen, Peder, and Österberg, Torun (2015), 'Immigrant child poverty: the Achilles heel of the Scandinavian welfare state', in Thesia I. Garner and Kathleen S. Short (eds), *Measurement of Poverty, Deprivation, and Economic Mobility*, Bingley: Emerald Group, pp. 185–219.

Government of Norway (2018), Prop. 74 L (2017–2018) *Endringer i folketrygdloven og kontantstøtteloven*, Oslo: Barne- og likestillingsdepartementet.

Government of Sweden (2018), *Sveriges nationella reformprogram 2018*, Stockholm: Regeringskansliet.

Hakovirta, Mia, and Eydal, Guðný B. (2020), 'Shared care and child maintenance policies in Nordic countries', *International Journal of Law, Policy and Family*, 34 (1), 43–59.

Hakovirta, Mia, and Jokela, Merita (2019), 'Contribution of child maintenance to lone mothers' income in five countries', *Journal of European Social Policy*, 29 (2), 257–72.

Halleröd, Björn, Ekbrand, Hans, and Bengtsson, Mattias (2015), 'In-work poverty and labour market trajectories: poverty risks among the working population in 22 European countries', *Journal of European Social Policy*, 25 (5), 473–88.

Hemerijck, Anton (2013), *Changing Welfare States*, Oxford: Oxford University Press.

Hiilamo, Heikki, and Kangas, Olli (2009), 'Trap for women or freedom to choose? The struggle over cash for child care schemes in Finland and Sweden', *Journal of Social Policy*, 38 (3), 457–75.

Kamerman, Sheila, and Kahn, Alfred J. (eds) (1978), *Family Policy: Government and Families in Fourteen Countries*, New York, NY: Columbia University Press.

Karila, Kirsti (2012), 'A Nordic perspective on early childhood education and care policy', *European Journal of Education*, 47 (4), 584–95.

Korpi, Walter (2000), 'Faces of inequality: gender, class, and patterns of inequalities in different types of welfare states', *Social Politics*, 7 (2), 127–91.

Leira, Arnlaug (2006), 'Parenthood change and policy reform in Scandinavia, 1970s–2000s', in Anne Lise Ellingsæter and Arnlaug Leira (eds), *Politicising Parenthood in Scandinavia: Gender Relations in Welfare States*, Bristol: Policy Press, pp. 27–52.

Lundkvist, Marina, Nyby, Josefine, Autto, Janne, and Nygård, Mikael (2017), 'From universalism to selectivity? The background, discourses and ideas of recent early childhood education and care reforms in Finland', *Early Childhood Development and Care*, 187 (10), 1543–56.

Morel, Natalie, Palier, Bruno, and Palme, Joakim (2012), 'Beyond the welfare state as we knew it', in Natalie Morel, Bruno Palier and Joakim Palme (eds), *Towards a Social Investment State*, Bristol: Policy Press, pp. 1–30.

NOSOSCO (2017), *Social Protection in the Nordic Countries 2016/2016*, Copenhagen: Nordic Social Statistical Committee.

Nyby, Josefine, Nygård, Mikael, and Blum, Sonja (2018), 'Radical reform or piecemeal adjustments? The case of Finnish family policy reforms', *European Policy Analysis*, 4 (2), 190–213.

Nygård, Mikael, Lindberg, Marja, Nyqvist, Fredrica, and Härtull, Camilla (2019), 'The role of cash benefit and in-kind benefit spending for child poverty in times of austerity: an analysis of 22 European countries 2006–2015', *Social Indicators Research*, 146 (3), 533–52.

OECD (2019a), 'Employment rate', accessed 19 November 2019 at https://data.oecd .org/emp/employment-rate.htm.

OECD (2019b), 'Social expenditures, aggregated data', accessed 23 November 2019 at https://stats.oecd.org/Index.aspx?datasetcode=SOCX_AGG#.

OECD (2020), 'Enrolment rate in early childhood education', accessed 29 January 2020 at https://data.oecd.org/students/enrolment-rate-in-early-childhood-education .htm.

Ólafsson, Stefan (2016), 'The strategy of redistribution: Iceland's way out of the crisis', in Valur Ingimundarson, Philippe Urfalino and Irma Erlingsdóttir (eds), *Iceland's Financial Crisis: The Politics of Blame, Protest and Reconstruction*, London: Routledge, pp. 156–82.

Povlsen, Lene, Regber, Susann, Fosse, Elisabeth, Karlsson Eklund, Leena, and Gunnarsdottir, Hrafnhildur (2018), 'Economic poverty among children and adolescents in the Nordic countries', *Scandinavian Journal of Public Health*, 46 (20), 30–37.

Rostgaard, Tine, and Lausten, Mette (2015), 'The coming and going of the father's quota in Denmark: consequences for fathers' parental leave take-up', in Guðný B. Eydal and Tine Rostgaard (eds), *Fatherhood in the Nordic Welfare States*, Bristol: Policy Press, pp. 277–302.

Salmi, Minna, and Närvi, Johanna (2014), 'Perhepoliittiset uudistukset ja pienten lasten vanhempien mielipiteet', *Yhteiskuntapolitiikka*, 79 (4), 413–23.

Skevik, Anne, and Hatland, Axel (2008), 'Family policies in Norway', in Ilona Ostner and Christoph Schmitt (eds), *Family Policies in the Context of Family Change*, Weisbaden: VS Verlag, pp. 89–106.

Skinner, Christine, and Hakovirta, Mia (2020), 'Separated families and child support policies in times of social change: a comparative analysis', in Rense Nieuwenhuis and Wim Van Lancker (eds), *Palgrave Handbook of Family Policy*, London: Palgrave, pp. 267–301.

Søgaard, Jakob Egholt (2018), 'Top incomes in Scandinavia: recent developments and the role of capital income', in Rolf Aaberge, Christophe André, Anne Boschini et al. (eds), *Increasing Income Inequality in the Nordics: Nordic Economic Policy Review 2018*, pp. 66–94.

Sørvoll, Jardar (2015), *The Norwegian Welfare State 2005–2015: Public Attitudes, Political Debates and Future Challenges*, Canterbury: University of Kent.

Tammelin, Mia, Malinen, Kaisa, Rönkä, Anna, and Verhoef, Melissa (2017), 'Work schedules and work–family conflict among dual earners in Finland, the Netherlands, and the United Kingdom', *Journal of Family Issues*, 38 (1), 3–24.

Thévenon, Olivier (2011), 'Family policies in OECD countries: a comparative analysis', *Population and Development Review*, 37 (1), 57–87.

Wennemo, Irene (1994), *Sharing the Costs of Children*, Stockholm: Swedish Institute for Social Research.

5. Family policy support for the earner-carer and traditional-family models in Lithuania and Sweden[1]

Katharina Wesolowski, Sunnee Billingsley and Gerda Neyer

INTRODUCTION

Social policies are a key tool governments have to address societal developments and respond to social needs. How policies shape behaviour and social structures is a fundamental question in understanding intended and unintended effects of policies. For example, low fertility is one issue that has worried policy-makers, as it has become a widespread feature of post-industrial Eastern and Western countries since the last quarter of the 20th century. Low fertility contributes to a shrinking labour force, and many fear this might make it difficult to sustain an ageing population. Family policies have been suggested as a remedy to low fertility because they offer support to families. This support may affect the division of paid and unpaid work in the family to different degrees. Family policies can support a stay-at-home-mother/male-breadwinner family – that is, a gender-traditional family – and/or a family in which both parents are in paid work and share the upbringing of their children; that is, an earner-carer family.

Discussions among researchers and policy-makers, however, have not only been about a remedy for low fertility, but also about gender equality. McDonald (2000) and Goldscheider et al. (2015) argue that supporting both partners' earning and caring and enhancing gender equality may be a precondition to increased fertility. They maintain that as long as women have to do most of the unpaid work at home at the same time as being in paid work, a common feature of post-industrial societies, they will rather forego childbearing than shoulder the dual burden of work and care, or give up employment altogether for having children (England 2010; Goldscheider et al. 2015; McDonald 2000). Therefore, family policies facilitating the combination of paid and unpaid work for both mothers and fathers would make it easier for couples to have the number of children they want.

Research has shown that family policies may have an impact on fertility, but the results are not consistent (Gauthier 2007; Neyer 2005). We take the discussion around family policy effects on fertility as a starting point for thinking about how policies are measured and assessed. We argue that the conceptualisations and measurements of family policy have contributed to this inconclusiveness. For example, some research has used gender regimes to denote a country's support for different family models (Pfau-Effinger 1998). Classifications based on regime types make it difficult to capture how family policies vary over time. There is also the danger that regime-type approaches mix causes and outcomes in their typologies (see the argument in Korpi and Palme 1998). Another example is the conceptualisation of family policies on a continuum from support of a gender-traditional family model to support of an earner-carer family model (Mandel and Semyonov 2006). The drawback here is that countries' family policies can support both family types simultaneously to different degrees. Lastly, the use of expenditures on family policies in total, on single policies or on combinations of policies as measures (see, for example, Luci-Greulich and Thévenon 2013), has the drawback that it captures governmental spending, not the amount to which individuals are entitled.

Thus, we argue that in order to assess the impact of policies, we need a different approach towards the measurement of family policies. First, we need to acknowledge an essential feature of family policies, namely that they are multidimensional (see Ferrarini 2003; Korpi 2000). Multidimensionality refers to two aspects: On the one hand, it denotes that family policies usually comprise several policies that may belong to different policy fields, such as parental leave policies, child subsidies and tax policies. On the other hand, it signifies that family policies may have different functions, such as supporting a gender-egalitarian or a gendered family model. Often the functions are not clear-cut; they may be ambivalent or even contradictory. Some policies may support a gender-egalitarian behaviour and others a gendered behaviour. Second, we need to acknowledge that family policies are time-variant. Changes in family policies may shift the functions of those policies, for example, towards more forceful support of a gender-egalitarian family behaviour or towards a stronger support of a gendered family model. Third, we also need to consider what individuals can expect to receive when they have a child, and whether this support backs a more gender-egalitarian childrearing behaviour or a traditional gender-divided family form. To study the link between family policies and fertility we need measures that capture these various dimensions of family policies. The Social Policy Indicator database (SPIN) provides such measures. SPIN is a longitudinal database that acknowledges a variety of different policies that support families. Moreover, it gives the possibility to synthesise these policies into indicators of two types of family support simultaneously offered in many countries, and thus captures not only what a prospective parent can expect to receive when on leave with a newborn child, but also what share of the support favours a gendered and what share a gender-egalitarian behaviour.

In this chapter, we explore these harmonised data on social policies over time to describe how policies support earner-carer and traditional-family models in Lithuania and Sweden. We use these cases to describe how measures of earner-carer and traditional-family support have been constructed, and compare the policy developments over time. We highlight areas of convergence and divergence in family policy in these two countries with very different histories. We introduce the logic behind the SPIN data in the next section, detailing which policies fit within the two measures and how they are calculated. We then describe the measures specifically as they refer to Lithuania and Sweden from 1995 to 2015, illustrating both how the measures reflect the policies and how support for earner-carer and traditional-family arrangements have shifted over time in the two cases. These developments in Lithuania and Sweden are then contextualised by locating them among other Baltic and Nordic countries for which these measures have been produced in the SPIN database. Finally, we discuss the convergences and divergences we observe in Lithuania's and Sweden's family policy development, both in relation to each other and in relation to Baltic and Nordic countries.

BACKGROUND: THE SOCIAL POLICY INDICATOR DATABASE

Contrary to most other databases, SPIN is a theory-driven database. It is based on the so-called institutional or social rights approach (Ferrarini 2003; Korpi 2000; Nelson et al. 2020). This approach to classifying social policies builds on T. H. Marshall's idea of social citizenship and the social rights citizens of a country have as written in country legislation. According to Marshall (1950), citizens in a country have civil, political and social rights. He argues that social citizenship entitles citizens to at least a basic level of welfare. Building on that idea, Korpi and Palme (1998) developed indicators[2] that are based on legislation of social insurances, capturing what citizens are entitled to receive when they are not able to be in paid work. An important indicator developed in this connection is what a typical worker earning an average production worker's wage is entitled to receive in a percentage of her/his wage, called the replacement rate.

In regard to family policies, Korpi (2000) created a typology based on both the institutional or social rights approach and a gender approach. This typology captures the degree to which family policies support a gender-equal and/or a gender-traditional division of paid and unpaid work. Countries were said to have earner-carer forms of family support when their policies attribute high levels of support to earner-carer families, in which both partners work and share childrearing, and when they have low levels of support for a gender-traditional family behaviour. When low support is given to both types of division of work in the family, countries are said to have market-oriented family policies. When high levels of support are directed to a gender-traditional division of work in the family, and low support is allocated to an earner-carer family, countries are deemed to have traditional-family policies. When high support is assigned to both family arrangements, countries are said to have a contradictory family policy model (see Ferrarini 2003; Korpi 2000; Korpi et al. 2013). This approach accounts for the multidimensionality as well as the potential ambiguities of family policies by measuring the extent to which both family arrangements are supported in a country. Moreover, it allows policies to change over time and does not use static regime types. Finally, it avoids the use of expenditures that measure total governmental spending on families by taking into account what individuals can expect to receive.

The information in the Parental Leave Benefit dataset (see endnote 2) builds on this logic. Here replacement rates are calculated for every fifth year for parental leave insurance, childcare leave and child benefits given in cash and through tax deductions, as well as tax rebates given to a male breadwinner, also called marriage subsidies.

The model family used for the calculation of the replacement rates consists of two grown-ups and two children. One of the children is the newborn for which one of the parents is on leave; the other child is below school age. The inclusion of a second, older child in the model family allows the measure to estimate what is allocated to a two-child family in cash child benefits, where some allocations depend on the age of the child.

Parental leave insurance is the income-related benefit paid to the parent on leave after the birth of a child, including income-related maternity leave benefit. To meet the eligibility requirements for income-related parental leave benefits in all countries, the parent on leave is assumed to have worked for two years on an average production worker's wage before going on leave with the newborn. Since the amount of parental leave payment, the length of payment and sharing options between parents differ among countries, the measures in the Parental Leave Benefit dataset are standardised in the following way: Information on leave weeks allocated to the mother, the father and leave that can be shared among the parents is collected and summarised. In addition, the level of the weekly and yearly income-related benefit in a country's currency is collected both gross and net of taxation. The information on cash benefits and duration per week and during the first year after the child's birth is then used to calculate weekly and yearly replacement rates. The net replacement rate for the first year after the child's birth is used to denote the extent of a country's support for earner-carer families, called earner-carer support.

To classify earner-carer vs. traditional gender support, the Parental Leave Benefit database distinguishes between income-related parental leave benefit and childcare leave. Childcare leave is a benefit mostly given in low flat-rate amounts, not related to previous employment, for leave after the termination of the income-related parental leave. Childcare leave information is collected in a similar way as parental leave; however, the yearly standardised replacement rate for the duration of the childcare leave benefit is calculated for the 12-month period after the termination of the income-related parental leave. Cash and fiscal child allowances, as well as maternity grants and marriage subsidies, are calculated as yearly sums, which are then divided by both the gross and net yearly wage of an average production worker. The net replacement rates for childcare leave and child allowances given in cash and through the tax system, as well as maternity grants and marriage subsidies, are summed up to reach the replacement rate denoting the extent of support to a traditional family with a stay-at-home mother and a working husband, called traditional-family support.[3]

One advantage of calculating a yearly replacement rate in this manner is that the measure takes into account both the taxation and duration of benefits. Taking taxation into account avoids mixing taxable and non-taxable benefits that could bias comparisons between countries (Ferrarini et al. 2013). Moreover, accounting for the duration of benefits avoids giving too much weight to high replacement rates with short duration. These result in lower replacement rates when the duration is short. So, 100 per cent replacement over 10 weeks will result in a lower annual replacement rate compared to 70 per cent over 40 weeks. Finally, the approach also uses legislated benefit ceilings instead of formal replacement rates that do not account for earnings ceilings that might take effect for an average production worker in some of the countries (Wesolowski and Ferrarini 2018).

The information used to construct the measures is taken from various sources, both international and national ones. One frequently used source is Missoc, the Mutual Information System on Social Protection of the European Union (see www.missoc.org). For countries associated with the Council of Europe, MISSCEO (Mutual Information System on Social Protection of the Council of Europe; www.missceo.coe.int) has been used as a source. SSPTW, *Social Security Programs Throughout the World*, published by the United States Social Security Administration in collaboration with the International Social Security Association, is another repeatedly used source (www.ssa .gov/policy/docs/progdesc/ssptw/). For the calculation of net wages and replacements, information from the European Tax Handbook from the IBFD

(International Bureau of Fiscal Documentation, www.ibfd.org/) has been extremely helpful throughout the years.

COUNTRY COMPARISON

Lithuania

The development of family policies in Lithuania since 1990

According to Stankūnienė and Juknienė (2009), Lithuanian family policy began forming a few years before the Soviet Union broke apart and Lithuania became an independent country in 1991. Before the break-up of the Soviet Union, Lithuania was a Soviet republic during most of the 20th century and, therefore, had the same family policy as other republics (Stankūnienė and Juknienė 2009). The goal for the development of Lithuanian family policies was to improve the economic situation of families with children, but policy-makers also advocated that parents were responsible for the upbringing and well-being of their children, not the state (Aidukaite 2006). However, after the decline of fertility to its lowest low levels at the beginning of the 2000s, more pronatalist goals entered into family policy formation (Stankūnienė and Juknienė 2009).

As early as 1989, the partly paid parental leave was expanded until the child turned 18 months old, while unpaid leave was extended until the child turned 3 years old. Although the Population Programme of Lithuania, developed by researchers and policy-makers, suggested family policies that expanded the opportunities for parents to reconcile work and care, the conservative government in power opted to support stay-at-home mothers. Between 1990 and 1992 it introduced a number of low paid benefits for families to promote a gendered family behaviour. At the same time, many pre-school institutions were closed down (Stankūnienė and Juknienė 2009). Family policy goals changed again with the Social Democratic Party coming to power in 1993. In 1994, under the influence of international and national initiatives, steps were taken to emulate the family policy of social-democratic welfare states. This implied a turn to reconciliation policies supporting the combination of paid work and childcare for both women and men (Stankūnienė and Juknienė 2009), in our typology called earner-carer support. However, in 1996 a conservative government came to power and the system of low paid benefits was expanded, while policies supporting work–family reconciliation were neglected, but not abandoned. After 2001, when a government that was rather social-democratically influenced came to power, work–family reconciliation policies were expanded, but the maternity (birth) grant as well as child benefits were also increased (Stankūnienė and Juknienė 2009). As an example, the age span for the child cash benefit was expanded from the child's third to seventh birthday in 2004 (Aidukaite 2006). Since 2006, fathers are entitled to receive a paternity benefit ('daddy days') with a replacement rate of 100 per cent of earnings for the first month after a child's birth. Moreover, as of 2008, the maternity and parental leave benefits amount to 100 per cent of a wage during the first year and 85 per cent for the second year (Stankūnienė and Juknienė 2009).

Since independence, changes in government thus led to inconsistencies and changes in goals and ideas from a conservative and rather patriarchal focus on traditional-family support to a more social-democratic focus on earner-carer support. According to Stankūnienė and Juknienė (2009), this seems to be typical for the other Baltic countries as well. However, overall one can see an expansion of what in our typology is called earner-carer support in Lithuania. According to Aidukaite (2006), Lithuania has more means-tested benefits inherited from the Soviet system compared to other Baltic countries. The reliance on means-tested benefits also became clear in interviews with social policy experts. The experts tended to emphasise that targeting benefits to families in need would be more efficient in alleviating poverty and less expensive for a country with restricted financial resources (Aidukaite 2006). This emphasis on means-tested benefits also seems to have been met with approval by the population (Aidukaite 2004).

Aidukaite (2019) states that after the financial crisis of 2008–2010, retrenchment of social policies took place and, especially in the field of family policy, family benefits were cut back. Earnings-related maternity and parental leave benefits were reformed, and parents can now choose between a one-year leave at 100 per cent replacement of earnings or two years' leave with a rate of 70 per cent of previous earnings during the first year and 40 per cent of earnings during the second year. The paternity leave of one month after the child's birth has been kept in place (Aidukaite 2019). Thus, in terms of the typology used in this paper, it is rather the traditional-family support that decreased, while earner-carer support increased and was diversified.

Earner-carer support and traditional-family support in Lithuania, 1995–2015

Using SPIN data, we describe family policies in Lithuania from 1995 to 2015 using the typology of earner-carer and traditional-family support, as defined in the background section. Figure 5.1 shows the replacement rates of earner-carer support and traditional-family support from 1995 to 2015 for every fifth year. The replacement rates show how much an average production worker can expect to receive in per cent of her/his annual net wage when on leave with the newborn (second) child.

In 1995, earner-carer support was made up of eight weeks maternity leave at a replacement rate of 100 per cent and 44 weeks of shareable dual parental leave at 60 per cent of previous earnings until the child's first birthday.

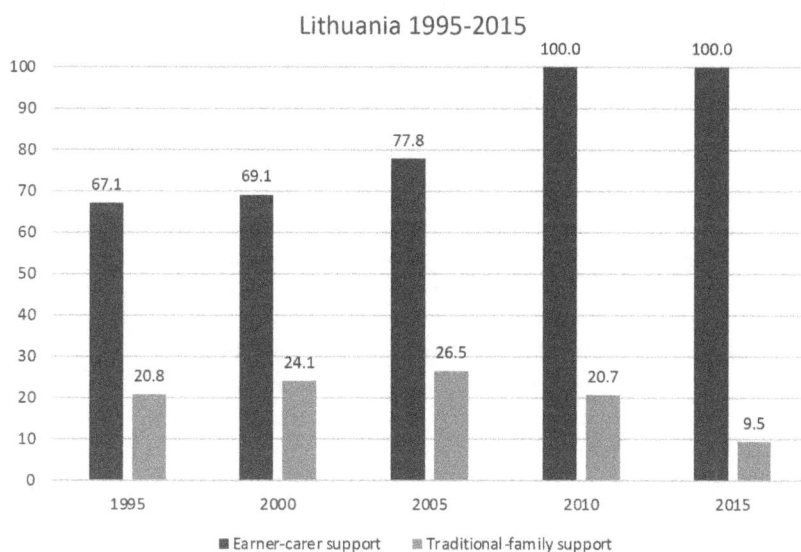

Lithuania 1995-2015

Source: SPIN, 2019 (partly unpublished data).

Figure 5.1   *Earner-carer support and traditional-family support in Lithuania, 1995–2015*

Therefore, an average production worker could expect to receive around 67 per cent of an annual net wage (4,326 Lithuanian litas, or LTL) for the first year after the child's birth. Traditional-family support was made up of a maternity grant of 360 LTL and 540 LTL in cash child benefit in total for 12 months, summing up to almost 21 per cent of an annual net wage for an average production worker.[4]

In the year 2000, as in 1995, earner-carer support consisted of eight weeks maternity leave at a replacement rate of 100 per cent and 44 weeks of shareable dual parental leave at 60 per cent of previous earnings until the child's first birthday. So, an average production worker could expect to receive 69 per cent of an annual net wage (7,790 LTL) for the first year after the child's birth. An earnings ceiling was in place, but the average production worker's wage did not hit the ceiling. Traditional-family support comprised a maternity grant of 750 LTL and 1,125 LTL in cash child benefit in total for 12 months, summing up to around 24 per cent of an annual net wage for an average production worker.[5]

In the year 2005, earner-carer support was made up of eight weeks maternity leave at a replacement rate of 100 per cent and 44 weeks of shareable dual parental leave at 70 per cent of previous earnings until the child's first birthday. An average production worker could then expect to receive 78 per cent of an annual net wage (11,146 LTL) for the first year after the child's birth. An earnings ceiling was in place, but the average production worker was not affected by it. Traditional-family support was made up of a maternity grant of 1,000 LTL, 1,725 LTL in cash child benefit and 229 LTL in fiscal child benefit in total for 12 months, summing up to almost 26.5 per cent of an annual net wage for an average production worker.[6]

For 2010, earner-carer support encompassed eight weeks maternity leave at a replacement rate of 100 per cent and 44 weeks of shareable dual parental leave at now 100 per cent of previous earnings until the child's first birthday. An average production worker could now expect to receive 100 per cent of an annual net wage (18,155 LTL) for the first year after the child's birth. Again, the earnings ceiling did not affect the average production worker.[7] Traditional-family support was constituted of a maternity grant of 1,000 LTL, 1,794 LTL in cash child benefit and 540 LTL in fiscal child benefit in total for 12 months, summing up to almost 21 per cent of an annual net wage for an average production worker.[8]

In 2015, Lithuania joined the Euro zone. Earner-carer support consisted of a maternity leave at 100 per cent of earnings paid for eight weeks after birth. Thereafter, parents could draw dual parental leave at 100 per cent of earnings until the child turned 1 year old. An average production worker could expect to receive 100 per cent of an annual net wage (6,662 EUR) for the first year after the child's birth. The average production worker's wage did not hit the earnings ceiling.[9] Traditional-family support comprised a maternity grant of 418 EUR plus 216 EUR in fiscal child benefits in total for 12 months, summing up to a mere 9.5 per cent of an annual net wage for an average production worker.[10]

Changes over time captured in the measure

As Figure 5.1 shows, the level of earner-carer support increased gradually from around 67 per cent to 100 per cent of an average production worker's yearly net wage from 1995–2015. However, the level of traditional-family support first increased from around 21 per cent in 1995 to almost 27 per cent in 2005, only to clearly decrease down to around 10 per cent in 2015. This mirrors the description of Stankūnienė and Juknienė (2009) of a shift in focus of family policy depending on which parties were in power. The focus on traditional-family support increased, while earner-carer support stayed about the same until it was clearly increased under a social-democratically influenced government. By 2015, the replacement rate for traditional-family support had decreased, which Aidukaite (2019) attributes to the economic crisis that took place in 2008–2010. We need to point out that the development of the replacement rate does not solely reflect increases or decreases of benefits and thus political decisions about family benefits. The replacement rate is also driven by the development of the average production worker's wage. For example, between 2005 and 2010 wages increased substantially, while benefits increased only slightly. The result of these different developments is that cash benefits in 2010 replaced a lower share of an average production worker's wage than in 2005 despite the increase in benefits.

Sweden

The development of family policies in Sweden since 1990
According to Kälvesten (1955), family policy in Sweden was expanded after Alva and Gunnar Myrdal drew attention to the risk of depopulation in their seminal book *Kris i befolkningsfrågan (Crisis in the Population Question)* in 1934. Most relevant for our comparison is the income-related, gender-egalitarian parental leave insurance that was first introduced in 1974 and was developed mostly by the social-democratic and liberal parties (Ferrarini and Duvander 2010). Nevertheless, we will concentrate on the developments since 1990 to give the reader the possibility to compare the development of family policies in Sweden and Lithuania during the same time period.

During the economic crisis in the 1990s, the level of the parental leave benefit was cut back to 75 per cent and then increased again to 80 per cent of the pre-leave wage (Ferrarini and Duvander 2010). At the end of the rule of a coalition of conservative and liberal parties from 1991 to 1994, the government announced that one month of parental leave would be reserved for each parent, becoming effective by 1995. The same year, shortly before the social-democratic party regained power, a home-care allowance was introduced, but was in place for only a few months. In 2002, during the social-democratic rule, the reserved period for one parent was extended from one to two months, and the duration of parental leave from 15 to 16 months. Thirteen months were paid at 80 per cent of pre-leave income, while three months were paid at a low flat-rate amount.[11]

By 2008, the centre-right government that had come to power in 2006 revived the home-care allowance of the early 1990s. The new regulation permitted municipalities to pay a flat-rate allowance of maximally 3,000 SEK per month for children up to age 3 provided they did not use public childcare. The home-care allowance constituted a paradox among the otherwise gender-egalitarian, labour-market oriented earner-carer Swedish family policies (Lundqvist 2011). To counter this move towards a traditional-family model, the government introduced a tax relief for couples in which the father used more than the legally allocated share of parental leave, the so-called 'gender-equality bonus' (Ferrarini and Duvander 2010; Lundqvist

2011). Ferrarini and Duvander (2010) warned that the introduction of the home-care allowance might lead to increased inequality in care and undermine the gender-egalitarian reconciliation of work and childrearing. Neither the home-care allowance nor the gender-equality bonus gained popularity. Only half of the municipalities offered the home-care allowance benefit, and only 4 per cent of all parents took it; 90 per cent were women and most had only a weak attachment to the labour market (Duvander and Ellingsæter 2016). Not least because of an initially complicated regulation, the gender-equality bonus was equally unsuccessful. It did not immediately or noticeably increase fathers' use of parental leave or promote gender equality (Duvander and Johansson 2012).

When the social-democratic party regained power with the help of the Green and Left parties, it abolished the home-care allowance in 2016 (Sveriges riksdag 2016), and the gender-equality bonus in 2017. Instead, in 2016 it extended the reserved part of parental leave to three months, so that the current regulation allocates three months of the income-related parental leave to one parent, three months to the other, and seven months that can be shared as parents prefer (Försäkringskassan 2019). The introduction and every expansion of the reserved part of the leave increased fathers' uptake of parental leave, but the most influence on fathers' uptake of parental leave was related to the first reserved month in 1995 (Försäkringskassan 2019).

Ferrarini and Duvander (2010) state that parental leave is used by basically all mothers and around 90 per cent of fathers. The high earnings ceiling ensures most parents 80 per cent of their pre-leave income. Commonly, collective bargaining agreements state that the employer pays an additional 10 per cent of the wage below the wage ceiling and, when an employee reaches the wage ceiling, the employer pays the difference to ensure a total of 90 per cent wage replacement. Since most parents are covered by a collective agreement, this substantially reduces the income loss during parental leave. Parental leave in Sweden is also very flexible; benefits are calculated in days and can be drawn in full, half-days, quarter-days or one-eighth-of-a-day shares. If a parent takes only part of a day, the leave extends accordingly. But flexibility has been reduced somewhat since 2014, as a larger part of parental insurance has to be taken before the child turns 4 years old (Duvander et al. 2015).

In Sweden, as in Lithuania and many other countries, family policy development was influenced by the political orientation of the different governments in power. Every time a more conservative government was in power, the conservative parties introduced reforms that rather supported a traditional-family model, while reforms supporting a more gender-equal division of paid and unpaid work were more on the agenda of the liberal party and strongly promoted by the social-democratic party. The practical failure of the latest home-care allowance demonstrated that gender equality in parental leave is by now firmly anchored in Swedish society.

Earner-carer support and traditional-family support in Sweden, 1995–2015

We now turn to a description of family policies in Sweden from 1995 to 2015 using our typology of earner-carer and traditional-family support. Figure 5.2 shows the replacement rates of earner-carer support and traditional-family support from 1995 to 2015 for every fifth year. To recall, the replacement rates denote how much an average production worker can expect to receive in per cent of her/his annual net wage when on leave with the newborn (second) child during the first year of its life.

Sweden 1995-2015

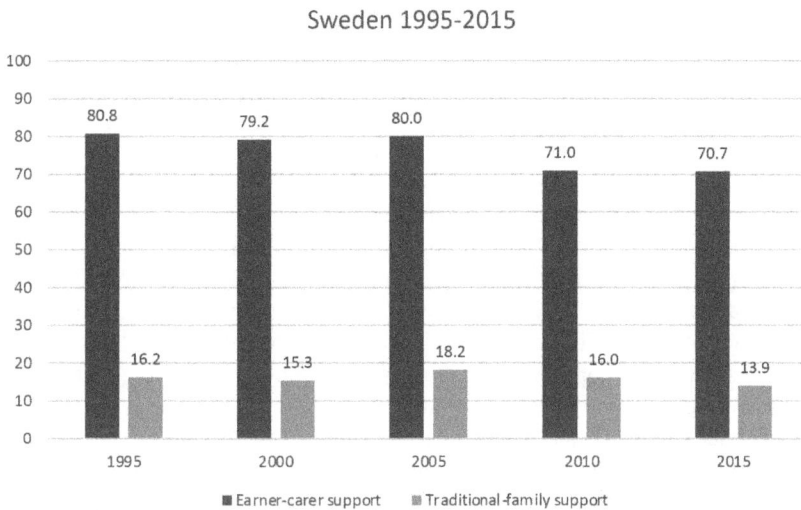

Source: SPIN, 2019 (partly unpublished data).

Figure 5.2   *Earner-carer support and traditional-family support in Sweden, 1995–2015*

In 1995, earner-carer support consisted of 12 months of shareable parental leave at 80 per cent of pre-leave income, with one month reserved for each parent. Therefore, an average production worker could expect to receive almost 81 per cent of an annual net wage (134,976 Swedish kronor, or SEK). Traditional-family support consisted of the three months of flat-rate paid leave after income-related parental leave at 60 SEK/day, as well as 18,000 SEK of cash child benefit, amounting to a replacement rate of around 16 per cent of an average production worker's wage.[12]

In 2000, earner-carer support consisted of 12 months of shareable parental leave at 80 per cent of pre-leave income (156,511 SEK), with one month reserved for each parent. An average production worker could then expect to receive around 79 per cent of an annual net wage. The decline from 81 per cent in 1995 is due to differences in taxation. Traditional-family support again consisted of three months of flat-rate leave after income-related parental leave at 60 SEK/day and 20,400 SEK of cash child benefit, summing up to around 15 per cent of an average production worker's wage.[13]

In the year 2005, earner-carer support consisted of 13 months of shareable parental leave at 80 per cent of pre-leave income (187,015 SEK), with two months now reserved for each parent. It is important to note that, as described in the background section, only the first 12 months of this leave are included in the SPIN measure since it is calculated as the replacement rate for the leave during the first year after the child's birth. So, an average production worker could expect to receive 80 per cent of an annual net wage. Traditional-family support still consisted of three months of flat-rate leave after income-related parental leave at 180 SEK/day and now 22,800 SEK of cash child benefit, giving a replacement rate of around 18 per cent.[14]

In 2010, earner-carer support consisted of 13 months of shareable parental leave at 80 per cent of pre-leave income (239,282 SEK), with two months reserved for each parent (12 months coded). By then, however, the social insurance agency multiplied the pre-leave income by a factor of 0.97, so that the effective gross replacement rate was 77.6 per cent. Further, changes in taxation rules with the introduction of an earned-income tax credit (EITC) led to a higher pre-leave net income. An average production worker could thus expect to receive 71 per cent of an annual net wage. Traditional-family support included the three months of flat-rate leave after income-related parental leave at 180 SEK/day and 27,000 SEK of cash child benefit. The net replacement rate was thus 16 per cent.[15]

In the year 2015, as in 2010, earner-carer support consisted of 13 months of shareable parental leave at 80 per cent, with two months reserved for each parent (12 months coded). As the same calculation rule applied in 2015 as in 2010 and the EITC was also still in effect, an average production worker could expect to receive around 71 per cent of an annual net wage (273,445 SEK). Traditional-family support included three months of flat-rate leave after income-related parental leave at 180 SEK/day, as well as 27,000 SEK of cash child benefit. Since the amount of the cash child benefit had not increased, while the pre-leave income had, the replacement rate was around 14 per cent of an average production worker's net wage.[16]

Changes over time captured in the measure
As Figure 5.2 shows, there are only small changes to be seen in the strength of support to both dimensions during our observation period. Effectively, however, earner-carer support has been reduced to around 70 per cent of pre-leave net income due to changes in the calculation of benefits and tax effects of the EITC that was introduced after the change in government in 2007. The EITC is only granted on earned income, not on parental leave benefits, and thus gives a higher net income compared to before. For traditional-family support, the only changes are small fluctuations in the effect of the cash child benefit, while the three months of leave paid in flat-rate amounts had not changed during the time period.

Lithuania and Sweden compared to other Baltic and Nordic countries
The SPIN database offers measures of the degree of traditional-family and earner-carer support for many other countries besides Lithuania and Sweden. All measures were calculated in the same manner as described for Lithuania and Sweden and therefore are comparable across countries. Figures 5.3 and 5.4 display the measures of earner-carer support and traditional-family support from 1995 to 2015 for every fifth year for the Baltic and Nordic countries, excluding Iceland because it is not included in the Parental Leave Benefit data. As evident, these measures capture significant shifts over time in policy support for earner-carer and traditional-family arrangements. Earner-carer and traditional-family support for the Baltic countries is presented in Figure 5.3. In the top panel we see that Lithuania offered the most earner-carer support in the late 1990s and early 2000s, whereas Latvia offered the least. The difference was substantial, with support hovering around 70 per cent of an average production worker's wage in Lithuania and only 20 per cent in Latvia. By 2005, this gap had reversed, with both Estonia and Latvia offering almost full coverage (93 per cent in Estonia and 100 per cent in Latvia). Lithuania followed suit and offered full support (100 per cent) by 2010. This high coverage remained mostly the case thereafter, with the exception of Latvia reducing support to around 74 per cent by 2015. Less dramatic shifts in support for traditional-family arrangements are evident in the bottom panel of Figure 5.3. The trend indicates reduced support of this kind over time in Lithuania and Estonia since 2000, but levels have remained relatively steady in Latvia regardless of the marked increase in earner-carer support in the same time period.

Regarding the Nordic countries, Figure 5.4 shows that Denmark began with the lowest levels and remained at the lowest level even after a substantial increase. In the late 1990s and until even 2000, Denmark provided less than 30 per cent of an average production worker's net annual wage in the form of benefits that encouraged an earner-carer family arrangement. From the data

Earner-carer support 1995-2015, Lithuania and other Baltic countries

■ Earner-carer support, 1995 ■ Earner-carer support, 2000 ■ Earner-carer support, 2005
■ Earner-carer support, 2010 ▨ Earner-carer support, 2015

Traditional-family support 1995-2015, Lithuania and other Baltic countries

■ Traditional-family support, 1995 ■ Traditional-family support, 2000 ■ Traditional-family support, 2005
■ Traditional-family support, 2010 ▨ Traditional-family support, 2015

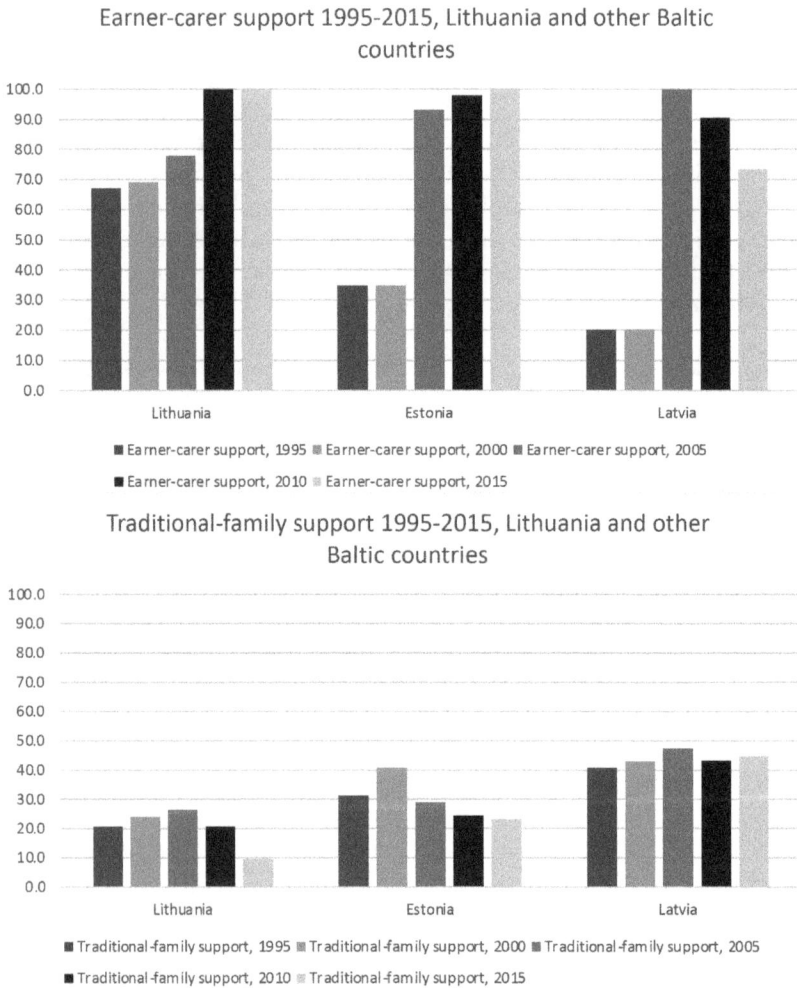

Source: SPIN, 2019 (partly unpublished data).

*Figure 5.3   Earner-carer support and traditional-family support over
time in the Baltic countries*

point of 2005 onwards, this support had increased and hovered around 45 to
50 per cent. On the other end of the distribution, Norway consistently offered
the strongest support for earner-carer family arrangements, which ranged from
a low of 77 per cent in 2005 to around 89 per cent in 2015. We see a convergence between Sweden and Finland over time in which Sweden offered around

Earner-carer support 1995-2015, Sweden and other Nordic countries

■ Earner-carer support, 1995 ■ Earner-carer support, 2000 ■ Earner-carer support, 2005
■ Earner-carer support, 2010 ■ Earner-carer support, 2015

Traditional-family support 1995-2015, Sweden and other Nordic countries

■ Traditional-family support, 1995 ■ Traditional-family support, 2000 ■ Traditional-family support, 2005
■ Traditional-family support, 2010 ■ Traditional-family support, 2015

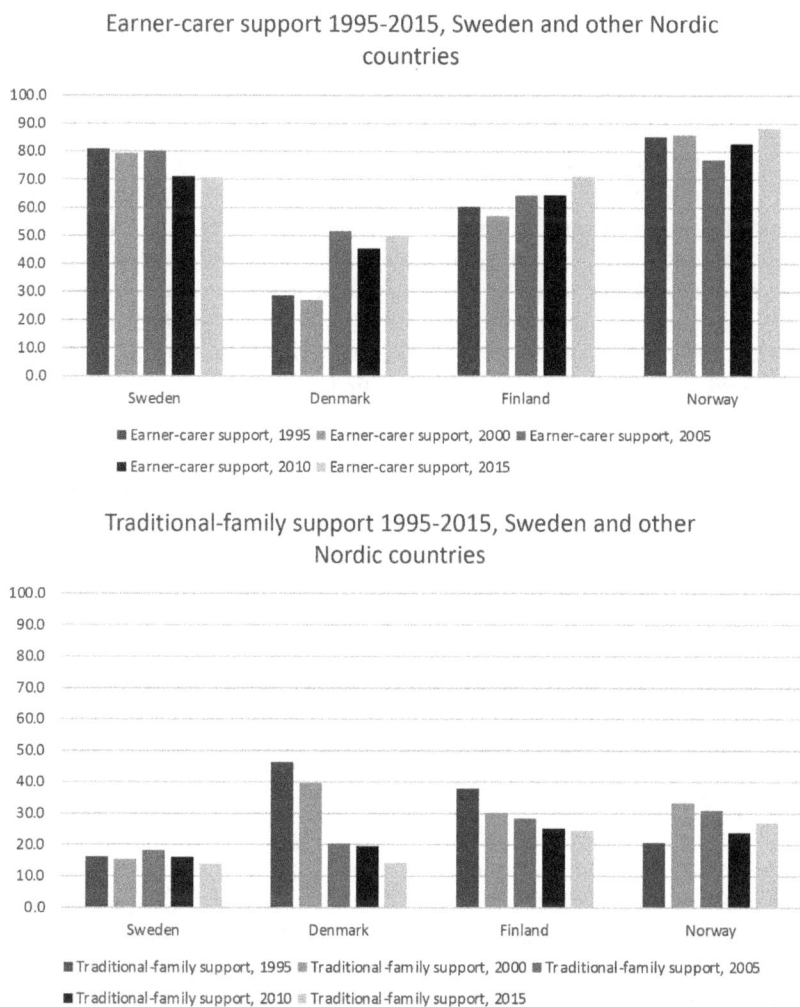

Source: SPIN, 2019 (partly unpublished data).

Figure 5.4   *Earner-carer support and traditional-family support over time in the Nordic countries*

20 percentage points more support in the early years measured here, but by 2015 Finland had slightly surpassed Sweden in earner-carer support. The bottom panel of Figure 5.4 shows that when support for earner-carer families decreased, support for traditional families tended to increase. In particular, we see this trend in Denmark and Finland. Traditional-family support declined

over the years observed here in those two countries, but not in Sweden and Norway. By 2015, the difference between the Nordic countries had narrowed to a span of 14 per cent in Sweden and Denmark to 27 per cent in Norway.

Although the data reveal differences among the Nordic and Baltic countries, we still see similarities among the countries within a group, such as parallel trends or convergence. When comparing the two groups of countries to each other, we similarly see convergence towards the same levels of earner-carer support over time among them all. In 1995, the data reveal that Lithuania's policies resembled the Nordic countries' policies in terms of what a family could expect to receive in the first year following a birth, whereas Denmark's policies resembled those in the Baltic countries. As early as 2005, the Baltic countries were already leading in earner-carer support offered, and this continued until the end of our time-series. This finding may come as a surprise, as the Nordic countries are often used as examples of policies strongly supporting gender equality, instead of the Baltic countries. By 2015, however, only Denmark stood out from the countries in both groups as offering particularly low support. In terms of traditional-family support, declines by 2015 in all countries except Latvia and Norway have resulted in similar, low shares of an average production worker's wage that would be expected by families. Only Latvia stands out as having relatively high support for traditional-family arrangements in these two groups of countries. In summary, we see remarkable similarities among the Baltic and Nordic countries in the orientation of their different policies and how they support couples during the years in which they are having children.

DISCUSSION

In this chapter, we presented arguments for family policy measures that distinguish between support of gender-egalitarian earner-carer family arrangements and traditional gendered family arrangements. We used the example of fertility research to demonstrate the importance of this distinction according to prevailing fertility theories; these distinct orientations of family policies shape the division of labour in the home and have implications for women's childbearing behaviour. How couples divide home and care work has implications for other individual and family developments across the life course, lending relevance to these measures for a wide range of family and demographic research.

We outlined the principles and logic behind SPIN's complex harmonisation effort and used the cases of Lithuania and Sweden to illustrate how real policies are transformed into these measures. The development of these measures over time reflects important changes in support to families in each country. Although SPIN data may provide the best measures available for comparative research of the link between family policies and family dynamics, it is not without limitations, and in this section we discuss these in light of these two country contexts. We conclude by acknowledging additional advantages to what we already outlined that became evident in the course of this exercise.

First, one disadvantage with the approach adopted in the SPIN data is that it reflects only what a four-member family with one or two average production worker earners can expect after having a child. The model family approach has the advantage of being simple and reflecting the most common family norm in post-industrial countries or the reality for a portion of the population. It is also used in other indexes, such as poverty indexes. A comparison with alternative model families could inform us about potentially relevant variations in policy design. Incorporating eligibility criteria such as pre-requisites for receiving benefits and income ceilings would tell us whether there are substantial sub-groups of individuals that receive a very different level of support than the average production worker model family. In particular, we could see how the replacement rate varies for groups such as high earners as well as immigrants with no work experience yet in the host country. Measures related to other model families are already being calculated by the social policy group at the Swedish Institute for Social Research. Single parents represent another model family that would be useful to explore because some countries offer specific support to these families. Moreover, given that single parents are overwhelmingly mothers, pegging the replacement rate to a wage in a male-dominated occupation (average production worker) may not yield the most accurate or generalisable information. Although the average production worker wage is widely published and easily available, it may be worth collecting information on an average female worker's wage or an average wage in areas with many women employees, such as a service worker's or public employee's wage, for example. This would also be more in alignment with the fact that it is the woman's wage in the family that is being replaced in the majority of the benefits.

A few other aspects in how well the measures represent the family policies and support different family arrangements became noticeable in the discussion of our specific case studies. The measures only consider the replacement rate in terms of one earner in a household when policies can be directed specifically to both parents as earners and/or offer support that is conditional on the other partner taking the benefit. A more complete picture of earner-carer support may therefore emerge with a replacement rate of both parents' income rather than one parent's income.

Third, the measures focus on the first 12 months after a child is born, as a way of estimating the share of a replaced annual wage. This narrow window of time can lead to an under-representation of actual support received that is relevant to the division of labour. Already, SPIN data step over the one-year boundary in an effort to capture support given through the childcare leave benefit, which increases the accuracy of the traditional-family arrangement measure. By not doing the same for the earner-carer measure, the SPIN data might underestimate some of the parental leave provisions, for example, if parental leave is shorter or longer than one year (see, for example, Nieuwenhuis et al. 2017). However, deciding the correct length of time to observe is not straightforward, and some policy features may always be lost. At the least, the time frame considered for calculating the measures needs to be explicitly discussed in relation to whether certain policies are excluded that may be relevant to an outcome of interest.

A fourth feature to discuss is that beyond the level of earner-carer support, the calculation of the earner-carer support measure in the SPIN data does not acknowledge policies that incentivise both parents taking parental leave. For example, it does not take into account the paternity leave that may be taken simultaneously with maternity leave. It also does not account for leave that is reserved for either parent. Considering the emphasis in contemporary theory and public discussion on gender equality in both the private and public spheres, this omission is important. Weighting the measures in terms of shareability or reserved months may be one avenue of bringing dual carer support into the measure, as would changing the construction to potentially include both parents' wages.

Finally, SPIN data are collected for every fifth year. Changes in between that may affect family behaviour are not reflected. Yearly data may provide a more accurate picture of the development of family support. An expansion of the database to annual data is already planned by the social policy group at the Swedish Institute for Social Research.

This discussion of limitations illustrates the complexity of calculating a simple, comparable measure across very different policy designs. It may also hide the advantages that SPIN data have and do injustice to those who collected them. As discussed in our introduction and the background section, other databases of comparative family support may provide some of the information we found missing in SPIN but lack other features that are essential for some types of research. To our knowledge there is no other database that provides (a) comparable, (b) standardised family policy measures (c) over time, which (d) distinguishes the aims of family policies and (e) recognises support from different policy areas in the calculation (for example, taxation, social insurance). SPIN data can be used for research on a variety of social policy issues, both at the aggregate and individual levels, and are particularly useful for comparative and longitudinal research. The exercise in comparing Lithuania and Sweden revealed a few additional advantages to highlight besides the arguments stated earlier in this chapter and the brief summary above. In the discussion of why the measures were calculated as they are, we mentioned an important principle in SPIN data, which is that measures reflect what couples can actually expect to receive after having a child, instead of a more abstract or aggregated level of support. This principle became even clearer when observing both changes in the policies and the measures simultaneously, because it is evident that changes in other arenas, such as taxation and wage-setting, impact the policy support. For example, we saw that two small tax-related changes essentially lowered earner-carer support by 10 percentage points in Sweden. In Lithuania, traditional-family support declined due to wage growth even when there had been small increases in benefits. These fluctuations are unintended consequences that are relevant to individuals but do not necessarily speak to any shift in policy-makers' support. They highlight the fact that individuals' experience of social insurances is vulnerable to many forces. The SPIN measures, therefore, provide an important check for analysts and policy-makers to ensure that the policy continues to provide as strong a support as was intended.

ACKNOWLEDGEMENTS

The policy measures were derived from the SPIN database, which has been extended by Katharina Wesolowski and colleagues at the Swedish Institute for Social Research. The construction of the dimensions follows Ferrarini (2003) and Korpi et al. (2013). We presented a draft of this chapter at the workshop Challenges to the Welfare State Systems in Baltic and Nordic Countries organised by Jolanta Aidukaite at the Lithuanian Social Research Centre in Vilnius, Lithuania, and would like to thank the participants for their input. Gerda Neyer acknowledges financial support by the Swedish Research Council, research grant Dnr 2020-01976, on fertility intentions, fertility considerations and fertility decline in Sweden.

NOTES

1. An earlier version of this chapter was published in *Demographic Research* with a more detailed description of the dataset and a comparison of more European countries (Wesolowski et al. 2020). The authors thank the editors for the permission to republish parts of the article.
2. At first, the data collected covered information from 18 Organisation for Economic Co-operation and Development (OECD) countries on four main social insurances connected to working life: unemployment, sickness, work accident and old age. As of 2019, the Social Policy Indicators database (SPIN), as it is called now, covers additional social insurance and social assistance programs for up to 34 countries (see www.spin.su.se). One of the modules included in SPIN is the Parental Leave Benefit dataset (PLB). The data available cover institutional information on parental leave insurance for 18 OECD countries from 1950–2015. For an overview over the SPIN database and planned expansions, see Nelson et al. (2020).
3. Indicators on childcare leave and maternity grants used in this chapter have been taken from an earlier unpublished version of the Parental Leave Benefit dataset.

Data on cash and fiscal child allowances are taken from the Child Benefit dataset module, while marriage subsidies are calculated by subtracting the net wage of a single average production worker's wage from the net wage for a couple that can be found in the SIED module (Social Insurance Entitlement dataset).

4. Sources for 1995: SSPTW 1995, law on state benefits for the family 1994, law on state social insurance 1993, provisional law on income tax of natural persons 1990 (as of 1993); government regulation on minimum amounts Jan 4 1995, answer from Ministry of Social Security and Labour 26th April 2013.

5. Sources for 2000: SSPTW 1999 and 2002, Missceec 1999 and 2002, Missceo 2000, law on state benefits for families with children, answer from Ministry of Social Security and Labour 26th April 2013.

6. Sources for 2005: Missoc 2005; Missceo 2005; SSPTW 2004 and 2006; national laws; direct information; European Tax Handbook 2005.

7. There was also the possibility to continue on parental leave for one more year at 85 per cent of previous earnings, but our measure of earner-carer support only takes into account the duration of earnings-related leave during the first year after the child's birth.

8. Source for 2010: Missoc 2010.

9. Parents could choose between two options for parental leave: 100 per cent of earnings until the child is 1 year old, or 70 per cent of earnings until the child is 1 year old and 40 per cent of earnings until the child is 2 years old. For the calculation of earner-carer support, the first option, maximising parental leave during the first year, was chosen. A paternity leave (daddy days) of 1 month at 100 per cent of earnings was given simultaneously with maternity leave and is therefore not included in earner-carer support.

10. Sources for 2015: 11th International Review of Leave Policies and Related Research 2015, Missoc 2015.

11. These three months paid at a flat rate existed from 1980, when this benefit's duration was expanded from one to three months (SOU 2017:101).

12. Sources for 1995: SPIN calculations.

13. Sources for 2000: SPIN calculations.

14. Source for 2005: International Review of Leave Policies and Related Research 2005.

15. Source for 2010: International Review of Leave Policies and Related Research 2010.

16. Source for 2015: International Review of Leave Policies and Related Research 2015.

REFERENCES

Aidukaite, J. (2004), *The Emergence of the Post-Socialist Welfare State: The Case of the Baltic States; Estonia, Latvia and Lithuania*, Huddinge: Södertörns Högskola.

Aidukaite, J. (2006), 'Reforming family policy in the Baltic states: The views of the elites', *Communist and Post-Communist Studies*, 39 (1), 1–23.

Aidukaite, J. (2019), 'The welfare systems of the Baltic states following the recent financial crisis of 2008–2010: Expansion or retrenchment?', *Journal of Baltic Studies*, 50 (1), 39–58.

Duvander, A.-Z., and A. L. Ellingsæter (2016), 'Cash for childcare schemes in the Nordic welfare states: Diverse paths, diverse outcomes', *European Societies*, 18 (1), 70–90.

Duvander, A.-Z., T. Ferrarini and M. Johansson (2015), *Familjepolitik för alla?: en ESO-rapport om föräldrapenning och jämställdhet*, Stockholm: Finansdepartementet, Regeringskansliet.

Duvander, A.-Z., and M. Johansson (2012), 'What are the effects of reforms promoting fathers' parental leave use?', *Journal of European Social Policy*, 22 (3), 319–30.

England, P. (2010), 'The gender revolution: Uneven and stalled', *Gender & Society*, 24 (2), 149–66.

Ferrarini, T. (2003), *Parental Leave Institutions in Eighteen Post-War Welfare States*, Stockholm: Stockholm University.

Ferrarini, T., and A.-Z. Duvander (2010), 'Earner-carer model at the crossroads: Reforms and outcomes of Sweden's family policy in comparative perspective', *International Journal of Health Services*, 40 (3), 373–98.

Ferrarini, T., K. Nelson, W. Korpi and J. Palme (2013), 'Social citizenship rights and social insurance replacement rate validity: Pitfalls and possibilities', *Journal of European Public Policy*, 20 (9), 1251–66.

Försäkringskassan (2019), *Reserverade Dagar Ökar Pappors Uttag Av Föräldrapenning*, Korta analyser 2019:1, Stockholm: Försäkringskassan.

Gauthier, A. H. (2007), 'The impact of family policies on fertility in industrialized countries: A review of the literature', *Population Research and Policy Review*, 26 (3), 323–46.

Goldscheider, F., E. Bernhardt and T. Lappegård (2015), 'The gender revolution: A framework for understanding changing family and demographic behavior', *Population and Development Review*, 41 (2), 207–39.

Kälvesten, A.-L. (1955), 'Family policy in Sweden', *Marriage and Family Living*, 17 (3), 250.

Korpi, W. (2000), 'Faces of inequality: Gender, class, and patterns of inequalities in different types of welfare states', *Social Politics: International Studies in Gender, State & Society*, 7 (2), 127–91.

Korpi, W., T. Ferrarini and S. Englund (2013), 'Women's opportunities under different family policy constellations: Gender, class, and inequality tradeoffs in Western countries re-examined', *Social Politics: International Studies in Gender, State & Society*, 20 (1), 1–40.

Korpi, W., and J. Palme (1998), 'The paradox of redistribution and strategies of equality: Welfare state institutions, inequality, and poverty in the Western countries', *American Sociological Review*, 63 (5), 661–87.

Luci-Greulich, A., and O. Thévenon (2013), 'The impact of family policies on fertility trends in developed countries', *European Journal of Population*, 29 (4), 387–416.

Lundqvist, Å. (2011), *Family Policy Paradoxes: Gender Equality and Labour Market Regulation in Sweden, 1930–2010*, Bristol: Policy Press.

Mandel, H., and M. Semyonov (2006), 'A welfare state paradox: State interventions and women's employment opportunities in 22 countries', *American Journal of Sociology*, 111 (6), 1910–49.

Marshall, T. H. (1950), *Citizenship and Social Class and Other Essays*, Cambridge: Cambridge University Press.

McDonald, P. (2000), 'Gender equity in theories of fertility transition', *Population and Development Review*, 26 (3), 427–39.

Nelson, K., D. Fredriksson, T. Korpi, W. Korpi, J. Palme and O. Sjöberg (2020), 'The Social Policy Indicators (SPIN) database', *International Journal of Social Welfare*, 29 (3), 285–89.

Neyer, G. (2005), 'Family policies in Western Europe: Fertility policies at the intersection of gender, employment, and care policies', *Österreichische Zeitschrift für Politikwissenschaft*, 34 (1), 91–102.

Nieuwenhuis, R., A. Need and H. van der Kolk (2017), 'Is there such a thing as too long childcare leave?', *International Journal of Sociology and Social Policy*, 37 (1/2), 2–15.

Pfau-Effinger, B. (1998), 'Gender cultures and the gender arrangement: A theoretical framework for cross-national gender research', *Innovation: The European Journal of Social Science Research*, 11 (2), 147–66.

SOU (2017:101), *Jämställt Föräldraskap Och Goda Uppväxtvillkor För Barn: En Ny Modell För Föräldraförsäkringen: Slutbetänkande Av Utredningen Om En Modern Föräldraförsäkring*, Stockholm: Wolters Kluwer.

Stankūnienė, V., and R. Juknienė (2009), 'Family policies in the Baltic countries: 1989–2008 – 3.1 Lithuania', in V. Stankūnienė and D. Jasilionis (eds), *The Baltic Countries: Population, Family and Family Policy*, Vilnius: Institute for Social Research, pp. 91–100.

Sveriges riksdag (2016), *Lag Om Upphävande Av Lagen (2008:307) Om Kommunalt Vårdnadsbidrag*.

Wesolowski, K., and T. Ferrarini (2018), 'Family policies and fertility: Examining the link between family policy institutions and fertility rates in 33 countries 1995–2011', *International Journal of Sociology and Social Policy*, 38 (11/12), 1057–70.

Wesolowski, K., S. Billingsley and G. Neyer (2020), 'Disentangling the complexity of family policies: SPIN data with an application to Lithuania and Sweden, 1995–2015', *Demographic Research*, 43, 1235–62.

6. The sustainability of family support systems in the 21st century: comparing Sweden and Lithuania

Jolanta Aidukaite and Kristina Senkuviene

INTRODUCTION

Family policies and policies that impact on families (such as health care, education and housing policy) have not been constant over time and space. Public support systems for families were transformed in reaction to socioeconomic pressures, socio-demographic change, cultural norms and changes in family forms (Hantrais 2004). Today we live in a world where pressures on public support for families are especially high due to deinstitutionalisation of the family, ageing of the population and increased female education and labour force participation. Scientists and policy makers still pose a rhetorical question: What kind of family policy measures are best equipped to help families cope in 21st-century Europe? This study seeks to contribute to a better understanding of the challenges that public family support systems experience in the 21st century by closely focusing on two rarely compared country cases of Sweden and Lithuania. It asks questions: What are the challenges that the public family support systems experience in two countries? What are the differences and similarities? How do citizens evaluate the state support for families with children in Sweden and Lithuania? What could be learned from it?

To answer these questions, the authors of this study conducted 20 expert interviews with social policy makers and scientists in Sweden and Lithuania. Additionally, nationwide surveys were conducted in 2018 (December, in Lithuania) and 2019 (January, in Sweden), providing unique information on how citizens evaluate public support for families. The semi-structured expert interviews and nationwide surveys were conducted under the project Challenges to the Welfare State Systems in Lithuania and Sweden, financed by the Research Council of Lithuania, grant number No. S-MIP-17-130.

We chose to compare Sweden and Lithuania as both countries have rather generous parental leave policies, yet they are also compatible according to the female labour force participation and fertility rates (see OECD 2020a). However, when it comes to child poverty, we see sharp differences, with Sweden being among a group of countries with the lowest child poverty, while Lithuania has the highest child poverty if Baltic and Nordic countries are compared (see Chapter 2 in this volume). This raises serious questions for social policy research. Lithuania has reformed its support system for families (especially parental leave policies), exporting many schemes from the Nordic countries. However, as stated by Ferge (2001, p. 14), there are "problems in family policy [in] that the outcome may not necessarily be what was sought or intended". The analogous schemes do not necessarily generate similar results in different countries. Therefore, we raise the questions: How sustainable is the family support system in Lithuania? Do citizens approve of the public family policy system after 30 years of drastic reforms?

Methodologically, this chapter combines qualitative and quantitative data, which is not common in social policy research. However, its benefit is that we draw a broad picture of problems and challenges in Sweden and Lithuania, allowing us to hypothesise on the sustainability of the family support systems in two countries. Experts' views allow us to delineate major challenges, and citizens' attitudes allow us to test the legitimacy. According to Wendt, Mischke and Pfeifer (2011), there have been limited comparative studies analysing attitudes towards public support for family policies. This could be partly explained by the lack of data. However, the citizens' attitudes are an important indicator for the legitimacy of existing institutions, and the citizens' dissatisfaction should be understood as a mismatch between the public's preferences and the institutional status quo (Wendt, Mischke and Pfeifer 2011).

The chapter is arranged as follows. First, some theoretical consideration is presented. Second, we provide the methodology of the chapter. Third, we present the comparative analysis of the similarities and differences in public support systems between Lithuania and Sweden. Fourth, we analyse the experts' interviews. Fifth, we analyse a nationwide survey of 2018–2019 data on residents' attitudes towards the public support system for families, and explore how much their attitudes mirror the experts' views. Finally, we offer a discussion and conclusions.

THEORETICAL CONSIDERATIONS

Social policy development has been driven by many factors, including structural (demographic, economic, technological), institutional (veto points, the impact of the World Bank and the European Union, or EU) and power-resource-related (unionisation, Left parties) (Brady and Young Lee 2014; Deacon 2000; Korpi and Palme 2003). Family policy, which is an integral part of social policy, has been influenced by similar forces. However, it has been widely agreed that family policy, unlike other fields of social policy such as pensions or unemployment, is largely defined by cultural factors – predominant ideals and attitudes towards gender roles in society and family (Lohmann and Zagel 2016; O'Connor 1996; Orloff 1993; Sainsbury 1996). Therefore, it is important to examine not only real structures of support systems for families, their problems and the reasons behind their development, but also public opinions and attitudes.

Countries that hold more egalitarian views on gender roles have developed welfare and family policy systems involving support for female labour force participation and the redistribution of caring work within the family. Countries with more traditional views on women's roles in the family and society have developed systems that encourage homemaking. Nordic countries usually fall within the former category, while South European countries and Continental Europe fall into the latter cluster. Central and East European countries had inherited high female labour market participation rates since the fall of the communist regimes. Although under the communist regime women's paid work was supported and encouraged by the state, the unpaid work at home was not monetised and equally divided between the sexes, resulting in a double burden for women. They actively participated in the labour market on equal terms with men, but the unpaid household work and caring responsibilities were left to women only. Since the fall of the communist regimes, women have become even more familialised due to a collapse in social services (childcare and elderly care), a decline in wages and an increase in unemployment (see Pascall and Manning 2000). Nevertheless, this situation has been rapidly replaced by the necessity of the dual-earner family, due not only to low wages in many post-communist societies, but also to high female job aspirations and increasing gender-equality values coming from the West and emphasised by the European Commission. Gender equality has been increasingly taken into account in Lithuania and has been addressed to varying extents in the systems of support to families with children (Aidukaite 2016).

Korpi (2000) identified three types of gender/family policy models: general family support, dual-earner support and market-oriented policies. He focused on social insurance programs and the taxation relevant for children and parents, as well as on social services for children and the elderly.

Central to the dual-earner model are care facilities, available on a continuous basis, for the youngest preschool children, as well as earnings-related maternity and paternity leave. This model is found precisely in what is elsewhere known as social democratic welfare states. Sweden, Norway, Finland and Denmark are examples of dual-earner and social democratic models. Cash benefits to minor children and family tax benefits, given via tax allowances or tax credits, are a form of general family support, formally neutral with respect to the labour force participation of the spouses. However, the tax benefits to housewives can be expected to encourage homemaking. Childcare services are underdeveloped in this model. The general family model is usually found in the conservative welfare states, and such countries as Italy, Germany, Austria and Holland are examples of both models. Countries such as the United States, the United Kingdom, New Zealand and Australia, where maximum private responsibility for childcare prevails, are described as having a market-oriented gender policy (Korpi 2000). Korpi's gender/family policy typology is useful in many ways, as it shows how gender relations are produced and reproduced by various welfare policies. The availability of public childcare, elderly services and generous maternity and paternity leave produces a most egalitarian society as it supports female labour market participation. However, other positive outcomes could also be observed, such as lower poverty among children and higher birth rates compared to countries that cluster into the traditional/general or market-oriented gender/family types. Thus, there seems to be a far-reaching consensus among researchers that is implicitly in favour of the dual-earner family policy model. The well-being of the children often depends on that of the parents, which becomes much easier to maintain if both parents participate in paid employment (Aidukaite 2004, 2006; Ferrarini 2006; Korpi 2000; Orloff 1993; Sainsbury 1996; Wennemo 1994).

In recent decades, the shift from dual-earner to dual-earner/dual-carer has slowly appeared in European countries. Sweden is known to have had a dual-earner/dual-carer family policy model since the 1970s (Duvander and Ferrarini 2013). The dual-earner/dual-carer model implies not only state support for both parents' (particularly the mother's) employment through various welfare provisions, but also encourages fathers' participation in childcare (Saraceno 2013). Fathers' participation in childcare is encouraged through shared parental leave and/or paternity leave policies specifically designed for the father.

In Western countries, the motives behind the introduction and extension of family policy were important for the establishment of benefits systems and the mixture of various forms of support for families (Wennemo 1994). Wennemo highlighted four main reasons that explicitly influence family legislation: population reproduction, poverty reduction, the breadwinner ideology and gender equality.

English-speaking countries, which, according to Korpi's typology, are mainly grouped into the market-oriented gender/family policy model, put strong emphasis on poverty reduction. The reproduction of the population is an important reason that features in the general family support model. Scandinavian countries, which are classified as the dual-earner/dual-carer family support model, put strong emphasis on gender equality; another crucial role in these societies is played by poverty reduction, particularly among single mothers.

For the purposes of this study, we rely on Korpi's family support models. Korpi's typology allows us to observe major differences between countries in their support of the family's arrangements, and explains how these differences account for varying outcomes. To identify major challenges, we focus on exploring the major underlying motives behind family policy legislation in each country and how well equipped the family support systems are, according to the experts, to deal with poverty reduction among children, to solve demographic problems and to increase gender equality.

METHODOLOGY AND DATA

As noted, this study combines qualitative and quantitative data to reach its goals. The qualitative approach helps to uncover major problems and challenges of family support systems. The analysis is based on semi-structured interviews with social policy experts conducted in 2018 in Lithuania and Sweden. Twenty interviews were conducted (10 in each country). The analysis of expert interviews passed through major stages of the qualitative analytical process as described by Meuser and Nagel (2009, pp. 35–36): transcription, paraphrasing, coding, thematic comparison, sociological conceptualisation and generalisation. This chapter displays the final stages of the interview analysis – the thematic comparisons, conceptualisation and generalisation. To maintain confidentiality and the anonymity of our experts, we assigned the codes *LT1–10* and *SE1–10* to our interviewees.

While examining interviews, we raise the following questions: What major changes were implemented in family support systems of Sweden and Lithuania over the last 10 years? How well does the family support system support the dual-earner family or dual-earner/dual-carer model in Sweden and Lithuania? What are the major goals of family support system reforms? How well do family support systems ensure gender equality, reduce poverty among children and solve demographic problems?

The citizens' attitudes (quantitative indicators) for this study come from a questionnaire carried out in Lithuania and Sweden. The questionnaire in Lithuania was administered and carried out in December 2018 by the market and opinion research centre Vilmorus. In Sweden, the identical questionnaire was carried out by NorStat. A multi-stage probability sample with a random route procedure was used for the survey in both countries. One thousand respondents were questioned in each country. The response rate was between 28 and 36 per cent, which is in a normal range. There was no representation bias (distributions regarding some socio-demographics that are similar to the population). In Lithuania, the questionnaire was completed through personal, face-to-face interviews at the homes of respondents by trained and supervised interviewers. In Sweden, the survey was carried out online. To capture the citizens' satisfaction with the support for families, the respondents were asked "Generally how satisfied are you with the state support to families with children in your country?" and were asked to rate each family support scheme provided by the state (Very good, Good, Fair, Poor, Very poor, Don't know).

We grounded our methodology on comparative case study. Comparative case studies encompass the analysis of the differences and similarities across two or more cases that share a common focus. Comparative case studies usually use both qualitative and quantitative data. It is important in such studies to describe each case in depth from the beginning, as this enables a successful comparison (Goodrick 2014).

FAMILY SUPPORT SYSTEMS IN LITHUANIA AND SWEDEN: A COMPARATIVE OVERVIEW

Family policy in Sweden has developed consistently over time, placing a great importance on gender equality and individualism, and putting emphasis on providing public services instead of cash benefits (Hantrais 2004; Leitner 2003). Swedish family policy is also characterised by universal child allowances, weak pronatalism, a relatively good economic position of single mothers, income equality among families with children and a high level of female income from paid work (Hiilamo 2002a, 2002b). Gender equality has been a cornerstone of the family policy in Sweden. In support of gender equality, work–family reconciliation policies were developed to facilitate female labour force participation and to ensure gender equality within a family by incentivising fathers to take parental leave (Duvander and Ferrarini 2013; Grødem 2017; Tunberger and Sigle-Rushton 2011; see also Chapters 3, 4 and 5). Hence, the Swedish family support system exhibits a high degree of defamilialism, with highly developed public services for children and the elderly.

Family policy in Lithuania has undergone dramatic reconfigurations over 29 years (1990–2019), especially in the early 1990s, right after the collapse of the communist regimes (Aidukaite 2006). The family policy in Lithuania has gone through many reforms, which have been described by a number of studies (see, for example, Aidukaite 2006, 2016; Javornik 2014; Stankūnienė 2001; Žalimienė 2015), and has been developed quite inconsistently. The means-tested benefits have been an important part of the financial support for families in Lithuania, together with earnings-related benefits. The emphasis was placed on financial support, while services have been not so well developed (Aidukaite 2006, 2016). The general reform paths have been observed from defamilialism (the Soviet system supported maternal employment through well-developed childcare services) to familialism (the period from 1990 to 1996 saw a massive decline in childcare services), and from familialism to defamilialism again (the period from 1997 and onwards, when

Table 6.1   *Number of children in preschools in Lithuania*

	2012	2013	2014	2015	2016	2017	2018
Urban areas	92 836	96 838	99 465	100 699	101 470	103 688	105 089
Rural areas	11 694	13 287	14 192	14 875	15 344	15 648	15 763
Total	104 530	110 125	113 657	115 574	116 814	119 336	120 852

Source: Statistics Lithuania, 2019.

Table 6.2   *Number of preschool institutions in Lithuania*

	2012	2013	2014	2015	2016	2017	2018
Urban areas	547	563	581	614	633	639	632
Rural areas	113	112	109	107	104	99	99
Total	660	675	690	721	737	738	731

Source: Statistics Lithuania, 2019.

emphasis was again placed on policies encouraging a mother's employment), with, however, some coexistence (or elements) of familialism at the same time (Aidukaite 2016). These changes in family policy in Lithuania are best illustrated by the change in the number of preschool facilities over the last three decades. The network of preschools has declined significantly since independence was restored. At the beginning of independence, between 1989 and 1990, there were 1808 preschools in Lithuania (1003 in urban areas and 805 in rural areas). In 2003 there were only 672 of the preschool institutions left (489 in urban areas and 183 and rural areas; Kavoliūnaitė-Ragauskienė 2012, p. 26). Data provided by the Lithuanian Department of Statistics shows that the situation has improved in recent years: the number of children in preschool education increased by several thousand from 2012 till 2018, which can be considered a positive trend. In 2012, there were about 93 000 children in the preschool institutions in urban areas and almost 12 000 in rural areas. In 2018, there were 105 000 in urban areas and almost 16 000 in rural areas (see Table 6.1).

However, the development of these institutions in Lithuania remains uneven. If the number of preschool facilities in urban areas is growing steadily, in rural areas several such establishments are closed each year (see Table 6.2). During the period from 2012 to 2018, the number of preschool institutions increased from 547 to 632 in urban areas. But in rural areas, the number of preschool institutions declined from 113 (in 2012) to 99 (in 2018).

In Sweden, a heavy emphasis is placed on the provision of childcare institutions (nurseries and preschool facilities). According to the Organisation for

Economic Co-operation and Development (OECD) data for the year 2016, the enrolment rate of children from 3 to 5 years old in Sweden was about 96 per cent, while in Lithuania it was 84 per cent. The differences are much higher if the enrolment rates of children up to 2 years old are examined. The enrolment rate for Sweden was 46.5 per cent, while for Lithuania only 23 per cent, which is lower than the EU (31 per cent) or OECD (33 per cent) averages (for details please see Chapter 2).

But let us take a closer look into the current systems of support for families of Lithuania and Sweden in more detail.

The state support system for families with children in Lithuania comprises two main parts: universal benefits (paid irrespective of the family's assets and income) and the assistance paid to poor families according to their income level. In Sweden, most of the benefits are universal. That is why Sweden's public spending on family benefits is one of the highest in Europe – it totals 3.5 per cent of its gross domestic product (almost 1.5 per cent in cash and the rest in services; OECD 2020b). Spending in other social policy areas such as health and housing support also assists families but is not included here. Therefore, Sweden's support for parents with children is comprehensive and effective but expensive.

Both countries have similar parental leave systems with a slight difference in duration and flexibility. Though in Lithuania, parental leave is longer – it is one of the longest in Europe. Before 2019, if a one-year period was preferred, 100 per cent of the salary was compensated. If the benefit was preferred to be received for two years, during the first year (until the child turns 1 year old) the benefit was 70 per cent of previous salary and 40 per cent afterwards (until the child turns 2 years old). According to new amendments implemented in January 2019, a parent can choose to receive a benefit until the child is 1 year old (he/she will be paid 77.58 per cent of the compensated recipient's wages) or to receive a benefit until the child is 2 years old – from the end of the pregnancy and childbirth or the paternity leave until the child is 1 year old, he will be paid 54.31 per cent and later, until the child is 2 years old, 31.03 per cent (SODRA 2019). But there is no possibility to use the parental leave more flexibly as in Sweden (until a child turns 8 years old) (Swedish Social Insurance Agency 2018). The main difference between the parental leave schemes of both countries is who can take the leave. In Lithuania, this leave can be used optionally by the mother or the father. In Sweden, each parent receives sharable 240 days (480 in total) of parental leave. Mother and father have an equal part of a non-transferable period of parental leave (90 days each – mother's quota and father's quota), which can be used in parts (months, weeks, days, hours), while the remaining 300 days (from which 90 days' flat rate is paid; it does not depend on previous salary) can be shared voluntarily, until the child is aged 12 years old (Aidukaite and Telisauskaite-Cekanavice 2020; MISSOC

Table 6.3   *Parental leave benefits recipients by gender*

	2014		2015		2016		2017		2018	
	1st year	2nd year	1st year	2nd year	1st year	2nd year	1st year	2nd year	1st year	2nd year
Women	16 368	13 550	17 364	12 747	18 628	13 877	18 839	15 318	18 345	14 907
Men	1539	4779	1656	6187	1670	7291	1480	8234	1409	8913

Source: Statistics Lithuania, 2019.

2018; Swedish Social Insurance Agency 2018; see also Chapter 3). This means that in this case fathers spend more time caring for their children and this promotes gender equality. Still, in general both countries have rather generous parental benefits.

It should be mentioned that in Sweden, the maternity, paternity and parental leave policies are merged, while in Lithuania a clear distinction is made and they consist of separate schemes (see also Aidukaite and Telisauskaite-Cekanavice 2020). For instance, the paternity benefit reserved exclusively to the father is longer in Lithuania than in Sweden: 30 days at any time from the birth of a child until the child reaches 3 months. Paternity leave is becoming increasingly popular in Lithuania (see Table 6.3). In Sweden, this type of benefit is called temporary parental benefit – 10 days of leave can be used to be at the delivery or take care of other children (SODRA 2019; Swedish Social Insurance Agency 2018).

The data in Table 6.3 show that by the time a child reaches 1 year old, the number of women in parental leave exceeds the number of men by 10–13 times. For instance, in 2018, there were more than 18 000 women taking parental leave during the first year, while only 1400 men were on parental leave at the same time. In the second year (for the first to second years of the child's life) the recipients' distribution by gender is somewhat more even, and each year more and more men stay at home with their children till they become 2 years old. In 2018, there were about 15 000 women taking parental leave during the second year, with almost 9 000 men taking parental leave. According to Reingardė and Tereškinas (2006), the most common explanation by men who do not take parental leave is the financial reason; that is, men usually earn more than women, so women stay home. But there are also deeper cultural and ideological aspects in the understanding of gender roles and fatherhood as well as motherhood. For many men, such leave is beyond the scope of understanding of their masculine and paternal identities. Childcare is generally considered to be a "woman's job". The understanding that a mother is the main carer for children is quite strong in Lithuania (Reingardė and Tereškinas 2006).

Child benefit in both countries is universal – in Sweden slightly larger, but Lithuania has an additional amount for children from poor families. The same

additional amount is paid for children from large families (three or more children) in Lithuania, whereas Sweden pays a large family supplement for families with two children. An additional amount of money for large families is
not only paid beginning from different numbers of children, but these amounts
differ considerably (for example, for three children both parents receive EUR
60.42 (20.14 x 3) in Lithuania, and EUR 34 each (EUR 68 for both) in Sweden;
for four, EUR 80.56 (20.14 x 4) and EUR 82 each (EUR 164 for both) accordingly; for five, EUR 100.7 (20.14 x 5) and EUR 141 each (EUR 282 for both)
accordingly (SODRA 2019; Swedish Social Insurance Agency 2018).

In both countries the care conditions for a sick child are similar, with
only a slightly higher percentage of salary compensated in Sweden (80 per
cent), while in Lithuania from 1 January 2019 the sickness benefits to take
care of a sick child make up 65.94 per cent of the recipient's compensated
wage (Aidukaite and Telisauskaite-Cekanavice 2020; SODRA 2019; Swedish
Social Insurance Agency 2018).

A comparative overview of both countries' benefits for and assistance to
families with children shows some difference in their social support systems'
orientation. The Lithuanian social support system is more oriented to support
those in need. Therefore more assistance is paid to poor families according to
their income level: additional child benefit; social benefit for low-income families; compensation for the costs of house heating and hot and drinking water;
and social support for pupils from low-income families.

The Swedish social support system is more oriented towards gender equality: the emphasis is on child care services and shared parental leave.

EXPERTS' VIEWS ON CHALLENGES TO FAMILY SUPPORT SYSTEMS IN LITHUANIA AND SWEDEN

Advantages and Disadvantages of Family Support in Lithuania

What is strikingly evident from the expert interviews in Lithuania is that the
family support system is very fragmented; namely it has been developed
fragmentally, focusing on separate aspects of the family support system but
not having a systematic, long-lasting view on how family policy should be
reformed and which path (universal or targeted) it has to follow. Family
support measures are targeted at the early life of children (infants and preschool children) and families with small children; there is little support in
the later stages of children's lives and little support to families having other
special needs. As our experts note: "There is a big problem here, because we
are still jumping from one measure to another, and in reality, no one sees an
overall picture" (LT1); "Another thing that hinders our system is the lack of
a systematic approach" (LT9).

The lack of a systemic and long-lasting vision for family policy is partly explained by the fact that there is no separate institution to take care of family matters. Family policy problems are now being addressed by several institutions, which lack co-operation and co-ordination of their work. This situation is also confirmed by the research literature. According to Reingardienė (2004), the legal framework for family policy is in line with European standards, but it is not fully implemented. There are many reasons for this. First, there is no separate body responsible for the formulation and implementation of family policy, which leads to a lack of clear and common objectives for that policy. Second, the fragmentation and incoherence of family policy, which is often caused by the government's term of office, often lead to public distrust in the social system. Third, the orientation of family policy and its measures to families at social risk deprives other families of the feeling that the state supports them.

In the Lithuanian family support system, the means-tested benefits have played quite a significant role in supporting families since the 1990s. The experts see advantages and disadvantages in this. Social assistance benefits help families at a social risk. On the other hand, they create poverty traps, as in some cases it is better to live on benefits than to take paid work. The experts emphasised that the system itself does not encourage efforts, as minimum wages and social benefits are similar in size: "Why should I work if I get the same thing without working?" (LT9). The widespread view expressed among the experts is that the current social support system is not effective enough, creates poverty traps and dependency on benefits, and does not encourage people to return to the labour market soon enough.

The inefficiency of social assistance is also noted in the scientific literature. Previous studies (Gvaldaitė and Kirilova 2014; Stankūnienė, Maslauskaitė and Baublytė 2013; Žalimienė 2015) stressed that when evaluating family policy measures to reduce child poverty, it should be emphasised that Lithuania does not follow the principle of universality – financial support (except child allowance) is almost always dependent on the income of family members. Such a policy boomerangs: benefits to poor families become their livelihood and raising of children becomes a means of gaining benefits. The financial costs the state bears and the results it gets are absolutely inadequate.

Nevertheless, the universal child allowance (in Lithuania it is popularly called "child money") has been paid out to every child since its introduction on 1 January 2018. The experts' views of this are divided. Some see it as the state's attention for every child: "universal child money, I would regard this as an encouragement rather than a child support. Because it is, after all, a gesture of the state, a gesture of respect for every citizen" (LT1). Others expressed an unequivocal opinion on universal allowance. The decision to introduce a universal child benefit by cutting an additional tax-free income sized for working parents is called a mistake by some experts:

> These are different tools. ... These are different things, completely different. They cannot be opposed. The Tax Exempt Income is one, and if we look at all the more successful countries in the European Union that are slightly more successful, then there are the tax measures. ... And there is no need for opposition, it cannot be: this or that. In the case of a crisis, it is possible to remove one or temporarily remove it, but they should work together anyway. It's just that I think it's a mistake to separate them. (LT6)

Not everything is viewed so negatively by the experts. Speaking about advantages of the family support system in Lithuania, most experts mentioned first of all the long duration of parental leave: "the childcare leave system is probably one of the best in Europe" (LT5); "We are leaders here" (LT10). Bearing in mind that both mothers and fathers can choose to take parental leave in Lithuania, this measure is seen by the experts as "both family consolidation and gender equality" (LT4).

Another advantage of the parental leave system in Lithuania, as seen by the experts, is the possibility for grandparents to take parental leave (amendments to the law became effective from April 2018), as well as one month's paternity leave for fathers: "They contribute when it is the most difficult – just after the birth" (LT4). The paternity leave is viewed positively by scholars as it contributes to gender equality in childcare. However, the grandparents' involvement in childcare is seen as contradictory. A recent study (Aidukaite and Telisauskaite-Cekanavice 2020) claims that in Lithuania the state intentionally supports kinship familialism as grandparents are entitled to take parental leave.

How family support system in Lithuania ensures gender equality

When it comes to ensuring gender equality, the experts first of all emphasised the opportunity for both parents to take parental leave and the possibility for fathers to take paternity leave. This allows the father to participate more actively in the child's upbringing, and the mother to return to the labour market more quickly. The Lithuanian experts emphasise that access to childcare and education facilities is another tool that enables women to return to the labour market more quickly, and at the same time promotes gender equality. Unfortunately, the issue of preschool institutions is not fully resolved; this problem is particularly relevant in the largest cities of the country, where thousands of children are waiting for places in state care institutions.

Another measure to promote gender equality and women's participation in the labour market is, according to the experts, the creation of opportunities to reconcile work and family responsibilities: "It should be possible for parents raising children to choose flexible working hours, part-time work" (LT3); however, there is still much room for improvement here.

Previous studies (Bučaitė-Vilkė et al. 2012; Jančaitytė 2006; Reingardienė 2004) assessing the impact of family policy on women entering the labour market concluded that measures to combine professional and family commitments are not sufficient in Lithuania. Limitation of childcare services is the main concern. The conditions for parental leave are fairly good, but other family-friendly policy measures (part-time work, work at home, childcare centres at the workplace) are not developed for a variety of reasons (economic family status, the unfavourable attitude of employers, and so on).

During the interviews, several experts, when speaking about gender equality, drew attention to the difference between the salaries of women and men in Lithuania, which, according to one interviewee, "differs even in the public sector or state institutions" (LT1). This trend leads to the fact that, for example, the mother with the usually lower income is most likely to take parental leave.

Previous studies (Maslauskaitė 2004; Reingardienė 2004; Šarlauskas and Telešienė 2014) support the experts' view. Although there are more and more men taking parental leave, the process is not as fast as expected. Faster implementation of the gender-equality principle is largely impeded by cultural clichés still attributing the care of family members to women.

How the family support system in Lithuania reduces child poverty
Speaking about child poverty reduction measures, the experts emphasised the importance of ensuring equal opportunities for children regardless of the family's financial capacity. However, the social assistance support could be stigmatising for families receiving it. For instance, due to the fact that services such as free lunches are received only by children from poor families, children receiving them experience social exclusion. As one of the experts states: "There are certain tables in the schools' restaurants reserved for children who receive a free lunch subsidised by the state, everyone sees for whom they are. It stigmatises. Most of those children, even if they are hungry, do not eat at school" (LT4). Free school lunches were mentioned by many experts as an important child poverty reduction measure. But it was also mentioned here that differentiation of services stigmatises children from vulnerable families, they experience social exclusion, and this problem should be best addressed by the introduction of free meals for all preschool children.

Some of the experts suggested that the universal child allowance should also contribute to the reduction of child poverty, but also expressed doubts as to whether the money is used for the intended purpose in families at risk. Even a small amount is quite significant in families experiencing poverty, but when people do not have social skills, money is often wasted on secondary things and does not actually reduce poverty.

There was widespread awareness among experts interviewed that the problem of child poverty should be solved primarily by "enabling parents to work and earn money" (LT4). It was also proposed "to reform the tax system so that families with children would have more money to meet their basic needs" (LT6). And, as with the promotion of gender equality, almost everyone has emphasised that the problem of child poverty should be addressed through education and training. As one expert summarised, "cultural poverty is much more dangerous and deeper than economic poverty" (LT10).

Overall, there was a great concern among the experts interviewed about child poverty in Lithuania, and that the family support system should somehow intervene and help families to cope. However, there is also a lack of understanding that poverty is a structural problem, not only an individual one, and that universal measures could solve poverty more effectively than targeted ones.

Advantages and Disadvantages of Family Support in Sweden

In Sweden, our experts were mostly concerned with two major challenges affecting family policy: ageing and migration. Both social phenomena pose serious problems to ensure a smooth financing of the family support system, and to ensure the accessibility and quality of care services. Interestingly, these two problems are important in the Lithuanian case, too; however, experts in Lithuania have not mentioned them as a challenge to the family support system. Both Sweden and Lithuania are rapidly ageing societies (see Chapter 8). Both experience the migration challenge, too, but from different angles. Sweden is a receiving country with a high influx of migrants in recent years, while Lithuania is a sending country and outward labour migration poses serious challenges to the sustainability of public welfare financing, including family policy.

When it comes to the ageing problem, Swedish experts have highlighted the problem of a shortage of workers in the care sector: "Well, the aging population, of course, which is a problem we share with many other countries. That's a challenge, of course. And we are trying to combat that by employing people in the care sector or both care for the elderly and also healthcare" (SE1).

Migration is seen, on the one hand, as a blessing to solve the shortage of care workers in the service sector. As one expert noted: "It's a sort of a gift getting these people [recent migrants] and getting the opportunity to school them or to introduce them to sectors where we really need the labour force" (SE1). On the other hand, it is seen increasingly as a challenge to the sustainability of the Swedish welfare state model. A number of experts also expressed the concern that massive immigration of refugees, especially during 2015, created a lot of pressure on public finances and led to a change in the concept of solidarity:

> There has been this very shift in this notion of solidarity and who the welfare state should include in its people's home. ... [A] sense that those people who are not like us will be taking benefits away from Sweden has been a discourse that has given some right-wing [parties] a lot of discursive space and [votes] because it resonates in Swedish society. (SE5)

Despite some challenges expressed by the experts, the Swedish model still successfully holds to its gender-equality goal. According to most experts, the main advantage of the Swedish family support system is the emphasis on equality. As gender equality has already become a norm for many people in Sweden, it is natural that equal parenthood dominates in families with children, and many experts have identified that equal parenting is a priority of the country's family policy: "To work for an equal parenting, equal responsibility between men and women, or whatever gender you might have ... to increase equality between parents" (SE1).

Another important advantage highlighted by the experts is that the family policy system is perceived by the population as a guarantee of security. Everyone knows that the state will take care of you in emergency situations: "You can feel safe in different stages of your life. If the economy is bad or if you have a disabled child and so on, they should know that the state helps in those situations" (SE2). Certain elements of the family support system are immovable, irrespective of changes in government or other factors, and these are shared parental leave and childcare services: "Well, I think that certain things are untouchable. Nobody could take away the day care, it's just like a sacred cow. That's also true of parental leave and daddy leave. I don't think anybody's ever going to touch that" (SE5). The experts emphasised that there is great support for the Swedish welfare state model and for the family support system. This is confirmed with enthusiasm by numerous experts: "I think that most people here are fans of the welfare state" (SE1); "People are happy about the system, they like it. Most people do" (SE2); "Well, I think there is a very strong support for welfare state" (SE3); "Actually there is very, very strong support for the model in Sweden among families" (SE6).

How the family support system in Sweden ensures gender equality
Almost all of the experts, when speaking about the benefits of a family support system in Sweden, first of all emphasised the implementation of the principle of gender equality, which has become a norm in this country: "Gender equality is very, very normative in Sweden" (SE4). This has been one of the key prior-

ities of the country's social policy for many years; therefore, excellent results have been achieved in this area:

> We have worked with this since the sixties or something like that, with different family policies during different years. So, as you remember, in the fifties we had like over one million housewives in Sweden and today you can hardly find anyone. So, the society has changed from like [a] one-breadwinner system to [a] two-breadwinners system, I would say. (SE2)

Although much has been achieved, the experts are reluctant to idealise the situation, and think there is still room for improvement here: "we have a problem, that we always had – that of inequality between men and women, which is a high priority here, in Sweden" (SE1); "I would say that we haven't succeeded in it like a hundred per cent yet. ... We talk a lot about gender equality and so on, but I would say that maybe we have come half-way or something like that, but not more" (SE2).

Essentially, gender equality is implemented through greater involvement of women in the labour market and more active involvement of men in housekeeping and childcare. A majority of the experts see the fathers' involvement in childcare as a success of Swedish family policy:

> I think if we want to talk about something that has been successful in the Swedish family policy it is really this engagement of fathers in parental leave, because they are using a lot of leave, it is increasing all the time. ... So I think this is a successful policy. (SE4)

Despite the results achieved, some experts believe that changes could be faster: "It's really the division of labour inside the families. It's changing slowly, of course, but in a more gender-equal direction, and you are seeing fathers, they are really doing more of the housework" (SE6). It is also acknowledged that the situation in some cases depends very much on the father's background, social class and labour market participation: "Probably it's a question of a class. ... I think that the norms in the new middle classes in Stockholm [are] probably much more favourable in this direction, but I can imagine in the countryside that there is some resistance to this" (SE3); "Well, fathers who don't have a job and are outside the labour market, they don't use the parental leave to the same extent. So they are outside the social insurance system and they're outside the labour market, so they become marginalised in that way" (SE4). This situation is especially applicable to migrant families. Previous studies (Ma et al. 2020) have also acknowledged this situation, referring to the finding that migrant fathers take parental leave less often than native-born fathers. Experts expressed concern that the issue of gender equality takes on a completely different character when it comes to immigrant families living in Sweden. In some cases, such families adhere to a patriarchal worldview and to a single-breadwinner model: "in areas where you have a fairly strong representation of newcomers to Sweden, because ... females coming recently to Sweden with children, they don't work to the same extent" (SE3).

Swedish experts emphasised that family policy in Sweden is largely about ensuring gender equality in work and family life, about equality in childcare and household shared traditions. This kind of discourse was hardly prevalent in the Lithuanian expert interviews.

Despite long-standing efforts by the state and the results achieved in the area of gender equality, some experts believe that women are still responsible for the majority of household duties:

> The real question is how much does parental leave, which is a year and a half per child, affect the larger relationship in the family around paid and unpaid work. And that has not changed, the amount of unpaid work. Still mainly women take the lion's share and tend to work part time. (SE5)

Men, despite family-friendly policies and widely accepted shared parental leave practices, still spend more time on paid work:

> [There] is that kind of workplace culture about expectations that men will work more and they have more flexibility to work longer hours and they do work longer hours than women. And Sweden actually has a high proportion of men to work over 40 hours a week. Given the fact that there's this family friendly policy. (SE5)

How the family support system in Sweden reduces child poverty

Another important priority of Swedish family policy is to ensure the equality between families with and without children. This is achieved by a universal child allowance, which is shared equally by both parents. Child allowance is seen as a means of redistributing money between families with and without children. The experts are aware that because child allowance is universal, it prevents stigmatisation of poor people and at the same time reduces child poverty in low-income families. This discourse was not prevalent among Lithuanian experts, where in many cases poor families were blamed for depending on a social assistance system instead of working. Both Swedish and Lithuanian experts share the same understanding that the best policy to reduce child poverty is to ensure that both parents are working. However, many Lithuanian experts, contrary to the Swedish, see preschool as a means to ensure the parents' (usually the mother's) participation in the labour market, but not so much as a means to reduce poverty among families with children and without.

Swedish experts stated: "pre-schools [are] always like the key to good economic standard" (SE1). In addition, generous parental leave support encourages people to work and earn money before they have children, which also prevents child poverty:

> I think the parental leave is good in reducing child poverty because, normally, it really means that you wait before having children, until you have a job. So both of you have a good benefit while at home. But you have a job to go back to. So children don't live so often with unemployed parents. Of course, it's going to reduce poverty. (SE4)

None of the Lithuanian experts mentioned that the generous parental leave is a means to reduce poverty among children; it is seen more like a means to ensure childcare.

True, given the high level of the Swedish economy and the generous social system in the country, the problem of child poverty exists only relatively. This is not the absolute poverty when the minimum needs of the child are not met. Experts pointed out that families in which parents have a weak attachment to the labour market and poor skills and education are most vulnerable to falling into the poverty trap:

> But of course we have a group that ... have a very weak position at the labour markets and the poverty among children is among groups that haven't, that don't have any work and perhaps haven't, the parents haven't worked either, earlier on ... So of course, among migrants who haven't succeeded in getting established in the labour market ... a lot of them are poor, I would say, according to our way of measuring poverty. (SE6)

Experts also point out that the problem of child poverty is more relevant in families where one parent is raising children, as the economic situation of two-breadwinner families has improved significantly more than in single-breadwinner families.

PUBLIC OPINION ON FAMILY POLICY SUSTAINABILITY

In this section we review citizens' attitudes and opinions on the family support system in Lithuania and Sweden to see how much they correspond to the experts' views and problems raised during the interviews.

We asked whether the respondents are in general satisfied with the state support for families with children in their country. Figure 6.1 displays the results. The contrast between Lithuania and Sweden is striking. In Sweden, more than a half of the interviewees reported that they are very satisfied with the family support system, and more than 80 per cent are satisfied (Very satisfied + Satisfied). In Lithuania, slightly more than 1 per cent of respondents reported that they are very satisfied with the family support system. Those who are unsatisfied (Not really satisfied + Not at all satisfied) comprise a slightly larger group of 35 per cent than the satisfied group (Very satisfied + Satisfied), which amount to 31 per cent.

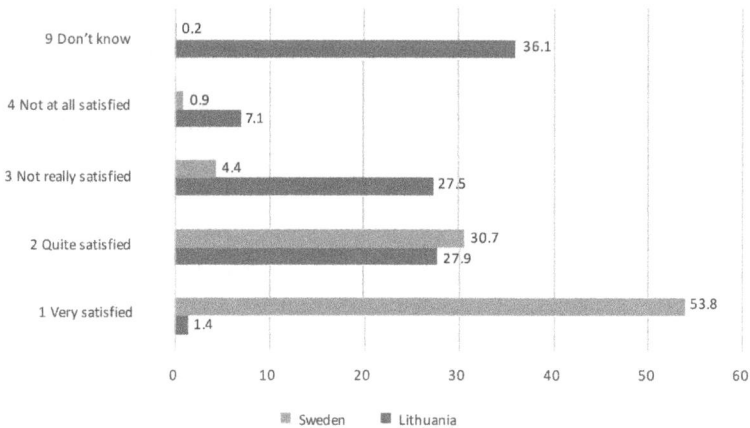

Figure 6.1   Satisfaction with the family support system in general in Lithuania (N1000) and Sweden (N1002)

The first data inspection tells us that family policy is a matter of national pride in Sweden, well entrenched in the social policy system and sustainable in the future. The case of Lithuania shows that the family support system is not backed up by citizens' expectations; it divides society into supporters and critics of the system. But let us look at how each family support scheme is rated; this will provide us with more accurate information on satisfaction with the system.

The ratings of each family support scheme are provided in the Appendix, in Table 6A.1 for Lithuania and Table 6A.2 for Sweden. In Lithuania, parental, maternity and paternity leaves are rated rather high by respondents. More than 40 per cent rated them as "Good" and about 10 per cent as "Very good". About a quarter rated them as "Fair". Together with a birth grant and sick leave policy related to children, these public support schemes have rather high approval among the population, while support schemes that rated "Poor" and "Very poor" are social assistance benefits (maintenance support and housing assistance) and support services for elderly care.

In Sweden, we find that the worst rating received for support services was for the elderly care as well as care services and financial support related to disabled children. The latter were also rated low in Lithuania, but not as low as support services for elderly care. The highest approvals were received for parental leave, universal child allowance and sick leave policy related to children. Overall, in Sweden the public support schemes were rated much better than in Lithuania, as expected. There were only about 5 per cent on average who reported "Poor" and "Very poor" ratings for each scheme, except for elderly services and support for a sick child, where more than 20 per cent reported dissatisfaction. In Lithuania, dissatisfaction was ranging from about 7 per cent for parental benefits to up to 30 per cent for elderly care. The satisfaction (Very good + Good) was ranging from more than 80 per cent for parental leave to about 35 per cent for elderly care and support for a disabled child in Sweden; in Lithuania, from 55 per cent for maternity leave to less than 20 per cent for maintenance support.

Overall, we see similar patterns for both countries – paternal leave policies are on the top of the ratings, elderly care and disabled children's support at the bottom. Yet in Lithuania means-tested benefits got very poor approval from the population.

DISCUSSION AND CONCLUSIONS

The Lithuanian and Swedish family support systems are at very different stages of development. Lithuania is still shaping its own system due to the lack of a systematic approach and strategic direction, which was developed in Sweden decades ago. Meanwhile, in Sweden family support is sustainable, generous and valued by the country's own population. Sweden is facing "new" challenges in this regard: problems caused by massive immigration and possible difficulties in financing the country's support system. Lithuania is still facing "old" challenges: combating child poverty and helping parents to facilitate work–life balance.

Despite the new challenges faced by the welfare state in Sweden, the family support system is very sustainable, and much appreciated by the population. Evaluation of the family support system in Lithuania shows ambiguous results. Some parts of the family support system have quite high approval among the population, especially parental leave policies (parental, maternity, paternity). However, since they are not backed up by other complementary policies such as childcare services, they contribute neither to the overall higher approval of the family support system nor to gender equality awareness or practices.

Striving for gender equality is still the cornerstone of the Swedish family system. Despite high achievements in this field, the policy makers and the general population see possibilities and the need for improvements. Lithuanian experts, while talking about gender equality, were more concerned with measures to ensure mothers' participation in the labour market; less concern was expressed about fathers' engagement in childcare. Gender equality was not mentioned as the goal of the family support system. However, the parental leave system was evaluated as contributing to gender equality by the Lithuanian respondents to a greater extent than by the Swedish residents. This allows us to make the assumption that the framing is important in family policy reform. In Lithuania there is little discourse about the gender (in)equality and how and why it is important to address it in reforming family policy, while in Sweden there is a high awareness among policy makers and the general public about gender (in)equality issues and what negative/positive outcomes they generate for individuals and society.

The findings of this study show that in the 21st century, the policies that address gender equality, such as parental leave policies, are highly appreciated and needed. However, they have to be backed up by care services. The low ratings of elderly care and disabled children's support shows that in the future policy makers in both countries have to fulfil the increasing demands for them if they want to have sustainable family support systems. In Lithuania, the emphasis on means-testing in family support systems does not prove to be a sustainable strategy. Despite the long-lasting tradition in supporting families according to proven need, the respondents view the means-tested benefits as the least adequate support.

REFERENCES

Aidukaite, J. (2004), *The Emergence of the Post-Socialist Welfare State: The Case of the Baltic States – Lithuania, Latvia and Estonia*, Södertörn University College.

Aidukaite, J. (2006), "The formation of social insurance institutions of the Baltic states in the post-socialist era", *Journal of European Social Policy*, **16** (3), pp. 259–270.

Aidukaite, J. (2016), "Support to families with children in the Baltic States: pathways of expansion and retrenchment from 2004 till 2016", paper presented at the workshop Baltic States after the Crisis? The Transformation of Welfare Systems and Social Problems, 25–26 December 2016, Vilnius University.

Aidukaite, J., and D. Telisauskaite-Cekanavice (2020), "The father's role in child care: parental leave policies in Lithuania and Sweden", *Social Inclusion*, **8** (4), pp. 81–91.

Brady, D., and H. Young Lee (2014), "The rise and fall of government spending in affluent democracies, 1971–2008", *Journal of European Social Policy*, **24** (1), pp. 56–79.

Bučaitė-Vilkė, J., G. Purvaneckienė, R. Vaitkevičius and A. Tereškinas (2012), *Lyčių politika ir gimstamumo ateitis*, Kaunas: VDU.

Deacon, B. (2000), "Eastern European welfare states: the impact of the politics of globalisation", *Journal of European Social Policy*, **10** (2), pp. 146–161.

Duvander, A.-Z., and T. Ferrarini (2013), "Sweden's family policy under change: past, present, future", Working Paper 2013: 8, SpaDE, Stockholm University.

Ferge, Z. (2001), "European integration and the reform of social security in the accession countries", *European Journal of Social Quality*, **3** (1–2), pp. 9–25.

Ferrarini, T. (2006), *Families, States and Labour Markets: Institutions, Causes and Consequences of Family Policy in Post-War Welfare States*, Cheltenham, UK and Northampton, MA, USA: Edward Elgar Publishing.

Goodrick, D. (2014), "Comparative case studies: methodological briefs – impact evaluation No. 9", *Methodological Briefs*, Unicef Office of Research.

Grødem, A. S. (2017), "Family-oriented policies in Scandinavia and the challenge of immigration", *Journal of European Social Policy*, **27** (1), pp. 77–89.

Gvaldaitė, L., and A. Kirilova (2014), "Subsidiarumo apraiškos ir perspektyvos šeimos politikoje Lietuvoje", *Tiltai*, **66** (1), pp. 249–273.

Hantrais, L. (2004), *Family Policy Matters: Responding to Family Change in Europe*, Bristol: Bristol University Press.

Hiilamo, H. (2002a), "Family policy changes at the micro-level in Sweden and Finland during the 1990s", Working Paper No. 291, Luxembourg Income Studies, working paper series.

Hiilamo, H. (2002b), "Family policy models and family policy outcomes: a Nordic perspective", Working Paper No. 290, Luxembourg Income Study, working paper series.

Jančaitytė, R. (2006), "Palankios šeimai politikos įgyvendinimas Lietuvoje: problemos ir galimybės", *Socialinis darbas*, **5** (1), pp. 30–37.

Javornik, J. (2014), "Measuring state de-familialism: contesting post-socialist exceptionalism", *Journal of European Social Policy*, **24** (3), pp. 240–257.

Kavoliūnaitė-Ragauskienė, E. (2012), *Viešosios šeimos politikos kūrimo ir įgyvendinimo problemos Lietuvoje*, Teisės institutas.

Korpi, W. (2000), "Faces of inequality: gender, class, and patterns of inequalities in different types of welfare states", *Social Politics: International Studies in Gender, State and Society*, **7** (2), pp. 127–192.

Korpi, W., and J. Palme (2003), "New politics and class politics in the context of austerity and globalization: welfare state regress in 18 countries, 1975–95", *American Political Sciences Review*, **97** (3), pp. 425–446.

Leitner, S. (2003), "Varieties of familialism: the caring function of the family in comparative perspective", *European Societies*, **5** (4), pp. 353–375.

Lohmann, H., and H. Zagel (2016), "Family policy in comparative perspective: the concepts and measurement of familization and defamilization", *Journal of European Social Policy*, **26** (1), pp. 48–65.

Ma, L., G. Andersson, A.-Z. Duvander and M. Evertsson (2020), "Fathers' uptake of parental leave: forerunners and laggards in Sweden, 1993–2010", *Journal of Social Policy*, **49** (2), pp. 361–381.

Maslauskaitė, A. (2004), "Lytis, globa ir kultūriniai gerovės kapitalizmo barjerai Lietuvoje", *Sociologija. Mintis ir veiksmas*, **14** (3), pp. 39–51.

Meuser, M., and U. Nagel (2009), "The expert interview and changes in knowledge production", in A. Bogner, B. Littig and W. Menz (eds), *Interviewing Experts*, London: Palgrave Macmillan, pp. 17–42.

MISSOC (2018), Comparative tables database, accessed 25 January 2019 at www.missoc.org/missocdatabase/comparative-tables.

O'Connor, J. (1996), "From welfare state to gendering welfare state regimes", *Current Sociology*, **44** (2), 1–124.

OECD (2020a), Chart SF2.1.A. Total fertility rate, 1970, 1995 and 2018, accessed 2 January 2021 at www.oecd.org/els/family/database.htm/.

OECD (2020b), Social expenditure database, accessed 29 April 2020 at www.oecd.org/social/expenditure.htm.

Orloff, A. (1993), "Gender and social rights of citizenship: the comparative analysis of gender relations and welfare states", *American Sociological Review*, **58** (3), pp. 303–328.

Pascall, G., and N. Manning (2000), "Gender and social policy: comparing welfare states in Central and Eastern Europe and the former Soviet Union", *Journal of European Social Policy*, **10** (3), pp. 240–266.

Reingardė, J., and A. Tereškinas (2006), "Darbo ir šeimos gyvenimo suderinimas Lietuvoje bei lyčių lygybė: iššūkiai ir galimybės", in J. Reingardė (ed.), *(Ne) apmokamas darbas: šeimai palanki aplinka ir lyčių lygybė Europoje*, Vilnius, pp. 47–103.

Reingardienė, J. (2004), "Europos lyčių lygybės strategija: kintančios lyčių politikos privalumai ir grėsmės", *Sociologija. Mintis ir veiksmas*, **14** (3), pp. 13–27.

Sainsbury, D. (1996), *Gender Equality and Welfare States*, Cambridge: Cambridge University Press.

Saraceno, C. (2013), "Family policies", in B. Greve (ed.), *The Routledge Handbook of the Welfare State*, London: Routledge, pp. 381–400.

Šarlauskas, T., and A. Telešienė (2014), "The regulation of state social insurance: structure and choices of beneficiaries", *Public Policy and Administration*, **13** (1), pp. 95–108.

SODRA (Lithuanian Social Insurance Board) (2019), Ligos ir motinystės išmokų atvejai (gavėjai) [Cases of sickness and maternity benefits (recipients)], accessed 2 September 2019 at https://atvira.sodra.lt/lt-eur.

Stankūnienė, V. (2001), "Family policy of Lithuania: a changing strategy", paper presented at the European Population Conference 2001, Helsinki, Finland, 7–9 June 2001.

Stankūnienė, V., A. Maslauskaitė and M. Baublytė (2013), *Ar Lietuvos šeimos bus gausesnės?* Vilnius: Lietuvos socialinių tyrimų centras.

Statistics Lithuania (2019), Child care institutions, accessed 21 April 2020 at https://osp.stat.gov.lt/EN/statistiniu-rodikliu-analize?hash=8129a443-c9dd-4839-b828-914f89b9fc3a#/.

Swedish Social Insurance Agency (2018), Parental benefits, accessed 2 January 2019 at www.forsakringskassan.se/privatpers/foralder/nar_barnet_ar_fott/foraldrapenning.

Tunberger, P., and W. Sigle-Rushton (2011), "Continuity and change in Swedish family policy reforms", *Journal of European Social Policy*, **21** (3), pp. 225–237.

Wendt, C., M. Mischke and M. Pfeifer (2011), *Welfare States and Public Opinion: Perceptions of Healthcare Systems, Family Policy and Benefits for the Unemployed and Poor in Europe*, Cheltenham, UK and Northampton, MA, USA: Edward Elgar Publishing.

Wennemo, I. (1994), "Sharing the cost of children: study on the development of family support in the OECD countries", *Doctoral Dissertation Series*, No. 25, Swedish Institute for Social Research, Stockholm University.

Žalimienė, L. (2015), "Šeimos paramos politika Lietuvoje: ar galime identifikuoti paradigminius pokyčius 1996–2013 metų laikotarpiu?", *Tiltai*, **70** (1), pp. 39–61.

APPENDIX

Table 6A.1   Evaluation of family support schemes in Lithuania (answers in per cent)

Family support scheme	1 Very Good	2 Good	3 Fair	4 Poor	5 Very poor	9 Don't know
Parental leave	6.1	40.6	24.4	5.7	1.8	21.4
Preschool facilities	3.7	31.4	32.7	11.4	2.0	18.8
Child allowance	5.9	35.7	27.7	9.8	2.9	18.0
Paternity leave	8.4	42.9	19.8	4.7	1.0	23.2
Maternity leave	10.2	45.3	20.0	4.3	1.2	19.0
Birth grant	8.9	40.2	24.0	5.3	1.7	19.9
Maintenance support	2.5	17.3	31.2	20.3	7.6	21.1
Housing assistance	3.1	23.3	32.9	14.0	5.8	20.6
Possibility to work flexible hours	5.7	26.3	21.2	14.0	1.6	28.2
Possibility to work from home	6.4	26.7	19.8	12.5	4.4	30.2
Sick leave policy related to children	8.9	40.7	21.1	7.2	2.3	19.8
Support services for elderly care	2.3	16.8	27.7	22.1	7.6	23.5
Care services and financial support related to disabled child	4.2	19.3	23.1	13.1	5.2	35.1

Table 6A.2   Evaluation of family support schemes in Sweden (answers in per cent)

Family support scheme	1 Very Good	2 Good	3 Fair	4 Poor	5 Very poor	9 Don't know
Parental leave	53.8	30.7	4.4	0.9	0.2	10.0
Preschool facilities	27.4	44.6	11.9	3.9	0.4	11.8
Child allowance	36.6	40.1	9.9	3.3	0.9	9.2
Maintenance support	14.1	26.5	14.6	3.2	0.4	41.2
Housing assistance	15.9	32.6	15.7	4.5	0.7	30.6
Possibility to work flexible hours	24.8	35.9	11.8	3.1	0.9	23.3
Possibility to work from home	22.0	34.9	15.6	4.6	1.6	21.4
Sick leave policy related to children	44.1	37.2	6.0	1.1	0.5	11.1

Family support scheme	1 Very Good	2 Good	3 Fair	4 Poor	5 Very poor	9 Don't know
Support services for elderly care	9.1	26.2	21.2	15.1	5.0	20.5
Care services and financial support related to disabled child	11.8	22.9	15.3	16.0	6.8	27.3

7. Cost of childcare: evolution of regional diversity in Estonia

Mare Ainsaar and Mona Sõukand

INTRODUCTION

Early childhood education creates a solid foundation for future life chances and for children's development. Studies (Stolk et al. 2013) show that childcare has a positive impact on children's development: it reduces educational inequalities and poverty in society, helps parents to reconcile work and family life and creates additional opportunities for disadvantaged families (Baizán 2009; Haan and Wrohlich 2011; OECD 2011; Dumčius et al. 2012; Ainsaar 2013; Ainsaar and Riisalu 2014; Ainsaar and Themas 2015). Studies in Estonia found that the availability of kindergarten services even shapes fertility plans of young families (Oras 2003; Oras and Unt 2008; Ainsaar 2013). A positive link between childcare and fertility is also confirmed by other studies (Hank and Kreyenfeld 2003; Rindfuss et al. 2007; OECD 2011).

It is not surprising that several international organisations, like the Organisation for Economic Co-operation and Development (OECD) and the European Union (EU), have been active in targeting and promoting childcare standards in the last decade. According to the 'Europe 2020' strategy (European Commission 2010), the EU member states should achieve at least a 95 per cent participation rate of children in childcare from the fourth year of age to compulsory school age. Although Estonia is very close to this threshold (Figure 7.1), the essential regional differences remain a problem.

Analyses of family policy often concentrate only on the central government level and regional diversity is neglected, despite large spatial differences (Dunkan and Goodwin 1988; Gauthier 1996; Forssén 1998). With this chapter we fill in the gap in Estonia, record regional inequality in childcare and analyse the mechanisms behind the sources of regional diversity.

This chapter provides an overview of long-term trends in childcare in Estonia and analyses the regional differences and mechanisms behind regional childcare price diversity. In countries with relatively high levels of child poverty, the high cost of childcare services can be an important barrier to the

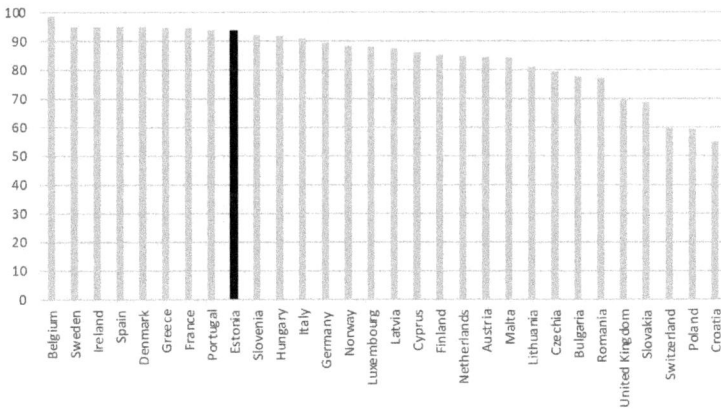

Source: Eurostat.

Figure 7.1   Share of children attending formal childcare in 2018, from age 3 up to school age

take-up of services. To analyse regional differences we use data from special surveys collected since 1999 in Estonia. This is the first time we are able to bring together the data from these surveys and provide standardised analyses. We focus on the total cost of childcare services and regional diversity of fees for parents.

THE CHILDCARE SYSTEM IN ESTONIA

Estonia has a solidarity-based universal family policy system with all the classical components of a family policy: universal child benefits, long parental leave with a high replacement rate, extra support for families with three and more children, and well-developed childcare services (Ainsaar 2019). Verbist and van Lancker (2016) analysed poverty reduction through family transfers and how much family policy covers all costs of children in Europe, and argued that Estonia is in the middle position in the EU in both of those categories. Compared to the EU average, Estonia has fewer young (1–3 years old) children in formal childcare, but more children over 3 years old compared to the EU average (Eurostat 2017). A low childcare participation rate in younger age groups is likely influenced by a long and generously supported parental leave system in Estonia (Ainsaar and Tarum 2016).

An accessible childcare service is the main cornerstone of services for families with small children and has been an important policy agenda for a long time in Estonia. Kindergartens were already a priority area of the family policy in the Soviet Union when the economic goal was to capture the successful industrialised countries. This task required mothers to return to work as quickly as possible after giving birth (Põder et al. 2015). However, the main problem was a constant lack of childcare places. In 1980 nearly 63 per cent, and in 1985 69 per cent of children participated in preschool childcare (Figure 7.2). As a result of the efforts to create additional childcare places and workplace-related kindergartens, the queues for kindergarten places began disappearing despite the growing number of small children in the society in the mid and late 1980s. After the change of the political system, a new trend in family behaviour emerged in the beginning of the 1990s. Many mothers preferred to remain home with their children in a newly emerged state of freedom of choice. As a result, the children's participation rate dropped below 50 per cent, and many childcare institutions were closed.

The participation rate of children in childcare and the demand for places gradually began to grow again in the middle of the 1990s (Ainsaar and Tarum 2016). However, as a result of a reorganisation of kindergartens and the reduction of places at the beginning of the 1990s, new queues emerged and remained the main family policy challenge for a long time. Before 1992, the provision of childcare services was the responsibility of the central government. Since 1992, according to the Local Government Organisation Act, the issues of organisation and administration of preschool children's institutions became the duties of the local government. This also caused regional differentiation of price levels and availability of the services for parents. As a result, a nationwide law about preschool educational institutions was worked out to guarantee the availability of childcare places and to regulate the price. However, in the beginning reality provided relatively vague messages regarding the certainty of obtaining a place for a child in a kindergarten, although the law provided some guarantees.

Since 1999, a special tool for monitoring the family policy at the local level, including information about childcare, was established under the auspices of the Minister of Population Affairs in Estonia. This survey also provides information for our chapter. Due to the national survey, the debate about childcare availability became a natural part of national family policy. The regular results of monitoring provided information about the situation and indicated the best local municipalities, but also shortcomings. Due to growing demand and active policy debate, the participation rate and the number of children in formal childcare started to grow from the end of the 1990s. At the beginning of the 21st century, 67 per cent of the 1- to 6-year-old children attended kindergarten, which was roughly the same level as in the 1980s (Figure 7.2). The participation rate was higher in towns (over 70 per cent) and lower in rural areas (50 per cent), although queues were particularly characteristic for towns.

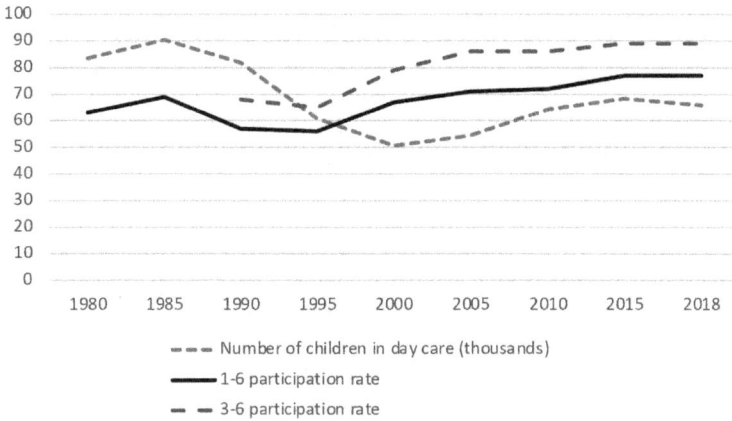

Number of children in day care (thousands)

1-6 participation rate

3-6 participation rate

Source: Ainsaar (2000) and Eurostat.

Figure 7.2   *The number of children and participation rates in formal childcare in Estonia, 1980–2018*

As the childcare service may differ in terms of objectives (education or only care) and childcare forms, here is an overview of the main features of the current system in Estonia in the 21st century. In Estonia there has never been a pre-primary education obligation, but the division of social welfare between central and local governments is similar to the one in the Scandinavian countries, and childcare belongs to the educational system. In line with the educational aim, preschool children's institutions are the responsibility of the Ministry of Education and Research. Furthermore, the Ministry of Social Affairs plays an important role in the development of childcare policy. The activity of the Ministry of Social Affairs in the field of legislation, monitoring and funding stems from the motivation of the ministry to address gender-equality and parents' employment issues.

Pursuant to the Local Government Organisation Act, local authorities are the main authorities responsible for the well-being of local residents and provision of services to inhabitants in Estonia. Additionally, financing of childcare services is decentralised and the responsibility of local municipalities in Estonia. In 1992, central funding for kindergartens was terminated in Estonia, and local municipalities became responsible for financing and providing childcare services. The main principles of the financing of childcare were established by the Preschool Child Care Institutions Act, according to which the cost of childcare can be covered by the state, local governments, parents and donors.

In practice, the majority of the costs have been covered by the local authorities (management costs, wages and educational tools), and the state support was project-based: bigger capital investments and renovations of buildings. Parents pay different fees (see the next section). The state does not centrally cover the salaries of kindergarten teachers as is the case for primary and secondary school teachers. This leads to the large variations among municipalities.

Despite regional diversity in financing the childcare, the main childcare standards are fixed by laws on the central government level. The 2002 Preschool Child Care Institutions Act states that the primary obligation of childcare is to ensure early childhood education, and also sets special stand-ards and requirements for childcare institutions and education of teachers (Ainsaar 2000, 2008). The Act also states that each municipality must create an opportunity for formal childcare in kindergarten for all children at 1–7 years of age residing in that municipality. Although such a requirement is imposed by law, nearly half of the local governments in Estonia had problems providing childcare places for all in 2014 (Ainsaar et al. 2015). While parents prefer kindergartens, it is often impossible to obtain a childcare place due to the lack of the latter. Even though both municipal and private childcare exists simultaneously, the majority of parents prefer municipality-provided child-care, and 90 per cent of Estonian children in formal childcare used municipal kindergartens in 2015 (Ainsaar et al. 2015). The Social Welfare Act allows municipalities to also provide alternative childcare services in addition to the municipality-owned childcare, like private care, home services, etc. It has to be considered as an additional option that can be used only with the consent of the parents in Estonia. Namely, since 2015, legal changes allow the offering of nursery services instead of municipal kindergartens only with the parents' consent. The law also obliges the local government to cover any possible price gap between municipality-provided and private childcare for parents.

Previous surveys (Roots 2013) show that parents with a lower education tend to use formal childcare services less often compared to parents with a higher education, but the use of formal childcare is not related to the parents' wealth.

SOURCES OF REGIONAL INEQUALITY

Large regional differences in childcare raise questions about the equality of families with children in different regions of the country. Measurement of regional differences is particularly important because the space itself seems to have an influence on the well-being and equality of people. A distinction is often made between equality and equity (Champernowne and Cowell 1998) in social policy studies. Compared to equality, equity is more dependent on an understanding of the fair treatment of people in a society. A discussion of spatial equity and equality is a mixture of principles of justice, rights and local-level democratic choices. Although spatial equality does not necessarily lead to social equity, the dream of equity remains in the (good) society. Generally, people seem to support an idea that unjust inequalities should be reduced and, if possible, eliminated, and 'welfare could be seen as a situation in which all members of the society enjoy similar levels of well-being in terms of the material and non-material resources' (Curtis 1989: 4). The main challenger seems to be a contradiction between the general aspirations towards spatial equality and the right of local governments to self-determination and diversity of regional circumstances. Therefore, an increasing local autonomy is usually associated with greater variations in the well-being of people, and greater centralisation of social policy with greater uniformity and equality (Page 1982; Brown and Jackson 1986).

We have five hypotheses about sources of regional inequality of childcare costs and prices. The hypotheses are based on previous research in economics and political science, and we shall test them in this chapter. They can shape the situation simultaneously or individually and, therefore, make the final output complex (Table 7.1). The hypotheses about the sources are as follows:

1. Regional inequality in costs and fees is a result of the diversity of the effectiveness of childcare service because of the economic scale effect (Panzar and Willig 1977). According to the scale effect, parents pay less for childcare in local municipalities and institutions where there are more children and therefore the price per child is lower. Larger kindergartens allow for the provision of a cheaper service per child due to the scale effect, which creates lower fees for parents. This effect does not always affect the parents' share of the total cost.
2. Regional inequality is a result of political representation and size of the interest group. According to the political representation theory (Rehfeld 2006), families with children have more strength to stand up for their interests in places with a higher share of parents of small children in the total population (or more children in the population). A higher proportion of children from the whole population should lead to a lower parental share of the total cost. For example, social policy history in Estonia reveals there have been protests by parents against rising childcare fees in some municipalities. In 2017, parents in one of the biggest towns in Estonia collected signatures to freeze the growth of day care prices and organised public protests. The political scientist Anu Toots (2011) calls this type of interest group an *anomic group*, which arises as a response to political action but without a longer-term plan and a formal structure. Such parents' groups might disappear when a political issue is resolved or loses its significance.

3. A childcare fee is a result of a community size effect. Previous studies (Sootla and Grau 2005) proved that political decision-making might depend on the size of the local government unit. Because of the closer social contacts of people in smaller communities, we can expect greater solidarity in smaller municipalities and higher motivation to care for local children. We assume that smaller places help more families with children and the fees for childcare are lower.
4. Regional inequality in childcare fees is a result of the inequality of resources. In more prosperous municipalities, parents pay a smaller share of the total cost of the kindergarten, because the municipality itself has more resources to cover the costs of the kindergarten. The total costs of the childcare may be higher for a municipality because rich municipalities have better prospects for investing in the childcare, but the parents' share can be lower due to resources.
5. Regional inequality is a result of market forces. Municipalities with a higher proportion of children and greater demand for kindergarten places or with higher incomes have a higher demand for kindergarten places, and these municipalities have higher childcare fees for parents, in terms of both absolute and relative costs.

METHOD

The analysis is based on local-level family policy monitoring surveys conducted in all local municipalities since 1999 (1999, 2000, 2003, 2004, 2005, 2007, 2009, 2011, 2014) in Estonia. This is the first time the information from all surveys has been merged and standardised, and longitudinal analyses provided.

The data were collected in the form of a questionnaire from the local municipalities. The local government authorities were asked to answer questions about childcare costs, fees and the components of those fees as well as the role of the local municipality in financing these actions. The surveys were financed by the Office of the Minister of Population Affairs and Ministry of Social Affairs in Estonia and conducted by the University of Tartu. Only local-level expenditures are taken into account, and targeted financial resources received directly from the central government for development of childcare are excluded because the local municipalities did not have influence on the central investment rules.

The number of municipalities changed with administrative reforms in Estonia and, therefore, so did the number of units of the analyses (1999: 212 municipalities, 2000: 217, 2004: 214, 2005: 219, 2007: 217, 2009: 227, 2011: 226, 2014: 213). The survey holds great value as it provides a representative

Table 7.1   Five hypotheses (in the brackets are explanations of mechanisms) about the formation of the cost of childcare services

	Total childcare cost for a municipality	Parents' share from the total fee
Large % of children	No effect	Smaller (bigger interest group of parents forces a lowering of the prices)
Large size of municipality (urban/rural)	Smaller per child (economic scale effect because a large number of children lowers the price per child)	Bigger (there is less solidarity in bigger communities)
More municipal resources	Bigger (richer municipality can afford more municipal investments)	Smaller (richer municipality can afford more municipal investments)
Individual poverty	No effect	Smaller (according to market forces explanation, parents with lower incomes can contribute less)
Higher income level and greater demand	No effect	Bigger (according to market forces explanation, parents with higher incomes can buy more expensive services)

picture from all regional units and represents full regional variability in the country. For the analyses, the survey data are combined with the statistical background data about municipal budget revenue per capita, the size of the population, the percentage of children (0–18 years old) in the population, poverty (number of applications for low-income subsistence benefits per 1,000 inhabitants) and an average income of the population. These data are derived from the Office of Statistics of Estonia.

Our main dependent variables are the cost of one municipal childcare place and the share of the costs covered by parents per one child in one month. We consider the parents' contribution from the total costs as the best social justice measure because the objective total childcare costs can vary due to regionally different economic and demographic situations, including income levels.

RESULTS: CHANGES AND DIFFERENCES IN THE TOTAL COST OF THE CHILDCARE

Table 7.2 shows that with economic development and the rise of inflation, the total cost of childcare constantly rose simultaneously. The increase was

Table 7.2   *The total cost (euros) of a full-time childcare place in municipality-owned childcare, 1999–2014*

	Min	Max	Average	Rate between min and max
1999	10	321	84	32
2000	38	380	90	10
2003	nd	452	138	nd
2004	66	428	148	6
2005	79	903	172	11
2007	50	1,579	242	31
2009	114	1,762	305	15
2011	122	1,985	266	16
2014	123	1,092	298	9

Note: nd – no data.
Sources: Data from Ainsaar and Kozlov (2001), Ainsaar and Aidarov (2003), Ainsaar et al. (2004), Ainsaar and Soo (2006, 2008, 2009, 2012), Ainsaar et al. (2015).

especially fast during the period of 2005–2008, and it stopped only temporarily in 2009 – a year of the economic crisis. By 2014, the average cost had again reached the pre-crisis level. The average costs increased about three times in 15 years. Along with the increase in the total cost, the differences between municipalities remained large. The difference between minimum and maximum ranged from nine to 32 times in various years (Table 7.2).

Figure 7.3 presents the total costs of the childcare service per one child and its value if considering the inflation in the country – the relative cost. We use an average salary of a full-time worker as a reference and divide the childcare cost per child by an average salary and get the relative costs of the childcare (Figure 7.3). The relative costs of the childcare have a similar but steeper growth trend compared to the total costs of the childcare. The only exceptions in this growing trend are a decline of the total cost in 2000–2003 and a remarkable drop during the 2009 economic crisis, when both the absolute and relative cost of the childcare declined.

We are interested in factors that shape the total cost of the childcare, and use correlation analysis to investigate the relationship between childcare costs and the other municipality indicators in different years. As a conclusion (Table 7.3), we see that only one factor has more or less systematic association with childcare total cost: municipality resources. Other factors, such as percentage of children in population, size of the municipality (urban/rural), the poverty rate in the municipality and parents' income level, have no effect on the total cost. More prosperous municipalities tend to have a greater total childcare cost per child in some years, but not always. Other links have a rather incidental nature, from which no definite conclusion can be drawn.

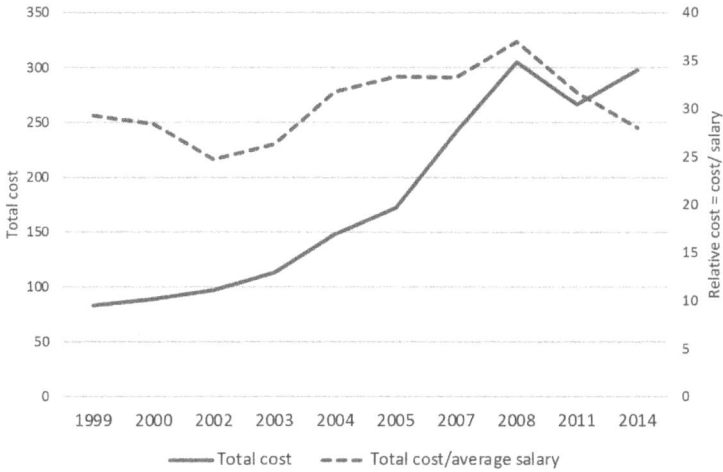

Figure 7.3   Total childcare costs per one child in a month and the relative cost of childcare (dividend with an average salary) in 1999–2014

Table 7.3   Correlations between total childcare cost per one child and municipality indicators

	1999	2000	2003	2004	2005	2007	2009	2011	2014
% of children in population	0	nd	Neg	0	0	0	0	nd	Pos
Size of municipality	0	nd	Pos	0	0	0	0	Neg	0
Municipal resources	Pos	Pos	0	0	0	0	0	nd	Pos
Poverty	0	nd	nd	0	0	Pos	0	nd	0
Income level	nd	nd	Pos	0	0	0	0	nd	nd

Note: Pos – positive correlation, Neg – negative correlation, 0 – no stat.sign. correlation, nd – no data.

RESULTS: CHILDCARE COST FOR PARENTS

The cost of childcare influences the use of childcare and accessibility; the lower the cost of childcare for parents, the smaller the barriers for them. Some preliminary studies (Ainsaar and Aidarov 2003) let us assume that the cost of childcare may be influenced by market forces in Estonia. Even though the maximum childcare fee is regulated by law and cannot exceed 20 per cent of the current minimum wage (plus the cost of meals), there are large distinctions in the amounts that parents need to pay for childcare in different municipalities (Table 7.4). In addition to the childcare service fee, municipalities can demand the cost of meals and additional fees (under different names) from parents, which will not be counted as childcare fees, and the wage ceiling rule does not apply for these additional fees. This increases the hidden costs of childcare for parents.

Before 1990, parents only had to pay extra for the meals as a supplement to the childcare fee. In 1996, the city of Valga was the first that added a partici-pation fee, which initially raised the question whether it was lawful, but it was announced as legal by the Chancellor of Justice. Several other municipalities started to introduce additional fees after this case (also referred as a 'charge' or a 'fee'). Additionally, other expenditures, such as extra money for visits to cultural events or money for kitchen repairs (Ainsaar and Kozlov 2001), emerged in the list of additional costs of childcare for parents since 2000. These additional costs were asked only in about 6 per cent of municipalities. In 2002, 44 per cent of municipalities asked for extra participation fees (Ainsaar and Aidarov 2003), and a year later 51 per cent (Ainsaar 2004). As a result of the lack of specific control over childcare fees and manipulations with the price list (slicing the total price into different fees), the real childcare cost was revealed to be sometimes higher than allowed by law. For example, the total costs for parents exceeded the legal ceiling in 35 municipalities in 2003 (Ainsaar et al. 2004).

From Table 7.4 we see that there are municipalities with a total cost for parents twice as high as the average in Estonia, but at the same time there are municipalities without any fee for childcare services in all years. Positively, we do not see any systematic increase of parents' share of the total costs of the childcare. It had remained close to 15 per cent of all the costs related to child-care. A large part of childcare expenses is still covered by local municipalities in Estonia throughout the period.

Interestingly, the share of the 'official childcare fee' from all costs for parents had increased, but still formed only 20–30 per cent of all childcare costs in 2011–2014.

For example, on average, parents paid 44 euros a month per one child in 2014; however, parents' cost for childcare varied from zero to 85 euros per child (Table 7.4). The participation fee, which has a ceiling according to the law, formed only 33 per cent of the total childcare cost for parents, 56 per cent of the total cost was related to the cost of meals, and 9 per cent all other extra fees (Ainsaar et al. 2015).

To put the value of the fee for parents into the context of life expensiveness in the country, we compare the total childcare cost for parents with an average salary, and with child allowances for the first child in the period of 1999–2004

Table 7.4   *The total cost of one full-time childcare place for parents in municipality-owned childcare, 1999–2014*

	Cost for parent (euros)			Childcare fee % of the total cost for parents	Costs for parents as % of total day care cost in municipality
	Min	Max	Average		
1999	0	32	12.5	10	15
2000	0	35	16	15	17.9
2003	10	42	20	16	17.7
2005	0	39	21	15	12.2
2007	0	59	27	30	11.2
2009	0	98	29	19	9.5
2011	0	93	36	22	13.5
2014	0	85	44	33	14.7

(Figure 7.4). The figure shows that although the total cost for the childcare increased, the relative cost in comparison with wages remained steady or even decreased. Moreover, the comparison of child allowance is interesting because the allowance should cover child-related expenses for parents. We see essential fluctuations related to the change of the value of the child allowance and rising childcare costs throughout the period. In 1999, parents were able to cover about 80 per cent of the childcare cost with a child allowance, and 90 per cent in 2004, but the declining line is the most common for most years, and in 2003 and in 2014 it is only about 50 per cent.

In the situation of high regional diversity, it is interesting to know from where regional differences stem. Reports related to the surveys in particular years (Ainsaar and Kozlov 2001; Ainsaar 2008) found negative correlations between the total cost of childcare and the share of parents. The higher was the total cost of the kindergarten for the municipality, the smaller was the parents' relative contribution to the childcare. Some other reports (Ainsaar and Aidarov 2003; Ainsaar et al. 2004; Unt and Krusell 2004; Ainsaar and Soo 2005, 2006) had indicated that the cost of childcare might be shaped by market forces, namely by the gap between the demand and the provision. Furthermore, the link between higher incomes of the population and higher costs for the parents has been found (Ainsaar et al. 2004, Ainsaar and Soo 2006, 2008, 2009). The childcare fee for parents was higher in larger municipalities (Ainsaar 2008; Ainsaar and Soo 2008), with a larger share of children from the population and higher demand for childcare places (Ainsaar and Soo 2015). In conclusion, we can argue that previous fragmented reports let us assume that the fees for parents are the result of a combination of market forces and political factors.

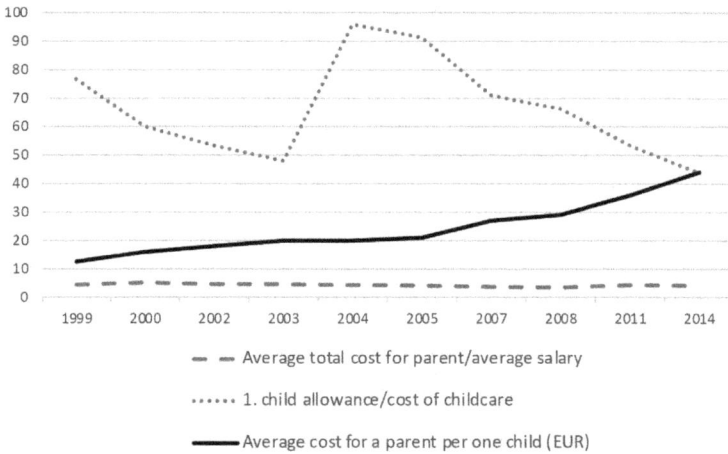

Sources: Ainsaar (2000, 2008), Ainsaar and Kozlov (2001), Ainsaar and Aidarov (2003), Ainsaar et al. (2004), Ainsaar and Soo (2006, 2009, 2012), Ainsaar et al. (2015).

Figure 7.4   *Indicators of childcare costs for parents*

Table 7.5   *The correlations among the relative childcare costs (from the total costs) for parents per one child and municipality background indicators*

	1999	2000	2003	2004	2005	2007	2009	2011	2014
% children	0	0	Neg	Neg	0	Neg	nd	nd	0
Size of municipality	0	Pos	Pos	Pos	Pos	Pos	Pos	Pos	Pos
Municipal resources	0	0	Pos	0	0	0	nd	nd	0
Poverty	0	0	0	0	0	Pos	Neg	nd	0
Income level of population	0	0	Pos	Pos	Pos	Pos	Pos	nd	0

Note: Pos – positive correlation, Neg – negative correlation, 0 – no stat.sign. correlation correlation, nd – no data.
Sources: Ainsaar and Kozlov (2001), Ainsaar and Aidarov (2003), Ainsaar et al. (2004), Ainsaar and Soo (2006, 2008, 2009, 2012), Ainsaar et al. (2015).

This chapter initially merges data from the different sources and provides systematic analyses.

Table 7.5 presents standardised results from all previous years and provides a coherent overview of trends for the first time. We see that the greater share of children in the total population of the region is related to the lower childcare fee for parents in some years but not always. Parents in children-rich municipalities paid relatively less in 2003, 2004 and 2007 than parents in municipalities with less children. The impact of the size of municipality and population income level to the relative fees was even stronger. In large municipalities and in those with a higher income level of the population, parents' relative fee was higher, and in smaller municipalities with lower individual incomes, the local government tends to cover a bigger share from the total childcare cost for parents.

Poverty and local government wealth indicators did not provide any consistent results. Consequently, the result seems to indicate that the fees for parents are shaped by a combination of an effect of market forces, political and economic scale effects and local solidarity. The hypothesis (Table 7.1) about the impact of resources on the relative childcare fees of parents did not find support, and also the link with poverty remained unclear.

CONCLUSION

Access to childcare services is important for a child's development and for equal opportunities for both children and parents. Therefore, it is essential to explore the childcare situation and the opportunities for parents. This chapter analysed the expenses related to the development of the childcare system in Estonia over nearly 15 years. Unique childcare survey data were used, and a special interest was paid to regional diversity of cost. In Estonia, local governments are responsible for the childcare services and pricing policy. The upper ceiling of the fee paid by the parents is set by the law, and cannot exceed 20 per cent of the minimum wage, but this regulation does not include many components of the total childcare cost for parents; for example, an extra fee related to meals and other running costs.

The results of analyses showed significant regional disparities within a country, indicating large regional inequalities of parents. We also analysed the sources of regional disparities using five hypotheses – the diversity of effectiveness, diversity of size of interest group, community size effect, resource diversity and market diversity. These all were either economically or politically rational explanations for the regional diversity.

We used these hypotheses in analysing the total cost of a childcare place for a local municipality and the share of the costs paid by parents. The analyses showed an increase of the total cost of the childcare place for municipalities in better economic times and the fall of costs during an economic recession period. This result is anticipated and directly demonstrates the impact of market forces on the childcare market. Simultaneously with the cost rise, regional diversity of total costs also increased.

The total fee for parents increased throughout the period and did not fall even during the economic crisis. A regional diversity of municipalities in terms of the childcare cost for parents also increased throughout the period. Parents paid relatively more for childcare services in larger and wealthier municipalities and in places with a smaller proportion of children in the population. Consequently, the results indicate that the fees for parents are formed in combination with an effect of market forces, political and economic scale effects and local solidarity. This might partially explain the differences in regional unequal treatment of parents. The justified or unjustified grounds for equity of these differences need further investigation.

REFERENCES

Ainsaar, M. (2000), 'Eesti laste- ja perepoliitika otsingul', in M. Ainsaar (ed.), *Laste-ja perepoliitika Eestis ja Euroopas*, Tartu: Johannes Esto Society, pp. 153–170.

Ainsaar, M. (2004), 'Muutused laste päevahoiu teenuse maksumuses', *Sotsiaaltöö*, 3, 37–39.

Ainsaar, M. (2008), 'Lastepäevahoiu regionaalsed erinevused Eestis', in T. Hallik and L. Haugas (eds), *Linnad ja vallad arvudes 2008. Cities and Rural Municipalities in Figures*, Tallinn: Statistics Estonia, pp. 60–74.

Ainsaar, M. (2013), 'Eestlaste ja vähemusrahvuste esindajate erinevad probleemid töö- ja pereelu ühitamisel ja hoiakud perepoliitika suhtes', in K. Espenberg, M. Ainsaar, K. Kasearu, L. Lilleoja, O. Nahkur, A. Roots, A. Rämmer, M. Sammul, K. Soo and T. Vihalemm (eds), *Vähemusrahvustest inimeste töö- ja pereelu ühitamise võimaluste analüüs*, Tartu: RAKE, pp. 126–134, accessed 20 March 2019 at www.ec .ut.ee/sites/default/files/www_ut/vahemusrahvuse_raport_25.09.2013.pdf.

Ainsaar, M. (2019), 'Economic crisis, families, and family policy in the Baltic states, 2009–2014', *Journal of Baltic Studies*, 50 (1), 59–77.

Ainsaar, M., and A. Aidarov (2003), 'Lastepäevahoid Eesti kohalikes omavalitsustes aastal 2002', *Sotsiaaltöö*, 2, 73–78.

Ainsaar, M., and A. Kozlov (2001), 'Lastepäevahoid Eesti kohalikes omavalitsustes, *Sotsiaaltöö*, 5, 50–53.

Ainsaar, M., and H. Riisalu (2014), 'Towards pronatalism: Baltic family policy in European comparison in 2002 and 2010', *Baltic Journal of Political Science*, 3, 67–82.

Ainsaar, M., and K. Soo (2005), 'Changes in child friendliness in local governments in 2001–2003', in M. Servinksi, M. Kivilaid and M. Lehto (eds), *Cities and Rural Municipalities in Figures 2005*, Tallinn: Statistical Office of Estonia, pp. 40–43.

Ainsaar, M., and K. Soo (2006), *Omavalitsuste toetus lastega peredele 2004–2005*, Tartu: University of Tartu, accessed 20 March 2019 at www.sm.ee/sites/default/files/ content-editors/Ministeerium_kontaktid/Uuringu_ja_analuusid/Sotsiaalvaldkond/ kov_2006.pdf.

Ainsaar, M., and K. Soo (2008), *Kohalike omavalitsuste toetus lastega peredele Eestis 2007*, Tartu: University of Tartu, accessed 20 March 2019 at www.sm.ee/ sites/default/files/content-editors/Ministeerium_kontaktid/Uuringu_ja_analuusid/ Sotsiaalvaldkond/kov_2007.pdf.

Ainsaar, M., and K. Soo (2009), *Kohalike omavalitsuste toetus lastega peredele 2008 ja laste päevahoid 2008–2009 Eestis*, Tartu: University of Tartu, Office of the Minister of Population Affairs, accessed 7 July 2016 at www.sm.ee/sites/default/files/

content-editors/Ministeerium_kontaktid/Uuringu_ja_analuusid/Sotsiaalvaldkond/
kov_2009.pdf.

Ainsaar, M., and K. Soo (2012), *Kohalikud omavalitsused ja lastega pered 2011*, Tartu:
University of Tartu, Ministry of Social Affairs, accessed 7 July 2016 at www.sm.ee/
sites/default/files/content-editors/Ministeerium_kontaktid/Uuringu_ja_analuusid/
Sotsiaalvaldkond/aruanne_2011_kovraport_final_21.08.2012.pdf.

Ainsaar, M., and K. Soo (2015), *Kohalike omavalitsuste tegevus eelkooliealiste
laste lapsehoiu tagamisel. Alushariduse ja lapsehoiu uuring* (16–31), Tartu. Tartu
Ülikool, accessed at https://www.sm.ee/sites/default/files/content-editors/Uudised
_pressiinfo/alusharidus_ja_lapsehoiu_uuring_2015.pdf

Ainsaar, M., K. Soo and A. Aidarov (2004), *Omavalitsuste toetus lastega peredele
2002–2003*, Tartu: University of Tartu, accessed 13 March 2019 at www.sm.ee/
sites/default/files/content-editors/Ministeerium_kontaktid/Uuringu_ja_analuusid/
Sotsiaalvaldkond/kov_2003.pdf.

Ainsaar, M., K. Soo and T. Puolokainen (2015), 'Kohalike omavalitsuste tegevus
eelkooliealiste laste lapsehoiu tagamisel', in A. Themas, H. Tarum, K. Soo, L.
Reisberg, M. Aksen, T. Puolokainen, T. Lauri and E. Themas (eds), *Alushariduse ja
lapsehoiu uuring*, Tartu: University of Tartu, pp. 16–31.

Ainsaar, M., and H. Tarum (2016), 'Eesti rakendab Euroopa Liidu lapsehoiu soovitusi
– kas ajast ees või ajal jalus?', *RITo*, 34, 179–192.

Ainsaar, M., and A. Themas (2015), 'Pere ja lapsed', in A. Themas, M. Ainsaar, K. Soo,
M. Sammul, A. Uusküla, H. Tarum, R. Hendrikson, T. Arak, K. Espenberg and U.
Varblane (eds), *Eesti meeste hoiakute ja käitumise uuring: tervis, haridus, tööhõive,
ränne ja pereloome*, Tartu: University of Tartu, pp. 19–32.

Baizán, P. (2009), 'Regional child care availability and fertility decisions in Spain',
DemoSoc Working Paper, 31, Department of Political and Social Sciences,
Universitat Pompeu Fabra, accessed 7 July 2016 at www.upf.edu/demosoc/_pdf/
DEMOSOC31.pdf.

Brown, C.V., and P.M. Jackson (1986), *Public Sector Economics*, 3rd edition, Oxford:
Blackwell.

Champernowne, D.G., and F.A. Cowell (1998), *Economic Inequality and Income
Distribution*, Cambridge: Cambridge University Press.

Curtis, S. (1989), *The Geography of Public Welfare Provision*, London: Routledge.

Dumčius, R.P.J., N. Hayes, G. Van Landeghem, H. Siarova, L. Peciukonytė, I. Cenerić
and H. Hulpia (2014), *Study on the Effective Use of Early Childhood Education and
Care in Preventing Early School Leaving: Final Report*, European Commission
EAC/17/2012, Luxembourg: Publications Office of the European Union, accessed 7
July 2016 at www.fruehe-chancen.de/fileadmin/PDF/Archiv/Final_report.pdf.

Dunkan, S., and M. Goodwin (1988), *The Local State and Uneven Development:
Behind the Local Government Crisis*, Cambridge: Polity Press.

European Commission (2010), *Europe 2020: A Strategy for Smart, Sustainable and
Inclusive Growth*, Brussels: Communication from the Commission.

Eurostat (2017), Database: participation in early childhood education by sex (children
aged 3 and over) (sdg_04_31).

Forssén, K. (1998), 'Decentralization of decision making: the case of payment policies
for children's daycare', *Scandinavian Journal of Social Welfare*, 7, 277–287.

Gauthier, A.H. (1996), *A Comparative Analysis of Family Policies in Industrialised
Countries*, Oxford: Clarendon Press.

Haan, P., and K. Wrohlich (2011), 'Can child care policy encourage employment and
fertility? Evidence from a structural model', *Labour Economics*, 18 (4), 498–512.

Hank, K., and M. Kreyenfeld (2003), 'A multilevel analysis of child care and women's fertility decisions in western Germany', *Journal of Marriage and Family*, 65 (3), 584–596.

OECD (2011), *Doing Better for Families*, Paris: OECD Publishing, accessed 7 July 2016 at www.keepeek.com/Digital-Asset-Management/oecd/social-issues -migration-health/doing-better-for-families_9789264098732-en#page1.

Oras, K. (2003), 'Perekonda soovitava laste arv ja ootused riigi perepoliitikale', in D. Kutsar (ed.), *Millist perekonnapoliitikat me vajame?* Tartu: Tartu University Press, pp. 71–87.

Oras, K., and M. Unt (2008), *Sündimust mõjutavad tegurid Eestis*, Tallinn: Office of the Minister of Population Affairs, accessed 6 March 2019 at www.sm.ee/ sites/default/files/content-editors/Ministeerium_kontaktid/Uuringu_ja_analuusid/ Sotsiaalvaldkond/sundimust_mojutavad_tegurid_eestis_2008.pdf.

Page, E. (1982), 'The value of local autonomy', *Local Government Studies*, 8 (4), 21–42.

Panzar, J., and R.D. Willig (1977), 'Economies of scale in multi-output production', *Quarterly Journal of Economics*, 91 (3), 481–493.

Põder, K., T. Lauri and K. Kross (2015), 'Eesti kui väikese üleminekuühiskonna pere-poliitika – ei uus Põhjala ega vana Euroopa', *Riigikogu Toimetised*, 31, 168–183.

Rehfeld, A. (2006), 'Towards a general theory of political representation', *Journal of Politics*, 68, 1–21.

Rindfuss, R.R., D. Guilkey, S.P. Morgan, Q. Kravdal and K.B. Guzzo (2007), 'Child care availability and first-birth timing in Norway', *Demography*, 44 (2), 345–372.

Roots, A. (2013), 'Koolieelikutest lastega eestlastest ja vähemusrahvustest emade kasutatavate lastehoiu tüübi seos nende tööhõive ja sissetulekutega', *Ariadne Lõng*, 35–41.

Sootla, G., and K. Grau (2005), 'Institutional balance in local government: council, mayor and city manager in local policymaking', in G. Soos and V. Zentai (eds), *Faces of Local Democracy*, Comparative Papers from Central and Eastern Europe, Budapest: Open Society Institute, Local Government and Public Service Reform Initiative, pp. 275–300.

Stolk, A., S. Hunnius, H. Bekkering and I. Toni (2013), 'Early social experience pre-dicts referential communicative adjustments in five-year-old children', *PLOS ONE*, 8 (8), accessed 21 December 2020 at https://journals.plos.org/plosone/article?id=10 .1371/journal.pone.0072667.

Toots, A. (2011), 'Huvirühmad', in L. Kalev and A. Toots (eds), *Poliitika ja valitsemise alused*, Tallinn: University of Tallinn, pp. 235–255.

Unt, M., and S. Krusell (2004), '*Lastehoid Eesti Peredes*', Tallinn: Office of the Minister of Population Affairs, accessed 17 March 2019 at www.sm.ee/ sites/default/files/content-editors/Ministeerium_kontaktid/Uuringu_ja_analuusid/ Sotsiaalvaldkond/lastehoid_eesti_peredes_01.pdf.

Verbist, G., and W. van Lancker (2016), 'Horizontal and vertical equity objectives of child benefit systems: an empirical assessment for European countries', *Social Indicators Research*, 128 (3), 1299–1318.

PART II

Perspectives on pension protection in the era of
ageing

8. Ageing and the welfare state: welfare policies and attitudes in the Baltic and Nordic countries

Jolanta Aidukaite, Sven E. O. Hort and Mare Ainsaar

INTRODUCTION

Ageing – with the goal of a later life of decency and dignity – is perhaps the greatest achievement in the global history of modern humanity. Welfare states, in particular medical and pension policies, have contributed immensely to the increase in health and well-being among the elderly in general. Harold Wilensky (1975) early on argued that demographic pressure and the material resources of a country together with different ideological-political orientations shaped national social policies around the globe. This may yet be the case. Due to increasing numbers of retirees in Europe and elsewhere, governments are taking measures to reform pension insurance and expand on long-term care. As stated by Wacker and Roberto (2011), 'We are living in a unique period in history and at a time in which governments will be compelled to consider myriad ageing social policy questions' (p. 3). A few questions include: What can be done to protect the financial sustainability of the pension systems? How should responsibility be shared between the state, market and family regarding providing social security (financial and care) in old age? Should the state be a primary caregiver for the elderly, or should the responsibility be shared or even transferred to the family? At present, there is a great variation among European countries on how governments respond to these questions.

This chapter seeks to contribute to a growing body of literature on ageing and how different welfare state systems are trying to address it (Aidukaite, Ainsaar and Hort 2021). We aim to (1) capture the current trends in the Baltic and Nordic[1] welfare policies on ageing from a comparative perspective, (2) highlight differences and similarities, and (3) reveal senior citizens' subjective perceptions of their socioeconomic situation and their attitudes towards the role of government in ensuring safety. The goals of social policy are to reduce economic insecurity and to improve the life chances of the population. In evaluations of goal achievement, policy makers and scientists should not only take into account the actual social policy arrangements, but also citizens' perceptions and their subjective feeling of security (Svallfors 1997; Wendt, Mischke and Pfeifer 2011). Therefore, citizens' views in this chapter should add vital information to the overall understanding of the Baltic and Nordic welfare policies on ageing.

The methodology is mainly comprised of the analysis of previous literature on the topic of ageing and related international data sources (Eurostat; the Organisation for Economic Co-operation and Development (OECD)). Influenced by the literature on welfare state typologies (Arts and Gelissen 2002; Esping-Andersen 1990), we employ welfare state regimes and welfare state political ideologies (Hemerijck 2017) to delineate major differences between the Baltic and Nordic countries. For our purposes, we choose to focus on pension protection as the main policy of income security for older citizens and on long-term care (LTC) as the key policy to ensure autonomy for older people. A review of senior citizens' subjective expectations is based on the European Social Survey (ESS) data 2018.

The chapter is organised as follows: First, we discuss the ideal-typical features of the Nordic and Baltic welfare state models and how they address the issues of ageing. Then, we look at welfare state expenditure to illustrate the differences between the Nordic and Baltic countries and within each group. This is followed by a summary of the major differences between the Baltic and Nordic welfare models. We then analyse senior citizens' subjective perceptions of their socioeconomic situation and their attitudes towards the role of government in ensuring safety, and whether they correspond to the prevailing welfare models and ideologies in these countries. Finally, we discuss the results and reach our conclusion. The major argument of this chapter is that the state still remains, with variations, a major agent in ensuring the financial security and autonomy of older citizens (Aidukaite, Ainsaar and Hort 2021).

KEY FEATURES OF THE NORDIC (SOCIAL-DEMOCRATIC) WELFARE STATE

The welfare state can be understood as the government's intervention in people's lives through provisions that reduce their vulnerabilities during their life, such as loss of income, childbirth, old age, unemployment, disability and illness, and empower them by providing social services, such as health care, education, social housing and long-term care (LTC). Welfare state provisions include social security, labour market policies, health care, education, social services and housing policies (Aidukaite, Bogdanova and Guogis 2012; Kemeny 2001; Titmuss 1974; Wilensky 1975). These provisions have evolved in European nations, and have been improved over time and become entrenched into state, market and family relationships.

Numerous studies (for example, Esping-Andersen 1990; Korpi and Palme 1998) have shown that access to welfare provisions varies across countries and nations. The Nordic welfare state or 'social-democratic welfare regime' (Esping-Andersen 1990) has been praised for being the most universalistic and exhibiting the highest levels of solidarity, lowest levels of poverty and inequality compared to the rest of Europe and the world. In the social-democratic regime, the state is the main agent for guaranteeing the well-being of its citizens. All inhabitants benefit from the welfare state, and, at the same time, they are all dependent and, therefore, will presumably feel obliged to pay their contribution/tax (Esping-Andersen 1990; Korpi and Palme 1998). 'The social-democratic regime seeks to emancipate the individual from both the family and the market through generous and universal state-sponsored social rights' (Danforth 2014, p. 166). This means that the state seeks to ensure the economic independence and social security of all, irrespective of gender, class, ethnicity, place of residence and age. In our chapter, age is in focus, namely older age. Governments ensure economic independence and social security for older people through generous pension benefits and the widespread network of social service provision. It is possible to claim that the elderly in the Nordic countries are the least dependent on their families (financially and caring) compared to the rest of the world. As stated by Danforth (2014), the social-democratic regime is committed to social equality through economic redistribution. It seeks to safeguard its citizens' welfare 'from the cradle to grave'. This regime is also committed to full employment and social benefits based on citizenship/residency and earnings. Numerous scholars (see, for example, Alestato, Hort and Kuhnle 2009; Danforth 2014; Hort 2014) have emphasised the state's commitment to deliver extensive and high-quality social services in the Nordic countries. It can be argued that the 'Nordic model' rests on the social investment paradigm. This paradigm seeks to enhance human capital and the potential of the entire population; therefore, it targets all age cohorts, but with an emphasis on the young. It aims to enhance human development and break the intergenerational reproduction of poverty and inequality through high levels of employment. This can be achieved through capacitating social services, lifelong learning/education, family-friendly and gender-sensitive benefits, and active labour market policies (Hemerijck 2017).

To sum up, the social-democratic regime implies high levels of universalism and solidarity across classes and generations, with a stress on public financing, commitment to full employment, relatively strong weight placed on the delivery of social services rather than income transfers compared to other welfare states, and an emphasis on the individual and its emancipation from the family and market. What do these characteristics mean for the elderly population of the Nordic countries? This will be analysed in the subsequent section.

AGEING AND WELFARE STATES IN THE NORDIC COUNTRIES

The Nordic welfare states have become the epitome of 'the social-democratic welfare regime'. With the initial exception of Finland, their welfare systems evolved concomitant to a rather peaceful nation-building process. The Scandinavian or Nordic countries together with Japan have among the oldest and healthiest populations on earth (Kuhnle, Selle and Hort 2019). Older people in Denmark, Finland and Sweden nowadays have a strong position in their respective societies, which is reflected in individual well-being, associational configurations and systemic solutions. Ageing and welfare are top priorities in the national as well as local public agendas.

The social welfare approach to old age in the Nordic countries rests on one primary principle and two general public practices. First, an official recognition (in white papers) and respect for a life of dignity and decency long before death, and, after 67 or so, support in cash as well as public support in-kind; the actual retirement age on the rise, averaging round age 63 at present (2018); and policies pushing the age of withdrawal from the labour market upwards. Financial security is ensured through well-developed pensions systems.

The work-first principle has governed the construction of pension systems from the start, although they have been modified over time. In the new millennium, the various central government authorities together with semi-public institutions under the auspices of joint labour market organisations – with earnings-related occupational benefits through nationwide agreements between the major 'social partners', employers and the organisations of employees (trade unions) – oversee and deliver cash from intricate transfer systems. Added to this, there are a variety of truly private (banking/financial) schemes operating 'on the market' but supported by public partnerships. The latter, 'private', schemes vary in generosity and regulatory framework. However, in practice, income maintenance through public–private channels in contemporary Scandinavia consists of a guaranteed income – a minimum pension benefit – for all persons with a residence record of at least 40 years, topped up with various 'tested' supplements, housing in particular. Depending on work records, most retirees of the baby-boom generation in the Nordic countries receive an income-related benefit far above the minimum (for more, see Chapter 10 in this volume and Aidukaite, Ainsaar and Hort 2021).

Income security is a central state obligation, while in-kind benefits, whether medical or 'social', are delivered by self-governing and tax-levying local governments: municipalities and county councils constitutionally on par. Hence, local government is a key to an understanding of the decentralised character of the 'Scandinavian welfare model', the 'subsidiarity principle'. Almost 1,000 municipalities all over Scandinavia have the obligation to oversee the general welfare and standard of living of the population residing in its respective territories. The services provided are again primarily paid out of local income taxes supported by national equilibrium systems, whereby rich municipalities support the poorer ones. For the elderly, these systems are geared to the 'most needy', and take the form of either 'home help services' or 'institutional care', in some cases even a combination of the two if one partner has to be temporarily or permanently taken care of by a support agency while the other person prefers to stay at home. Health services – whether in-patient at hospital or outpatient – also belong to these systems and are accessible to all residents irrespective of their nationality and are in general provided by county councils (regions in Denmark), though sometimes they are contracted out to private providers.

The Nordic countries have the most comprehensive and universalistic LTC systems for the elderly in the world. The systems are decentralised. Nevertheless, there are differences among the Nordic countries. Denmark has the most universal LTC system. In Denmark, LTC is financed through general taxation and generally provided for free (Kvist 2018). Recently, an 'ageing in place' policy has directed the performance and organisation of LTC in Sweden. This has led to a gradual reduction of institutional care. The other important development in Sweden is the outsourcing of public money to the private for-profit care providers. This leads to a strong marketisation of the service care sector with increased competition and diversity of providers (Schon and Heap 2018). In Finland, the entitlement to LTC services is based on residence in a municipality. Services are granted on the basis of an individual needs assessment (Kalliomaa-Puha and Kangas 2018). It is important to mention:

> Even though the LTC is a public responsibility, families play an important role (more than in the other Nordic countries) – not only as guides to finding services, but also as helpers and carers. Thus, Finland's care regime is a mixed one, a combination of public, private and individual provision. A characteristic of this care regime is a strong gender bias in care obligations, and hence gendered employment patterns (Kalliomaa-Puha and Kangas 2018, p. 4).

A previous comprehensive report (Meagher and Szebehely 2013) has also confirmed that 'market ideas and rationalities have started to frame and shape the eldercare sector in all the Nordic countries' (p. 241). However, Finland and Sweden are clearly more affected by marketisation than is Denmark. In particular, the for-profit sector is more extensive in Finland and Sweden, and the growth of its share has been faster and large corporations have a stronger position. Yet, the share of for-profit organisations in eldercare has grown significantly in recent decades in Finland as in Sweden (Meagher and Szebehely 2013, pp. 241–247).

To sum up, the Nordic countries provide universal and comprehensive support for their aged. They are provided with income support through universal old-age pensions, which are topped up by the earnings-related occupational benefits (see Chapter 10). Services for the elderly are decentralised and provided by the local municipalities. Health care, home help services or institutional care services are provided universally according to needs and are based on the principle of the subsidiarity. The state is responsible for ensuring the well-being of the elderly. However, recently there has been an increase in market-based private pension insurance. The exclusional elements have been visible, especially in pension insurance, as 40 years of residency is required to qualify for the full pension (Aidukaite, Ainsaar and Hort 2021).

BALTIC WELFARE STATES

In contrast to the Scandinavian/Nordic/social-democratic welfare state regime or model, which is highly researched and internationally recognised and praised, the Baltic welfare state model is hardly visible in any well-established welfare state typologies. In the social policy literature, especially in the earlier writings, the three Baltic states were considered to represent similar cases of neoliberal transition (see Bohle and Greskovits 2007; Lendvai 2008). They were, and still are, 'blamed' for being neoliberal economies and neoliberal welfare states, based on their low public spending on social protection, high income inequality and limited social dialogue (see Lazutka, Juška and Navickė 2018; Sommers, Woolfson and Juska 2014). On the other hand, scholars claimed that the three Baltic states were not uniform and their development could not be simply tied to the neoliberal transition. Studies (Aidukaite 2006; Bernotas and Guogis 2006; Kuitto 2016) showed that the three Baltic states do not fall into any of Esping-Andersen's welfare regimes, and instead argued that they form hybrid cases exhibiting a mix of features taken from liberal, conservative-corporatist and even social-democratic regimes. The most recent study (Aidukaite 2018) indicated that the three Baltic states have developed differences in their welfare state systems. The detailed examination of social security institutions over the recent period (2004–2016) revealed emerging divergent patterns among the three countries. It appeared that Estonia has more in common with the social-democratic model, based on its generous parental leave policies and stress on universal child allowances. Latvia has many signs of the conservative-corporatist model with an emphasis on benefiting those participating in the labour market; while Lithuania, with a heavy reliance on means-tested benefits and low replacement rates for the unemployed, shares some similarities with the liberal model. Hence, the three Baltic states are not uniform in their social security arrangements. However, some similar patterns can be identified, if a broader comparison of the Baltic and Nordic countries is made. As indicated by Kuitto's (2016) study, in all three Baltic states social services are much less developed than in the Nordic countries, and in general they comprise a group of countries which spend relatively heavily on income security rather than services. More details on spending are coming in the subsequent sections.

However, if we want to distinguish the ideal-typical features of the welfare state model of the three Baltic states, it is useful to turn to the earlier studies on Baltic social policy development. Features such as the supremacy of the social insurance system, high coverage but relatively low benefit levels and poor outcomes of the performance of social security systems can be attributed to the Baltic (or post-communist) welfare regime (Aidukaite 2009, 2011). Although at present we observe variation among the three Baltic states in their social policy outcomes and welfare programs, it is still possible to claim that decommodification is not as high as in many developed Western welfare states, meaning that Baltic populations have to rely more on the market and/ or family to ensure their well-being and social security. The importance of the state (especially in Estonia) is evident, but the benefits provided and their levels are in many cases relatively low, ensuring only minimum levels of security. This fact strongly affects the social policy outcome indicators. They are still at the bottom of the ladder, with some variation within when comparing them – according to the minimum wage, relative poverty (especially for Latvia and Lithuania, less for Estonia), social security spending, income inequality, satisfaction with life and well-being – to the 'old' and some 'new' European Union (EU) countries (Aidukaite 2019; Ainsaar 2019; Gataūlinas 2013). In-work poverty is also widespread in the Baltic states (see Atas 2019), and this puts a significant proportion of the population at a greater risk of poverty. However, it must be noticed that Estonia stands out compared to Latvia and Lithuania, with its higher benefit levels and wages, lower unemployment, more financially sustainable social welfare system (see Aidukaite 2019) and higher life satisfaction (see Ainsaar 2011).

Overall, the Baltic welfare state is not uniform across the three countries, but general patterns can be identified: heavy reliance on social insurance contributions; relatively low levels of benefits (lower than in the developed Western welfare states); services are less developed than income security programs, and characterised by low social protection expenditures (among the lowest in the EU); and high income inequalities (among the highest in the EU) (see Aidukaite 2009, 2019). The neoliberal welfare state paradigm has dominated the three Baltic states since the fall of the Soviet regime in the 1990s. However, a pattern of social investment can be detected though generous family policies (see, for example, Ainsaar 2019). In the following section we will explore what this situation means for older citizens in the Baltic states.

THE SITUATION OF OLDER PEOPLE IN THE BALTIC STATES, AND WELFARE STATE POLICIES

Older citizens in the Baltic states, as in many other Central and East European countries, could be considered to be 'a lost generation' since the fall of the communist regime in 1990s. Their pensions have been heavily devaluated, as well as their labour market skills (namely, the transition from a socialist to a market economy required new skills and education), due to dramatic economic changes, making this group very vulnerable to poverty and social exclusion (Aidukaite, Ainsaar and Hort 2021). This is confirmed by the recent Eurofound report (2019) *Age and Quality of Life: Who Are the Winners and Losers?* The key findings of the report show that older generations experience a lower quality of life than the younger age groups in Eastern Europe, while for Western Europe the opposite is true. The 'Baltic' welfare state, as it is described in the previous section, provides only minimal support to its citizens, forcing them to rely heavily on the market and/or family for support. The elderly make up the poorest part of the population in the Baltics. They are more willing to stay in the labour market longer after retirement, and more often depend on family support than in Western Europe. According to the latest EU Statistics on Income and Living Conditions (SILC) data for 2017, the poverty rate among the population 60 years and over was slightly above 15 per cent in the EU-27, while in Estonia it was 36 per cent, in Latvia above 36 per cent and in Lithuania 31 per cent, making older people in the Baltic states most deprived compared to the rest of the EU countries. The corresponding figures for the poverty rate among the population aged 60 years and over for Denmark (8.3 per cent), Finland (11.4 per cent) and Sweden (14.1 per cent) are among the lowest in Europe. Thus, in the Baltics the elderly, especially those living alone, are often trapped in poverty. It should be mentioned that the aggregate replacement ratio for pensions is low in the Baltics – in Estonia 0.45 and in Latvia and Lithuania 0.43, lower than the EU-27 average, which is 0.58 (Eurostat 2019; see also Aidukaite, Ainsaar and Hort 2021).

To improve the financing of old-age pensions, and to solve demographic problems (rapid ageing, high outworld labour migration), the governments in the Baltic states initiated pension insurance reforms from the mid 1990s. The pension insurance system has gone through drastic reforms over a period of thirty years (for details, see Aidukaite 2006, 2019; Casey 2004). Currently, the pension insurance system in the Baltic states is established with the 'Three Pillar' model advocated by the World Bank (for details, see Chapters 11, 12 and 13). At present, it is the first pillar that bears the lion's share of pension financing. However, the introduction of the second and third pillars shows that the private responsibilities of the welfare systems have increased progressively in the Baltic states. Despite the numerous reforms of the pension system, the sustainability of old-age pension financing is still a significant challenge in the Baltic states.

Due to the low replacement rate for pensions, many older people prefer to stay in the labour market as long as possible. The Baltic states have employment rates for the population aged 55 to 64 that are well above 60 per cent (ranging from 62 per cent in Latvia to almost 70 per cent in Estonia), while the EU-27 average is 50 per cent (based on Eurostat data for 2019). The Nordic countries have a similar or an even higher employment rate for the population aged 55 to 64, ranging from 63 per cent in Finland to slightly above 74 per cent in Sweden, making them the most employment-friendly for older people (based on Eurostat data for 2019). However, we should keep in mind that the retirement age is lower in the Baltic countries than in the Nordic ones and life expectancy is shorter. In the Baltics, the retirement age is about 63. There is a plan to raise this age to 65 by 2025/2026 for both sexes (Aidukaite, Ainsaar and Hort 2021).[2]

For the Baltic states, high employment rates among older people are impressive, as age discrimination at work is evident and age stereotypes prevail (see Brazienė 2017; Mikulionienė 2008). Employers prefer younger workers as they believe they have better skills, are eager to learn and have better adaptation abilities than older people.

Health care services are universally provided in Estonia and Lithuania, but their quality is questioned, especially in Lithuania. In Latvia, however, the inequalities in health care are increasing as high patients' fees have been introduced since the 1990s. Given that the elderly need health care most and their pensions are low, age inequities in health are increasing in Latvia (Roots, Ainsaar and Nahkur 2019). Alongside public health care, private health care clinics and hospitals have expanded in the Baltic states. This has created unequal access to health care between those who can afford private health care and those who have to rely on a public health care system, which is characterised by long waiting lists and generally lower quality of services.

LTC services have developed in all three countries since the 1990s. However, they are far from sufficient to meet all needs. The Baltic states have had and still have the lowest share of institutional care among the 75-plus population (Monnier 2007). One obstacle for the development of institutional care is general negative attitudes among the population. These attitudes were developed in the Soviet period and were influenced by the extremely low standards and bad reputation of LTC institutions. Because of high regional inequality and the low density of populations in the Baltic countries, the big regional differences in access to and provision of LTC exist. Municipalities are expected to ensure similar levels of quality and services to those stated in the national laws, regardless of their geographical location, density of population and available budget. This, however, remains one of the challenges (Aidukaite, Ainsaar and Hort 2021).

The Baltic states have similar approaches in building up LTC systems (see Lazutka, Poviliunas and Zalimiene 2018; Paat-Ahi and Masso 2018; Rajevska 2018). The institutional system for LTC is divided into health and social care systems, and there is a need for strengthening the social and health care policy coordination and implementation of common models for LTC. The health-care system usually provides nursing care, geriatric assessment, services and nursing care at home. The welfare system provides LTC in welfare institutions, day-care services, home care and housing services, as well as other social services run by public or private owners (Aidukaite, Ainsaar and Hort 2021).

One of the particularities of the Baltic countries is the considerable burden on and responsibility of families when it comes to LTC. Although in all countries solutions outside of the family exist, the family is seen as a primary source of financing and practical solutions for LTC. This familialistic approach has prevented the development of a modern solution for LTC. The informal care prevails over the formal care. For example, Estonian family law states that the family is responsible for preventing the need for external help, and although there are options for institutional LTC, often the family is responsible for financing this type of care, or only old persons without a family are in priority positions in the waiting lists for LTC. Only in recent years has the burden of caregivers emerged on the political agenda. Also, in Latvia and Lithuania the LTC policy approaches have a strong informal-care orientation based on the family care tradition (Aidukaite, Ainsaar and Hort 2021; Lazutka, Poviliunas and Zalimiene 2018; Rajevska 2018).

The future development plans for LTC for Estonia and Latvia refer to the need to guarantee access to services and avoid poverty (Paat-Ahi and Masso 2018), and to ensure that the quality of life will not deteriorate for a person due to old age or functional disorders (Rajevska 2018). In Lithuania, the main goal is more explicit regarding the increased availability and quality of outpatient rehabilitation (Lazutka, Poviliunas and Zalimiene 2018).

All in all, the Baltic welfare state provides some basic protection for the aged. Everyone is covered and no one is left out. However, the aged have a weak position in the national welfare communities. Their interests are poorly represented in the political landscape of the Baltic states, and they are poorly organised. The major public support is provided by income protection and health care. However, these securities are provided only on a basic/minimal level; they do not ensure the full and equal participation of the older citizens in all aspects of social life. Although there are some LTC services in all three countries, the family plays a primary caregiver role.

STATE EXPENDITURE ON PENSION PROTECTION AND LONG-TERM CARE IN THE NORDIC AND BALTIC COUNTRIES

In this section, we focus on aggregate social protection expenditure to demonstrate state commitment to ensure the welfare of the elderly and the differences within and between the Nordic and Baltic clusters.

As stated by Castles (2009), the aggregate social security expenditures do not reveal all the information about the performance of the welfare state. It is still worthwhile to examine overall welfare efforts. A previous study (Aidukaite, Ainsaar and Hort 2021), while examining the trends in social spending in the Baltic and Nordic countries, has identified the patterns that were called a move towards the EU and OECD average. For the Nordics it means a decline in social expenditure, for the Baltics, catching up with the Nordics'.

Figure 8.1 shows the spending on social protection in the Nordic and Baltic countries since 2014. For total public social spending it is noteworthy that at least since 2014 the Baltic states have caught up and are gradually moving from more than 15 per cent towards the OECD average of 20 per cent. For the Nordic countries we can identify a pattern of slow decline in social spending, which is highest in Finland. The social expenditures in Finland went down from 30.1 per cent in 2014 to 28.7 per cent in 2018, with a slight increase to 29.1 per cent (see also Aidukaite, Ainsaar and Hort 2021).

As expected, spending on public pensions as a percentage of gross domestic product (GDP) shows that the Nordic countries spend relatively more than the Baltic ones. In 2019 (the latest available data), Estonia (6.5 per cent), Latvia (6.8 per cent) and Lithuania (6.2 per cent) spent less than the OECD average (7.7 per cent) on public pensions. Nevertheless, there is also a great variation among the three Nordic countries in our analysis. Finland is on top, as it spent 11.8 per cent of its GDP on public pensions; Denmark spent only 8.0 per cent and Sweden was at the bottom with only 7.2 per cent (see also Aidukaite, Ainsaar and Hort 2021; OECD 2021).

The ageing of the population puts great pressure on the social protection systems of both Baltic and Nordic countries. While the Baltic states, resources-wise, seem to have a way to go in adapting to invest in older people's needs, the Nordic ones are well equipped to solve frail elder care issues. This is noticeable if we examine public spending as a percentage of GDP on health care. Latvia spent only 6.3 per cent of its GDP, and Estonia and Lithuania 6.8 per cent, on health care in 2019 according to OECD data. This is way below the OECD average (8.8 per cent). Sweden (10.9 per cent), Denmark (10 per cent) and Finland (9.1 per cent) were higher spenders. The Nordics were in the group of the highest OECD-17 spenders, while Estonia and Latvia were

■ 2014 ■ 2015 ■ 2016 ■ 2017 ▨ 2018 ▨ 2019

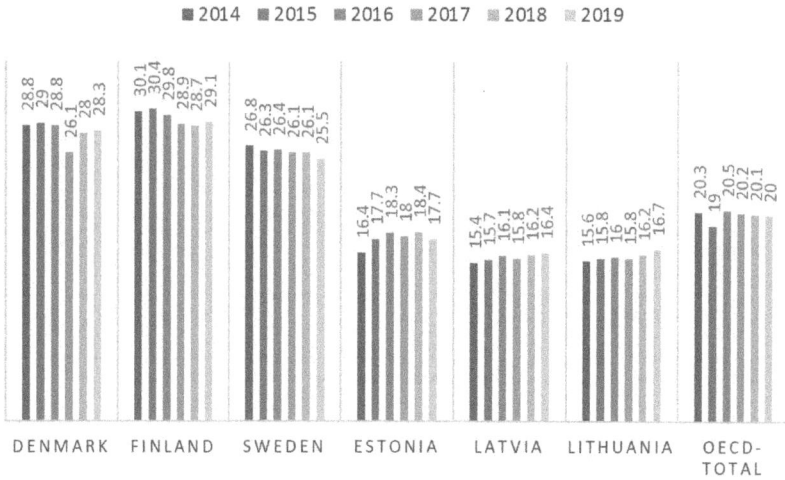

	DENMARK	FINLAND	SWEDEN	ESTONIA	LATVIA	LITHUANIA	OECD-TOTAL
2014	28.8	30.1	26.8	16.4	15.4	15.6	20.3
2015	29	30.4	26.3	17.7	15.1	15.8	19
2016	28.8	29.8	26.4	18.3	16.1	16	20.5
2017	26.1	28.9	26.1	18	15.8	15.8	20.2
2018	28	28.7	26.1	18.4	16.2	16.2	20.1
2019	28.3	29.1	25.5	17.7	16.4	16.7	20

Source: OECD (2021).

Figure 8.1   *Trends in social spending in the Baltic and Nordic countries, 2014–2018*

at the other end, among the countries with very poor spending on social and medical LTC in 2017. Spending in the Baltic countries was much lower than the OECD-17 average (1.7 per cent), approaching only 0.4 per cent in Latvia, 0.2 per cent in Estonia and 0.9 per cent in Lithuania, while the Nordics spent about 2.2–3.2 per cent of their GDPs on social and medical LTC (based on OECD 2020a, 2020b; see also Aidukaite, Ainsaar and Hort 2021).

The need for LTC is usually related to the health conditions of people and life expectancy. They both determine the relative need and absolute number of people who need LTC. In a European context, the Baltic countries have one of the lowest healthy life expectancies, and the general length of life is short. On the contrary, in the Nordic countries life expectancy is high (Aidukaite, Ainsaar and Hort 2021).

The proportion of people aged 65 and over who receive LTC is fairly small in Estonia (5.7 per cent in 2015), while in the OECD-18 the average proportion was 13 per cent. In the Nordic countries, a much higher share of those aged 65 and over received LTC. The figure was 11.5 per cent in Finland, 16 per cent in Denmark and 17 per cent in Sweden (Muir 2017).

Overall, as expected, the data on expenditures show significant differences between the Nordic and Baltic groups. The Baltic states have a long way to go to reach the level of the Nordic countries (Aidukaite, Ainsaar and Hort 2021).

*Table 8.1   Ideal-typical features of the Nordic and Baltic welfare
                  regimes and policies on ageing*

Features	Nordic welfare regime	Baltic welfare regime
The main agent in guaranteeing the well-being for the elderly	The state	A mix of state support, family and market
The state approach to ageing	Encompassing view of the life course	Financial sustainability of pension insurance
The aim of the policy towards the elderly	Independence and dignity	Poverty prevention
The level of poverty among the aged	Low	High
The major form of state support	Income support and provision of services	Minimal income support, provision of services is low
Marketisation and privatisation elements in the social security for the aged	Increasing	Increasing
Prevailing ideology of the welfare state	Social investment	Neoliberal
Familialisation in elderly care	Low	High

COMPARISON: NORDIC AND BALTIC WELFARE STATES AND AGEING POLICIES

The analyses provided above show a sharp contrast, or even sharper than expected, between welfare state models and approaches taken by the governments in the Nordic and Baltic countries. Table 8.1 summarises the ideal-typical features of the Baltic and Nordic welfare regimes. The major characteristics of the Nordic model, such as inclusiveness, solidarity, universalism and dignity, have shaped policies for the aged. The state's approach to the aged is defined by an encompassing view on the life course, meaning that the state takes care of its citizens from 'cradle to grave' and prepares and helps them to move smoothly from one stage of life to another. This is in line with the social investment paradigm. The bulk of support for the aged concentrates on the high quality of services, whether health care, institutional care or home care, making the elderly largely independent of their families. Nevertheless, we observe differences among the three Nordic countries in our analysis. Finland follows a more familialistic path in elderly care. In Denmark, Finland and Sweden, the government gives higher benefits for people who have resided for 40 years or more in their country, and they are entitled to a higher old-age pension benefit or housing supplements.

In the Baltics, the state does not provide a comprehensive approach to the life course, allowing a smooth transition from one stage of life to another. The state's support is centred on providing basic income security and health care. However, in Latvia, universal access to health care is declining (Roots, Ainsaar and Nahkur 2019). Other services (institutional care, home care) are less developed in the Baltics. Therefore, the family is an important agent for guaranteeing both income security and care support in old age. Even more, the constitutions of the Baltic states reinforce family dependencies, as it is stated that children are the primary caretakers of their elderly parents (see Chapter 2). Therefore, it is possible to claim that the ageing policies are highly familialised. The 'Baltic welfare state', with some variation among the three countries, seeks to reduce poverty by providing minimal income protection and/or social assistance. Income replacement by the old-age pension is still low in the Baltics. This is not true for the Nordic countries, where the state provides universal basic support to all, and for those who actively participated in the labour market income replacements are higher. However, higher income replacement in the Nordic countries has created a higher degree of stratification among the elderly than in the Baltic states, where pensions are more equalised (see Chapter 12; Medaiskis and Eirošius 2019).

The analyses revealed that the Nordic welfare state is increasingly being characterised by marketisation elements; for example, outsourcing of public services to private providers (Meagher and Szebehely 2013). In the Baltic states we see increasing market domains for pension provisions, health care and elderly care services (see Chapters 10, 11, 12, 13; Roots, Ainsaar and Nahkur 2019). The privatisation and marketisation of welfare provisions for the elderly will likely increase inequalities in the future. This means that unless policy reforms are introduced, both the Baltic and Nordic countries may be faced with more inequality among the elderly in coming decades.

THE SITUATION OF OLDER PEOPLE AND THEIR ATTITUDES TOWARDS THE ROLE OF THE GOVERNMENT

This section reviews citizens' perception of their socioeconomic situation and their attitudes towards the role of government in ensuring a safety net. According to Brooks and Manza (2007), the development of modern welfare states cannot be adequately understood without paying attention to public attitudes. Therefore, we ask: Do public attitudes about the support of elderly and social policy differ in the Nordic and Baltic countries?

We analyse the subjective life satisfaction of older people, assessments of their household income, views on the importance of a strong government for social security and attitudes towards means-testing. All data are analysed in two population groups: people below 60 and those 60 and over. The age of 60 is selected as an age when people start to make arrangements for their retirement.

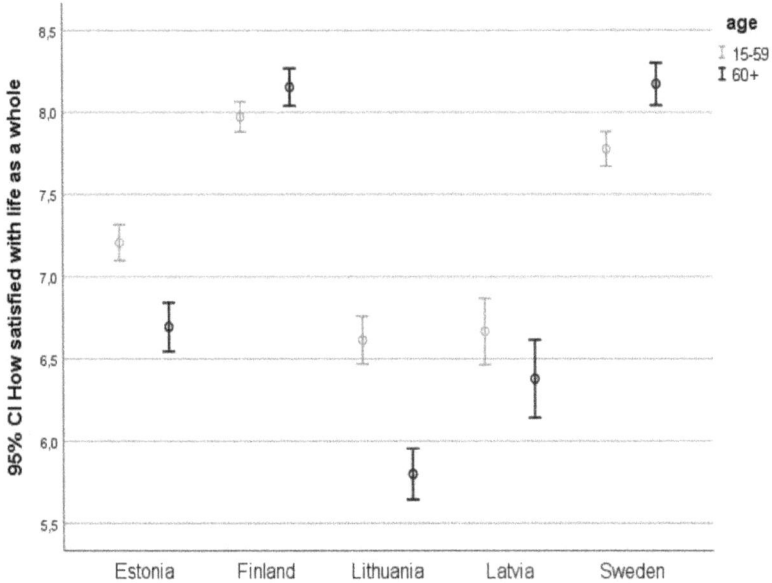

Source: ESS data 2018.

Figure 8.2   *Subjective life satisfaction (0 – not at all satisfied, 10 – very satisfied)*

To understand the situation of senior citizens, we first analyse their satisfaction with life (see Figure 8.2). As expected, the Nordic countries demonstrate higher subjective satisfaction, both for the population below 60 and for older age groups. The subjective well-being in older ages is higher compared to the younger population in Scandinavian countries. The Baltic countries lag behind and demonstrate the negative gap between life satisfaction of older and younger persons. The Baltic welfare state, with its lower level of public safety net, tends to generate lower satisfaction with life among the elderly. Some previous surveys (Ainsaar 2011) showed that income policy and health care in combination with social trust are the most important determinants of well-being of older people in the Baltic countries.

Perceived discrimination because of age is a direct indicator of the welfare of people and attribution of their problems to specific age-related reasons. The ESS data from 2018 do not reveal systematic differences in Baltic and Scandinavian countries compared to the rest of Europe.

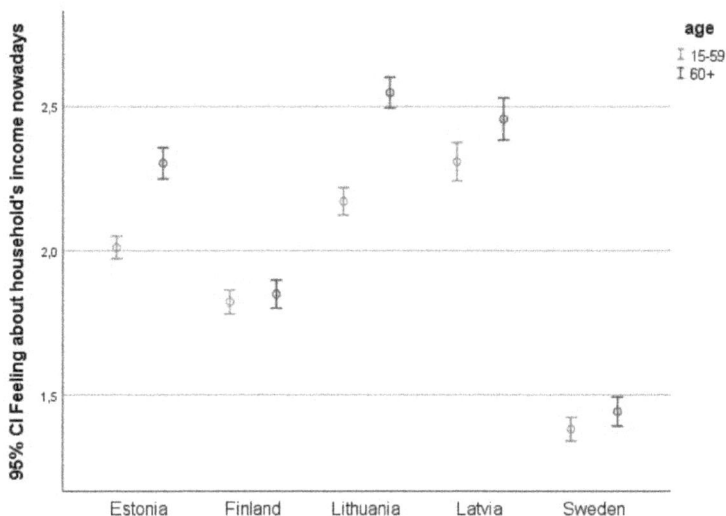

Source: ESS (2018).

Figure 8.3   *Evaluation of the household's income situation (1 – living comfortably, 4 – very difficult)*

Interestingly, the perceived discrimination does not correspond with the self-perceived income situation of older people (see Figure 8.3). However, as expected there are no differences among older and younger age groups in the Nordic countries, but an essential gap exists in the Baltic countries. On the scale from 1 to 4, the perceived standards of living of pensioners are the best in Sweden and Finland. The situation is worst in Lithuania and Latvia.

We can argue that once the perceived situation is miserable, more people would support government intervention in the social policy field. Figure 8.4 demonstrates the results about the need for safety guaranteed by the government (it is important that the government is strong and ensures safety). We see that the attitudes correspond to a certain level to perceived living standards, but are more diverse. The need for a strong government is lower and does not depend on age in Sweden. In Latvia, Estonia and Lithuania, we see first of all essential age gaps where older people support the government much more as a safety network provider. This might be explained by the greater vulnerability of older generations in those countries, which is reflected in the feelings about the household income.

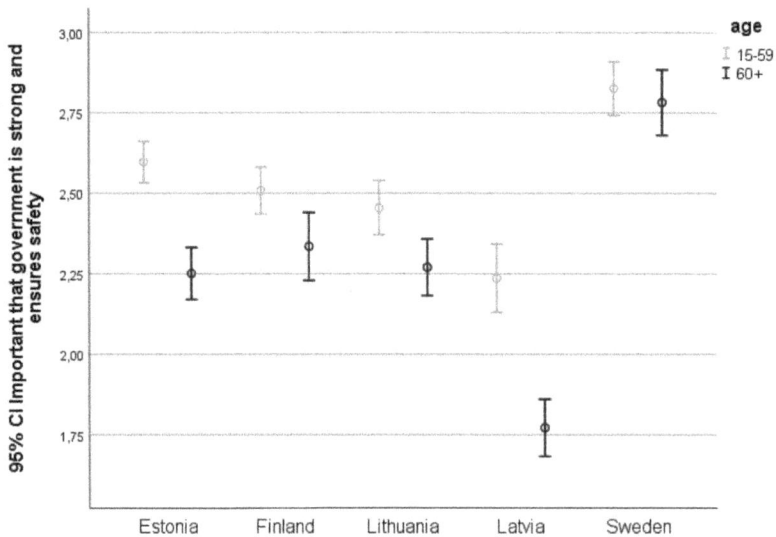

Source: ESS (2018).

Figure 8.4   Important that government is strong and ensures safety (1 – very much like me, 6 – not like me at all)

In order to see whether citizens' attitudes correspond to the prevailing welfare state ideologies and models in a country, we look at the attitudes towards means-testing. The attitudes could tell us which distributional principles the citizens favour. We should expect that in the Nordic countries citizens would be less in favour of means-testing than in the Baltic countries. In all countries older people tend to support more means-tested benefit distribution (see Figure 8.5). Lithuania is the only country with overlapping opinions of older and younger persons. The support for means-testing is generally higher in Lithuania, probably because of the influence of existing practices. In Lithuania, social assistance (benefits and in-kind) has always played a much greater role

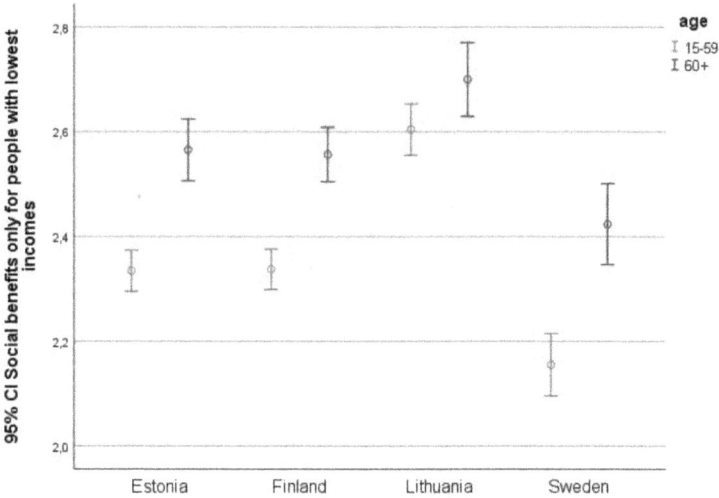

Note: No data for Denmark and Latvia.
Source: ESS (2016).

Figure 8.5   *Social benefits only for persons with lowest income (0 –*
            strongly against, 4 – strongly in favour)

than in Estonia (see Aidukaite 2009, 2011). Estonia and Finland are very similar, and Sweden has the most universalistic attitudes about distribution.

Overall, the attitudes correspond to the previous discussion about the welfare state models and support for the aged in the Baltic and Nordic countries. In this sense, we can say that, in general, citizens' attitudes comply with the welfare state models of the Nordic and Baltic countries. However, Finland, surprisingly, deviates from Sweden and joins the Baltic group when attitudes towards social assistance, feelings about household income and 'strong government' are examined.

DISCUSSION AND CONCLUSIONS

This chapter has reviewed the development of social policy arrangements to address older people's income security and autonomy through service provision in the Baltic and Nordic countries. The analyses have offered a short overview of pension insurance, LTC and senior citizens' perceptions of their socioeconomic situation and attitudes towards the role of government in ensuring safety. The Baltic states reformed their social policies, often learning from the best practices in the far north. Now, after 30 years of development, do we find any similarities between the Baltic and Nordic countries?

The findings of this chapter are in line with the previous research (Aidukaite, Ainsaar and Hort 2021) which shows that senior citizens remain in a precarious situation according to objective and subjective indicators. The analyses reveal essential existential gaps among younger and older generations, if poverty and income security are taken into account. The situation is, as expected, more positive in the Nordic countries. However, Finland exhibits similarities with Estonia and Lithuania in terms of the overall satisfaction of elderly people with their household income situation, support for the means test and their attitudes towards the government; namely that it is 'important that government is strong and ensures safety'.

Our analysis confirms that there are some developments towards marketisation and familiarisation of elderly care in the Nordic countries. It also shows that individualisation (service provision based on individual needs assessment instead of universal provision) and familiarisation (a greater role for family care, especially mothers' or daughters' care provisions for a family member) of elderly care seem to be more pronounced in Finland, and this leads to a lower subjective satisfaction of older people with their household income and a higher desire for a stronger state role in ensuring safety compared to Sweden. The support for means-testing is also stronger in Finland – to the same extent as in Estonia – than in Sweden. This can be explained by the fact that care services in Estonia, Finland and Lithuania are granted on the basis of the individual's needs assessment, and this further strengthens the perceived support for the means test in these countries, especially in Lithuania.

Second, our chapter reveals the vastness and scope of the differences among the Baltic and Nordic countries, which have not been documented to the same extent before. Some of the differences are very pronounced, especially in the service sector (LTC) development and its funding. In the Baltic countries, the LTC services are underdeveloped and very poorly financed. Yet familialism is entrenched by law in the Baltic societies. It is stated in the constitutions of Estonia, Latvia and Lithuania that children are obliged to take care of their elderly parents (see Chapter 2). However, the negative attitudes towards institutional care still prevail in the Baltic societies because of the low standards and bad reputations of the LTC institutions.

The pension insurance shows similarities between the two groups of countries as to the replacement rates, financing principles and design. However, the privatisation elements in pension insurance are more pronounced in the Baltic countries than in Finland and Denmark. Sweden shows more similarities with the three-pillar system of the Baltic states than with the Danish or Finnish pension systems (Aidukaite, Ainsaar and Hort 2021; see also Chapter 10, 12).

ACKNOWLEDGEMENTS

This study was financed by the project Construction of Older People's Well-being: The Empowerment Policy, Monitoring Indicators and the Voice of Older People, grant No. DOTSUT – 09.3.3-LMT-K-712-01-0063. The authors would like to thank Inga Blažienė, Igna Gaižauskaitė and Sarmite Mikulionienė (project team members) for useful comments in developing this chapter.

NOTES

1. We focus on public support to older adults in the three Baltic and three Nordic states: Estonia, Latvia and Lithuania on the one hand, and Denmark, Finland and Sweden on the other.
2. At present, the pension age in Estonia is 63 for both sexes; in Latvia, 62 years and 9 months for both sexes; in Lithuania, 63 years and 4 months for men, and 61 years and 8 months for women.

REFERENCES

Aidukaite, J. (2006), 'The formation of social insurance institutions of the Baltic states in the post-socialist era', *Journal of European Social Policy*, 16 (3), 259–227.

Aidukaite, J. (2009), 'Transformation of Welfare Systems in the Baltic States: Estonia, Latvia and Lithuania', in A. Cerami and P. Vanhuysse (eds), *Post-Communist Welfare Pathways: Theorizing Social Policy Transformations in CEE*, New York: Palgrave Macmillan, pp. 96–112.

Aidukaite, J. (2011), 'The "Baltic Welfare State" after 20 Years of Transition', in M. Lauristin and M. Aisaar (eds), *Estonian Human Development Report: Baltic Ways of Human Development: Twenty Years On*, Tallinn: Eesti Koostoo Kogu, pp. 70–74.

Aidukaite, J. (2018), '"Baltic Welfare State" or "Welfare States"? A Comparative Analysis of Social Security Systems in Estonia, Latvia and Lithuania', in M. Sengoku (ed.), *The Great Dispersion: The Many Fates of Post-Communist Society*, Sapporo: Slavic-Eurasian Research Centre, Hokkaido University, pp. 3–23.

Aidukaite, J. (2019), 'The welfare systems of the Baltic states following the recent financial crisis of 2008/2010: expansion or retrenchment?', *Journal of Baltic Studies*, 50 (1), 39–58.

Aidukaite, J., M. Ainsaar and S. E. O. Hort (2021, forthcoming), 'Current trends in social welfare policies towards the older people in the Baltic and Nordic countries: an exploratory study', *Journal of Baltic Studies*.

Aidukaite, J., N. Bogdanova and A. Guogis (2012), *Gerovės valstybės raida Lietuvoje: mitas ar realybė?* Vilnius: Lietuvos socialinių tyrimų centras.

Ainsaar, M. (2011), 'Changes in the Well-Being of Social Groups in the Baltic States from 1990–2009', in M. Lauristin and M. Aisaar (eds), *Estonian Human Development Report: Baltic Ways of Human Development: Twenty Years On*, Tallinn: Eesti Koostoo Kogu, pp. 82–87.

Ainsaar, M. (2019), 'Economic crisis, families, and family policy in the Baltic states, 2009–2014', *Journal of Baltic Studies*, 50 (1), 59–79.

Alestato, M., S. E. O. Hort and S. Kuhnle (2009), *The Nordic Model: Conditions, Origins, Outcomes, Lessons*. Working papers, No. 41, June, Hertie School of Governance.

Arts, W., and J. Gelissen (2002), 'Three worlds of welfare capitalism or more? A state-of-the-art report', *Journal of European Social Policy*, 12 (2), 137–158.

Atas, N. (2019), 'The immediate impact of the global financial crisis and neo-liberal austerity policies on in-work poverty dynamics in Lithuania', *Journal of Baltic Studies*, 50 (1): 105–124. doi:10.1080/01629778.2019.1553792.

Bernotas, D., and A. Guogis (2006), *Globalizacija, socialinė apsauga ir Baltijos šalys*, Vilnius: MRU leidybos centras.

Bohle, D., and B. Greskovits (2007), 'Neoliberalism, embedded neoliberalism, and neocorporatism: paths towards transnational capitalism in Central-Eastern Europe', *West European Politics*, 30 (3), 443–466.

Brazienė, R. (2017), 'Age and Workplace Discrimination in Lithuania', in Ł. Tomczyk and A. Klymczuk (eds), *Selected Contemporary Challenges of Aging Policy*, Krakow: Uniwersytet Pedagogyszny w Krakowie, pp. 53–69.

Brooks, C., and J. Manza (2007), *Why Welfare States Persist: The Importance of Public Opinion in Democracies*, Chicago, IL: University of Chicago Press.

Casey, B. H. (2004), 'Pension reform in the Baltic states: convergence with "Europe" or with "the World"?', *International Social Security Review*, 57 (1), 19–45.

Castles, F. (2009), 'What welfare states do: a disaggregated expenditure approach', *Journal of Social Policy*, 38, 45–62.

Danforth, B. (2014), 'Worlds of welfare in time: a historical reassessment of the three-world typology', *Journal of European Social Policy*, 24 (2), 164–182.

Esping-Andersen, G. (1990), *The Three Worlds of Welfare Capitalism*, Cambridge: Polity Press.

Eurofound (2019), *Age and Quality of Life: Who Are the Winners and Losers?* Luxembourg: Publications Office of the European Union.

Eurostat (2019), Database, accessed 1 April 2019 at https://ec.europa.eu/eurostat/data/database.

Gataūlinas, A. (2013), *Lietuvos visuomenės subjektyvioji gerovė Europos Sąjungos šalių kontekste* (Lithuanian public subjective well-being in the context of the European Union countries), Vilnius: Vilnius University.

Hemerijck, A. (2017), *The Uses of Social Investment*, Oxford: Oxford University Press.

Hort, S. E. O. (2014), *Social Policy, Welfare State and Civil Society in Sweden*, Volumes I and II, Lund: Arkiv.

Kalliomaa-Puha, L., and O. Kangas (2018), *ESPN Thematic Report on Challenges in Long-Term Care: Finland*, Brussels: European Commission.

Kemeny, J. (2001) 'Comparative housing and welfare: theorizing the relationship', *Journal of Housing and the Built Environment*, 16, 53–70.

Korpi, W., and J. Palme (1998), 'The paradox of redistribution and strategies of equality: welfare state institutions, inequality and poverty in Western countries', *American Sociological Review*, 63 (5), 661–687.

Kuhnle, S., P. Selle and S. E. O. Hort (eds) (2019), *Globalizing Welfare: An Evolving Asian-European Dialogue*, Cheltenham, UK and Northampton, MA, USA: Edward Elgar Publishing.

Kuitto, K. (2016), *Post-Communist Welfare States in European Context: Patterns of Welfare Policies in Central and Eastern Europe*, Cheltenham, UK and Northampton, MA, USA: Edward Elgar Publishing.

Kvist, J. (2018), *ESPN Thematic Report on Challenges in Long-Term Care: Denmark*, Brussels: European Commission.

Lazutka, R., A. Juška and J. Navickė (2018), 'Labour and capital under a neoliberal economic model: economic growth and demographic crisis in Lithuania', *Europe–Asia Studies*, 70 (9), 1433–1449.

Lazutka, R., A. Poviliunas and L. Zalimiene (2018), *ESPN Thematic Report on Challenges in Long-Term Care: Lithuania*, Brussels: European Commission.

Lendvai, N. (2008), Incongruities, Paradoxes, and Varieties: Europeanization of Welfare in the New Member States, paper presented at the ESPAnet Conference, September 2008, Helsinki.

Meagher, G., and M. Szebehely (eds) (2013), *Marketisation in Nordic Eldercare: A Research Report on Legislation, Oversight, Extent and Consequences*, SSW 30 Stockholm Studies in Social Work.

Medaiskis, T., and Š. Eirošius (2019), 'A comparison of Lithuanian and Swedish old age pension systems', *Ekonomika*, 98 (1), 38–59.

Mikulionienė, S. (2008), 'Diskriminacijos dėl amžiaus samprata viešajame diskurse: asmenų, dirbančių viešajame sektoriuje, atvejis', *Socialinis darbas*, 7 (1), 19–25.

Monnier, A. (2007), 'Baby-boomers: towards the end of an era', *Population and Societies*, 431.

Muir, T. (2017), *Measuring Social Protection for Long-Term Care*, OECD Health Working Paper No. 93, Paris: OECD Publishing.

OECD (2020a), Long-term care, accessed on 18 August 2020 at www.oecd.org/els/health-systems/long-term-care.htm.

OECD (2020b), Health spending (indicator), accessed on 18 August 2020 at https://doi.org/10.1787/777a9575-en.

OECD (2021), Social spending (indicator), accessed on 1 January 2021 at https://data.oecd.org/socialexp/social-spending.htm.

Paat-Ahi, G., and M. Masso (2018), *ESPN Thematic Report on Challenges in Long-Term Care: Estonia*, Brussels: European Commission.

Rajevska, F. (2018), *ESPN Thematic Report on Challenges in Long-Term Care: Latvia*, Brussels: European Commission.

Roots, A., M. Ainsaar and O. Nahkur (2019), 'Economic inequality in satisfaction with healthcare in the Baltic countries during and after the economic crisis, 2008–2014', *Journal of Baltic Studies*, 50 (1), 21–37.

Schon, P., and J. Heap (2018), *ESPN Thematic Report on Challenges in Long-Term Care: Sweden*, Brussels: European Commission.

Sommers, J., C. Woolfson and A. Juska (2014), 'Austerity as a global prescription and lessons from the neoliberal Baltic experiment', *Economic and Labour Relations Review*, 25 (3), 397–416.

Svallfors, S. (1997), 'Worlds of welfare and attitudes to redistribution: a comparison of eight Western nations', *European Sociological Review*, 13 (3), 283–304.

Titmuss, R. M. (1974) 'What Is Social Policy?' and 'Social Administration and Social Welfare', in R. M. Titmuss (ed.), *Social Policy: An Introduction*, London: George Allen and Unwin.

Wacker, R. R., and K. A. Roberto (2011), *Aging Social Policies: An International Perspective*, London: SAGE.

Wendt, C., M. Mischke and M. Pfeifer (2011), *Welfare States and Public Opinion: Perceptions of Healthcare Systems, Family Policy and Benefits for the Unemployed and Poor in Europe*, Cheltenham, UK and Northampton, MA, USA: Edward Elgar Publishing.

Wilensky, H. (1975), *The Welfare State and Equality: Structural and Ideological Roots of Public Expenditures*, Berkeley, CA: University of California Press.

9. Gender inequalities in family leaves, employment and pensions in Finland

Kati Kuitto and Susan Kuivalainen

INTRODUCTION

Over the decades, women's and men's life courses have become more similar and more equal in terms of labour market participation and division of homework and professional life. Some welfare states have put more emphasis on gender equality by developing institutional solutions supporting women's employment and economic independence by, for example, offering public childcare and social security based on the individual's rather than the partnership's status (Esping-Andersen 2009). Despite these efforts and the positive developments, even in the most gender-equal countries large gender differences in economic well-being over the life course persist. Those inequalities culminate in a gap between women's and men's pensions, which was 25 per cent on average in the Organisation for Economic Co-operation and Development (OECD) countries in 2016. This gender pension gap has diminished only slowly (OECD 2019). Although the Nordic and the Baltic countries, with the exception of Sweden, fare better than the OECD average, the gender pension gap remains an issue in these countries, too. Although more and more women obtain pension income in their own right as a result of the maturing of pensions systems, increasing labour market participation of women over generations, and ever fuller careers of women, retired women still suffer much more often than men from old-age poverty. Older women are particularly affected by old-age poverty, and the lower pensions affect women longer due to their greater longevity.

In most of the pension systems today, pension income more or less directly reflects the employment and earnings history of the retiree. Therefore, gender differences in careers and breaks in them result in the gender pension gap. Parenting is the main reason for career breaks during early stages of the working life and one of the factors causing gender inequalities in labour markets and beyond. Even after decades of attempts to engage fathers more intensively in child-rearing by a variety of family policy measures, women still bear the main load of childcare and family-related homework. For women, childbearing is, therefore, still partly related to considerable labour market risk and a 'motherhood penalty' (Budig et al. 2012; Angelov et al. 2016; Kleven et al. 2019). Cumulating over the life course, the gendered careers also manifest themselves in a gender gap in pensions (Frericks et al. 2009; Betti et al. 2015).

In this chapter, we examine gender inequalities in employment and pensions related to parenting in Finland, which, along with Iceland, Norway and Sweden, has continuously scored highly in international comparisons of gender equality (World Economic Forum 2020). The Nordic welfare state has in general been considered as woman-friendly and promoting gender equality (Hernes 1987; Orloff 1993), but Finland is an interesting and in part contradictory case. Finland takes a somewhat deviant position when it comes to a female labour market position and the division of child-rearing between genders. On the one hand, women's labour market participation has been traditionally high, and women work full-time more often than they do in many other countries. In the Nordic model, social citizenship is based on the individual rather than family status, and the welfare state provides social policies and public services enabling women's paid employment. On the other hand, the Finnish labour market is highly segregated to a greater extent than in the other Nordic countries, with only every tenth Finn in 2015 being employed in so-called equal occupations, where the share of the different sexes is 40 to 60 per cent (European Commission 2009; Boll et al. 2016; Statistics Finland 2018). Furthermore, the Finnish family leave scheme includes a comparatively long home care allowance, available until the child's third birthday, that poses an institutional incentive for a longer drop-out from the labour market. This leads to comparatively long home care spells for Finnish children that are nearly exclusively taken by mothers (Sipilä and Korpinen 1998; Hiilamo and Kangas 2009; Sipilä et al. 2010; Ellingsæter 2012). This, in turn, generates considerable gender gaps in labour market positions, earnings and, later in life, also in pensions (Koskenvuo 2016; Kela 2018; Kuitto et al. 2019).

Resting upon cross-sectional data on family leave use, employment and retirement, we point out gender inequalities over the life course and show how Finland relates to the other Nordic and Baltic countries. Furthermore, we report results of a recent cohort study of young Finns based on longitudinal population data consisting of different administrative registers and focusing on early career developments and the use of family leave benefits. The assessment of the Finnish case shows how gender inequalities persist despite gender-neutral family and pension policies, and lead to gender gaps in income throughout the life course.

In the next section, we describe the Finnish family leave scheme and the pension system, which set the institutional frame for gender inequalities relating to employment, parenting and old-age income. In the third section, we look at how employment, wages and retirement of men and women differ. The fourth section provides insights into the division of family leaves between men and women and how they relate to career developments. The fifth section concludes by discussing the challenges the Finnish welfare state faces regarding a more equal division of work, family and related social security over the life courses of men and women.

FAMILY AND PENSION POLICIES IN FINLAND: THE INSTITUTIONAL FRAMEWORK

The Finnish Family Leave Scheme

The family leave scheme in Finland has evolved over time since the implementation of paid maternity leave in 1964. Initially, about two months' maternity leave was extended to nine months by 1980. From the 1980s on, fathers gradually got more paid leave days, the maternity allowance was extended to maternity, paternity and parental leave allowances, and in 2003 a father quota of one month's parental leave was introduced (Kellokumpu 2007). Increasing fathers' use of parental leave and thereby enhancing gender equality in childcare and the labour market has been the leitmotiv of the family leave reforms of the past decades (Lammi-Taskula 2007, 2017).

At the same time, from the 1970s the public childcare system was developed. The Child Day Care Act, passed in 1973, granted the right to day care for all children who needed it. In 1996, the subjective right to day care was extended to cover all children of preschool age. In 2014, the government decided to restrict the universal right to day care. The child is entitled to day care on a part-time basis only if a parent is not working or studying full-time. Currently, the government aims to restore the subjective right to full-time day care for all children.

After the latest major reform in 2013, the Finnish family leave scheme today offers a comparatively long possibility of stepping out of employment for childcare. The scheme is presented in a simplified form in Figure 9.1. Mothers can stay on paid maternal leave for 105 days around the birth. After that, either the mother or the father can stay home on paid parental leave for 158 working days. Parents can split the parental leave as they wish or only one parent can go on leave. Parental leave can also be taken simultaneously, but only when both take it part-time. For fathers, there is a paid paternity leave of about nine weeks, of which up to 18 days can be taken simultaneously to the maternity or parental leave of the mother, and the rest after the parental leave. All these leave allowances are earnings-related with a replacement level of around 90 per cent for the first 56 days of maternity leave and 70 per cent for paternity and parental leaves (National Institute for Health and Welfare 2019a). A flat-rate benefit is granted for those not entitled to the earnings-related benefits, such as students or persons outside the labour market.

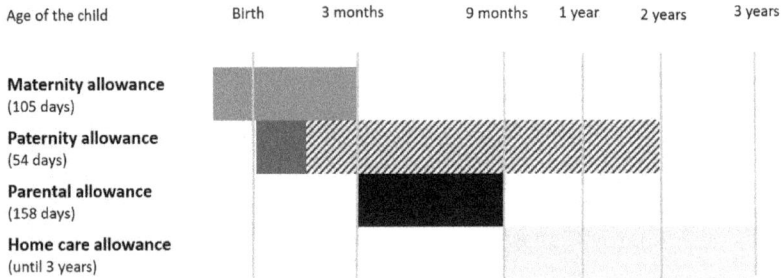

Source: Own compilation based on Kela (2020).

*Figure 9.1		Finnish family leave scheme (2020)*

A rather specific feature of the Finnish family leave scheme, though, is the long home care allowance that allows the parents to take care of their child at home until the age of 3. Only a minority of OECD countries provides this kind of cash-for-childcare benefits. The Finnish home care allowance is a flat-rate benefit with municipal supplements that vary regionally. Even though every child has a right to public childcare/early education after the parental leave, the majority of families choose to take care of their child at home on home care allowance at least for some time, most frequently until the child is about 2 years old (Kela 2018). Altogether, the Finnish family leave scheme offers one of the longest publicly paid possibilities to stay at home for child-rearing, and of the Scandinavian and Baltic countries only Estonia offers similarly long paid family leaves (Table 9.1). Although paid family leaves are long in Finland, they are less flexible in comparison to other Nordic countries (Hakovirta et al. 2013).

The Finnish Pension System

The first-pillar pension scheme dominates the Finnish pension system. Owing to comprehensive statutory earnings-related pension schemes, the roles of second- and third-pillar pensions are marginal. The Finnish statutory pension system (the first pillar) consists of the earnings-related employment pension, a residence-based national pension and a guarantee pension. The employment pension aims to maintain the income level achieved during the working career, while the tasks of the national and guarantee pensions are to ensure basic income security and protect against old-age poverty. The national pension

Table 9.1   Maximum lengths of parental leaves in different schemes (2016, in weeks)

Country	Maternity leave	Parental leave with job protection	Paid maternity and parental leave total	Paid father-specific leave
Estonia	20.0	146.0	166.0	2.0
Latvia	16.0	78.0	94.0	1.4
Lithuania	18.0	148.0	62.0	4.0
Denmark	18.0	32.0	50.0	2.0
Finland	17.5	143.5	161.0	9.0
Iceland	13.0	30.3	26.0	13.0
Norway	13.0	78.0	91.0	10.0
Sweden	19.9	65.1	55.7	14.3
OECD	*19.1*	*65.7*	*55.2*	*8.2*

Source: OECD Employment Database (www.oecd.org/employment/emp/onlineoecdemployme ntdatabase.htm, accessed on 27 February 2020).

complements the pension income of those who have not earned a sufficiently large pension through the earnings-related pension. The national pension is phased out as the employment pension increases. In 2020, pensioners whose earnings-related pension is more than 1,368.21 euros per month are no longer entitled to any national pension. The full national pension (662.86 euros in 2020) is granted with 40 years of residence since the age of 16. A guarantee pension was introduced in 2011 to guarantee a minimum pension level of 834.52 euros in 2020 for those with the lowest pension income. The amount of the guarantee pension is reduced by any other pension income the recipient may receive from Finland or from abroad.

The Finnish earnings-related pension scheme is very comprehensive and encompassing. It is mandatory and statutory and covers nearly all those in gainful employment; all employees over 17 years with earnings exceeding 60.57 euros per month (the limit in 2020) are insured. Moreover, the conditions of receiving benefits are uniform: all employees, notwithstanding their con-tracts, occupations, branch or sector, are insured according to the same rules. The scheme also operates without any earnings or benefits ceiling; thus, all income levels are covered equally. Since the earnings-related pension scheme covers practically all types of employment and has no ceilings, the role of second-pillar employer-specific occupational pensions or third-pillar provi-sion based on individual private pension insurance is very modest in Finland (Kangas and Luna 2011; Barr 2013). The Finnish earnings-related pension system is characterised as a functional hybrid that incorporates features from both first and second pillars (Börsch-Supan 2005; Ebbinghaus 2011).

As such, the Finnish pension system is gender-neutral and can be viewed as quite women-friendly. In contrast to many other countries in which earnings-related and occupational pension schemes often leave work typical for women and low-wage occupations uncovered (Ginn and Arber 1992; Gruber and Wise, 2004), the Finnish statutory earnings-related employment pension covers almost all earnings with uniform benefits and conditions of receiving benefits. Additionally, the national and guarantee pension schemes ensure basic income security for those with no or only limited earnings-related pension accrual. The national pension has an important role in cushioning and moderating income differences created throughout the working life (Möhring 2015; Kuivalainen et al. 2018). This is a case particularly for women; without the national pension, women's overall pension income would have been 10 per cent lower, and 39 per cent of women receive national pension in addition to earnings-related pensions. For men, owing to their higher earnings-related employment pension, the national pension has a less significant role, and 25 per cent also have income from the national pension (Finnish Centre for Pensions 2020). Additionally, the survivor's pension adds to the old-age income package of many elderly and/or widowed women, and in Finland the survivor's pension, unlike in many other Nordic and Baltic countries, is paid until death (cf. OECD 2018a; see more in Takala et al. 2015).

Many reforms, a few major and numerous smaller changes, have been introduced into the Finnish pension system since the 1990s (Kuivalainen and Kuitto 2021). Reforms have further strengthened the dominance of the first-pillar pensions (Kautto 2017). As from 2005, the pension is calculated on the basis of the entire working career. *Ex ante* evaluations of the 2005 pension reform report that it does not create inequality between the genders (Tuominen 2004). Recent reforms have mainly been more favourable for women (Reipas and Sankala 2015; Kuivalainen et al. 2019). The most important improvement for women's pension adequacy has been the treatment of career breaks due to parenting.

How Career Breaks during Parenting Affect Pension Accumulation

As in many other countries, recent Finnish pension reforms have adjusted the rules for pension accumulation during family-related career breaks in order to acknowledge childcare periods (Frericks et al. 2009; OECD 2015). Most importantly, the 2005 pension reform improved pension provision for periods out of paid employment, and the provision for pension accrual related to these benefits was harmonised. Prior to 2005, in the private sector the pension accrued for maternity, paternity and paternal leaves according to the so-called one-year rule (Tuominen 2004). The one-year rule meant that breaks of shorter duration than 359 days in the contract of employment did not suspend pension accrual. This practice was adopted in the 1970s and concerned private sector employees. Similar rules applied for employees in the public sector (Koskenvuo 2016). Those without a contract of employment were not covered at all, and no pension accrued for periods of childcare prior to 2005.

As of 2005, pension has accrued for periods of childcare on more uniform bases. For periods of earnings-related maternity, paternity and parental allowance, the old-age pension accrues on a basis which is 121 per cent (in 2020) of the earnings on which the benefit is based regardless of sector or continuing contract of employment. The 2005 reform also improved the situation of those who are receiving a flat-rate maternity, paternity or paternal allowance. Prior to that, there was no entitlement for them. Furthermore, the 2005 reform introduced pension accrual for the period during which a parent stays at home to take care of a child under the age of 3 on home care allowance. For periods of home care allowance and for flat-rate maternity, paternity or paternal allowance, pension accrues based on a fixed euro amount (757.14 euros/month in 2020). A requirement for pension accrual for unpaid leaves is that one has earned a certain amount from work during one's preceding working life (a total of at least 18,171.43 euros in 2020). The accrual rate is the same for all unpaid periods and the same as for earnings, 1.5 per cent. Like most OECD countries, the Finnish pension system does not include a specific child credit in addition to the credit covering career breaks due to parenting (see OECD 2015).[1]

The reform of 2005 is so far the most momentous change in regard to acknowledging the family-related career breaks in pension provision. After 2005, no substantial changes were introduced to pension accrual for unpaid periods. Figure 9.2 illustrates pension accrual during the family-related care leaves compared to continuous employment. The example contrasts the pension accumulation over three years of either being continuously employed or on family leaves. The model calculation is based on the average earnings of a woman at the average age of having the first child (around 27): 2,400 euros per month. During the maternal/paternal and parental leaves, the amount of the accrued pension is even slightly higher than when working, as the base for pension accrual is 121 per cent of the previous wage level for those employed. However, during the home care allowance following the parental leave period – that is, after a child is 9 or 10 months old – there is a clear loss in one's pension accrual as the home care allowance period is credited on the basis of a flat-rate sum which is rather low in comparison to the average wage: only about one-fourth of the average wage. The higher one's earnings are, the greater is the loss in accrued pension compared to pension accrual when working. The longer the time spent at home taking care of a child, the larger are the losses. After a full three years at home, the pension accrual of these three years is only about half compared to continuous employment. According to the calculations by the OECD (2015), a five-year childcare-related employment break leads to an approximate 5 per cent pension loss (gross) compared to a situation of uninterrupted employment in Finland. The dent is above the OECD average and is higher than in Norway but lower than in Sweden and Estonia.

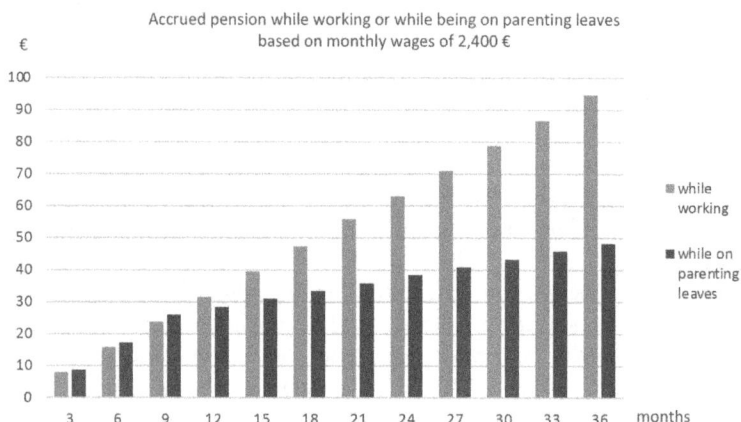

Accrued pension while working or while being on parenting leaves based on monthly wages of 2,400 €

Source: 'Pension for family leave' calculator, online at www.tyoelake.fi/en/how-much-pension/pension-for-family-leaves/ (accessed 11 March 2020).

Figure 9.2   *Pension accrual during parenting leaves compared to continuous employment*

GENDER GAPS IN EMPLOYMENT, RETIREMENT AND PENSIONS

Gender Gaps in Employment and Wages

In the Finnish pension system, the earnings-related scheme plays a key role in providing old-age income. Therefore, the working-life history throughout the life course is the main source of differences both between genders and, more generally, between individuals' pension incomes. Traditionally, the labour market participation rate of Finnish women has been high; at the time when an earnings-related pension scheme came into force in the early 1960s, the female employment rate was already over 60 per cent (Kuivalainen et al. 2019). With 76.3 per cent in 2018, the rate was similarly high as in the other Nordic and Baltic countries and much higher than the OECD or the European Union-28

Table 9.2   *Labour market participation and type of employment by gender (in per cent, 2018) and gender wage gap*

Country	Labour force participation rate (age 15–64)[a]		Part-time employment[a]		Temporary employment[a]		Gender wage gap	
							Hourly (unadjusted, 2017)[b]	Overall (2014)[c]
	Men	Women	Men	Women	Men	Women		
Estonia	82.5	75.7	5.8	12.8	3.6	3.3	25.6	38.4
Latvia	80.5	75.1	4.2	8.8	3	2.4	15.7	22.8
Lithuania	78.9	75.8	4.5	8.8	1.7	1.5	15.2	19.2
Denmark	82.1	76.6	15.2	25.4	9.9	12.5	14.7	26.1
Finland	79.7	76.3	10.7	17.8	13.4	19.5	16.7	24.1
Iceland	89.9	84.5	11.4	23.4	7.7	10.8	15.5	34.0
Norway	80.4	75.5	11.7	27.7	7.4	9.5	14.3	31.5
Sweden	84.6	81.2	10.3	17.4	14.8	18.2	12.6	26.2
OECD	*80.4*	*64.6*	*9.4*	*25.4*	*11.3*	*12.1*	*-*	*-*
EU28	*79.4*	*68.4*	*8*	*26.5*	*13.7*	*14.7*	*16*	*39.6*

Notes and sources: (a) OECD Employment Database 2019; (b) Eurostat (online data code: sdg_05_20): difference between average gross hourly earnings of male and female employees as percentage of male gross earnings; (c) Eurostat (https://ec.europa.eu/eurostat/databrowser/view/teqges01/default/table?lang=en). The overall gender earnings gap is a synthetic indicator. It measures the impact of the three combined factors, namely: (1) the average hourly earnings, (2) the monthly average of the number of hours paid (before any adjustment for part-time work) and (3) the employment rate, on the average earnings of all women of working age – whether employed or not employed – compared to men. Accessed 15 July 2019.

(EU28) average (see Table 9.2). The gender gap in the participation rate (3.4 percentage points) was comparably low, too. Women's part-time employment is less common in Finland than in many other countries, but still more women than men do work part-time (17.8 per cent compared to men's 10.7 per cent). The gender gap in temporary contracts is larger than in other Nordic or Baltic countries; while nearly every fifth woman worked with a non-permanent contract in 2018, less than every seventh man did.

The relatively equal and mainly full-time labour market participation of women in Finland is also reflected in one of the lowest gender gaps in total earnings in Europe (24.1 per cent in 2014). However, when looking at gross hourly wages of male and female employees, the gender gap was 16.7 percentage points in 2018. This is slightly above the average of the EU countries and the second highest in the group of Nordic and Baltic countries. The gender gap in hourly wages reflects the differences in education, profession and experience, regardless of working time. This gender wage gap results mainly from the segregation of the Finnish labour markets, which is considerably strong in international comparison (European Commission 2009; Boll et al. 2016). Finnish women more often than men are employed in low-paid professions within health care, social services, restaurants and hotel businesses. Women are also over-represented in the public sector. Male-dominated professions, in turn, include sciences, technology, transport and construction in the private sector. Even when working in the same professions as men, women are less frequently in high-wage expert or managerial positions (Lilja and Savaja 2013; Kauhanen et al. 2015). Women also less frequently work overtime, so women work less and in less well-paid occupations overall. Gender differences in occupation choice and earnings have diminished only marginally over time (cf. Pietiläinen 2013).

GENDER GAPS IN RETIREMENT AND PENSIONS

When we look at retirement and length of working life, there are only minor differences between Finnish women and men. In 2018, the average expected duration of women's working life was 38 years, only 1.3 years less than that of men (Table 9.3). Finnish women thus work more years than women in the EU countries on average, but the length of their working life is close to the average of the Nordic and the Baltic countries. The effective retirement age in 2017 of women (63.1 years) was not much lower than men's (63.8 years), but it was one of the lowest in the group of the Nordic and Baltic countries and also below the OECD average.

Factors that shorten working lives include most notably unemployment, but also disability, sickness and family leaves. The most important factors generating gender differences in career breaks, though, are parenting leaves. In sum, however, Finnish women work almost as much and as long as their male counterparts and retire at similar ages. Socioeconomic differences in length of working life are very modest, too (Kuivalainen et al. 2018).

However, there are considerable differences in earnings and, consequently, in pension income and economic well-being between men and women. This is shown by the remarkable gender gap in pensions, which, in 2016, was 23.7 percentage points in Finland (Table 9.3). The figure is well below the EU average, but together with Sweden, considerably higher than in the other Nordic and Baltic countries. As in many other countries, the gender pension gap has diminished only slowly (Betti et al. 2015). Forecasts on the future development of pensions see further slight decreases in the gap, reflecting the wage and employment histories of current working-age generations. The median pension income of women in Finland was 74 per cent of men's pension

Table 9.3   *Duration of working life, retirement age and gender pension gap*

Country	Duration of working life 2018[a]		Effective retirement age 2017[b]		Gender pension gap 2016[c]
	Men	Women	Men	Women	
Estonia	39.7	38.4	65.8	65.2	1.8
Latvia	36.7	36.7	63.4	61.9	15.4
Lithuania	36.6	36.8	63.0	62.5	17.5
Denmark	41.5	38.3	64.6	62.8	7.8
Finland	39.3	38.0	63.8	63.1	23.7
Iceland	48.3	44.2	69.8	66.6	-
Norway	40.9	38.2	65.4	64.1	-
Sweden	42.9	41.0	66.0	65.1	28.3
OECD	-	-	*65.3*	*63.6*	-
EU28	*38.6*	*33.7*	-	-	*37.2*

Sources: (a) Eurostat LFS (lfsi_dwl_a) 12 July 2019; (b) OECD, www.oecd.org/els/emp/average
-effective-age-of-retirement.htm, 12 July 2019; (c) European Commission 2018 (PAR).

income in 2015, and the forecasts of the Finnish Centre for Pensions estimate the same figure to be 85 per cent in 2085 (Tikanmäki et al. 2019).

GENDER GAPS IN FAMILY LEAVES

Division of Family-Related Leaves and Attitudes

Even though the Finnish family leave policies offer a gender-neutral possibility to divide parenting-related career breaks equally between the mother and father, or even other persons, family leaves are still to a great extent taken only by the mothers. In 2018, 89.8 per cent of all parental leave days were taken by mothers, and 95 per cent of all home care allowance days (Kuivalainen et al. 2019). Most of the fathers take a short paternity leave after the birth during maternity or parental leave of the mother (1–18 days, 78 per cent of fathers in 2014), but only about one-third used the possibility to take the full length of the paternity leave after the parental leave (1–54 days). The share of fathers taking parental leave, which can be divided between the parents, has been very low, with only about 1–3 per cent of fathers using this opportunity and the ratio being more or less unchanged since the mid-1990s (Lammi-Taskula et al. 2017; National Institute for Health and Welfare 2019b). Research shows that disapproving attitudes both at workplaces and among fathers are one of the reasons why Finnish fathers do not use parental leave beyond the father's quota; the length of the quota seems to both set the norm of an acceptable absence from the workplace and also to support gendered perceptions of parental responsibilities. Lengthening the father's quota of parental leave might help in reaching a more equal division of parental care responsibilities (Närvi and Salmi 2019).

After the parental leave, when the child is around 9 to 10 months old, most of the families in Finland choose to take care of their children on home care allowance (89 per cent). In more than half of those families, home care allowance is taken for no more than 12 months, and around 16 per cent of the families care for their children at home until the age of 3 (National Institute for Health and Welfare 2019b). Attitudes supporting home care for small children and the perception of the mother being better suited to care for small children are still widespread in Finland and may in part explain the long leave spells and the unequal division of leave between mothers and fathers (Lammi-Taskula 2007; Närvi 2014). The home care allowance, however, is controversial in the public discourse and is justified and opposed on multiple ideological, economic and political grounds (Hiilamo and Kangas 2009; Sipilä et al. 2012). The home care allowance constitutes a strong incentive for women to stay out of the labour market for a longer time (OECD 2018b). Based on previous studies, we also know that long home care leaves are taken particularly by women with weak labour market positions and low education (Rissanen 2012; Haataja and Juutilainen 2014; Närvi 2014). Furthermore, mothers without employment contracts who take long home care leaves often experience weaker labour market attachment at a later point in time (Peutere et al. 2014).

Family Leaves, Early Career Labour Market Attachment and Pension Accumulation

The gender differences that emerge in the early stages of working life and accumulate over the life course may be exemplified based on a recent study of early career labour market attachment and parental leaves. In that study, we followed a young cohort of Finns born in 1980 during their early careers, at the ages of 25–36 (Kuitto et al. 2019). We used register data from the Finnish Centre for Pensions containing extensive information on employment and earnings on the basis of which earnings-related pensions accrue. The data also included information on different social security benefits related to career breaks such as family leaves, unemployment, disability and sickness, as well as different socioeconomic variables. With this data, we were able to trace the development of labour market attachment and earnings of the whole cohort (62,687 persons) during 12 years between 2005 and 2016.

On average, women had almost as many total days in employment as men (97 per cent) by the age of 36. However, great discrepancies in accumulated earnings between the genders had occurred already at this early stage of their careers. Women's earnings by the age of 36 were only 70 per cent of the earnings of men. The gender differences in occupations and working time at the Finnish labour market described above may explain the main part of this difference, but a further important reason can be found in the highly unequal distribution of parenting-related career breaks in the early career. About three out of four of the cohort's women and two out of three of the men had at least one child by the age of 36. Gender differences occurred first in the dynamics of childbearing and employment: while women in good labour market positions had fewer children on average and had them later, the opposite was true for men. Well-situated men had more frequent and more children than their counterparts with weak employment (cf. Kaufmann and Uhlenberg 2000; Koslowski 2011).

Of the parents in this cohort, mothers' career breaks due to family leaves were 13 times as long as those of the fathers (1,408 days compared to 111 days in sum during 2005–2016). While there were no significant differences in the length of days spent on maternity or parental leave across groups of mothers with different employment trajectories, long family leaves on home care allowance were much more common among women with weak labour market attachment (Kuitto et al. 2019). This is in line with previous research that shows long home care allowance spells to be popular among less educated mothers with no or non-standard employment (Närvi 2017; see also Evertsson and Duvander 2011). Especially for those women, long home care spells create a vicious circle. Of fathers, in turn, paternity and parental leave was used mostly by those with stable labour market positions.

The earnings gap between the gender and the 'motherhood penalty' or 'child penalty' is considerable in Finland and seems to be even larger than in many other countries (Kleven et al. 2019; Sieppi and Pehkonen 2019), having a major impact on the gender pension gap. Projections for future pensions and gaps due to parental leaves are hard to estimate, since many developments that impact pension accumulation over the life course of individuals are uncertain. Using some averages and simulation techniques, it is possible to make a rough estimate of the pension penalty caused by parenthood and family leaves of different lengths.[2] The following theoretical example illustrates the pension effects of different lengths of parental leaves for persons belonging to the cohort born in 1980. We assume the persons started their career at the age of 24 and keep working to the earliest old-age pension retirement age (66 years and 8 months). Earnings and price development follow the assumptions made in the long-term projections of the Finnish Centre for Pensions (Tikanmäki et al. 2019). The persons' monthly earnings in year 2018 are set at 2,400 euro, and at the birth of the first child in 2008, 1,900 euro, according to the above assumptions. Person A has no children, and person B has two children, born in 2008 and 2010, and he/she has spent two years at home with each of them (10 months of maternity/paternity and parental leave, 14 months of home care allowance). Person C also has two children, born in 2008 and 2011, and he/she has spent the full three years at home with each of the children (10 months of maternity/paternity and parental leave, 26 months of home care allowance). When retiring, the difference in person B's to person A's earnings-related pension benefit is 60 euros per month, and person C's difference 117 euros per month. Given the average pension income of women of 1,533 euros per month (in 2019, Finnish Centre for Pensions 2020), this gap is considerable.

The analysis of the career trajectories and family-related career breaks of this Finnish cohort born in 1980 exemplifies the problems of gender inequalities with far-reaching consequences. Gaps in earnings and careers evolve at an early stage of the life course, and catching up to the men's lead will be hard for women.

CONCLUSIONS

In this chapter, we discussed how family-related career breaks and gender inequalities in employment relate to the gender pension gap in Finland. As one of the Nordic welfare states, the country provides favourable institutional conditions for women's equal participation in the labour market. Great attention is paid to gender equality in the political agenda, affordable and good quality public childcare is provided for everyone and the pension system can be considered women-friendly. Still, considerable differences in the level of men's and women's pensions exist, and the gender pension gap is among the highest in the group of Nordic and Baltic countries.

The reasons for this large gap can be found in the gendered working lives of Finnish men and women. Women's labour market participation is nearly as high and intensive as men's, but in an early stage of the career a considerable gap in earnings evolves. This is, first, related to the strong segregation of the Finnish labour market in women's and men's professions and the lower wages of women associated with that. Second, career breaks due to child-rearing affect women's careers much more than men's. Over 90 per cent of all family leave days are still taken by mothers, and women with a lower educational level and socioeconomic status step out of the labour market for a particularly long time when having children. Long family leaves, in turn, are also related to lower earnings and less stable labour market attachment after the phase of caring for small children. The example of early career development and parental leaves of the Finnish women and men born in 1980 points to the fact that unequal parenting and its effects on careers are not a problem of older generations. Instead, even in this relatively young cohort, gender inequality is so obviously visible, casting a cloud far into the future of women's incomes and making a rapid decrease of the gender pension gap unlikely.

Even though the Finnish pension system is highly inclusive, granting earnings-related pensions for everyone with the same rules and topping up low earnings-related pensions with the national and guarantee pension, as well as providing women-friendly features such as wide coverage and uniform rules across sectors and occupations, women's pensions continue to be about one-fifth lower than men's (Finnish Centre for Pensions 2020). The gender pension gap has diminished only slowly. From the perspective of the pension system, it seems like most means to diminish the gender pension gap have already been implemented. However, the effects of the reforms will show only in the long run. Occasionally, discussion about the need to improve pension accrual for a period of home care allowance has popped up. However, so far this has not gained support as it is seen to weaken even further the incentives for women to uphold their labour force participation.

Instead, labour market and family policies play a key role in narrowing the gender gap and in making women's and men's careers more equal. Efforts for achieving equal pay and diminishing labour market segregation are essential for more equal labour market outcomes, and for reducing the gender pension gap of future retirees. Furthermore, combating pregnancy discrimination in working places and policies to promote family-friendly attitudes among employers, as well as flexible working-time solutions, help against gender inequality in labour markets and in combining family and work for both women and men. Easier and more flexible possibilities to combine work and family are wished for by many Finns in their family-forming years, but at the same time an overwhelming majority of working parents in today's Finland feel that they can easily combine family and working life (Sorsa and Rotkirch 2020).

The key challenge for family policy is achieving a more equal division of family-leave-related career breaks between women and men. One of the main problems causing long breaks in careers and losses in earnings and pension accumulation is the long home care spell, which is still mainly used by the mothers. In 2016, the OECD recommended reducing the combined duration of parental leave and home care allowance to encourage female labour market participation, but so far nothing has happened in this direction (OECD 2016, 2018b). Shortening the home care leave seems to be a highly sensitive issue in Finnish politics, and therefore it is unlikely that it will be shortened or abolished.

Family policy reforms of past decades have strongly concentrated on increasing earmarked quotas for fathers, and encouraging fathers to make use of their right for parental leave. However, quotas are not highly favoured by Finnish people; rather, they wish that families had more freedom and flexibility to decide on the use of parental leaves (Kontula 2018). As it stands, the decision is nearly always that the mother stays at home and cares for a child. Freedom to choose does not thus appear an effective way to promote gender equality. To attain more equal division of family leaves, attitudes of both employers and employees need to change. A change in attitudes in workplaces and society towards more acceptance of fathers equally taking the responsibility for childcare not only adds to the rights of the fathers as carers and the rights of the child to the care of both parents (Lammi-Taskula 2017). Longer parental leave spells of fathers have further positive effects on the commitment of fathers in childcare and homework in the longer perspective (Tamm 2018). Changes in attitudes and culture, however, take place at a very slow pace.

The Finnish case draws our attention to the fact that, even in a nominally gender-equal country, considerable inequalities in careers, earnings and pension exist. These inequalities also reflect some of the challenges that the Nordic – and also other European – welfare states face. First, women's strong labour market participation is a cornerstone of the Nordic welfare model, and in order to secure the tax base for the kind of welfare systems the Nordic countries are pursuing, employment rates and working-life lengths need to be increased (this in particular in Finland; Kautto and Kuitto 2021). However, in its current form the Finnish welfare state relies heavily on the less expensive labour provided by women in the public sector (Koskinen Sandberg 2018) and diminishing the labour market segregation may have some consequences for the provision, esteem and price of public welfare services as well.

Second, decreasing fertility is a serious problem not only in Finland, but in many other countries as well. An ageing population challenges the financial sustainability and the generational justice of pension systems (Birnbaum et al. 2017; OECD 2017). Persistent inequalities in child-rearing and the career risk that comes with it are not positive incentives for having children for young women. By aiming clearly at a more equal division of family leaves and offering high-quality public childcare easily available for all, family policy can potentially help to overcome institutional barriers for having children, and support family-friendly attitudes in society.

This Finnish example is but one piece of evidence on how life courses affect pensions and inequalities in old age; in the words of Gøsta Esping-Andersen, 'a good retirement policy must begin with babies' (Esping-Andersen 2009: 163). Social policies, early education and family policies in particular that combat inequalities from the beginning of the life course are likely to be more effective in levelling out gender inequalities in the labour market and later in retirement than any reforms of the pension system alone (Esping-Andersen 2009; Morel et al. 2012; Bonoli 2013).

NOTES

1. Only France, Germany, Italy, and the United Kingdom (up to an earnings threshold) grant some child credit for pensions regardless of whether parents stop working or not (OECD 2015).
2. We thank Suvi Ritola from the Finnish Centre for Pensions for these model calculations.

REFERENCES

Angelov, N., P. Johansson and E. Lindahl (2016), 'Parenthood and the gender gap in pay', *Journal of Labor Economics*, **34**(3), 545–579.

Barr, N. (2013), *The Pension System in Finland: Adequacy, Sustainability and System Design*, Helsinki: Finnish Centre for Pensions.

Betti, G., F. Bettio, T. Georgiadis and P. Tinios (2015), *Unequal Ageing in Europe: Women's Independence and Pensions*, New York, NY: Palgrave.

Birnbaum, S., T. Ferrarini, K. Nelson and J. Palme (eds) (2017), *The Generational Welfare Contract: Justice, Institutions and Outcomes*, Cheltenham, UK and Northampton, MA, USA: Edward Elgar Publishing.

Boll, C., A. Rossen and A. Wolf (2016), *The EU Gender Earnings Gap: Job Segregation and Working Time as Driving Factors*, HWWI Research Paper 176, Hamburg: Hamburg Institute of International Economics.

Bonoli, G. (2013), *The Origins of Active Social Policy*, Oxford: Oxford University Press.

Börsch-Supan, A. (2005), *The 2005 Pension Reform in Finland*, Working Papers 2005:1, Helsinki: Finnish Centre for Pensions.

Budig, M., J. Misra and I. Böckmann (2012), 'The motherhood penalty in cross-national perspective: the importance of work–family policies and cultural attitudes', *Social Politics: International Studies in Gender, State & Society*, **19**(2), 163−193.

Ebbinghaus, B. (2011), 'Introduction: studying pension privatization in Europe', in B. Ebbinghaus (ed.), *The Varieties of Pension Governance: Pension Privatization in Europe*, Oxford: Oxford University Press, pp. 3–22.

Ellingsæter, A.L. (2012), *Cash for Childcare: Experiences from Finland, Norway and Sweden*, Friedrich Ebert Stiftung International Policy Analysis, April 2012, Berlin: Friedrich Ebert Stiftung.

Esping-Andersen, G. (2009), *The Incomplete Revolution: Adapting Welfare States to Women's New Roles*, Oxford: Oxford University Press.

European Commission (2009), *Gender Segregation in the Labour Market: Root Causes, Implications and Policy Responses in the EU*, Luxembourg: Publications Office of the European Union.

Evertsson, M., and A.Z. Duvander (2011), 'Parental leave: possibility or trap? Does family leave length effect Swedish women's labour market opportunities?', *European Sociological Review*, **27**(4), 435–450.

Finnish Centre for Pensions (2020), Statistical database, accessed 13 March 2020 at https://tilastot.etk.fi/pxweb/en/ETK.

Frericks, P., T. Knijn and R. Maier (2009), 'Pension reforms, working patterns and gender pension gaps in Europe', *Gender, Work and Organisation*, **16**(6), 710–730.

Ginn, J., and S. Arber (1992), 'Towards women's independence: pension systems in three contrasting European welfare states', *Journal of European Social Policy*, **2**(4), 255–277.

Gruber, J., and D.A. Wise (2004), *Social Security Programs and Retirement around the World*, Chicago, IL: University of Chicago Press.

Haataja, A., and V.-P. Juutilainen (2014), *Kuinka pitkään lasten kotihoitoa? Selvitys äitien lastenhoitojaksoista kotona 2000-luvulla*, Working Papers 58, Helsinki: Kela Research Department.

Hakovirta, M., S. Kuivalainen and M. Rantalaiho (2013), 'Welfare state support of lone parents: Nordic approaches to a complex and ambiguous policy issue', in I. Harslof and R. Ulmestig (eds), *Changing Social Risk in the Nordic Countries*, London: Palgrave Macmillan, pp. 50–74.

Hernes, H. (1987), *Welfare State and Woman Power: Essays in State Feminism*, Oslo: Norwegian University Press.

Hiilamo, H., and O. Kangas (2009), 'Trap for women or freedom to choose? The struggle over cash for child care schemes in Finland and Sweden', *Journal of Social Policy*, **38**(3), 457–475.

Kangas, L., and P. Luna (2011), 'Finland: from the public dominance towards private schemes', in B. Ebbinghaus (ed.), *Varieties of Pension Governance: Pension Privatization in Europe*, Oxford: Oxford University Press, pp. 210–239.

Kaufmann, G., and P. Uhlenberg (2000), 'The influence of parenthood on the work effort of married men and women', *Social Forces*, **78**(3), 931–947.

Kauhanen, A., M. Kauhanen, P. Laine, R. Lilja, M. Maliranta and E. Savaja (2015), *Työelämän muutosten vaikutukset naisten ja miesten työmarkkina-asemaan ja samapalkkaisuuteen*, Ministry of Social Affairs and Health Reports 2015:10, Helsinki: Ministry of Social Affairs and Health.

Kautto, M. (2017), 'Reforming pensions in Finland: multi-pillar stability in the context of changes within the first pillar', in D. Natali (ed.), *The New Pension Mix in Europe: Recent Reforms, Their Distributional Effects and Political Dynamics*, Brussels: P.I.E. Peter Lang, pp. 99–124.

Kautto, M., and K. Kuitto (2021), 'The Nordic countries', in D. Béland, S. Leibfried, K. Morgan, H. Obinger and C. Pierson (eds), *The Oxford Handbook of the Welfare State*, 2nd edition, Oxford: Oxford University Press (forthcoming).

Kela (2018), Perhevapaat tietopaketti, accessed on 28 April 2018 at www.kela.fi/perhevapaat-tietopaketti.

Kela (2020), Families, accessed on 8 December 2020 at www.kela.fi/web/en/families.

Kellokumpu, J. (2007), *Perhevapaiden kehitys 1990-2005: Isillä päärooli uudistuksissa, sivurooli käyttäjinä*, Labour Institute for Economic Research Reports 10, Helsinki: Labour Institute for Economic Research.

Kleven, H., C. Landais, J. Posch, A. Steinhauer and J. Zweimüller (2019), *Child Penalties Across Countries: Evidence and Explanations*, NBER Working Paper No. 25524 February 2019, Cambridge, MA: National Bureau of Economic Research.

Kontula, O. (2018), *2020-luvun perhepolitiikka. Perhebarometri 2018*, Katsauksia E52/2018, Helsinki: Väestöntutkimuslaitos.

Koskenvuo, K. (2016), 'Perhevapaiden vaikutus eläkkeeseen 1980-luvulta 2000-luvulle', in A. Haataja, I. Airio, M. Saarikallio-Torp and M. Valaste (eds), *Laulu 573566 perheestä*, Helsinki: Kela, pp. 116–135.

Koskinen Sandberg, P. (2018), 'The corporatist regime, welfare state employment, and gender pay inequity', *NORA: Nordic Journal of Feminist and Gender Research*, **26**(1), 36–52.

Koslowski, A.S. (2011), 'Working fathers in Europe: earning and caring', *European Sociological Review*, **27**(2), 230–245.

Kuitto, K., J. Salonen and J. Helmdag (2019), 'Gender inequalities in early career trajectories and parental leaves: evidence from a Nordic welfare state', *Social Sciences*, **8**(9), 253.

Kuivalainen, S., N. Järnefelt, K. Kuitto and S. Ritola (2019), *Naisten ja miesten eläke-erot. Katsaus tilastoihin ja tutkimuksiin*, Sosiaali- ja terveysministeriön raportteja ja muistioita 2019:66, Helsinki: Sosiaali- ja terveysministeriö.

Kuivalainen, S., and K. Kuitto (2021, forthcoming), 'Pension reforms in Finland', in J. Kolaczkowski, M. Maher, Y. Stevens and J. Werbrouk (eds), *The Evolution of Supplementary Pensions: 25 Years of Pension Reform*, Cheltenham, UK and Northampton, MA, USA: Edward Elgar Publishing.

Kuivalainen, S., S. Nivalainen, N. Järnefelt and K. Kuitto (2018), 'Length of working life and pension income: empirical evidence on gender and socioeconomic differences from Finland', *Journal for Pension Economics and Finance*, DOI:10.1017/S1474747218000215.

Lammi-Taskula, J. (2007), *Parental Leave for Fathers? Gendered Conceptions and Practices in Families with Young Children in Finland*, Research Reports 166, Helsinki: Stakes.

Lammi-Taskula, J. (2017), 'Fathers on leave alone in Finland: negotiations and lived experiences', in M. O'Brian and K. Wall (eds), *Comparative Perspectives on Work–Life Balance and Gender Equality*, Life Course Research and Social Policies 6, Springer Online, pp. 89–106.

Lammi-Taskula, J., M. Salmi and J. Närvi (2017), 'Isien perhevapaat', in M. Salmi and J. Närvi (eds), *Perhevapaat, talouskriisi ja sukupuolten tasa-arvo*, Helsinki: National Institute for Health and Welfare, pp. 105–134.

Lilja, R., and E. Savaja (2013), *Sukupuolten välinen palkkauksellinen tasa-arvo yksityisillä palvelualoilla. Selvitys miesten ja naisten palkkakehityksestä vuosilta 2007–2010 kaupan alalla, kiinteistöpalvelualalla sekä matkailu-, ravintola- ja vapaa-ajan palveluissa*, Reports 24, Helsinki: Pellervo Economic Research.

Möhring, K. (2015), 'Employment histories and pension incomes in Europe', *European Societies*, **17**(1), 3–26.

Morel, N., B. Palier and J. Palme (eds) (2012), *Towards a Social Investment Welfare State? Ideas, Policies and Challenges*, Bristol: Policy Press.

Närvi, J. (2014), 'Äidit kotona ja työssä – perhevapaavalinnat, työtilanteet ja hoivaihanteet', *Yhteiskuntapolitiikka*, **79**(5), 543–552.

Närvi, J. (2017), 'Äitien perhevapaat ja osallistuminen työelämään', in M. Salmi and J. Närvi (eds), *Perhevapaat, talouskriisi ja sukupuolten tasa-arvo*, Report 4/2017, Helsinki: National Institute for Health and Welfare, pp. 64–204.

Närvi, J., and M. Salmi (2019), 'Quite an encumbrance? Work-related obstacles to Finnish fathers' take-up of parental leave', *Community, Work & Family*, **22**(1), 23–42.

National Institute for Health and Welfare (2019a), *Perhevapaajärjestelmä ja korvaukset*, accessed on 15 August 2019 at https://thl.fi/fi/tutkimus-ja-kehittaminen/tutkimukset-ja-hankkeet/perhevapaatutkimus/perhevapaajarjestelma-ja-korvaukset.

National Institute for Health and Welfare (2019b), *Tilastotietoa perhevapaiden käytöstä*, accessed on 16 July 2019 at https://thl.fi/fi/tutkimus-ja-kehittaminen/tutkimukset-ja-hankkeet/perhevapaatutkimus/tilastotietoa-perhevapaiden-kaytosta.

OECD (2015), *Pensions at a Glance 2015*, Paris: OECD.

OECD (2016), *OECD Economic Survey Finland 2016*, Paris: OECD.

OECD (2017), *Preventing Ageing Unequally*, Paris: OECD.

OECD (2018a), *OECD Pensions Outlook 2018*, Paris: OECD.

OECD (2018b), *OECD Economic Survey Finland 2018*, Paris: OECD.

OECD (2019), *Pensions at a Glance 2019*, Paris: OECD.

Orloff, A.S. (1993), 'Gender and the social rights of citizenship: the comparative analysis of gender relations and welfare states', *American Sociological Review*, **58**(3), 303–328.

Peutere, L., A. Haataja, J. Vahtera, M. Kivimäki, J. Pentti and P. Virtanen (2014), 'Heikentääkö kotihoidon tuen kuntalisä äitien kiinnittymistä työelämään?', *Yhteiskuntapolitiikka*, **79**(3), 291–305.

Pietiläinen, M. (ed.) (2013), *Työ, talous ja tasa-arvo*, Helsinki: Statistics Finland.

Reipas, K., and M. Sankala (2015), *Effects of the 2017 Earnings-Related Pension Reform: Projections Based on the Government Bill*, Reports 08/2015, Helsinki: Finnish Centre for Pensions.

Rissanen, T. (2012), 'Kotiin, töihin, työttömäksi – siirtymät työelämän ja kotihoidon tuen välillä', in J. Sipilä, M. Rantalaiho, K. Repo and T. Rissanen (eds), *Rakastettu ja vihattu kotihoidon tuki*, Tampere: Vastapaino, pp. 151–182.

Sieppi, A., and J. Pehkonen (2019), 'Parenthood and gender inequality: population-based evidence on the child penalty in Finland', *Economic Letters*, **182**(2019), 5–9.

Sipilä, J., and J. Korpinen (1998), 'Cash versus child care services in Finland', *Social Policy & Administration*, **32**(3), 263–277.

Sipilä, J., M. Rantalaiho, K. Repo and T. Rissanen (eds) (2012), *Rakastettu ja vihattu kotihoidon tuki*, Tampere: Vastapaino.

Sipilä, J., K. Repo and T. Rissanen (eds) (2010), *Cash-for-Childcare: The Consequences for Caring Mothers*, Cheltenham, UK and Northampton, MA, USA: Edward Elgar Publishing.

Sorsa, T., and Rotkirch, A. (2020), Työ ja perhe ne yhteen soppii? *Vanhemmuuden ja työn yhteensovittaminen suomalaisissa lapsiperheissä*, Katsauksia E42/2020, Helsinki: Väestöntutkimuslaitos.

Statistics Finland (2018), *Sukupuolten tasa-arvo: Työelämä*, accessed 18 July 2019 at www.tilastokeskus.fi/tup/tasaarvo/tyoelama/index.html#segregaatio.

Takala, M., J. Salonen and J. Lampi (2015), *Survivors' Pensions in Finland*, Working Papers 02/2015, Helsinki: Finnish Centre for Pension.

Tamm, M. (2018), *Fathers' Parental Leave-Taking, Childcare Involvement and Mothers' Labor Market Participation*, SOEP Papers 1006-2018, Berlin: DIW.

Tikanmäki, H., S. Lappo, V. Merilä, T. Nopola, K. Reipas and M. Sankala (2019), *Statutory Pensions in Finland: Long-Term Projections 2019*, Reports 07/2019, Helsinki: Finnish Centre for Pensions.

Tuominen, E. (2004), *Gender Mainstreaming in the Finnish Pension Reform 2005*, Working Papers 10, Helsinki: Finnish Centre for Pensions.

World Economic Forum (2020), *Global Gender Gap Report 2020*, Geneva: World Economic Forum.

10. Approaches to minimum-income protection in old age: comparing the three Scandinavian countries

Axel West Pedersen

1. INTRODUCTION

The provision of relatively generous minimum benefits in old age has traditionally been an important distinctive feature of the Nordic pension systems and, arguably, one of the hallmarks of the ideal type notion of the Nordic welfare state. This chapter offers a comparative study of the current minimum-income protection schemes for old-age pensioners in Denmark, Norway and Sweden.

The primary purpose of the chapter is to describe and assess developments in the overall generosity of minimum protection provided through the pension system proper and other relevant instruments. To what extent has the historical legacy of generous minimum protection been upheld in the three countries, despite extensive reforms intended to improve the financial sustainability of the respective systems?

Second, the interaction between minimum protection and the earnings-related components of the respective pension systems will be analysed with a view to the implications it might have for distributive outcomes and labour market incentives. Additional aspects covered in the comparison are the implicit equivalence scales, residency requirements and flexibility offered with respect to the timing of benefit take-up.

It is a central premise of the chapter that the overall distributive outcome among old-age pensioners in each country is strongly dependent on the generosity of minimum protection schemes and the way they are designed to interact with the contributory, earnings-related parts of the respective national systems. Deciding on the level of minimum protection, and on the way minimum benefits are integrated with the earnings-related parts of the system, poses intricate dilemmas for policy makers that over the last decades have been met with rather different responses in the three Scandinavian countries.

After providing a brief sketch of the historical background in Section 2, the current architecture of minimum protection is described in Section 3. Section 4 presents findings on the development over time in the generosity of minimum protection, while Section 5 investigates the interaction between minimum protection and contributory (public and private) pensions. The findings are summarised and discussed in the concluding section.

2.   A SKETCH OF THE HISTORICAL BACKGROUND

The pension systems in the three Scandinavian countries are rooted in what we might call a Nordic/Anglo-Saxon tradition for redistributive minimum protection in old age. This tradition is characterised by providing flat-rate (universal or means-tested) benefits to all elderly people based on citizenship or residence. The approach that is sometimes somewhat ahistorically referred to as 'Beveridgean' can be contrasted with the 'Bismarckian' social insurance tradition, with its emphasis on prior contributions and earnings-related benefits, that has tended to dominate in Continental Europe.

Denmark pioneered the development of this minimum protection approach in 1891 by introducing a law that required municipalities to provide cash benefits to the elderly without alternative means of subsistence. However, this first Danish pension law was little more than a system of poor relief targeted towards the elderly. Therefore, it can be argued that a distinctive Scandinavian approach to pension provision was only fully developed during the 1930s, when Denmark, Sweden and Norway introduced reforms that led to significantly improved levels of minimum-income protection for all elderly residents in the form of (mainly) tax-financed, flat-rate benefits (Hort 1990; Pedersen and Kuhnle 2017; cf. Baldwin 1990). While old-age benefits from these reformed systems were subject to both income and asset testing, little administrative discretion was involved, and the tapering rules were relatively mild. As a consequence, these old-age benefits were firmly rights-based and only a minority of the elderly population was excluded from receiving benefits (see Pettersen 1982; Hort 1990; Petersen and Petersen 2009). Also in Finland, where the pension system had previously followed the insurance path, a tax-financed minimum benefit for the elderly was introduced in the late 1930s (Salminen 1993).

In the early post-war period, a common reform trend in the three Scandinavian countries was to abandon or limit the use of means-testing and introduce full universalism in the provision of old-age benefits. In Sweden (1946) and Norway (1959), means-testing of old-age benefits was completely abolished, and minimum protection began to take the form of a truly universal, flat-rate income transfer to all residents above a specific age (67 in Sweden and 70 in

Norway) (Elmér 1986; Pettersen 1987). Also, in Denmark universal old-age benefits were introduced through legislation enacted in the 1950s, but here the introduction and expansion of a basic universal benefit was combined with the preservation of an income- and asset-tested supplementary benefit (Petersen and Petersen 2009).

These moves towards more universalistic systems of minimum protection were quickly followed (or even partly preceded) by debates on the possible introduction of a more insurance-like second tier of earnings-related pensions. In Sweden (1961) and Norway (1967) this debate resulted in major reforms of the respective public pension systems, introducing a second tier of earnings-related benefits on top of the existing first tier of flat-rate benefits (Molin 1965; Pedersen 1990). The national pension systems of these two countries have since been characterised by a compromise between a residency-based minimum protection of the first tier and a contributory insurance logic of the second tier. Both the Swedish 'ATP' system (*Allmän tilläggspension*) and the somewhat more modest Norwegian *Folketrygdens tilleggspensjon* were 'point systems' where benefits were linked to the earnings levels enjoyed over a number of the best years (15 and 20 years respectively) and requiring a longer contribution period (30 and 40 years, respectively) to receive full benefits.

In Denmark, however, a general, obligatory second tier of earnings-related pensions was never introduced. A rather modest obligatory contributory pension scheme (ATP; *Arbejdsmarkedets Tillægspension*) was introduced in the 1960s, but benefits and contributions in this scheme were tied to years of employment and not the level of earnings. Several attempts were made in both the 1970s and late 1980s to introduce a more substantive, earnings-related second tier, but they all failed (Vesterø Jensen 1985). Thus, the Danish public pension system has remained faithful to the goal of providing flat-rate (partly means-tested) benefits only. Instead, a comprehensive system of negotiated defined-contribution occupational pension schemes was developed in the 1990s. These industry-wide schemes automatically enrol all workers covered by the relevant collective wage agreement, and they encompass more than 80 per cent of the Danish workforce (Kangas, Lundberg and Ploug 2010).

In the 1970s and 1980s, the structure of minimum protection was gradually changed in both Sweden and Norway. In the early 1970s, a targeted supplementary benefit was introduced to top up the universal basic pensions in both countries. The supplementary benefits were only tested against benefits from the earnings-related second tier, but with a 100 per cent taper. In this way they functioned as a sort of guaranteed-minimum-earnings-related benefit. Over time these supplementary benefits were systematically increased in order to compensate for the fact that the level of universal basic pensions was lacking behind developments in average wages. However, an unintended side effect of the expansion of the targeted supplements was that individuals with relatively low lifetime earnings (like women working part-time for significant parts of their life course) would not in reality benefit from having contributed to the earnings-related part of the system.

In the 1990s, Sweden once again pioneered a radical reform path by replacing the existing defined-benefit system with a notional defined contribution (NDC) system and a smaller, fully funded (FDC) system in which the accumulation of pension rights is proportional to earnings up to an annual ceiling just around a full-time average wage (7.5 times the 'income base amount') and featuring both automatic longevity adjustments of benefits and a flexible, actuarially neutral system for claiming benefits (Könberg et al. 2000). At the same time, the provision of a universal benefit floor was abandoned in favour of a targeted minimum benefit (guarantee pension) that is tested (tapered off) against benefits from the NDC and FDC systems.

About ten years later, Norway followed suit by introducing an NDC reform that started to take effect from 2011 (Christensen et al. 2012). Just like the Swedish prototype, the Norwegian reform introduced automatic longevity adjustments of benefits and a flexible, actuarially neutral system for claiming benefits, and it also involved the abandonment of a universal benefit floor in favour of a targeted minimum pension ('guarantee pension') that is tapered off against benefits from the NDC system.

3.   THE CURRENT CONTEXT AND ARCHITECTURE OF MINIMUM PROTECTION

While Denmark has developed a private, negotiated system of earnings-related pension schemes, Sweden and Norway both feature an obligatory public scheme with contributory, earnings-related benefits. Despite these differences in the institutional set-up, all three systems can be seen as having an earnings-related core aimed at providing (contributory) benefits that are roughly proportional to lifetime earnings.

In the Danish negotiated schemes, contribution rates range from 12 to 18 per cent of annual earnings, where one-third is typically paid by the employee and two-thirds by the employer (Pedersen et al. 2018). In Sweden contributions to the NDC system are fixed at 16 per cent of annual earnings, but on top of that a small, fully funded FDC system (*premiepension*) takes the combined contribution rate up to 18.5 per cent of annual earnings below the ceiling. The Norwegian NDC system is financed out of general taxation. The accrual rate is fixed at 18.1 per cent of annual earnings up to a ceiling of 720,000 NOK in 2020, corresponding to approximately 120 per cent of an average full-time wage.

The proportionality between lifetime earnings and retirement benefits comes with important modifications in all three countries. The Norwegian and

Swedish NDC systems contain (or are flanked with) a number of redistributive features, like a ceiling on annual earnings that count for the accrual of pension rights, subsidised accrual for parents with low earnings due to caring for small children, and accrual based on the receipt of social security benefits. These modifications are generally missing in the private, decentralised Danish system. In addition, the Norwegian and Swedish NDC systems are free from the inegalitarian implications of the exposure to capital market risks that are present in the fully funded Danish schemes, and differences in longevity between men and women, and between occupational groups, do not enter the annuity conversion upon retirement. Annuity conversion is required to be sex-neutral within each of the Danish negotiated schemes, but differences in the gender composition of the risk pools of the respective schemes are not compensated for (see Pedersen et al. 2018).

On the other hand, the Danish ATP system, with its flat-rate accrual formula, is a potentially equalising component that has no equivalent in the two other Scandinavian countries. The lack of risk pooling between different labour market segments in the Danish FDC schemes will also, to some extent, have egalitarian implications since groups of workers with relatively low education/ earnings and low life-expectancy are not required to enter a common risk pool with high-education/earning groups and high life-expectancy. Finally, both Sweden and Norway have developed occupational pension schemes on top of the earnings-related public schemes with benefit profiles that tend to be more or less regressive in contrast to the largely proportional Danish occupational pension schemes. The regressive nature of the schemes is primarily related to the fact that contribution rates are higher for earnings above the ceiling in the public NDC systems.

Hence, in terms of their implications for the distribution of income among old-age pensioners, the pay-as-you-go financed NDC systems of Sweden and Norway, and the fully funded Danish defined-contribution schemes, cannot be expected to be strongly divergent. None of them will in and by themselves rule out the risk of income poverty in old age, and none of them are explicitly designed to achieve significant and systematic income redistribution towards people with low lifetime earnings. These tasks are left to be handled by the respective minimum protection schemes.

The Nature of Minimum Pensions

All rich countries offer some kind of minimum-income guarantee for old-age pensioners – either through the pension system proper or in the form of social assistance (see OECD 2019, pp. 134–136). The minimum pension can be either universal or targeted or a combination, and targeting can be narrowly related to public pension income, or broader, including other income components like private pensions and income from capital, and possibly also involve an assets test.

While the three Scandinavian countries for several decades provided universal flat-rate benefits as an important part of the minimum protection system, this is no longer the case in the reformed Swedish and Norwegian systems. Only in Denmark does a universal basic benefit (*Folkepensionens grundbeløb*) continue to be the backbone of the minimum protection offered to old-age pensioners. The Danish basic benefit is in fact subject to a (relatively mild) earnings test, but it is not tested against other pension income nor against income from capital. Since a possibility has been introduced to voluntarily postpone the take-up of the basic benefit on actuarially neutral terms, the significance of the earnings test has been further reduced and the universalistic nature of the benefit has been strengthened. As already mentioned, a means-tested supplementary benefit (*Pensionstillæg*) has always been part of the minimum pension in Denmark, but its role was increased in the mid-1990s when the supplement was raised to constitute roughly half of the total minimum pension for a single pensioner. Until 2018 the minimum pension (*grundbeløb* and *pensionstillæg*) could be claimed at age 65, but beginning in 2019, and over the next three years, the pensionable age is to be raised by half-a-year per calendar year to reach 67 by 2022. The indexation of minimum pensions in Denmark is linked to the development in gross wages. For many years, a deduction of 0.3 percentage points was made from the wage indexation (but only in years when wages rose by at least 2.3 per cent), but this practice was abandoned in 2018, introducing full wage indexation of the minimum pension taking effect from 2019.

In both Sweden and Norway, the introduction of a guarantee pension to replace the former dual minimum protection schemes was associated with an explicit intention to uphold the same level of minimum protection as under the old system.

In Sweden, the design of the minimum pension guarantee was discussed in relation to three basic concerns: (a) not seriously reduce compensation levels for lower earnings levels compared to the existing system, (b) guarantee that all pensioners would have at least some effect of accrued NDC pension rights and (c) limit the share of the population whose marginal pension accrual was affected by the withdrawal of the benefit guarantee (SOU 1994, p. 214). While the first and second of these concerns require that the rate of withdrawal should be mild and always lower than 100 per cent, the third calls for a steep and rapid withdrawal. In the legislation adopted in 1998 it was decided to combine an initial 100 per cent withdrawal with a taper of 48 per cent for earnings-related benefits in excess of a certain threshold. This solution ensures that all except a small minority in the very lowest part of the earnings distribution will have at least some effect of contributions paid into the NDC and FDC schemes, and it ensures that the combined benefit profile is progressive over a larger part of earnings distribution. However, the downside is that a substantial share of the Swedish population – given the present ratio between average earnings and the minimum guarantee – can expect to be affected by the 48 per cent taper and, hence, have their effective marginal pension accrual seriously curtailed (Scherman 2001). Although the Swedish reformers in this way made significant concessions to distributive concerns in the short run, they gave priority to the principle of proportionality between contributions and benefits and, hence, to strengthening labour market incentives in the longer run. While all parameters and pension rights accrued in the NDC scheme are to be indexed with the development in average wages, the guarantee pension is indexed with prices only. In this way the minimum benefit guarantee is programmed to be gradually marginalised in line with the growth in real wages.

The Swedish guarantee pension can be claimed from age 65. It offers no possibility to postpone the take-up with actuarial adjustments, but there is no earnings test affecting the right to claim benefits and the size of benefits received.

In Norway, policy makers chose a somewhat different approach. In the detailed reform proposal prepared by the Stoltenberg government in 2006, it was suggested a constant taper of 80 per cent be applied against earned (contributory) pension rights. In this way all wage earners will always be guaranteed an increment in pension income from even the smallest lifetime earnings/contributions. However, as long as you remain within the taper interval, the marginal gain will be relatively modest (20 per cent; see Pedersen 2010), and the taper interval effects a large part of the distribution of lifetime earnings. The Norwegian policy makers chose indexation rules that link the minimum pension to developments in average wages, but with a deduction for increases in longevity among successive birth cohorts similar to the longevity adjustment integrated in the annuity divisor for the NDC benefits. In this way the benefit structure (the balance between minimum benefits and NDC benefits) should remain constant in the long run while benefit levels were set to decline in relative terms in line with future increases in longevity. In Norway the normal age of withdrawing the guarantee pension is set at age 67 (similar to the normal retirement age in the old system), but in contrast to the Swedish system an opportunity is offered to start claiming benefits earlier and postpone the claiming of guarantee benefits with full actuarial adjustments. However, early benefit claiming is strongly limited by a rule saying the resulting total annual pension benefit (the sum of NDC and guarantee benefits) should at least be at the minimum pension level at age 67 (Pedersen 2018).

Taxation, Housing Benefits and Schemes for Individuals with Short Residence

In Denmark, since the mid-1990s the taxation of old-age pensioners and of the minimum retirement benefits has been completely normalised, with the consequence that the recipients of minimum benefits pay a significant share of gross benefits in taxes. The income taxation of old-age pensioners and pension income in Sweden has also been largely normalised. In fact, after the introduction of an in-work tax credit (the so-called *jobbskatteavdraget*) in the 2000s, the taxation of a certain income from work has in periods been milder than the taxation of a similar income from pensions, but in recent years new special tax reliefs have been granted to old-age pensioners. By contrast, Norway has maintained favourable tax rules for pensioners with a view to making sure that pensioners who depend on minimum pensions only will not pay any income tax. After the pension reform of 2011 this was achieved primarily through a special targeted tax credit to old-age pensioners with low pension incomes (Pedersen 2010).

In all three countries old-age pensioners can apply for housing allowances on different (more generous) terms than the general population, and the provision of housing benefits can be seen to add to the minimum protection offered to old-age pensioners. As we shall see, the significance of housing allowances for minimum protection in old age is currently largest in Sweden, followed by Denmark and Norway. In all three countries the housing allowances are subject to means-testing (testing against income and wealth of the household) and depend on the size of housing expenditure. In Denmark a number of supplementary means-tested benefits should also be counted in as part of the minimum protection offered to old-age pensioners, including, for example, a special means-tested supplement (*Ældrecheck*), and a supplement to help cover expenditures on heating (*Varmetillæg*) (see Forsikring og Pension 2019).

In all the Scandinavian countries a residency test is applied to the receipt of minimum pensions. To receive full minimum benefits, 40 years of residency as an adult (four-fifths of the adult life phase) before reaching the pensionable age is required, and minimum benefits are reduced proportionally in cases where the residency period is shorter than this. In Denmark it was decided in 2018 to sharpen this criterion. Beginning in 2026 a person will be required to have been a resident for nine-tenths of the period between age 15 and the pensionable age in order to receive the full minimum pension, and the minimum pension is reduced proportionally if the share of life between age 15 and the pensionable age spent abroad exceeds one-tenth (Forsikring and Pension 2019, p. 163).

However, in the 2000s in Sweden and Norway it was decided to introduce subsidiary minimum schemes to cater to immigrants and others with a shorter residency record before reaching the pensionable age. In Sweden the subsidiary scheme (*Äldreförsörjningsstöd*) was introduced in 2003 while a similar scheme (*Supplerende stønad*) intended for elderly people who failed to meet the residency requirement to receive a full minimum pension was put in force in Norway in 2005. In the Norwegian version, benefit levels are identical to the levels provided through the normal minimum pension benefits. The only difference is that benefits from this residual scheme are strictly means-tested with a 100 per cent taper against all other incomes of the individual or the household, and benefits cannot be exported to other countries. The latter also applies to the Swedish equivalent, but here benefit levels are significantly lower than the guarantee pension offered to old-age pensioners with a full residency record.

4.   THE GENEROSITY OF MINIMUM PROTECTION

Figure 10.1 depicts the development in the level of minimum pensions (for single pensioners) net of taxes provided in the three countries between 1998 and 2019.

The top panel presents the development in the real value of minimum benefits measured in national currencies (2019 price levels). It shows how the real value of minimum pensions over the observation period has grown very fast in Norway, while it has been more stable in the two other countries. Over this period the real value of the minimum pension for a single pensioner in Norway has increased from NOK 10,500 per month to NOK 16,900 per month adjusted to 2019 prices, corresponding to an accumulated real increase of 61 per cent. In addition to full wage indexation that has prevailed until the onset of the Norwegian pension reform, the level of the minimum pension was raised by discrete political decisions on a number of occasions. However, the latest increases only apply to the minimum benefits offered under the old system that is still in the process of being phased out, and, therefore, the development of the minimum pensions can be expected to become less spectacular in the coming years as the longevity adjustment factor will start to take its toll. In Denmark the real value of the net minimum pension has increased from DKR (2019) 8,100 to DKR 10,700. Also, in Sweden the real value of the net minimum pension has increased from SEK 5,900 to SEK 7,900 adjusted to 2019 price levels. The real increase in the Swedish minimum pension is somewhat surprising, given the strict adherence to price indexation of the guarantee pension. However, part of the increase appears to be related to the transition to the guarantee pension and the parallel phasing out of the dual minimum benefit from the pre-reform pension system. In addition, reliefs in the taxation of old-age pensioners, and a discrete increase in the level of the guarantee pension taking effect in 2019, have contributed as well.

Real value in national currency (kroner), 2019

Real value in PPS US$, 2019

Relative value - per cent of average net wage

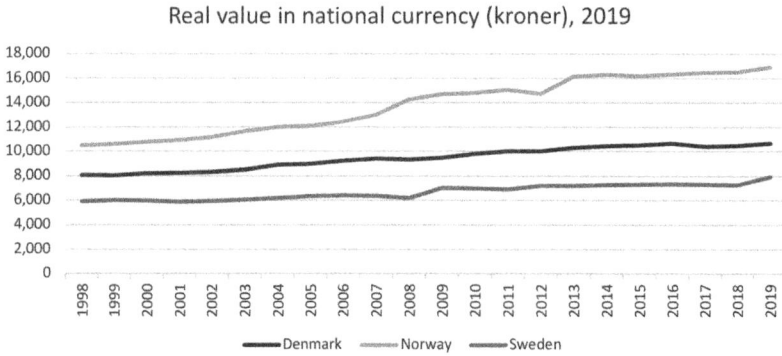

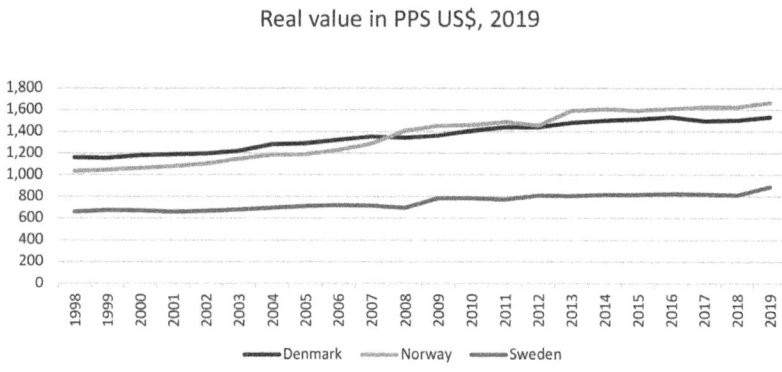

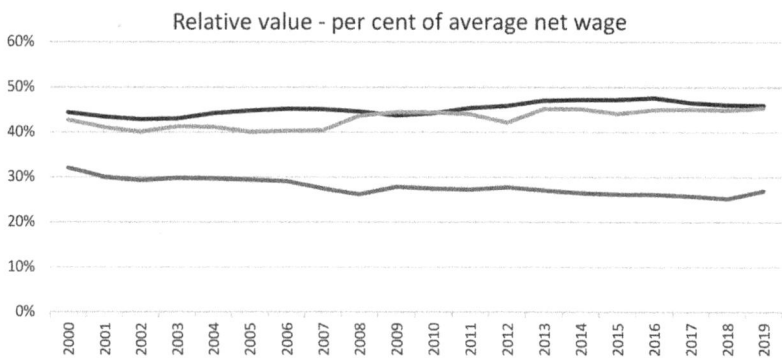

Source: NOSOSCO annual reports 1998 to 2016/2017, supplemented with author's calculations.

*Figure 10.1   Minimum pension net of tax for a single pensioner per month,
1998–2019*

In the middle panel, the real purchasing powers of the monthly net minimum pensions are made comparable across countries by converting them to purchasing power parities (PPS; US$) using 2019 conversion rates. Adjusting for cross-national differences in price levels shows that the purchasing power of the net minimum pension offered to single pensioners is roughly equivalent in Denmark and Norway, albeit with a slightly more positive development over time in Norway. Sweden, by contrast, lags seriously behind the two Scandinavian neighbours. In 2019 the purchasing power of the Norwegian net minimum pension is almost double the level found in Sweden, and the level in Denmark is only marginally behind. But these results must be seen in light of the significant differences in the general level of prosperity among the three countries, with Norway being by far the richest country.

Finally, therefore, the bottom panel of Figure 10.1 presents the development in minimum benefit levels measured relative to the national average wage net of taxes.[1] It shows that while the net relative generosity of minimum pensions has remained stable at a level around 45 per cent in both Denmark and Norway, the benefit level is much lower in relative terms in Sweden and shows a declining trend over time from about 32 per cent in the year 2000 to 25 per cent in 2018 and 27 per cent in 2019.

Implicit Equivalence Scales

An important caveat to the preceding comparison of the level of minimum pensions is that it has focused on single pensioners only. The finding that Denmark performs almost on a par with Norway both in terms of the purchasing power of minimum pensions and in terms of relative generosity (anchored in the net average wage) does not hold up for old-age pensioners living in couples.

As shown in Table 10.1, in both Norway and Sweden the minimum benefit offered to old-age pensioners living in couples is almost at the same level as the benefit offered to pensioners living alone. In Denmark, by contrast, the minimum pension for a single pensioner is significantly higher, presumably with a view to compensating for the lack of economies of scale and the higher living costs facing single-member households.

In inequality and poverty measurement, household incomes are routinely adjusted with equivalence scales that are supposed to reflect differences in economic needs between different household types. The widely used European Union (EU) equivalence scale assumes that a household with two adults (a pensioner couple) needs 1.5 times more income than a single-member household (a single pensioner) to achieve the same level of economic wellbeing. It is possible to extend this concept to compare the implicit equivalence scales embedded in the minimum pension system, by calculating the ratio between benefits offered to single and married/cohabiting pensioners.

Table 10.1   *Minimum pension benefit per month for single pensioners*
                 and pensioners living in a couple; national currencies
                 (Kroner) 2019

	Married/cohabitating pensioner	Single pensioner	Implicit equivalence scale
Denmark	11,247	14,717	1.31
Norway	15,159	16,902	1.11
Sweden	7,363	8,254	1.12

Sources: Forsikring and Pension 2019, www.nav.no/no/nav-og-samfunn/kontakt-nav/oversikt
-over-satser/minste-pensjonsniva, www.pensionsmyndigheten.se/forsta-din-pension/sa-fungerar
-pensionen/garantipension-om-du-har-lag-pension

The last column of Table 10.1 shows the implicit equivalence scale of minimum pensions in the three countries. While the implicit equivalence weight of the Danish minimum pension is 1.31, it is much lower in Norway and Sweden, at 1.11 and 1.12 respectively. Undoubtedly the implicit equivalence scales are more single-pensioner-friendly when housing benefits are taken into account.

In Norway the minimum pension system used to differentiate more strongly between single and married/cohabitating pensioners, but over the last decade the political emphasis has been on moving towards a more individualised benefit structure where the household situation is not taken into account (Pedersen 2018). In Sweden, by contrast, a recent white paper argues in favour of increasing the implicit equivalence scale of the minimum pension (Socialdepartementet 2018).

The Generosity of the Total Package of Minimum Protection

The three Scandinavian countries all operate housing allowance schemes with special provisions for old-age pensioners, and these schemes therefore should arguably be counted in as part of the minimum-income protection offered to old-age pensioners. The role of housing allowances is relatively modest in Norway and more important in both Denmark and (particularly) in Sweden. Therefore, the inclusion of housing allowances into the assessment of the generosity of minimum protection is likely to modify the picture of cross-national differences.

Figure 10.2 shows how pension benefits proper, housing allowances[2] and finally the payment of income taxes affect the level of minimum protection among old-age pensioners offered in the three countries in 2019. As in Figure 10.1, each panel in Figure 10.2 applies a different metric for the measurement of benefit levels: national currency, PPS US$ and finally a relative measure in terms of the respective average wage net of taxes.

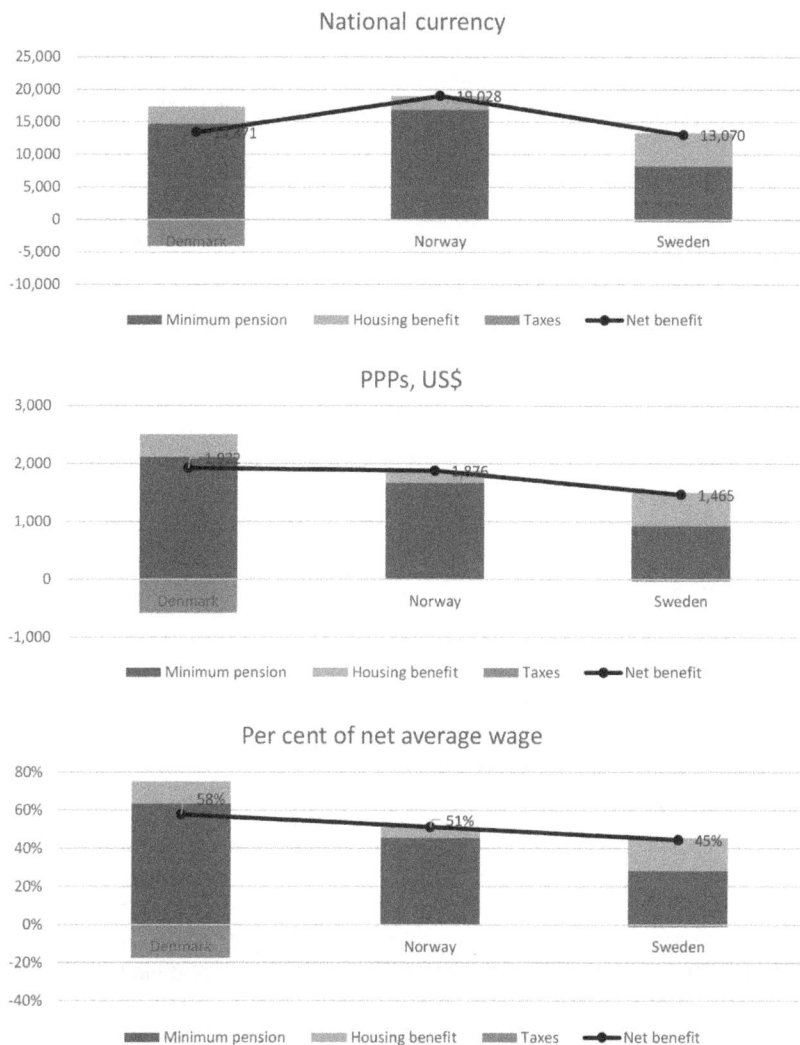

National currency

| | Denmark | Norway | Sweden |

Net benefit values: 15,271 (Denmark area), 19,028 (Norway), 13,070 (Sweden)

Legend: Minimum pension, Housing benefit, Taxes, Net benefit

PPPs, US$

Net benefit values: 1,922, 1,976, 1,465

Legend: Minimum pension, Housing benefit, Taxes, Net benefit

Per cent of net average wage

Net benefit values: 58%, 51%, 45%

Legend: Minimum pension, Housing benefit, Taxes, Net benefit

Sources: Author's calculations, Forsikring and Pension (2019), www.nav.no/no/nav-og-samfunn/
kontakt-nav/oversikt-over-satser/minste-pensjonsniva, www.pensionsmyndigheten.se/forsta-din
-pension/sa-fungerar-pensionen/garantipension-om-du-har-lag-pension

Figure 10.2   *The level and composition of minimum benefits for a single
pensioner, 2019*

The top panel confirms that the gross minimum pension is by far the highest in Norway, and that this is reinforced by minimum pensioners not paying any income tax. In Denmark the minimum pensioner pays a substantial amount in income tax, while the Swedish minimum pensioner only pays a very modest amount, primarily due to the general progressivity of the Swedish pension system and the low level of the minimum pension. The cross-national differences in the level of minimum protection are modified when housing allowances are taken into account. The housing allowance is most generous in Sweden and least generous in Norway.

The second panel shows that the ranking of the three countries is changed when we look at PPPs. The purchasing power of the minimum income offered to Danish single pensioners is slightly higher (1,922 US$) than the corresponding figure in Norway (1,876 US$) and significantly higher than in Sweden (1,465 US$). The same ranking appears in the bottom panel, where the generosity of minimum protection is measured in relative terms, in per cent of the net average wage in the respective country. While the net minimum pension amounts to 58 per cent in Denmark, it is 51 per cent in Norway and 45 per cent in Sweden.

As already mentioned, the performance of Denmark would have been less favourable if the comparison had been made for married/cohabiting pensioners, and most likely the ranking of Norway and Denmark in the second and third panels would have been reversed or at least equalised.

These differences in the generosity of minimum protection align with observed differences in the prevalence of financial poverty among the elderly in Sweden compared to Norway and Denmark. In 2018, 7.8 and 8.9 per cent of the Norwegian and Danish elderly (65-plus) were classified as financially poor according to the EU indicator, while the same applies to 14.6 per cent of the Swedish elderly.[3] While the poverty rates among the elderly have been falling very significantly in both Denmark and Norway over the last decade, they have remained stable at around 15 per cent in Sweden. This contrasts sharply with the situation in the 1980s, when Sweden featured one of the lowest financial poverty rates among the elderly in the Organisation for Economic Co-operation and Development (OECD) area (Kohl 1993; Smeeding 1993).

5.   INTEGRATION WITH EARNINGS-RELATED, CONTRIBUTORY PENSIONS

In all the three countries, minimum protection offered to old-age pensioners is, to a varying degree, targeted towards pensioners with a low accrual of earnings-related pension rights. As already pointed out, Denmark is the only country providing an unconditional universal basic pension to all retirees, but also in Denmark a significant part of the total minimum protection is subject to general income and asset testing. In Sweden and Norway, the guarantee pensions are targeted by being tested only against benefits from the respective earnings-related NDC systems,[4] and in these countries housing benefits offered to old-age pensioners are subject to broad income and assets testing.

Figure 10.3 illustrates how the various minimum benefits are related to the level of earnings-related pension benefits received. All values are expressed in relative terms using the average gross wage in each country as the anchor.

As illustrated in the Danish panel, the amount received from the basic pension is unrelated to the receipt of other pensioner income, and one could have chosen to let this be the first layer in the graph, before the contributory/ earnings-related benefit component. As already pointed out, contributory pensions in Denmark will have a smaller part stemming from the ATP system where only the number of years in employment count and a (much) larger part stemming from the system of earnings-related occupational pension schemes that reached a high coverage rate at the beginning of the 1990s. The remaining components of the Danish minimum protection system are all subject to general income and asset testing. The most important – at least for single pensioners – is the pension supplement, which operates with a rather high free amount and a relatively mild tapering of 30 per cent against incomes above the free amount. Consequently, the benefit is only tapered off completely when the level of contributory pensions reaches 75 per cent of the average wage. In addition, the tapering of the Danish housing allowance is relatively mild, which means that the benefit is only fully removed for single pensioners with contributory benefits equivalent to 56 per cent of the average wage.

The benefit structures in Norway and Sweden are simpler, with the guarantee pension being tapered off against earnings-related benefits from the public NDC/FDC schemes, and more broadly income-tested housing allowances. The latter component is much more important in Sweden compared to Norway.[5] Primarily due to the fact that the guarantee pension is relatively generous in Norway, the benefit is not tapered off completely before the earnings-related benefit reaches 41 per cent of the average wage, while the same happens in Sweden when the level of earnings-related benefits reaches a level equivalent to 30 per cent of the average wage. The opposite is the case for the respective housing allowance benefits that are much more generous in Sweden, and partly as a consequence of this, the tapering takes place over a longer interval. The housing benefit is tapered off in Sweden when the private/earnings-related pension exceeds 45 per cent of the average wage, while the same happens in Norway when the private/earnings-related pension reaches 31 per cent of the average wage.

Overall, it is apparent that the minimum protection systems are more strongly targeted towards pensioners with low earnings-related benefits (and, hence, with low lifetime earnings) in Norway and Sweden compared to Denmark. For a given level of minimum protection offered, less strict targeting means that

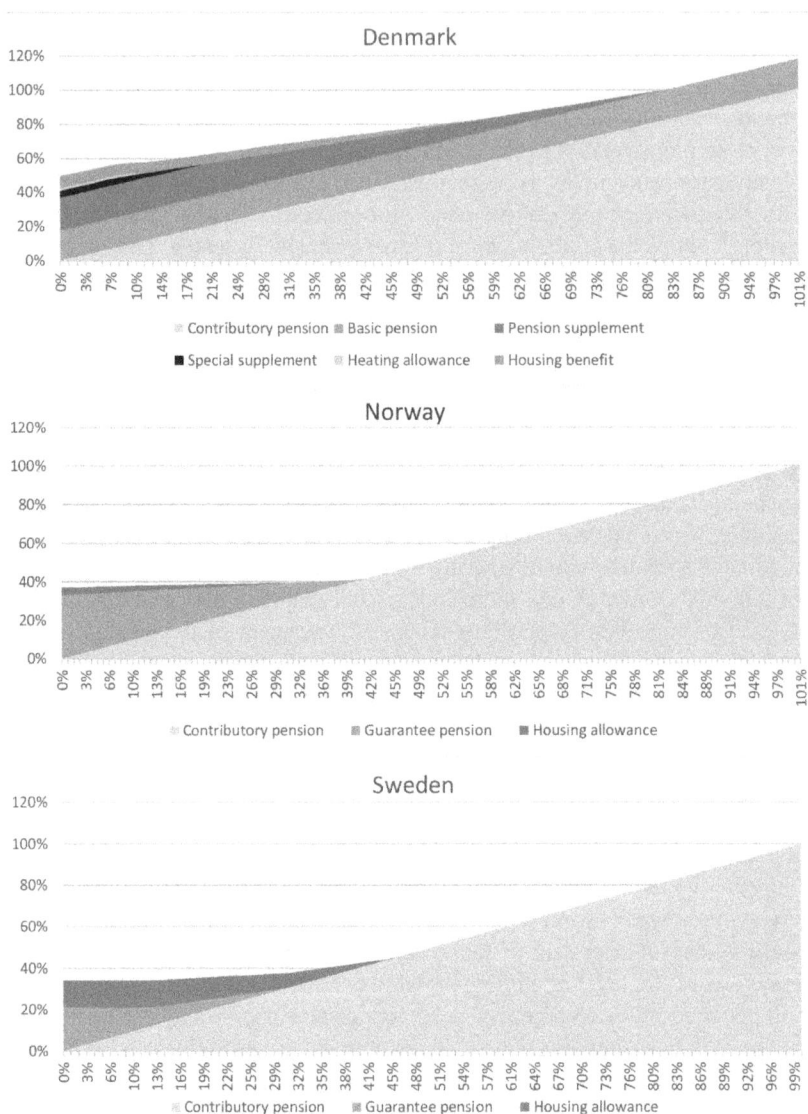

Source: Author's calculations – see endnote 2 about assumptions made related to housing costs and rents.

Figure 10.3   Pension benefits as a function of contributory pensions; per cent of average wage, 2019

the non-contributory benefits reach higher up in the income distribution among retirees and their redistributive effect is potentially stronger since it involves a larger share of the income distribution among old-age pensioners. The very strong targeting of the Swedish and Norwegian minimum protection systems mean that redistribution only affects the lower part of the income distribution among old-age pensioners, and for those who are affected the marginal gain in income from having built up contributory pension rights is seriously curtailed.

This is even more clearly brought out in Figure 10.4, which shows how the tapering/income testing of minimum pensions and the total package of minimum protection represents an implicit tax on contributory/earnings-related pension rights. The graph depicts how the total income of an individual is affected by an additional amount from contributory pensions. The tapering of minimum benefits implies that an additional amount received in contributory pensions is offset by reduced minimum benefits, and the effect is similar to a tax on contributory benefits. The rate of this implicit tax varies between 0 (no tapering) and 100 (when the additional contributory benefit is completely offset, leaving total income unchanged). The implicit tax rate can also exceed 100 per cent if the reduction in minimum benefits exceeds the increase in contributory pensions.

In Denmark the tapering of minimum benefits produces implicit marginal tax rates on contributory pensions which remain well below 50 per cent over the entire tapering interval. The only exception is the spike when contributory pensions constitute just above 10 per cent of the average wage, and the very high implicit tax in this short range is due to the joint tapering off of the two minor means-tested benefits, the special supplement and the heating allowance. But, of course, when ordinary income taxation is added to this, the compound marginal tax rate is significantly higher, and it has been shown to reach levels just above 70 per cent over a long range (Pensionskommissionen 2015, p. 17).

In Norway the implicit marginal tax rate associated with the tapering of the guarantee pension is 80 per cent. When adding the effect of means-testing of the housing allowance, we arrive at a total implicit marginal tax rate of 95 per cent over a broad interval. If the effect of income taxation had also been added to this, the marginal tax rate on contributory pensions comes very close to 100 per cent. In other words, contributory pension rights up to a level corresponding to 40 per cent of the average wage make very little difference to the recipients. Only when the guarantee pension is completely tapered off at a contributory pension corresponding to about 42 per cent of the average wage does the implicit marginal tax rate fall to zero, and the recipients actually start to benefit from additional earned pension rights.

In Sweden the implicit marginal tax rate associated with the guarantee pension is initially 100 per cent, but it is reduced to 48 per cent when the contributory benefit reaches about 14 per cent of the average wage, and it falls

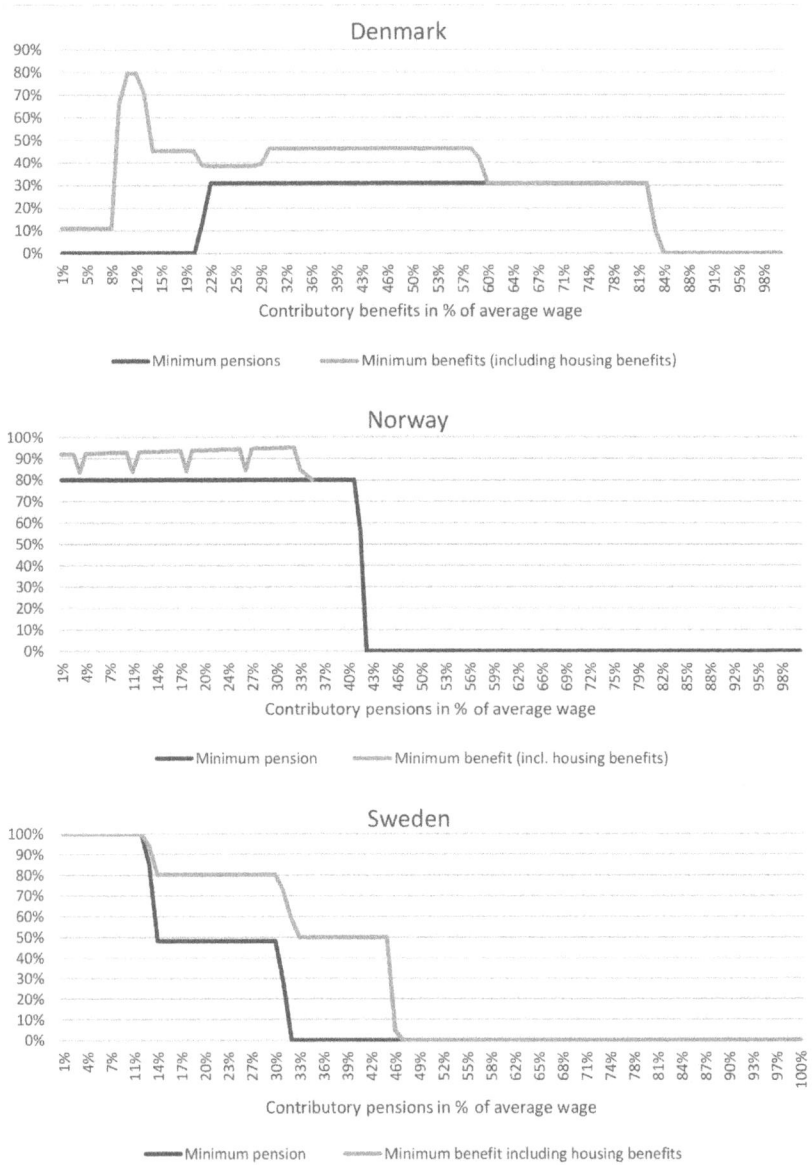

Source: Author's calculations.

Figure 10.4   Implicit marginal tax rates on contributory pensions, 2019

to zero when the contributory benefit reaches 30 per cent of the average wage.

The relatively short interval with very high marginal tax rates is primarily the result of the relatively low level of the Swedish guarantee pension. The Swedish housing allowance significantly improves the level of minimum protection offered to old-age pensioners (singles in particular), but it also significantly prolongs the interval with high marginal tax rates on contributory pensions.

6. CONCLUDING REMARKS

In Norway and Sweden minimum protection in old age has recently been reorganised in connection with major NDC pension reforms that are intended to improve the economic sustainability of the national pension systems, partly by limiting the growth of public pension expenditure and partly by stimulating higher labour force participation. The Danish system of minimum protection in old age that operates in the context of a mainly private, negotiated system of earnings-related pensions has been characterised more by continuity.

With respect to benefit generosity, the Danish and Norwegian systems of minimum protection are fairly similar, while the level of minimum protection offered to old-age pensioners in Sweden is significantly lower. This holds both in terms of absolute purchasing power and in terms of relative benefit levels measured against the average net wage. The difference is most pronounced when looking at the minimum pensions proper, but it holds up even when the relatively generous Swedish housing allowance is taken into account. Statistics provided by Eurostat (2021) confirm that financial poverty is much more prevalent among the aged (age 65 and beyond) in Sweden compared to the two other Scandinavian countries, where the financial poverty rates have declined significantly over the last decade.

The existing indexation rules in the respective countries indicate that these differences are likely to be perpetuated, and perhaps even amplified. The most generous indexation rules are found in Denmark, where full wage indexation was recently put in place. However, this must be seen in light of the fact that the age at which the minimum benefits can be taken out is about to be raised from the current 65 years to 67. Furthermore, it has been decided that the pensionable age will later be raised further in line with increases in longevity of the Danish population. In Sweden the guarantee pension is only indexed with prices, while in Norway full wage indexation is modified by the application of longevity adjustments to the guarantee pension.

As we have seen, the targeting of minimum pensions and minimum benefits more generally gives rise to high implicit marginal tax rates on contributory/ earnings-related pensions in all three Scandinavian countries. In both Sweden and Denmark this has figured as a serious concern in current policy debates.

In Sweden recent discussions about raising the level of minimum protection have resulted in only modest adjustments (Socialdepartementet 2018), and the main argument made against more resolute changes is that they would increase the taper interval and reduce the real gain associated with contributing to the NDC/FDC system for individuals with moderate lifetime earnings. In Norway stronger priority has been given to poverty prevention among the elderly, but with the cost of actually making participation in an earnings-related public pension system illusory for large segments of the workforce (see also Pedersen 2010).

Even if the implicit marginal tax rates are significantly lower in the Danish compared to the Norwegian and Swedish systems, the interaction between minimum protection and contributory pension rights has been pointed out as a serious problem in Denmark (Pensionskommissionen 2015), and a range of ad hoc measures have been taken recently to make sure that continued employment and payment of pension contributions for older workers actually pays off.

The fact that the Danish earnings-related schemes are private and have been built up as a result of trade unions giving up wage increases in exchange for pension contributions might help explain why high marginal tax rates on contributory pension benefits are politically less acceptable compared to Norway and Sweden, with a public, obligatory earnings-related system.

In all three countries, however, the same basic dilemma can be identified. On the one hand we have distributive concerns that require high minimum benefits. On the other we have concerns about improving or maintaining incentives for labour supply, and concerns about fairness in terms of maintaining a significant contribution/benefit link that requires implicit marginal tax rates on contributory pensions to be kept low for as many as possible. The Swedish and Norwegian system, combining an NDC pillar with a targeted minimum guarantee, does not in and by itself solve this dilemma, although it might help make it less politically controversial to uphold a minimum protection system that creates high implicit marginal tax rates on contributory pensions.

NOTES

1. Average net wages are obtained from the OECD Taxing Wages database: https://stats.oecd.org/Index.aspx?DataSetCode=AWCOMP.
2. Housing benefits are calculated using the following somewhat arbitrary assumptions about housing expenditures (rents) in the respective country cases. In Norway it is assumed that the housing expenditure of the single pensioner is equal to the maximum supported expenditure for a person resident in a major city (not Oslo): NOK 83,100. For the Swedish case a rent of SEK 60,000 is assumed, which gives a housing allowance of SEK 5,149 per month, which is close to the absolute maximum. For Denmark it is assumed a rent of DKR 60,000 per year (excluding expenditure on heating that is compensated for through a special heating subsidy).

3. The official label of this indicator is 'At-Risk-of-Poverty', and it classifies an individual as poor if the household income is less than 60 per cent of the population median. The figures are calculated by Eurostat based on data from European Union Statistics of Income and Living Conditions: https://ec.europa.eu/eurostat/ tgm/table.do?tab=table&init=1&language=en&pcode=tespn050&plugin=1.
4. In Sweden estimated benefits from the FDC system (*Premiepensionen*) also enter the calculation of the guarantee benefit.
5. The transition to the NDC system where the guarantee pension takes care of minimum protection will only take full effect for individuals born in 1963 or later. Even so, I have chosen to show the benefit structure of the new system while using 2019 figures for the level of minimum protection.

REFERENCES

Baldwin, Peter (1990), *The Politics of Social Solidarity: Class Bases of the European Welfare State 1875–1975*, Cambridge: Cambridge University Press.
Christensen, Arne Magnus, Dennis Fredriksen, Ole Christian Lien and Nils Martin Stølen (2012), 'Pension Reform in Norway: Combining an NDC Approach and Distributional Goals', in Robert Holzmann, Edward Palmer and David Robalino (eds), *Nonfinancial Defined Contribution Pension Schemes in a Changing Pension World, Volume 1: Progress, Lessons and Implementation*, Washington, DC: World Bank, pp. 129–154.
Elmér, Åke (1986), *Svensk socialpolitik*, Stockholm: Liber.
Eurostat (2021), European Union statistics of income and living conditions, https://ec .europa.eu/eurostat/tgm/table.do?tab=table&init=1&language=en&pcode=tespn050 &plugin=1.
Forsikring og Pension (2019), *Sociale ydelser - hvem, hvad og hvornår: håndbog i den sociale lovgivning med regler og ydelser 2019*, Hellerup: Forsikring og Pension.
Hort, Sven E. O. (1990), *Social Policy and Welfare State in Sweden*, Lund: Arkiv Förlag.
Kangas, Olli, Urban Lundberg and Niels Ploug (2010), 'Three routes to pension reform: Politics and institutions in reforming pensions in Denmark, Finland and Sweden', *Social Policy & Administration* **44** (3), 265–284.
Kohl, Jürgen (1993), 'Minimum Standards in Old Age Security and the Problem of Poverty in Old Age', in Anthony B. Atkinson and Martin Rein (eds), *Age, Work and Social Security*, New York, NY: St. Martin's Press, pp. 224–252.
Könberg, Bo, Edward Palmer and Annika Sundén (2000), 'The NDC Reform in Sweden: The 1994 Legislation to the Present', in Robert Holzmann and Edward Palmer (eds), *Pension Reform: Issues and Prospects for Non-Financial Defined Contribution (NDC) Schemes*, Washington, DC: World Bank, pp. 449–466.
Molin, Björn (1965), *Tjänstepensionsfrågan. En studie i svensk partipolitik*, Göteborg: Akademiförlaget.
NOSOSCO (1998 to 2016/2017), *Social Protection in the Nordic Countries*. All available publications. København: NOSOSCO.
OECD (2019), *Pensions at a Glance 2019*, Paris: OECD.
Pedersen, Axel West (1990), 'Fagbevegelsen og folketrygden. LOs målsetninger, strategi og innflytelse i pensjonspolitikken 1945–1966', Fafo-report no. 110, Oslo: Fafo.

Pedersen, Axel West (2010), 'Pensjonsreformen – status og konsekvenser for insentivene til arbeid', ISF-report no. 2010/1, Oslo: Institute for Social Research.
Pedersen, Axel West (2018), 'Assessment of Pension Adequacy in Norway 2017', ESPN Thematic Report, Brussels: European Commission.
Pedersen, Axel West, Jon Hippe, Anne Skevik Grødem and Ole Beier Sørensen (2018), 'Trade unions and the politics of occupational pensions in Denmark and Norway', *Transfer* **24** (1), 109–122.
Pedersen, Axel West, and Stein Kuhnle (2017), 'The Nordic Welfare State Model', in Oddbjørn Knutsen (ed.), *The Nordic Models in Political Science: Challenged, But Still Viable?* Oslo: Fagbokforlaget, pp. 219–238.
Pensionskommissionen (2015), 'Det danske pensionssystem - internationalt anerkendt, men ikke problemfrit', København: Pensionskommissionen.
Petersen, Jørn Henrik, and Klaus Petersen (2009), 'The Coalition of the Willing and the Breakthrough of the Welfare State: The Political History of the Danish People's Pension', in Jørn Henrik Petersen and Klaus Petersen (eds), *The Politics of Age: Basic Pension Systems in a Comparative and Historical Perspective*, Frankfurt: Peter Lang, pp. 19–40.
Pettersen, Per Arnt (1982), *Linjer i norsk sosialpolitik*, Oslo: Universitetsforlaget.
Pettersen, Per Arnt (1987), *Pensjoner, penger, politick*, Oslo: Universitetsforlaget.
Salminen, Kari (1993), *Pension Schemes in the Making: A Comparative Study of the Scandinavian Countries*, Helsinki: Central Pension Security Institute.
Scherman, Karl Gustav (2001), *Den nya pensionen. En reform med stora problem*, Stockholm: Sveriges Pensionärsförbund.
Smeeding, Timothy (1993), 'Cross-National Patterns of Retirement and Poverty among Men and Women in the Mid 1980s: Full Stop or Gradual Withdrawal?', in Anthony B. Atkinson and Martin Rein (eds), *Age, Work and Social Security*, New York: St. Martin's Press, pp. 91–114.
Socialdepartementet (2018), Ds 2018: 8 'Översyn av grundskyddet för pensionärer. Inriktning för ett nytt grundskydd', Stockholm: Regjeringskansliet.
SOU (1994), 'Reformerat pensionssystem', SOU 1994:20, Stockholm: Regjeringskansliet.
Vesterø Jensen, Carsten (1985), *Det tvedelte pensionssystem*, København: Forlaget Samfundsøkonomi og planlægning.

11. Pension systems as risk management: a case of the Baltic states

Olga Rajevska

INTRODUCTION

A pension system is a set of methods aimed at managing the risk of subsistence shortage in old age. Different elements of the pension system are focused on managing specific dimensions of this risk: the risk of low interest rates in funded schemes, risk of devaluation of savings, risk of longevity, risk of poor health, risk of a drop in living standards, and so on. Some of the risks are personal, while others are public or corporate, such as the risk of financial unsustainability or insolvency.

The aim of this chapter is to explore how risk perception and understanding have evolved by means of analysis and synthesis of experience in the functioning of pension systems under the circumstances of high uncertainty. It poses several questions: How do the existing pension schemes in the Baltic states reflect the way these risks are managed? What elements of pension systems are responsible for the implementation of these tasks? What similarities and differences can be found among Latvia, Estonia and Lithuania in the approaches to risk management?

The research is based on an analysis of the development of pension legislation in the three countries (laws and cabinet regulations), political documents (for example, reports of the World Bank; Organisation for Economic Co-operation and Development, or OECD; and European Commission, and documents from the International Labour Organization, or ILO) and statistical data (from the Eurostat online database, national social insurance agencies and financial supervisory authorities), demonstrating the performance of the considered pension systems. The author has also used numerous publications of pension system researchers from the Baltic states and their colleagues from other European countries.

The applicable risk management strategies are classified into four major groups: risk avoidance, risk reduction (mitigation), risk sharing (and risk transfer), and risk retention (acceptance) (see, for example, Dorfman and Cather

2013). We will consider what strategies and combinations of strategies can be found in the pension systems of the three Baltic states.

The study is organised as follows. First, a brief overview of the development of modern multi-pillar pension systems in Estonia, Latvia and Lithuania after restoration of their independence in the early 1990s, followed by an examination of the institutional design of the pension pillars, while at the same time looking at the risks that these pillars are supposed to manage. The development of financing principles of the Baltic pension systems and retirement age reforms are considered. There is a separate section for each of the three pillars, starting with a general description of its operational structure followed by a more detailed analysis of changes in recent years. In analysing pension pillars, their design and performance are assessed in terms of the effectiveness of managing the risks associated with pension provision. The risks specific to each pillar are reviewed, as well as the mechanisms aimed at controlling these particular risks. The chapter ends with conclusions, summarising trends in pension system development in the three Baltic states in recent years and assessing the set of risk management strategies used in them.

DEVELOPMENT OF MODERN PENSION SYSTEMS IN THE BALTIC STATES

Estonia, Latvia and Lithuania entered their new eras of independence with identical security systems for the elderly, inherited from the Soviet period. Pensions in the USSR were financed from the general state budget and no individual contributions by workers were made; entitlement to a pension was based on previous work experience and the amount of benefit linked to the size of wages during the last years of employment. Work record books were kept for all employees.

The processes of radical economic and political reforms in the early 1990s brought about the reform of the old social security system. All three countries promptly split financing of the pensions from the general budget by introducing social insurance budgets replenished by contributions made by employees and employers (or, in the case of Estonia, only by employers). While Lithuania did not reform the Soviet pension formula comprehensively until 1995, Estonia and Latvia adopted new pension laws in 1991, modifying into more generous pensions and keeping the amount of pension linked to preceding wages (Leppik and Võrk 2006; Vanovska 2006).

However, the new Estonian and Latvian laws had very short lives, having collided with the economic reality of collapsing enterprises, a sharp decrease in contribution bases and hyperinflation. In 1993, both Estonia and Latvia removed the earnings-related component from the formula, and pension benefit started to consist of two parts: a flat-rate basic pension and a component dependent on the length of service (that is, each year of employment and equalised periods amounted to a certain monetary value). Although the earnings-related component formally did exist in Lithuania, it took a very small fraction of the benefit, complemented with flat-rate supplements.

Thus, by the mid 1990s there was a strong demand for reformed pension systems capable of balancing assets and liabilities, and at the same time providing incentives for the population to pay contributions by linking the amount of pension to individual earnings for the whole working period. Lithuania was the first Baltic country to introduce contribution-based pensions, in 1995.

Pension reforms in the Baltic countries were very much influenced by the World Bank's seminal report 'Averting the Old-Age Crisis: Policies to Protect the Old and Promote Growth' (1994), which introduced the concept of the three-pillar pension system and actively propagated the substantial shift to privatisation of mandatory pensions. Redistribution in benefit formulas, widely regarded as excessive during the Soviet period, has been reduced or eliminated (Fultz and Hirose 2019).

So, by the middle of the 2000s, the structure of pension systems in all three countries included:

- Pillar I: state-managed compulsory pension schemes, operating on pay-as-you-go (PAYG) principles, financed by social insurance contributions ('pension tax') and offering earnings-related benefits;
- Pillar II: privately managed, compulsory and fully funded pension schemes, financed by social insurance contributions and participants' contributions;
- Pillar III: privately managed voluntary pension schemes, in the form of pension funds or life insurance policies offered by insurance companies.

PILLAR I: SOCIAL INSURANCE PUBLIC PAYG SCHEMES

International social security standards lay down certain general principles with regard to the organisation and management of social security systems. Thus, the ILO Social Security (Minimum Standards) Convention, 1952 (No. 102),[1] maintains that the state must accept general responsibility for the due provision of benefits and proper administration of the institutions involved, and that social security systems should be financed collectively by means of insurance contributions or taxation or both, so that the risks are spread among the members of the community. An essential part of the social security concept is pooling the risk through collective assumption of the financial burden of paying benefits (ILO 2017).

First pillars in the Baltic states are based on PAYG social insurance principles.

The Latvian first-pillar benefit is earned by all insured individuals by reg-
istering part of their social insurance contributions in personalised Notional
Pension Capital accounts. No actual money transfer takes place – this capital
exists only as a record in the State Social Insurance Agency database – and
the whole scheme is known as NDC: notional (or, in another reading of the
abbreviation, 'non-financial') defined contribution. The pension value is the
accrued notional capital at retirement divided by the projected life expectancy
at retirement age. The accrued notional capital is annually valorised (up-rated)
in line with the increase in the covered wage bill (that is, the total sum of all
socially insured wages in the country).

The first-pillar benefit in Estonia and Lithuania is comprised of two main
components: a general basic non-contributory one (in Estonia it is absolutely
flat, but in Lithuania it depends on the length of service), and an individual
insurance component, constructed quite similarly in the two countries and
based on variations of a pension point system (pension point is the ratio of
a person's social insurance contributions and the nationwide average social
contributions in a particular year).

In 2019, the system of financing the mandatory pillars in Lithuania was
radically changed. A fundamental reform was implemented: almost the whole
social insurance contribution was transferred to the employee's side, and only
the individual pension component based on pension points was funded from
social contributions, while the basic pension funding was transferred to the
general budget. This reform implied an essential change in the nominal wage,
rate of social insurance contribution and personal income tax. Despite all these
changes, the level of financing of the Pillar I pension system remained the
same (only indexed by the obligatory index prescribed by law).

Another important novelty was the introduction of a pension supplement
financed from the general state budget for those whose pension benefit
(general + individual) is lower than the minimum subsistence level (in 2020:
€257 per month). With this supplement, pensions are automatically raised to
the minimum, reducing the risk of poverty.

Both the basic component and monetary value of one pension point are
regularly revised (indexed). Pensions that are being paid are annually indexed,
taking into account the increases in the covered wage bill and consumer price
index (the latter in Estonia and Latvia only).

Risks of PAYG Schemes

From the state's point of view as the pension provider, the main systemic risk
in Pillar I is considered to be financial unsustainability of the social insurance
system and a pension budget deficit. Separating the social budget from the
general budget helped the payment of pensions to be covered by collecting

social insurance contributions from current employees. Automatic balancing mechanisms linking pension indexation and notional capital valorisation to the changes in the collected contributions (rather than changes in prices or average wages) have served this purpose in all three countries.

A rapid decline in population (mainly due to emigration) made it necessary for all Baltic States to take urgent measures to prevent social budget deficits. In order to increase the revenues, either the contribution rate or the number of contributors (or both) had to be increased. There was almost no direct increase in social contributions rate, but during the crisis years of 2008–2012 the share of pension contributions directed to Pillar II private funds was temporarily reduced in order to increase the revenues of the PAYG pillar. With the return to economic growth, the position of private funds has strengthened again, but in Latvia and Lithuania the pre-crisis proportions were not fully restored.

When the second pillars were established, Latvia and Lithuania financed them by carving out a share of social insurance contributions from the PAYG pillar, while Estonia introduced an additional contribution – 2 per cent of gross insured wage – to finance it (on top of carving out 4 percentage points, or p.p., from the social tax). This additional contribution was not formally considered an increase in the social tax though. Lithuania changed the financing scheme of the second pillar in a similar manner in 2014 by levying an additional 2 per cent on the gross wage of Pillar II participants, not changing the overall rate of social insurance contributions. Thus, in 2018 in Latvia 100 per cent of the second-pillar receipts were PAYG pension scheme transfers; in Lithuania, 80 per cent came from public sources (the PAYG pension scheme and state budget transfers) and 20 per cent came from private contributions from the participants (Lazutka, Poviliunas and Zalimiene 2018); while in Estonia two-thirds came from the collected social tax (PAYG scheme) and one-third from private contributions of the participants.[2] As a result of the aforementioned reform in 2019 in Lithuania, Pillar II is no longer financed from social contributions in that country.

To increase pension budget revenues, and reduce pension expenditures at the same time, another mechanism was used much more actively than the change in the social contribution rate. The number of contributors was increased by raising the statutory retirement age.

The author's calculations based on Eurostat data show that if Latvia had kept the retirement age at the 'Soviet' level, 55 years for women/60 years for men, there would be a 7 per cent increase in old-age pensioners in 2018 compared to 1990, with a simultaneous decrease of 33 per cent in the number of people of working age. Due to the increase of the statutory retirement age, which has been in place for more than 20 years, the number of both groups decreased proportionally, by 21 per cent by the end of 2018. Thus, it was possible to retain the old-age dependency ratio at the constant level.

The pioneer in raising the retirement age was Estonia, where it started in 1994. The initial regulation prescribed raising the statutory age by five years for both men and women (to reach 65 and 60 years of age respectively) in 10 years, increasing it by six months each year. In 1996, it was decided that the pace of growth was rising very fast, and was not fair to people born in different months of the same year, so it was reduced to four months per year (on average), and the finish line was shifted to 2007. In 1998, a whole package of laws on pension reform was adopted, changing the entire system. These included the equalisation of the age for men and women: the new goal was set at 63 years for both genders. Men reached this milestone in 2001, and for women the gradual increase lasted until 2016. At the same time, the possibility of early retirement with a reduced pension was introduced (Leppik and Võrk 2006).

Lithuania has been raising the retirement age since 1995. As in Estonia, it was planned to maintain the difference between men and women, but to make it smaller: to raise the age by 2.5 years for men and five years for women by 2009, increasing each year by two months for men and four months for women. In this country, in contrast to Estonia, the pace of growth was not slowed, but accelerated in 2001 to six months in a year, so the first stage of the statutory age increase was completed by 2003 for men and 2006 for women (Lazutka 2006).

Latvia has been raising the retirement age since 1996. Initially it was planned that only women's statutory age would be raised to 60 years, the same level as men. The rise was very fast; in the first year it was raised immediately by one year, and then by six months per year. In 1999, after the Russian default crisis,[3] the pension budget was threatened by a deficit, and it was decided to raise the retirement age by another two years in order to make it 62 years for both men and women. The government was planning to do it in one go, right from the following year, but opposition parties organised a referendum and the terms were relaxed, and the increase was kept to six months in a year. The raise was completed by 2003 for men and by 2008 for women.

There were talks about the need to further raise the retirement age in the early 2000s, but they did not receive sufficient support before the crisis. The shocks of 2008–2011, with falling employment, intensified emigration, sharp depletion of social budgets and austerity measures, all contributed to the adoption of the second wave of raising the retirement age in all three countries in 2010–2012.

Estonians were first to legislate the new increase: in 2010, despite criticism from the opposition and trade unions, a law was adopted, stating that from the point the female statutory age equalled the male one (63 years) in 2016, a further increase of three months a year would commence, to be completed by 2026, and reaching 65 years of age (Võrk, Leppik and Segaert 2010).

Similarly, at the beginning of 2010, a draft law was prepared in Lithuania to gradually raise the statutory retirement age to 65 years, starting in 2012 at a pace of six months per year. In the final version of the law adopted in 2011, the rate of growth slowed down to two months per year for men and four months per year for women, as in the 1990s. The goal is 65 years in 2026. At the same time, the rules on early retirement were relaxed (Jankauskiene and Medaiskis 2011, 2012).

In Latvia, the government first proposed raising the retirement age by six months a year, starting in 2016 and reaching the goal of 65 years by 2021. But in 2012 it was decided to halve the speed (as in Estonia), but to start two years earlier, in 2014, and extend the increase to 2025.

Thus, in 2020, the statutory retirement age in Estonia and Latvia is 63.75 years for both men and women, and in Lithuania 64 years for men and 63 years for women. Currently, the retirement age continues to rise in all three countries.

In December 2018, Estonia adopted the law with a new statutory pension age formula that will tie the statutory retirement age to life expectancy from 2027. That is, by 2026 it will reach 65 years of age, and then it will become 65 years plus an increase in life expectancy in comparison with the reference interval (2018–2022).[4] Also, from 2021, Estonia has introduced the so-called flexible pension instead of early/deferred retirement. The flexible pension will be actuarially neutral (the present system of deferred pensions is unfavourable for pension budgets) and should motivate people to prolong their working lives.

However, all these measures have not been able to fully protect pension budgets from deficit, and interventions from general tax budgets were necessary. ESSPROS (Eurostat) data show that old-age pensions[5] in the Baltic states are to a greater extent financed from social contributions compared to European Union (EU) countries. The average EU proportion in 2015 was as follows: 65 per cent of funding came from social contributions, 20 per cent from general taxation and 15 per cent from other revenues (interest on investments and other sources). The respective proportions in the Baltic States were: Estonia – 72.9 per cent + 23.2 per cent + 3.9 per cent, Latvia – 77.5 per cent + 17 per cent + 5.4 per cent, and Lithuania – 83.5 per cent + 16.1 per cent + less than 0.4 per cent (Spasova and Ward 2019). In Estonia and Lithuania deficits in the social insurance (PAYG) pension budget were covered by general tax revenue, while in the case of Latvia, formally the social insurance budget was not in deficit, but financing of the so-called pension supplements (a flat-rate allowance for pre-reform years of employment) was transferred from social insurance to general tax revenue. Similarly, since 2016 the state budget subsidises service pensions as well even after they are converted to old-age pensions when the pensioner reaches the official retirement age. There is a clear logical rationale in such a transfer of financing, since the rights to these benefits were not earned through social contributions.

Given the current demographic situation and the extremely low level of adequacy of old-age pensions, it seems inevitable that the general budget will increasingly participate in the financing of public pension insurance.

From the point of view of the risks borne by scheme contributors and not by the provider, PAYG schemes should safeguard them against the risk of poverty and ensuing social exclusion, the risk of declining living standards and the risk of devaluation of pension benefits with time.

Existing mechanisms do not sufficiently insure participants against these risks: statutory minimum pensions are well below the risk-of-poverty thresholds (particularly in Latvia), replacement rates are lower than the average EU indicators and are projected to decrease further (European Commission 2018), and indexation rules do not fully ensure that the purchasing power is maintained over time. This is the cause of a considerably higher level of poverty among old women than old men in the Baltics: in 2018, in the age group 65-plus, 53.3 per cent of women in Estonia were at risk of poverty or social exclusion as opposed to 36.1 per cent of men (the risk, therefore is 1.48 times higher for women), in Latvia 53.4 per cent of women and 40.1 per cent of men (risk ratio: 1.33) and in Lithuania 49.2 per cent of women and 29.8 per cent of men (risk ratio: 1.65). The EU-28 averages in 2017 equalled 20.6 per cent of women and 15.2 per cent of men (that is, 1.35 times higher for women). The basic pensions were not generous enough to keep women above the poverty risk, while men had additional income sources that reduced this risk. It should be noted that female pensioners tend to be older than men due to greater longevity, and they tend to be single (Ebbinghaus 2019).

The redistributive role of pensions is weaker in the Baltics than in the EU on average. The author has compared Gini coefficients before and after pensions; the calculations based on Eurostat dataset *ilc_di12c and ilc_di12b* were carried out in the same way as in the work of Dunajevas and Skučiene (2016), updated for the last available indicators of 2018. While including pensions (but not other social transfers) in disposable income causes a drop of 15.2 p.p. (that is, by 29.7 per cent) in the Gini coefficient in the EU-28, in Estonia the Gini coefficient drops by 10 p.p. (22.7 per cent), in Latvia by 9.9 p.p. (20.6 per cent) and in Lithuania by 10.5 p.p. (20.5 per cent). However, it can be argued whether the Gini coefficient is the best measure to assess the redistributive effect in the system.

As of 2021, the Estonian pension system will become more solidarity-based: if at present the number of points earned in a calendar year depends only on the amount of contributions made (the national average brings in one point, twice the national average brings in two points, and so on), then from 2021 the length of service will be taken into account along with the contributions paid.

Thus, an employee with half the average contributions, who has worked for a full year, will receive not 0.5 points as presently, but 0.75 (50 per cent × 1 year + 50 per cent × 0.5 of the average contributions). The employee with the insured income which is twice as high as the average and with a full year of service will receive 1.5 points (50 per cent × 1 year + 50 per cent × 2) instead of the current two points. An employee with an insured monthly income that is twice the average, but who has worked only six months, will receive 0.75 points instead of the current one point.

Risks associated with labour market turbulences, such as unemployment, the spread of precarious employment contracts, and bogus and true self-employment, have been largely the responsibility of workers themselves in the DC systems adopted in the Baltic states. Latvia, lacking a non-contributory element in its pension formula, has gone further than others in transferring risks to individuals. The author's calculations show that the drop in total length of insured employment from 40 years to 20 years brought an average-earner in Latvia a drop in replacement rate by 38 p.p. (from 62 per cent to 24 per cent) and in Lithuania by 27 p.p. (from 52 per cent to 25 per cent), while in Estonia the drop was only 15 p.p. (from 48 per cent to 33 per cent). For lower-earners the differences were even greater, although for higher-wage-earners shorter employment records affected their replacement rates to a lesser extent (Rajevska and Voroncuka 2019).

The share of inadequately low old-age pension benefits is quite significant in the Baltic countries: in 2018, the at-risk-of-poverty rates in the age group 65-plus reached 37.7 per cent in Lithuania, 45.7 per cent in Latvia and 46.3 per cent in Estonia (compared to the EU-28 average rate of 15.9 per cent), and the aggregate pension replacement rate was *c.*40 per cent in the three study countries (EU-28: 58 per cent). Not surprisingly, many pensioners continue working after reaching the statutory age, and employment rates in the age group 65-plus are high: 9.2 per cent in Lithuania, 9.4 per cent in Latvia and 13.4 per cent in Estonia, as opposed to 6.1 per cent in EU-28 (Eurostat). Willingness to remain in employment is higher in Latvia and Estonia than anywhere in the EU. The answer 'as late as possible' to the question 'Until what age do you want to work?' was given by about 40 per cent of respondents, which is more than twice as high as the EU-28 average (slightly below 20 per cent). Meanwhile, Lithuanians gave this answer in about 25 per cent of cases (Eurofound 2017).

Risk management strategies we consider in the PAYG pillar are mainly classified as risk sharing (among current pensioners, among current contributors and recipients) and risk transfer (for example, between PAYG and a funded pillar, also by attracting financing from general budgets). The state is mitigating the risks by proper organisation of the scheme elements, while individuals also demonstrate the tendency of risk avoidance by postponing effective retirement.

It should be noted that among the risks threatening the sustainability of the system, there are also political risks. They are designed to be mitigated by properly drafted legislation, a broad discussion of planned reforms, and constitutional review of accepted amendments and regulations.

PILLAR II: PRIVATELY MANAGED MANDATORY FULLY FUNDED SCHEMES

The main rationale for the introduction of private pension systems was the intention to reduce public pension liabilities in the long run. Thus, OECD estimations for Lithuania show that an average-earner who started their career in 2016 after retirement (at the statutory retirement age) would receive more than half of their pension income from private pre-funded schemes (Maciej 2018). The capital being accumulated in funded pillars has been growing constantly, and in 2018 net equity of households in mandatory and voluntary pension fund reserves accounted for 15.3 per cent of gross domestic product in Estonia, 13.8 per cent in Latvia and 7.1 per cent in Lithuania. In 2018, the second-pillar pension plans covered practically all the working population in Latvia, 96 per cent of the working population in Estonia and 92.8 per cent in Lithuania (Better Finance 2019).

Practically, the great majority of potential voluntary participants[6] in all three countries have exercised their right to join the scheme. Those who have joined the second pillar voluntarily do not have the right to opt out of the scheme, with the two temporary exclusions from this rule that occurred in Lithuania. The first time the 'door' was open was for nine months in 2013, before the introduction of a new financing model. The participants were then able to choose to either stay under the previous model, accept new rules or switch back to the fully PAYG scheme. But only 2.1 per cent of the second-pillar participants used this opportunity to withdraw from the funded scheme in 2013. Although they stopped contributing, the already accrued accumulations remained in pension funds and were not returned to the Pillar I scheme. The door opened for the second time in 2019, when a cardinal reform took place and the unit holders were again offered a choice: to accept new rules (chosen by 81 per cent of participants), take a temporarily contribution vacation (16 per cent) or quit participation in Pillar II and transfer the accumulations into individual social insurance pension schemes in Pillar I (3 per cent).

The risk of fluctuations in financial markets has been assigned to future pensioners, who therefore risk losing their savings in the event of a collapse of the markets (which happened during the global financial crisis in 2008–2009). Pension legislators in the Baltic states have not provided any protection to funded-pillar participants by the way of setting minimum guaranteed rates of return, unlike other Central and Eastern European (CEE) countries, where partial privatisation of public pensions took place at the turn of the 21st century. In the rest of the region, the guaranteed minimum yield was set on the basis of industry's average (as it was in Bulgaria, Croatia, Poland and Romania), or in the form of absolute return guarantees of protection of a nominal rate of return ('at least zero' in the Czech Republic, Romania and the Slovak Republic) or a real rate of return ('at least real value of accumulated assets' in Hungary) (Kawinski, Stanko and Rutecka 2012).

That means, in fact, that pension funds do not bear any financial risks: whatever the result of the investment, even if it is negative, managers in any case will receive their fixed fee (calculated as a percentage of the net value of assets). The fee rates of Baltic pension asset managers were seen as unduly high until recently, when significant cuts were introduced in all three countries and the fees were tightly linked to the effectiveness of pension plans.

As was stressed in the recent OECD review of Latvian pension systems (OECD 2018), when the fee rate is linked to the net asset value, a manager is more interested in boosting the assets not by more efficient investments, but by increased advertising campaigns. That is, while good performance can attract new members, advertising a fund may be more powerful. All financial operations of pension funds are carried out through a custodian bank. Therefore, asset managers pay commissions to their custodian bank, while the bank in turn can advertise products for which it is a custodian to its clients.

This is definitely the case in the two other Baltic countries as well. The market of pension fund managers is quite concentrated. The market leaders in all three countries are branches of the Sweden-based Swedbank. At the end of 2018, Swedbank controlled 41.8 per cent of all Pillar II assets in Latvia (having 42.2 per cent of all participants), 37.1 per cent of assets/39.9 per cent of participants in Lithuania and 41.7 per cent of assets in Estonia (in Estonia it is possible to have units in more than one plan, which makes it impossible to calculate the share of participants). The second place is occupied by subsidiaries of another Swedish bank, SEB: 24 per cent of assets/22.9 per cent of participants in Latvia, 25.4 per cent of assets/22.5 per cent of participants in Lithuania and 18.8 per cent of assets in Estonia. So, the two market leaders in asset management together constitute more than 60 per cent of the market (Bank of Lithuania 2020; Pensionikeskus 2020; State Social Insurance Agency 2019). Asset managers barely compete on fees, as most of them charge the maximum allowed by regulation (OECD 2018, p. 121).

Risks of Funded Schemes: Accumulation Stage

The state participates in the mandatory funded pillar as a general supervisory authority that licenses and controls market participants, virtually eliminating the risk of complete loss of pension capital or the appearance of unprofessional providers on the market. It also sets limits on the acceptable structure of invest-ment portfolios, management fees, and so on, that are designed to protect the interests of contributors.

The main risk for individual participants is to face a low return on their pension capital, insufficient to ensure the anticipated annuity during their retirement. In highly volatile financial markets, even long-term returns are very sensitive to entry and exit dates (both of them being beyond the control of an individual). 'Unless long term net returns are significantly positive (in the upper single digits), saving early and significantly will not provide a decent replacement income through retirement' (Better Finance 2019, p. 23). The experts (ibid., p. 32) list the following net real-returns drivers:

1.   asset allocation of pension products;
2.   performance of capital markets into which pension products are invested;
3.   skills of asset managers in terms of choosing securities and market timing;
4.   fees and commissions charged by asset managers and other financial intermediaries;
5.   and, ultimately, inflation and tax burdens.

An individual pension plan participant has some control (although quite limited) over only the first factor of the above list; that is, choosing a pension plan with the appropriate investment strategy. Funds participants in the Baltics may choose an investment strategy by selecting a conservative, balanced, active or aggressive pension plan, defined by the allowed share of stocks in a portfolio. Conservative plans do not allow stocks at all, so they are rec-ommended to people in their last 10 pre-retirement years to avoid excessive fluctuations of assets' values. Recently, life-cycle plans have been introduced as well, in which a portfolio composition changes as the participant gets older, thus mitigating the risk of choosing an inappropriate plan. The seriousness of that risk is backed by the Central Bank of Lithuania's 2016 report, which states that more than 50 per cent of participants have chosen the wrong pension fund considering their age. More than two-thirds are passive investors and choose one pension fund for their whole life. In 2014–2015, for example, only 2 per cent of all participants changed their pension fund or asset management pro-vider. Active clients follow short-term results and 92 per cent made the wrong decision during the financial crisis in 2008 (Better Finance 2019, p. 322). Similar conclusions have been reached by other researchers: most Pillar II participants are irrational in selecting participation rates; they make irrational choices on selecting the pension and changing it over the accumulation period. Pension fund participants are passive and tend not to change pension funds during the accumulation period, while those participants who did change funds made irrational decisions and chose inappropriate ones. So, in peak periods in stock markets, the majority of Pillar II participants in Lithuania switched from the funds with a lower proportion of equities to those with a higher proportion, or changed their pension fund to a fund in the same investment risk category. Moreover, in bottom periods in stock markets, most participants did the opposite, switching from funds with a higher proportion of equities to those with a lower proportion (Medaiskis, Gudaitis and Mečkovski 2018).

The recent (2018) reform of Pillar II in Lithuania introduced automatic enrolment of Pillar II participants into life-cycle plans according to their age. It is worth mentioning that Pillar II regulation in Lithuania allows a much riskier investment strategy: the allowed share of stocks for the most aggressive pension plans is from 50 per cent to 75 per cent in Estonia and Latvia, where these plans are not very popular: only 6.6 per cent of pension fund assets in Latvia and 18.2 per cent in Estonia were invested in such plans at the end of December 2019; meanwhile, Lithuanian life-cycle plans (for the people born in 1968 and later) that invest from 83 per cent to 98 per cent of their assets into stocks constituted 70 per cent of all Pillar II investments. Presently, there are no zero-stock pension plans in Lithuania at all. Is such a high investment risk justified?

To a marginal extent, an individual participant may have influence on the third factor, inducing 'natural selection' of the best-skilled fund managers by switching between providers. The idea that pension fund participants would actively monitor their savings and rationally switch from less successful plans to more successful ones found almost no evidence. The research showed that in fact people exercise almost no control over their pension accounts, and their decisions are driven by advertising campaigns rather than rational considerations (see Rajevska 2018). International research (Lussardi and Mitchell 2011) has also shown that people with higher levels of education, who as a rule have higher incomes, are generally better informed on financial matters and are less vulnerable to the risk of choosing an inappropriate pension savings product. Less educated people, whose incomes are lower, are more exposed to the risk of making the wrong investment choice. In this context, funded pillars are rendering a disservice to the lifetime poor, causing further distortion in income distribution in the old age.

Although an individual scheme participant has no control over the performance of capital markets, fees and commissions charged, as well as inflation and taxes, all possible negative consequences of these factors on the return on pension capital fall on the shoulders of an individual participant.

The rates of return demonstrated so far by private pension funds in the Baltic states are very disappointing. Yearly real returns of private pension funds were one of the lowest among European countries: during the period 2003–2018, Pillar II funds in Latvia demonstrated real growth of -0.72 per cent (that is, the investments were not even intact against inflation) and Pillar II funds in Estonia during the same period returned -0.01 per cent annually, while in Lithuania the real average growth rate was better: +0.67 per cent (but the reference period is one year shorter: 2004–2018) (Better Finance 2019). The year 2019 improved the cumulative results, as all three Baltic countries faced quite high nominal yields, but the beginning of 2020 was marked by the worst crisis, followed by a gradual recovery.

Underperformance was a 'family trait' of almost privatised public pension schemes established during the pension privatisation boom at the turn of the century, accompanied by high transition costs outreaching the initial over-optimistic projections. Mandatory privately managed fully funded 'second pillars' have been established in practically all post-communist CEE countries during pension reforms in the beginning of the century. In contrast to the situation in the Baltic states, their status in other countries of the region has seriously weakened in recent years following the crisis: the Czech Republic and Hungary have abolished their mandatory pillars, Poland made participation voluntary, and Bulgaria, Slovakia and Croatia eased opting out from the scheme (Fultz and Hirose 2019). Until recently, the governments of the Baltic states did not question the need to maintain mandatory private pension funds. There was also no possibility to leave the second pillar, except for the already mentioned temporary windows in Lithuania in 2013 and 2019.

In this regard, the pioneer (once again) in the region is Estonia, where in January 2020 the parliament voted for significant changes to the pension system. It foresees, in particular, that the statutory funded scheme will be maintained, but with very significant modifications. Despite automatic enrolment of all new labour market entrants, it will be possible to opt out of the pension fund at any time. The payouts will be made within two years and the beneficiary will have to pay income tax. In addition, it will be possible to transfer payments and shift the contribution from the pension fund to an individual investment account (that is, a personal bank account that can only be used for investment purposes). The payouts from the pension fund to an investment account will be made within two years of submitting an application. It will be possible to withdraw money from an investment account at any time, paying income tax. Calculations show that staying in the statutory funded scheme would be beneficial to people who earn more than 60 per cent of the average salary, while for lower-earners it might be more advantageous to opt out and direct all social tax to the PAYG pillar. However, the adopted law was not proclaimed by the president, who questioned its constitutionality and sent it to the Supreme Court for consideration (Piirits and Laurimäe 2020).

Although some people in Estonia welcome the anticipated reform as 'the abolition of serfdom', many others point out that financial myopia is the main economic rationale for guaranteed lifetime pensions. When workers are left to their own devices, many would save inadequately for retirement and recognise their error only when it is too late.

The risk management strategies at the Pillar II accumulation stage are mainly risk reduction and risk retention.

Risks of Funded Schemes: Payout Stage

When the accumulation phase is over and a fund participant retires, the pension fund transfers the money to a life insurance company chosen by the participant, which in reality means that the pension fund bears no more risks or obligations. All further obligations and risks are undertaken by the life insurance company.

This exit path is expected to become the mainstream one; however, as of today, the accumulated savings are often insufficient to buy a life insurance policy, and many of those who are retiring now have to use other options. Depending on the accumulated amount, in Estonia and Lithuania it can be receipt of the entire sum at once or receipt of regular payments from the pension fund. In Lithuania, where the funded pillar was launched later and contributions to the scheme were lower than in Latvia and Estonia, fewer than 1 per cent of retired participants received life insurance annuities in 2018 (Lazutka, Poviliunas and Zalimiene 2018).

In Latvia, quite a different payout mechanism is in operation. Should the accumulated amount be lower than necessary[7] for purchasing a life pension policy,[8] the capital would be transferred back to the state social budget from a private pension fund and added to the notional pension account in the PAYG scheme, and then the total would be converted into an annuity by dividing the total capital by the remaining life expectancy. This can be also done if the accumulated amount is sufficient for purchasing a life pension policy from a private insurer, should a pensioner not want to buy a life pension policy from a private provider. The choice is not an easy one. As shown by OECD experts (OECD 2018, pp. 125–126), when the capital is transferred to a notional account, its rate of return is actually equal to the indexation of pensions in payment – that is, inflation plus part of the real wage growth; however, only part of the pension up to a threshold is indexed. Meanwhile, traditional life annuities of insurance companies apply the risk-free rate of return when calculating annuity payments, leading to a larger retirement income from life pension insurance than from state social insurance. At the same time, in order to protect the lifetime payments from inflation, low- and middle-earners may prefer the option of appending Pillar II accumulations to a Pillar I notional account rather than buying life pension insurance. Other factors, such as a possibility to specify an additional beneficiary (heritability) and behavioural inertia, may tilt in favour of one of the other options, where risk assessment is in the hands of pensioners themselves.

Although insurance companies could offer inflation-indexed policies, in practice they do not, and life pensions are not safeguarded from inflation. In Estonia, the legislation stipulates that life insurance payments shall be equal or increasing (but the growth cannot be more than 3 per cent per year). In Latvia, life pension insurers offer either equal payments throughout the whole length of the policy or split the payout period into three sub-periods. The payments within each sub-period are equal, and it is possible to have the payment amount decreasing in each subsequent sub-period. So, the great majority of Pillar II pensions will not maintain their value over time. Only one country in CEE, Croatia, requires price adjustment of second-pillar pensions in the same manner as first-pillar public pensions. This requirement provides essential protection for pensioners but is designed in a way that poses a risk for the pension provider, due to the uncertainty of future inflation rates. Governments can mitigate such risks by issuing inflation-indexed bonds. Through investing in them, private insurers can shift the risk of uncertain inflation rates to taxpayers (Fultz and Hirose 2019, p. 13).

In Lithuania, from July 2020, private life insurance companies in the payout phase have been substituted by the State Social Insurance Agency. The agency offers three types of annuities:

- standard annuities (all accumulated capital is converted into an annuity that is not heritable);
- standard annuities with a guaranteed payment period (all accumulated capital is converted into an annuity that is heritable if a person dies before the end of the guaranteed payment period; that is, before reaching the age of 80. This option provides for lower payments than the option of simple standard annuities);
- deferred annuities (a part of the accumulated capital is frozen and is converted into an annuity only upon achieving a very old age (85 years), and this part is not heritable; the rest of the accumulations remain in the pension fund that provides the pensioner with periodic payments from the capital, and the pension capital remaining in the fund is heritable. Periodic payments are lower than the payments in the two previous options).

It is also important to note that in Estonia and Lithuania, the beginning of receiving payments from Pillar II accumulations does not necessarily coincide with the commencement of receiving pension benefits from Pillar I. Having reached the retirement age, a person may obtain the status of a pensioner and start receiving a social insurance pension, but do nothing with the accumulated pension capital in Pillar II, waiting, for example, for a more favourable market price for their pension fund units and keeping on earning interest on the capital. This was also the case in Latvia – but starting from 2020, applying for the Pillar I pension automatically means the simultaneous conversion of the Pillar II pension capital into an annuity. This puts those having to retire in times of crises, when the value of pension fund units falls, in a very unfavourable position. Latvian legislators recognised the problem, and in early April 2020 a transitional provision was added to the law: those who retire during the coronavirus crisis could keep their second-pillar accumulated capital untouched until the end of November 2021, waiting for a more favourable rate.

The mix of risk management strategies includes risk sharing (purchasing a life insurance policy, use of the state social insurance PAYG pillar), risk transfer (from pension fund to an insurance company), risk mitigation and risk acceptance (in individual strategies of pensioners).

PILLAR III: PRIVATELY MANAGED VOLUNTARY FULLY FUNDED SCHEMES

At the end of 2018 Pillar III schemes[9] covered 23 per cent of the economically active population in Latvia, 17 per cent in Estonia and 4.4 per cent in Lithuania (Better Finance 2019).

Although there are regulations for defined benefit plans or DC plans offering guarantees, in practice only DC plans with no guarantees are offered by private pension funds, where all the risks are borne by the members. The average annual real rates of return in Estonia and Latvia were slightly better than in Pillar II (although significantly underperforming when compared to most private pension savings providers in other European countries), and in Lithuania they were lower than in Pillar II.

In general, the risks in voluntary pension funds are almost the same as in Pillar II funds. In this regard, some important notes should be made:

• Pillar III investment strategies are far more aggressive (investing more in equities) than Pillar II funds; therefore the assets are more vulnerable to market fluctuations.
• Management fees in Pillar III funds are not capped and are significantly higher than in Pillar II; in addition, redemption fees are applied for withdrawal of the funds.

The most common forms of receiving benefits from voluntary private pension funds are a lump-sum payment or programmed withdrawals. Since acquisition of an annuity is not mandatory, the participants of Pillar III funds can be called participants in 'pension' accumulation with some reservations only (Pastukiene 2017, p. 9).

The mix of risk management strategies applied in Pillar III is similar to the Pillar II mix discussed above.

CONCLUSION

The pension systems of Estonia, Latvia and Lithuania were designed in the second half of the 1990s, when these countries were, to a much lesser extent, included in the global economic and financial markets. Small national states have limited ability to intervene in the market processes, and the systems were not prepared enough for the risks caused by globalisation as they were tailored for countries where people do not move abroad for work and pension funds make investments into the domestic economy.

There are more similarities than differences in the approaches to managing risks in pension systems in the Baltic states. The paradigm of mandatory privatisation of a significant share of state pensions that amplified the level of social inequality is being replaced by a new paradigm in which governments 'nudge' rather than require workers to contribute to supplemental private saving plans for retirement. At the same time, the focus on the relationship between pensions and earnings is being replaced by a focus on ensuring a decent pension standard for all. Another trend is the increase in the share of the general budget contributions in financing old-age pensions.

Development of the Baltic pension systems in the last decade shows that Estonia and, to a lesser extent, Lithuania are more in line with this paradigm shift than Latvia, with its invariably neoliberal approach to pension insurance. In the most recent years, the common features of the transformations in the Baltic pension systems include raising the retirement age, curbing management fees in Pillar II and enhancing the role of seniority. However, seniority plays a much more important role in pension formulas in Estonia and, particularly, in Lithuania than in Latvia. Estonia is reforming the early retirement scheme and links the statutory age to life expectancy. The tendency to a strong increase in vertical redistribution is present in Estonia and Lithuania, but it is achieved by different tools: Estonia changes the pension point calculation, while Lithuania has incorporated a subsistence minimum into the pension benefit. Lithuania has also considerably changed the financing of pensions and the design of the mandatory funded pillar. A fundamental reform of Pillar II is also expected in Estonia, but the essence of the planned changes is fundamentally different from the Lithuanian one.

The analysis of the existing pension schemes in the Baltic states proves that the countries use a wide range of different risk management strategies in designing their pension systems. Risk sharing is the major method of social insurance pension components in Pillar I, as well as in life pension insurance in the payout stage of funded pillars; risk mitigation is achieved on an individual level by maintaining individual pension accumulation accounts (notional accounts, points accounts, accumulations in the funded schemes) and on a state level by setting pension regulation and control over the performance of pension system actors. Risks are transferred between the pillars and between the actors, and a fair share of risk is transferred to parties outside the system (what is sometimes called the fourth pension pillar): other social security programs at state and municipal levels, families, charities. Certain risks are accepted as a necessary part of the system (for example, market fluctuations). Risk avoidance strategy can be traced as an individual intention to work as long as possible.

ACKNOWLEDGEMENT

The chapter has been prepared with the support from the Post-Doc Latvia Project No. 1.1.1.2/VIAA/1/16/056.

NOTES

1. The Convention is not ratified by any of the Baltic states. However, it is referenced as the basis for the European Social Security Code and serves as an instrument engaging the EU Acquis Chapter 19 (Social Policy and Employment).
2. Apart from the contributions made by the state budget for young parents as parental pensions.
3. The financial crisis that hit Russia in 1998 resulted in the Russian government and the Russian Central Bank devaluing the ruble and defaulting on debt. The crisis had severe impacts on the economies of many neighbouring countries.
4. The comparison will be made between the average life expectancy in 2018–2022 and the average life expectancy in further five-year periods. For example, to define the statutory retirement age in 2027, the average life expectancy in 2018–2022 will be compared with the average life expectancy in 2019–2023, and if the latter turns out to be higher, the statutory age will be increased by the difference (rounded to full months); in 2028, the average life expectancy in 2018–2022 will be compared to average life expectancy in 2020–2024, and so on.
5. Old-age pensions in the terms of ESSPROS (European System of Integrated Social Protection Statistics) data include not only social insurance pensions, but also social assistance pensions for those who do not have a sufficient contribution record. Social assistance pensions are financed from general taxation.
6. The second pillar is mandatory in Estonia for people born in 1983 and later, and in Latvia for people born on 1 July 1971 and later. Participation is voluntary in Lithuania irrespective of age; in Latvia it is voluntary for those born between 2 July 1951 and 30 June 1971; and in Estonia it was open for voluntary subscription until 31 October 2010 for those born in 1942–1983.

7. In contrast to Estonia, the said amount is set in absolute numbers in euros and not as a ratio to the annually indexed national pension. Lithuania switched from a relative benchmark to absolute numbers in 2020.
8. In Latvia, 'life pension' ('*mūža pensija*') is a special legal term, and it is different from life insurance ('*dzīvības apdrošināšana*'). This is a particular kind of life insurance policy that is designed specifically for Pillar II pensions and regulated separately.
9. Only pension funds' participants are counted, apart from life insurance companies' clients.

BIBLIOGRAPHY

Bank of Lithuania (2020). 'Performance indicators for pension accumulation: Results of 2nd pillar pension funds', accessed 20 March 2020 at www.lb.lt/en/pf-performance-indicators#ex-1-1.
Better Finance (2019). 'Pension savings: The real return 2019 edition', accessed 20 March 2020 at https://betterfinance.eu.
Dorfman, M.S., and D.A. Cather (2013). *Introduction to Risk Management and Insurance* (10th Edition), Prentice Hall Series in Finance, Boston: Pearson.
Dunajevas, E., and D. Skučiene (2016). 'Mandatory pension system and redistribution: The comparative analysis of institutions in Baltic States', *Central European Journal of Public Policy*, 10(2), 16–29.
Ebbinghaus, B. (2019). 'Pension reforms and old age inequalities in Europe: From old to new social risks?', paper presented at the 14th European Sociological Association Conference, Manchester, UK, August 20–23. Accessed 20 March 2020 at www.researchgate.net/publication/335228524_Pension_reforms_and_old_age_inequalities_in_Europe_From_old_to_new_social_risks.
Eurofound (2017). *Extending Working Life: What Do Workers Want?*, Dublin: Eurofound.
European Commission (2018). *Pension Adequacy Report 2018: Current and Future Income Adequacy in Old Age in the EU, Volume II – Country Profiles*, Brussels: European Commission.
Eurostat (2020). EU Statistics on income and living conditions (EU-SILC), The European System of Integrated Social Protection Statistics (ESSPROS). Accessed 20 March 2020 at https://ec.europa.eu/eurostat/data/database.
Financial and Capital Market Commission (2019). 'Valsts fondēto pensiju shēmas līdzekļu pārvaldīšana 2018. gada 4. ceturksnī' [State funded pension asset management in the IV quarter of 2018], accessed 20 March 2020 at www.fktk.lv/statistika/pensiju-fondi/ceturksna-parskati/.
Fultz, E., and K. Hirose (2019). 'Second-pillar pensions in Central and Eastern Europe: Payment constraints and exit options', *International Social Security Review*, 72(2), 3–22.
International Labour Organization (2017). *World Social Protection Report 2017–19: Universal Social Protection to Achieve the Sustainable Development Goals*, Geneva: ILO.
Jankauskiene, D., and T. Medaiskis (2011). *ASISP Annual National Report 2011: Pensions, Health Care and Long-Term Care – Lithuania*, Brussels: European Commission.

Jankauskiene, D., and T. Medaiskis (2012). *ASISP Annual National Report 2012: Pensions, Health Care and Long-Term Care – Lithuania*, Brussels: European Commission.

Kawinski, M., D. Stanko and J. Rutecka (2012). 'Protection mechanisms in the old-age pension systems of the CEE countries', *Journal of Pension Economics and Finance*, 11, 581–605.

Lazutka, R. (2006). 'Pension Reform in Lithuania', in E. Fultz (ed.), *Pension Reform in the Baltic States*, Budapest: ILO, pp. 267–350.

Lazutka, R., A. Poviliunas and L. Zalimiene (2018). *On-Going Discussions about the Financing of the Statutory Funded Pension in Lithuania*, ESPN Flash Report 2018/29, European Social Policy Network (ESPN), Brussels: European Commission.

Leppik, L., and A. Võrk (2006). 'Pension Reform in Estonia', in: E. Fultz (ed.), *Pension Reform in the Baltic States*, Budapest: ILO, pp. 17–142.

Lussardi, A., and O.S. Mitchell (2011). 'Financial literacy around the world: An overview', *Journal of Pension Economics and Finance*, 10, 497–508.

Maciej, L. (2018). 'Lithuanian pension system in the international perspective', presentation from the conference Lithuanian Pension System: How to Ensure Socially Just and Sustainable Pensions on 17 September 2018, accessed 20 March 2020 at www.lb.lt/uploads/documents/files/Lis_Maciej_OECD.pdf.

Medaiskis, T., T. Gudaitis and J. Mečkovski (2018). 'Second pension pillar participants' behaviour: The Lithuanian case', *Entrepreneurship and Sustainability Issues*, 6(2), 620–635.

OECD (2018). *OECD Reviews of Pension Systems: Latvia*, Paris: OECD Publishing.

Pastukiene, V. (2017). 'Lithuanian country fiche on pension projections 2018', accessed 20 March 2020 at https://ec.europa.eu/info/sites/info/files/economy-finance/final_country_fiche_lt.pdf.

Pensionikeskus [Pension Center] (2020). 'Statistics on funded pensions', accessed 20 March 2020 at www.pensionikeskus.ee/en/statistics/.

Piirits, M., and M. Laurimäe (2020). *Estonia's Statutory Funded Pension Scheme on the Way to Being Made Voluntary*, ESPN Flash Report 2020/07, European Social Policy Network (ESPN), Brussels: European Commission.

Rajevska, O. (2014). 'Pension statistics in Latvia: Resources and weaknesses', *Journal of Economics and Management Research*, 3, 65–74.

Rajevska, O. (2018). 'The Financial Illiteracy of Latvians Undermines their Well-being in Old Age', in F. Chybalski and E. Marcinkiewicz (eds), *Contemporary Problems of Intergenerational Relations and Pension Systems: A Theoretical and Empirical Perspective – Proceedings of PenCon 2018 Pensions Conference, 19–20 April 2018, Lodz, Poland*, Lodz: Lodz University of Technology Press, pp. 243–251.

Rajevska, O., and I. Voroncuka (2019). 'Modelling the Influence of Working Career Breaks on Pension Using Retrospective Simulation: A Case of the Baltic States', in N. Callaos, B. Peoples, B. Sánchez and M. Savoie (eds), *Proceedings of the 23rd World Multi-Conference on Systemics, Cybernetics and Informatics, July 6–9, 2019, Orlando*, Orlando: International Institute of Informatics and Systemics, Volume 4, pp. 54–58.

Spasova, S., and T. Ward (2019). *Financing Social Protection in Europe: A Study of National Policies 2019*, European Social Policy Network (ESPN), Brussels: European Commission.

State Social Insurance Agency (2019). 'Pārskats par valsts fondēto pensiju shēmas darbību 2018. gadā' [Review of the state funded pension scheme performance in

2018], accessed 20 March 2020 at www.vsaa.gov.lv/pakalpojumi/stradajosajiem/2
-pensiju-limenis/parskati-par-valsts-fondeto-pensiju-shemas-darbibu/.
Vanovska, I. (2006). 'Pension Reform in Latvia', in E. Fultz (ed.), *Pension Reform in the Baltic States*, Budapest: ILO, pp. 143–266.
Võrk, A., L. Leppik and S. Segaert (2010). *ASISP Annual National Report 2010: Pensions, Health and Long-Term Care – Estonia*, Brussels: European Commission.
World Bank (1994). *Averting the Old Age Crisis: Policies to Protect the Old and Promote Growth*, Oxford: Oxford University Press.

12. Looking for an adequate and sustainable old-age pension system: comparing Sweden and Lithuania

Teodoras Medaiskis and Šarūnas Eirošius

INTRODUCTION

Protecting the older population always was and still remains one of the main challenges of the modern welfare state. The ageing population is an important factor making this problem even more significant. The shared experiences among countries that implemented pension reforms in order to maintain adequate and sustainable pensions in the changing world may contribute to common progress in this field. Due to this, it appears valuable to compare the Lithuanian pension system, which is still in the process of changing, to the Swedish system, which is characterised by extensive experience, stability and modern reform. Most recently, a comparison of the Swedish and Lithuanian pension systems was carried by the authors in 2019 (Medaiskis and Eirošius 2019). This chapter presents renewed and extended previous research.

The Lithuanian pension system has been analysed primarily from the point of view of financial sustainability, effects on public finances and problems with the current system design (Medaiskis 2001; Lazutka 2008; Gudaitis 2009; Medaiskis 2011; Lazutka 2013; Bitinas and Maccioni 2014). The main challenges for the Lithuanian pension system were the ageing of the population, low financing of the system (and, consequently, the low benefits), emigration and the expected growth of the pension expenditures. Some of the studies compared the pensions of the participants and non-participants of the 'second pillar'. A comparison of the accumulated pension capital with losses in the pay-as-you-go system showed that the average accumulated amount in fully funded, private second-pillar pension funds slightly exceeds the evaluated current value of the lost part of social insurance pensions (Medaiskis and Gudaitis 2013).

The Swedish pension system has been widely analysed since the introduction of the Notional Defined Contributions (NDC) scheme. According to

Palmer (2018, interview), the NDC system was introduced as a measure to cope with the crisis of the 1990s. Studies have found it to be both advantageous and disadvantageous (Barr 2013). The NDC pension scheme in Sweden is equipped with a combination of a demographically adjusted annuity provision, indexation and a solvency ratio that maintains a near-perfect financial stability in the long run (Palmer 2014). On the other hand, Cichon (1999) noted that without any ad hoc adjustments to benefit levels and indexation provisions, the NDC system is not in an automatic equilibrium. The system does not automatically fully cope with the financial effects of population ageing. Scherman (2007) notes that any country that contemplates the introduction of the NDC system, such as Sweden – it being a system designed to keep the contribution rate unchanged – has to recognise that such a system maintains decreasing pension levels as the population continuously ages. After a comparison of different types of pension systems, Whitehouse states that 'notional accounts are an example of good practice [...] However, well-designed pension schemes of the alternative types – defined-benefit or points – share these characteristics' (Whitehouse 2010, p. 20).

The aim of this chapter is to compare the analogous statutory parts of the Swedish and Lithuanian pension systems, with special attention to similarities and differences in financing, indexation and benefit composition, and to evaluate whether following the Swedish approach would help improve the Lithuanian system.

This chapter consists of three parts: in the first part, the Lithuanian and Swedish pension systems are compared and their main differences are described and analysed based on national and international organisations' reports, other publications and interviews with experts. In the second part, a comparison of pension system adequacy in terms of replacement ratios and poverty rates is presented based on statistical data from the Organisation for Economic Co-operation and Development (OECD), Eurostat and national statistic sources. Finally, a simulation model is constructed and applied for the analysis of whether the Swedish NDC approach in the pension system would be more suitable in terms of financial sustainability and adequacy for Lithuania than the current approach of 'pension points'. Based on this model, individual pensions are calculated as if the NDC system had been introduced in Lithuania since 2001. The results allow comparison between the actual and simulated performance of the Lithuanian system and identification of the possible strengths and weaknesses of the NDC system if applied in Lithuania.

THE CURRENT PENSION SYSTEMS IN LITHUANIA AND SWEDEN: SOME DESIGN SIMILARITIES AND DIFFERENCES

The current Lithuanian pension system was shaped by several essential reforms. After the restoration of its independence in 1990, Lithuania inherited the system common for all the former Soviet Union states. The first national pension system of the 'first pillar' was designed in the years leading up to 1995 and became applicable from that year. The second essential reform was passed before 2004 and began in the same year. This reform introduced a 'second' and 'third' pillar of funded pensions. At the end of 2012, this system was modified because of the financial crisis. Recently, another reform regarding the funded part of the system was legislated and became effective in 2019.

The current Swedish pension system was introduced as a result of the consensus of the five largest political parties in Sweden. In 1994, after more than a decade of debate and research, the reform guidelines were adopted; four years later, all the necessary changes to the law were adopted. The new pension system began operation in 1999. The fact that the reform was carried out based on a consensus among the five parties creates a sufficiently high stability for the system and makes it resistant to political change. This stability is also evidenced by the fact that no significant changes have taken place since the start of the new system.

In comparing the origins and development of the pension systems over recent decades, it should be noted that the Lithuanian system has been reformed much more often and developed less than the Swedish one. This may be justified by the fact that Lithuania had to create the first national system from scratch, having insufficient experience in pension policy. A political consensus on the pension system reform was partially achieved at a time when funded pillars were introduced; nevertheless, no consensus in the political opinions regarding how to adapt the pension system to the consequences of the financial crisis was achieved, and decisions taken in 2004 and 2012 were robustly revised and partially abolished by the more recent political parties that came into legislative power in 2016. The permanent process of the reforms diminished the confidence that the society had in the pension system; thus, this confidence seems to be much weaker in Lithuania than in Sweden. In 2016, a survey found that the confidence of Lithuanians in their pension system dropped from 28 per cent to 18 per cent in one year, and not much has changed from that time. The main reason mentioned by the respondents was the frequent initiatives to change the pension system (SEB 2017, 2019).

To lay the foundation for further analysis, we will start with a short comparison of features of the Lithuanian and Swedish systems that are most important to this analysis. This is presented in Table 12.1.

A common feature of both the Lithuanian and Swedish pension systems is that both consist of the pay-as-you-go and funded components and are supplemented with 'guaranteed' or 'social' provisions for those who are not entitled to pension benefits at all or for whom these benefits are too low. Private pensions are available in both countries, yet occupational pensions are found only in Sweden.

Despite the similar composition, there are many essential differences in the design of the components. We discuss them below in more detail.

The Different Role and Weight of the Flat Part of Pensions

The Lithuanian 'first pillar' pension includes a general part paid for all recipients. Any individual earnings-related part is paid on the top. The general part is calculated according to the number of years of insurance, and it is related to the current amount of the 'basic pension'; the individual part depends on the number of pension points collected by the recipient and is multiplied by the current value of the pension points. One pension point per year is earned by the insured person if he or she pays the requested contribution from the country's average gross wage; not more than five pension points may be earned per year because of the ceiling of the contributions' base (an appropriate ceiling has been fully applied since 2021). The essential difference here from the Swedish system is that the general part of a pension is paid for all recipients, not only for those who receive a low amount of the individual part (unlike in Sweden, where a *guaranteed* pension is paid only to those with a low income pension). Instead of the Swedish guaranteed pension, the Lithuanian system applies two levels of semi-flat payments: the *general* and (if necessary) *social*. This part of the pension is not means-tested in either of the two countries.

The Swedish approach appears simpler and more transparent than the Lithuanian approach. Unfortunately, the efforts to follow this approach and to join the Lithuanian general and social pension into one 'zero-level' universal pension (similar to the Swedish guaranteed pension) were not successful due to the evaluated expenses of transformation.

The core of the differences in the benefits structure between the Swedish and Lithuanian pension systems is that the Lithuanian system is more redistributive among recipients than the Swedish one. Around 55 per cent of all pension expenditures in Lithuania are directed to the semi-flat general part. This is a consequence of the relatively low financing of the Lithuanian pension system: the low budget should be distributed among the recipients more evenly in order to guarantee necessary subsistence for the recipients with low

Table 12.1   A comparison of the Lithuanian and Swedish pension systems

Pillars

The main parts of the current Lithuanian old-age pension system are as follows:

First pillar:

First pillar (pay-as-you-go) pensions are divided into *general* (semi-flat, dependent on the number of years of insurance) and *individual* (earnings-related) parts.

This pillar is supplemented with 'social assistance pensions' granted to old and disabled residents who have no sufficient right to the other pillars' pensions.

Second pillar:

No occupational pensions are available. Instead, the 'second pillar' is legislated as a quasi-compulsory fully funded privately managed DC scheme. It is financed from personal contributions and matching state contributions.

Third pillar:

Individual voluntary private savings pillar.

The main parts of the current Swedish old-age pension system are as follows:

First pillar:

Income pensions (pay-as-you-go) and *premium* pensions (fully funded).

These pensions are supplemented with 'guarantee pensions' for those with insufficient pension rights as an addition to the income pension up to the threshold.

Older cohorts (born from 1938 to 1954) also receive part of the supplementary (ATP) pensions granted according to the rules before the reform.

Second pillar:

It is a quasi-compulsory pillar of occupational pensions. About 90 per cent of Sweden's wage-earners are covered by this pillar. Occupational pensions are financed by employers' contributions and fully funded.

Third pillar:

Individual voluntary private savings pillar.

First-pillar financing

From 2019, the general part became financed from general taxation, and the individual part from personal contributions (8.72 per cent of the wage for old-age, disability and survivors' pensions). Contributions are not shared by the employers.

Contributions are collected into the State Social Insurance Fund. Personal records of the earned 'pension points' are available from 1994.

The 'social pension' is non-contributory and financed from general taxation.

The income pension is financed from contributions. The contribution rate for old-age pensions is 16 per cent of pensionable income, which is divided between the employee and the employer.

All insured people have virtual accounts in the Swedish Pension Agency, where their accumulation balance is maintained.

Premium pensions are fully funded DC pensions managed by investment funds. The contribution rate for premium pensions is 2.5 per cent of pensionable income.

The 'guarantee pension' is non-contributory and financed from general taxation.

Benefit calculation and indexation	The general part of pension is semi-flat; that is, it is calculated as a flat 'basic pension' multiplied by the ratio of number of years of insurance earned by a person and the 'obligatory' years of pension insurance. The individual part is calculated on the basis of the 'pension points' approach. Both parts are indexed according to the seven years' average of the growth rate (reported and expected) of the national Labour Compensation Fund.	The income pension is calculated on the basis of the NDC scheme. It is indexed according to an index based on three years' growth of the real wage and reduced by 1.6 percentage points. The indexation of premium pension benefits depends on the performance of the funds and on the individuals' pay-out choice.
	The disability and survivors' pensions are included in the first-pillar system.	Disability and survivors' benefits are not tied to the old-age pension scheme and are managed by the Swedish Insurance Agency.
	All kinds of pensions are exempt from any taxation.	Pensions are subject to taxation like other forms of income.

Sources: Anderson and Backhan (2013), Fritzell et al. (2018), Ministry of Health and Social Affairs (2016), Swedish Pensions Agency (2019).

insurance records and a low number of earned points. For comparison: the expenditures for the Swedish guaranteed non-contributory pension are only 4 per cent of the total pension expenditure (this is calculated by the authors based on the data presented in Pensions Myndigheten, January 2020). This figure is not fully comparable with Lithuania's 55 per cent because of possible elements of redistribution in the ATP; nevertheless, the conclusion that the Lithuanian system directs a much larger part of pension expenditures to the semi-flat part is reasonable.

DIFFERENCES IN FINANCING

The different designs of the pay-as-you-go parts of the pension systems imply a different approach to the financing of these systems. Until 2019, both the general and individual parts of pensions in Lithuania were financed from contributions shared between the employers and employees. The pension insurance (including disability and survivors' pensions insurance) contribution rate in 2018 was 25.3 per cent (22.3 percentage points paid by the employer and 3 by the employee). In mid 2018, the essential tax and contributions reform was passed, the so-called 'tax revolution'. The main motive for this reform lies in an attempt to decrease the tax burden on labour. The whole financing of the general part of pensions was directed to the state (general tax) as the amount of this part is not related to contributions paid by the insured person. Only the individual part is now financed from contributions, and these contributions are paid solely by the employee. The consequence of this 'tax revolution' is that from January 2019 all wages were nominally increased by 28.9 per cent in order to transfer the contribution part of the employer to the employee and maintain previous net incomes after income tax increased from 15 to 20 per cent.

The Swedish 16 per cent and the current Lithuanian 8.72 per cent contributions for income and individual pensions respectively correspond to the differences in the pay-as-you-go pillar composition between Lithuania and Sweden. The Swedish pension composition, with a much higher weight of the earnings-related part of the pension, seems more fair for those who expect the pension system should serve as income replacement rather than poverty protection; the low Lithuanian expenditures for pensions, as stated above, act as an obstacle in following the Swedish approach. Another essential difference in pension contributions is that the whole Lithuanian contribution from 2019 is paid by the employee and not shared by the employer. The motive for this change, as presented by the politicians, is to show the employee 'the full cost of social insurance' and in this way encourage citizens to avoid shadow labour.

As mentioned above, the Lithuanian pension system is financed much less than the Swedish in absolute and in relative terms. The low financing of the Lithuanian pension system corresponds to the whole relatively low level of Lithuania's public resources. According to Eurostat data, total general government expenditures in 2019 were 34.9 and 49.3 per cent of the gross domestic product (GDP) in Lithuania and Sweden, respectively.[1] This shows that the pension financing problem is part of a larger problem associated with government revenue. Tax evasion, the shadow economy, and low direct taxation are usually cited as the main reasons for low government revenue (OECD 2018, pp. 186–187). Nevertheless, if the Lithuanian government collected taxes at the Swedish level and proportionally increased old-age pension financing, pension expenditure would amount to almost 7.9 per cent[2] of GDP, which would still be less than the current Swedish 9.2 per cent. This means that in Lithuania, not only is the whole government expenditure pie smaller, but that the slice of the pie is also smaller.

As mentioned above, both the Lithuanian and Swedish systems have fully funded components in their old-age pension systems. In Sweden, this is the premium pension, and in Lithuania the 'second pillar'. The Lithuanian second-pillar pension savings are managed by private pension-accumulation companies. There currently are four management companies and one life insurance company in Lithuania, while in Sweden there are more than 100 financial service companies (Fritzell et al. 2018). Despite the common purpose of additional savings and a common funded defined-contributions approach, several differences between these pensions should be noted.

A person who wished to participate in the Lithuanian second-pillar process may choose a pension-accumulation company and then a pension fund managed by this company. Before 2019, a person was allowed to direct 2 percentage points of the obligatory pension insurance contribution into a personal account under the condition that they would save an additional 2 per cent of the gross personal wage in this account. A matching state contribution of 2 per cent of the country's average wage was then added to this account. Participation in this system (usually referred to, in simple terms, as the '2+2+2') was voluntary: a person could choose either to pay the full contribution to the first pillar or join the second pillar; in the latter case, the first-pillar pension was proportionally reduced, but additional savings were earned. From 2019, this system became modified: participation in the second pillar is still voluntary, but a person who did not choose a pension-accumulation company was automatically enrolled and assigned to a randomly selected company. A person has the right to cancel this enrolment and stay solely in the first pillar; any default state-run fund is provided in this case, like in Sweden.

Pension funds managed by pension-accumulation companies are reorganised according to the life-cycle approach; thus, a participant is directed into the appropriate fund according to his or her age. The former 2 per cent pension insurance contribution is now joined with 2 per cent taken from a personal payment; so, the '2+2+2' system was transformed into 0 per cent of the obligatory pension insurance contribution, 4 per cent of the gross personal wage and 2 per cent of the country's average wage ('0+4+2') and then into '0+3+1.5' due to the above-mentioned 'tax revolution'.

The direct personal contribution to the second pillar made the Lithuanian system more similar to the Swedish premium pensions approach, but the main difference from the Swedish system remained: it matches the Lithuanian state's contribution to a person's account, which is not the case in Sweden. The contribution by the state (which may also be treated as tax relief) is justified as an incentive for those who are prudent and save their money for the future. It aims to encourage people to take more care about their future when pension protection from the first pillar is expected to be very modest due to population ageing.

It is difficult to directly compare the scale of the Swedish premium pension and Lithuania's second pillar by the rate of contribution, because the base of contribution (that is, the gross wage) is different due to different tax regimes. Nevertheless, it seems that the Lithuanian 4.5 per cent may accumulate relatively higher pension savings than the Swedish 2.5 per cent, and that in the future the pension part paid from the Lithuanian second-pillar savings will be higher than the corresponding part paid from the Swedish premium pension. This, in a certain sense, offsets the domination of the semi-flat general part of Lithuania's pay-as-you-go pension. According to the OECD's calculation, about 50 per cent of pensions in the future will be paid from the second-pillar savings (Lis 2018).

The question about the role and scale of the funded privately managed component in the pension system is a permanent topic of discussion in both countries. Swedish experts mention a trend towards pension system privatisation, but are sceptical about it. They mention high administrative costs of private management, difficulties for people in choosing among huge numbers of funds, and even criminal activities of some fund managers (Palme 2018, interview; Scherman 2018, interview). Also, saving for a pension is not easy for young people who have a relatively low income but have obligations for housing, child care, and so on (Kridahl 2018, interview).

DIFFERENCES IN THE CALCULATION AND INDEXATION OF BENEFITS

The main difference in how the Lithuanian and Swedish pensions are calculated lies in the distinction between the 'pension points' and the NDC approach. As mentioned above, the Lithuanian 'pension points' system was revised from 2018 to make it more consistent, but it was not recommended to change the whole system into a NDC approach. In the last sections of this chapter, we construct a simulation model that helps us to evaluate the possible advantages and disadvantages of an NDC system if it were to be applied in Lithuania.

The main factors determining the value of the Lithuanian pension are the amount of the basic pension (determining the general part) and the value of the pension point (determining the individual part). Despite efforts to introduce clear rules of the definition and indexation of these factors according to objective economic indicators, they were set by ad hoc decisions of the government during previous years. Clear pension indexation was introduced and made effective in Lithuania only since 2018.

As a starting point, the current values of the basic pension and the pension point at the end of 2017 were taken. Both factors are indexed according to the average growth rate of the national Labour Compensation Fund (LCF). For the calculation of this average, the data from three years before the current year, the expected value of the current year, and the forecasted growth rates of the coming three years are taken. Indexation is not applied if a decrease in GDP or the LCF is expected in the coming years. This rule is anticipated to ensure the financial sustainability of the pension system in the ageing population and additionally to help accrue a reserve fund to be used for maintaining pension values in case of a recession.

According to the new rule, both the general and individual parts were indexed by 6.9 per cent in 2018, 7.6 per cent in 2019 and 8.1 per cent in 2020. Until now there was no reason to apply the rules for the freezing of the paid amounts foreseen in the indexation scheme. Because of the pandemonium in

2020, a drop in GDP was expected, so the reasons to freeze pensions emerged. It was a serious challenge for the consistency-of-indexation rule and politicians decided to abolish the rule of freezing due to the GDP decline.

The application of the same index for both parts of the pension means that the ratio between these two parts for every recipient is fixed. Bearing in mind the rather low value of pension points (3.81 euros in 2020), it means that the Lithuanian pay-as-you-go system forever remains much more redistributive than the Swedish one (see above). This feature may discourage the participation of people with medium and higher incomes and force them to rely more on private funded provisions. Nevertheless, in 2020 the general part of pensions was increased more than the individual part by special legislative measures. It was justified as an additional protection for pensioners with low incomes.

The value of the Swedish pensions depends on the notional accounts of retirees, on the internal rate of return applied to these accounts, and on the rules regarding how they are converted into annuities and then indexed. Annuities are calculated in such a way that pensioners receive a part of the real growth in advance. This results in higher initial payments, but when benefits are indexed according to an income index based on a three-year growth of wages, this index is respectively reduced.

In order to ensure the financial sustainability of the Swedish pension system, it includes an automatic balancing mechanism (ABM). A formula for calculating the assets and liabilities of the system is prescribed by legislation. Assets and liabilities are valued at a three-year moving average. If the balance ratio falls below 1, the ABM is activated. It switches the indexation of pensions and notional pension capital to a new index series called the balance index. The balance index is calculated by multiplying the balance ratio (which is less than 1 if the balancing mechanism is activated) by the income index. Once the balance index catches up with the income index, the balancing mechanism is deactivated.

As a common feature of both systems, it should be mentioned that pension benefits are calculated based on lifetime contributions (the number of points collected or notional account accrued). However, in the Lithuanian case, it is fully true only for the individual part of the pension.

In both systems, pensions are indexed according to labour market performance, but this is taken into account in rather different ways: the growth rate of the LCF versus real wage growth, different periods of evaluation of the growth rates (seven or three years), and the choice of using growth rate forecasts or not.

Both systems have formal rules on how to slow down or stop the indexation, but these rules are quite different: the Lithuanian system relies directly on macroeconomic indicators, while the Swedish one relies on these indicators indirectly, via the ABM.

As a certain difference between Lithuanian and Swedish pension indexation it should be noted that the Swedish guarantee pension is indexed in another way (by price-base amount) than Lithuania's general part of the pension. The Swedish approach seems more rational because it allows for adaptation to real needs of the ratio between income support and earnings-related components in pension benefit composition. Nevertheless, as noted by Palme, due to the price indexing Sweden's guarantee pension is lagging behind the rest of pensions (Palme 2018, interview).

SOME ISSUES IN THE PERFORMANCE OF THE PENSION SYSTEMS

The comparison of pension systems should not be limited only to systemic design issues; it should also include a comparison of the performance of analysed systems. The most important aspects of pension system performance are without doubt the level of success in such essential issues as the smoothing of life income (evaluated as the replacement rate of income) and the protection from poverty (evaluated as the poverty rate of pensioners).

The Replacement Ratio

The aggregate replacement ratio, presented in Figure 12.1 and discussed below, is defined by Eurostat as the 'gross median individual pension income of the population aged 65–74 relative to gross median individual earnings from work of the population aged 50–59, excluding other social benefits'.[3]

In Sweden, the aggregated replacement ratio has not changed significantly from 2005 to 2016. The highest ratio was seen just before the last financial crisis, and it reached the lowest point in 2012. The slow impact of the crisis is caused by the adjustment mechanism, which uses indicators not from the last year but from the average of three years.

In Lithuania, this indicator shows a quite different situation: the replacement ratio is around 15 percentage points lower than in Sweden and much less stable. Surprisingly, the highest level was reached during the financial crisis. One of the main reasons for this is that pensions in Lithuania had no formal adjustment mechanism. The indexation of pensions was based only on political discretion. During the time of crisis, even though wages were significantly decreased, pensions were not reduced proportionally, and this caused an increase in the replacement ratio (including the social protection budget debt as well).

When looking at the gender aspect of the aggregate replacement ratio, it should be noted that during the whole of the last decade, the females' ratio went from 5 to 8 points lower than the males' ratio in Sweden, which is not

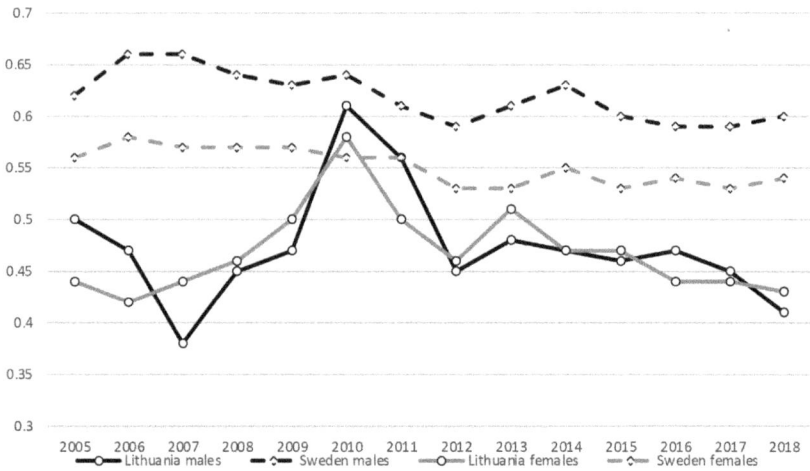

Source: Eurostat, Table tespn070.

Figure 12.1   Aggregate replacement ratio

the case in Lithuania. Despite some differences in certain years, the male and female replacement ratio in the averages does not differ so much in Lithuania as it does in Sweden.

This observation serves as evidence that the Swedish system provides better income protection and income smoothing during the life cycle but is more unequal from the gender point of view than the Lithuanian one. The main reason for this is the much lower financing of the Lithuanian pension system (see above), which results in a higher replacement rate for lower-wage-earners, usually females; gender inequality in Sweden may probably arise due to the fact that many women still devote more time to unpaid work and less time to paid work than men, which results in lower average incomes and, later on, in lower average pensions for women (Ahuja 2011). The relatively low level of pensions of single elderly women is also noticed by Swedish experts (Palmer 2018, interview).

The aggregate replacement rate shows the current average situation. Another important indicator of pension system performance is the net replacement rate, which is defined by the OECD as 'the individual net pension entitlement divided by net pre-retirement earnings, taking into account personal income taxes and social security contributions paid by workers and pensioners' (OECD Statistics Database 2020). According to the OECD's projections based on the situation of 2018, a person earning 50 per cent of the average wage has a 48.4 per cent replacement rate in Lithuania and 60.7 per cent in Sweden. On the other hand, a person earning 150 per cent of the average wage has only a 25.3 per cent replacement rate in Lithuania and 68.9 per cent in Sweden. Even the larger differences are seen in the projections for those who entered the labour market in 2012. A person earning 50 per cent of the average wage may expect a 101 per cent replacement rate in Lithuania and 68.8 per cent in Sweden. On the other hand, a person earning 150 per cent of the average wage may expect only a 62.4 per cent replacement rate in Lithuania and 72.9 per cent in Sweden (OECD Statistics Database 2020). These figures confirm the conclusion that the Lithuanian pension system is more redistributive in favour of the recipients of lower benefits.

The At-Risk-of-Poverty Rate[4]

One of the main indicators of the adequacy of a pension system is the percentage of retirees at risk of poverty. For this, Eurostat data for Lithuania and Sweden are presented in Figure 12.2.

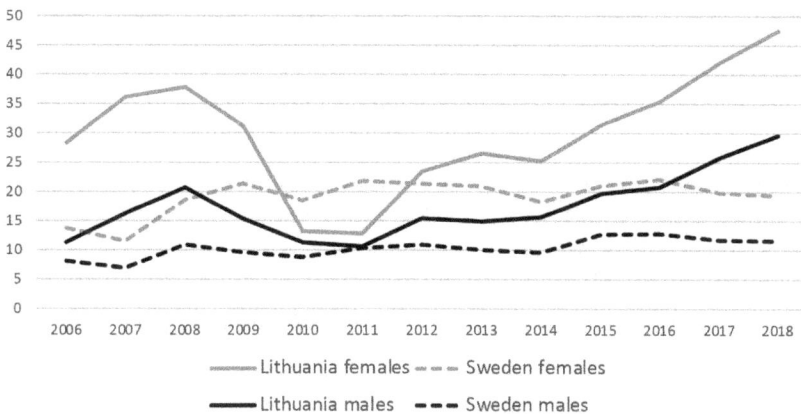

Source: Eurostat, Table tespn100.

Figure 12.2   The at-risk-of-poverty rate for pensioners

Swedish data show a stable or slightly increasing trend in the percentage of pensioners at risk of poverty, with small deviations. The gender gap is also more or less stable; the percentage of female pensioners at risk of poverty is above the male percentage by around 10 percentage points. It shows us that the Swedish system provides rather more stable protection, but the situation for women is visibly worse than it is for men. The reason for this is possibly similar to the reason behind the differences in the replacement ratio.

Lithuanian data are different: the percentage of pensioners at risk of poverty is much higher than in Sweden, except for the years 2010 and 2011, when, due to the economic crisis in Lithuania, the median income of the population fell more than the income of pensioners, which resulted in the low levels of the poverty rate. Outside of this period, the Lithuanian percentage of pensioners at risk of poverty is much higher than in Sweden and has a dangerous trend of rapidly increasing in the recent years. The gender gap is also bigger than in Sweden, by around 15 percentage points. Bearing in mind that the replacement ratio of men and women in Lithuania does not differ much, the most probable reason lies in the lower wage of women and the shorter insurance period due to an earlier retirement age applied in the former years, when the current generation of the pensioners had retired.

To conclude, these indicators show the better performance of the Swedish system; nevertheless, even in Sweden, women happen to be in a worse situation than men after retirement.

AN EVALUATION OF THE POSSIBLE APPLICATION OF THE NDC SYSTEM IN THE LITHUANIAN PENSION SYSTEM

As mentioned above, the Swedish NDC system is presented by some experts (Palmer 2018) as an example to follow in other countries due to its advantages in comparison with more traditional systems, like the Lithuanian 'pension points' system. Nevertheless, in our opinion NDC also has some disadvantages in comparison with the pension points system.

First is transparency. It is argued that NDC is ultimately transparent because it shows a retiring person the exact amount of pension savings, not something like 'mystical number of pension points'. But a retiring person is more interested how big his or her monthly benefit will be. The NDC answer is a complicated (and for many not transparent) rule of calculation and indexation of annuity. Here the pension point system seems more transparent: the number of personally earned pension points should be multiplied by the current value of pension points.

A second problem in our opinion may be named as 'intercohortal equality'. People of different birth cohorts with the same relationship of their wage to the average wage in the country and the same number of work years earn the same number of pension points; consequently their pensions are always equal. That is not the case in NDC. The notional capital of the older person is smaller than that of the younger person, just due to the growth of wages. It means that the older person retires earlier with the smaller pension and it is not necessarily automatically adjusted to the amount of the younger person's pension.

The NDC system is also presented as a system that helps to achieve pension adequacy and financial sustainability. In order to check this, in the Lithuanian case in the following part of our study we try to answer the following questions: if the Swedish NDC or current Lithuanian point-system approach had been implemented in Lithuania since 2001, what consequences would it have yielded? Would it have helped to improve the system's adequacy and sustainability? Would it have helped to cope with the crisis? Which model better protects Lithuanian individuals with different earnings?

Methodology of Constructing the Simulation Model

To answer these questions, we applied a simulation model based on the Swedish scheme and adapted it for Lithuania by modifying the formulae of the scheme and selecting the parameters suitable for Lithuania. Furthermore, a current Lithuanian pension model was applied, in order to evaluate adequacy from the perspective of individuals with different earnings. A similar methodology for NDC pensions' calculation was used in our previous research (Medaiskis and Eirošius 2019), but in this chapter, the analysis is more thorough. The calculations are performed not only on NDC pensions but also on pension points; much more attention is paid to pension adequacy.

The Equations of the Model and Data

In the NDC scheme, the sum $K_{i,T}$, accumulated by an individual i at the end of the time period T, is determined by the following formulae:

$$K_{i,T} = \sum_{t=1}^{T} cw_{i,t}I_t, I_t = \prod_{\tau=t}^{T-1}(1+\alpha_\tau), I_T = 1 \qquad (1)$$

Here, c stands for the pension contribution rate (or accumulation norm), $w_{i,t}$ stands for the individual wage in the time period t, I_t stands for an index calculated according to an internal yield in the time period t, and α_τ stands for the growth of the average wage. Apart from this, α_τ would also be used for indexing the pensions that are already being paid.

The factor of the annuity is calculated in the following way:

$$A_n = \sum_k P(k,n) F(k,n) \tag{2}$$

$$P(k,n) = L_k / L_n \tag{3}$$

$$F(k,n) = (1 + X/100)^{n-k} \tag{4}$$

Here, A_n is the annuity factor for an individual who retires at the age of n, $P(k, n)$ stands for the probability for the individual aged n to expect to live to the age of k, L_k stands for the number of population at age k, L_n stands for the number of population at age n, $F(k, n)$ is the discount factor from k years of age to n years of age, and X stands for the discount rate, which equals to 1.6 per cent, as in Sweden.

The pension paid for the individual i is calculated as an accumulated sum divided by the annuity factor: $K_{i,n} / A_n$ and then indexed by the growth rate of the average wage.

In the pension points scheme, which is applied now in Lithuania, the sum of pension points $P_{i,T}$, accumulated by an individual i at the end of the time period T, is determined by the following formulae:

$$P_i = \sum_{t=1}^{T} w_{i,t} \Big/ \overline{w}_t \tag{5}$$

The pension paid for the individual i is calculated as an accumulated sum of pension points multiplied by point value. The point value is indexed by the growth rate of the wage fund.

The period of 2001–2040 was chosen for the analysis. This period is sufficient for providing an overview of the economic cycle and evaluating the demographic changes.

The population data, especially the numbers of people of working age and those who retired, as well as data regarding the average wage in the years 2001–2018, were used as published by the Department of Statistics of Lithuania. For the period of the years 2019–2040, Eurostat population forecast data were applied. For the growth rate of the average wage, the short-term forecast of the Ministry of Finance was used, and for the later years, a 5 per cent growth of the average wage was presumed.

Scenarios of Calculation

Based on the previous formulae, the performance of the pension system was calculated according to three scenarios: NDC without a balancing mechanism, NDC with a balancing mechanism (an average of the past three years' social insurance incomes and expenditures' ratios), and the current Lithuanian pension points scheme. The accumulated amounts, benefits, and other indicators were calculated for the individuals who contributed to the simulated pension scheme the same rate from the average wage for 35 years before retirement. Contribution rates were taken in the terms of the years before 2019 (that is, before the 'tax revolution' spoken of previously). It was presumed that only 9.4 per cent of the full old-age pension insurance contributions are paid to the pension part which depends on previous earnings. The rest (9.01 per cent) is paid as a tax, while the general part of the pension is financed from the state budget. Since 2001, the pension amounts have been calculated for retiring persons each year. Pensions for persons who retired earlier than 2001 were transferred to the simulated scheme as well. It was performed by equating the benefits to the calculated pensions for the retired in 2001.

Scenario III is based on the current Lithuanian pension points scheme. The value of the points has been calculated since 2018; thus there is no historical data. For previous years the point value was calculated regressively based on the growth of the wage fund. It means that the point value for year t-1 is obtained by dividing the point value for year t by t-1 growth of the wage fund.

Model of Evaluation of Pension System Adequacy

System adequacy was evaluated from the perspective of four persons. Person A has earned the average wage during their whole career; Person B has earned half of the average wage, quite close to minimal wage; and Person C twice the average wage. Person's D income has been growing throughout all of their career, from 0.5 to 1.5 of the average wage. This means that during their working years Person D has earned almost the same amount as Person A. All four persons have participated in a pension system from 1980 to 2019. This means they have a 40-year history of participating in a pension system, and they retire in 2020. In addition, the weight of different years of participation was evaluated. Two possible scenarios of adequacy evaluation were added. First, all four persons entered the system five years later, and second, they left the pension system five years earlier.

Annuity Factor for Scenarios I and II

The annuity factor is calculated each year, and it might be slightly different annually. It increases in almost all periods because of growth of life expectancy. A higher annuity factor indicates that a pensioner will receive a smaller benefit because the virtual capital will be divided by a greater denominator. The dynamics of the annuity factor have significant changes in 2006–2011. People who had retired during this period were born at the time of the Second World War, and the number of such people is generally lower. The annuity factor is calculated according to formulae (3) and (4); thus, a lower number of people reaching the pension age causes a higher annuity factor. For example, the annuity factor in 2005 would be 14.87, and in 2007 19.28. A person with an average wage who retires in 2005 would have 10,500 euros in a virtual account and get a 62 euro monthly individual pension. A person with an average wage who retires in 2007 would have 12,600 euros and get a 54 euro monthly individual pension. From 2016 to 2025, the annuity factors are decreasing because of the changes in pension age. The older a person retires, the shorter the life expectancy that is used in annuity calculation. It means that the pension of a person with the same virtual capital in 2016 will be smaller than in 2025. Therefore, people who retire before the increase of the pension age will be in more of a disadvantageous situation. To avoid these problems, a linear extrapolation during this period was used to demonstrate a correct version of these calculations.

Results: Balance of the Pension System

According to the calculation results, all of the three scenarios indicate rather similar balances of the pension system, particularly until 2026. In later years, Scenario I, without a balancing index, suggests that liabilities exceed assets each year, and in 2040, the system gives a 19 per cent deficit. Therefore, indexation without a balancing mechanism is not sustainable, and if Lithuania had applied the NDC pension model, it could have worked only until 2026, while the pension age was increasing. Thus, the NDC scheme, if applied without a balancing mechanism, is not suitable for Lithuania.

On the other hand, Scenario II, with a balancing mechanism, helps stabilise the system. Also, it is notable that Scenarios I and II show identical results before the balancing mechanism is activated in 2011. Scenario II allows pensioners to collect a higher surplus of the social security fund during the peak of an economy cycle. It is important to mention that during 2003–2007, very high economy growth was visible in Lithuania. If the NDC system had been applied in Lithuania, it would have been indexed by wage growth, which would reach almost 20 per cent per year, and the pension insurance fund would have collected even more money because of the significantly decreased unemployment rate, which was 17 per cent in 2001 and only 4 per cent in 2007. During the crisis years, the negative balance would have not been as deep. Also, the surplus from the previous years could have been used to balance the system. Scenario III did create a quite similar surplus, because of the indexing by the wage fund. This includes both demographic and economic changes, so Scenario III allows pensioners to keep almost the same level of balance for the whole period. During the crisis in 2009–2010, the deficit was smallest in this scenario, because the pension point system does not use a three-year average of indicators; thus, it can react to changes faster.

Results: Replacement Ratio

Here the replacement ratio is described as the ratio between the average pension and the average wage of the same year. All scenarios would have quite a smaller amplitude in the dynamics of the replacement ratio; more significant differences are noticed in the beginning and the end of analysed periods. The replacement rate in Scenarios I and II would start at 46 per cent and would not be exceeded during all analysed periods. In Scenario III, the highest replacement rate, of over 43 per cent, would be reached in the years 2008 and 2009 at the beginning of the crisis. These years were the peak periods of the crisis, but benefits were increased due to the very high growth of the economy in previous years. The same also happened in the first two scenarios. An almost identical level of replacement would be kept in all scenarios during 2016 to 2025, but as was mentioned previously, differences appear in the end of analysed periods. From 2026, the replacement ratio significantly decreases in all scenarios, but the most significant decrease is notable in Scenario III, where in 2040 it would reach just 25 per cent. This means that during analysed periods the replacement ratio would decrease almost twice. In Scenario I it would stay at 32 per cent, but as was noticed before, this scenario would generate about 20 per cent of balance deficit.

Results: Perspectives of Persons with Different Earnings

As mentioned before, the adequacy of pension system models was evaluated in terms of four potential persons with different histories of incomes. It was assumed that all four persons would retire in 2020. As seen in Figure 12.3, Scenario I better protects persons who earn an average or higher wage. In this scenario, Persons A, C and D would get the highest pensions compared to other scenarios. On the other hand, Scenario III would be proffered for persons with a lower income. For Person B, who has half of the average wage income history, pension differences between scenarios would not be significant: only about 10 euros between different scenarios. Compared to their last year's wage, Person B would get from 62 per cent (Scenario II) to 64 per cent (Scenario III) of their previous income.

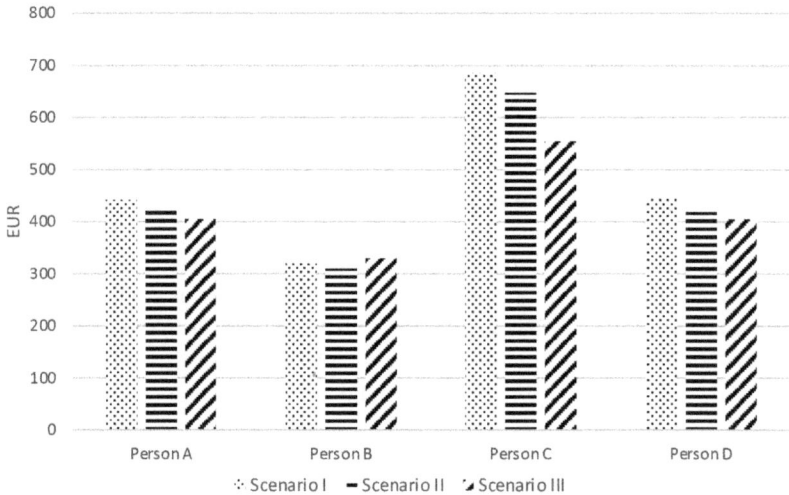

Source: Calculated by the authors.

Figure 12.3   Pension amounts for persons with different wage histories in 2020

The most significant difference between scenarios is noticed for Person C, who earned twice the average wage. Their pension would reach 685 euros, or 34 per cent of their previous earnings, if the NDC scheme was applied without a balancing mechanism. The worst situation for this person would be in Scenario III. Pension benefit would be 554 euros, or 131 euros less than in Scenario I. It would be less than 28 per cent of their previous income. For a person with a growing wage during their career years, all scenarios would provide almost the same pension as for Person A. Person D would contribute the same amount of money to a pension scheme as Person A, but neither NDC – with or without a balancing mechanism – nor a pension points scheme would give a significant advantage because of growing wages during the person's career. It is notable that for Person D, a pension would replace much less of their previous income. It would be 30 per cent in Scenario I and 27 per cent in Scenario III.

Another point of view to pension adequacy involves different breaks in a career. It was calculated how the pension amount would change if the same

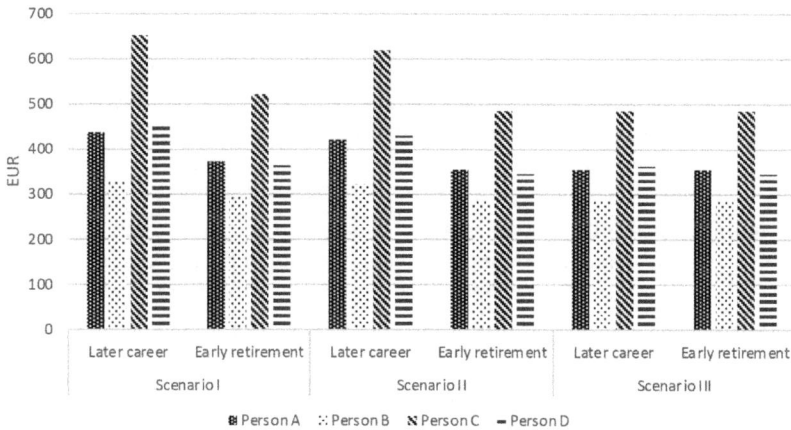

Source: Calculated by the authors.

Figure 12.4   Pension amounts for persons with different wage histories in 2020

persons as in previous calculations started their careers five years later or retired five years earlier (Figure 12.4). In Scenarios I and II, for all persons a later career generated higher pensions than early retirement. The difference is more significant for persons with higher incomes. For example, Person C in each case would have 35 years of contribution from an income of twice the average wage. If this person retires five years earlier, they would get a 20 per cent smaller pension than persons who started work five years later. For Person B, who had income close to the minimal wage, this difference would be about 10 per cent. In Scenario III there are no significant differences between both cases. So this means that an NDC scheme should motivate people to work longer, and does not damage pension amounts significantly if a person decides to make a career break in the early years. On the other hand, it is hardly possible that persons would calculate by how much their pension would increase if they stayed in labour for one additional year. Also, people who lose their job in later years or have to retire because of health problems would be damaged much more. Thus, more significant income in later years could not be a clear advantage of the pension system.

CONCLUSIONS

Both the Lithuanian and Swedish old-age pension systems are composed of pay-as-you-go and funded components, which are supplemented with additional provisions for those who are not entitled to pension benefits at all or for whom these benefits are too low.

The individual earnings-related component in Swedish pensions is much more significant than in the Lithuanian analogue. The relatively low financing of the Lithuanian pensions results in the necessity to distribute the available budget more evenly in order to guarantee necessary subsistence for the recipients with low insurance records. On the other hand, Lithuania's fully funded second-pillar pension component may accumulate relatively higher pension savings than the Swedish premium pension part due to the higher contribution rate and matching state contribution. This partially offsets the domination of the redistributive part of the Lithuanian pay-as-you-go pension.

Both the Swedish and Lithuanian pension benefits are calculated according to lifetime contributions. In both systems, pensions are indexed according to labour market performance, but this is taken into account in different ways: the growth rate of the LCF in Lithuania vs the real wage growth in Sweden. Also, both systems have formal rules on how to slow down or stop the indexation, but these rules are quite different: the Lithuanian system directly relies on macroeconomic indicators, while the Swedish one relies on these indicators indirectly using an ABM.

An analysis of statistical data shows that the Swedish system provides better income smoothing and income protection during the life cycle in terms of the replacement rate of old-age pensions and at-risk-of-poverty indicators for pensioners. However, Lithuanian replacement rates are more equal among genders, though they are below Swedish ones. On the other hand, Lithuania's at-risk-of-poverty gender gap among retired people is higher than in Sweden. Despite a more equal replacement rate, Lithuanian women may have lower income at retirement due to lower wages and shorter insurance records, and consequently be at higher risk of poverty.

The main difference between how Lithuanian and Swedish pensions are calculated is in the difference between the pension points and the NDC approach. The model used to simulate the possible application of an NDC system in Lithuania found a certain inequality effect of NDC: the people who retired at different years would receive pensions of considerably different amounts despite them having had the same length of service and similar wages (compared with the average wages of each year). The main reason for this is the influence of the growing life expectancy. The NDC scheme, only because of its balancing index, is able to maintain financial sustainability, but fluctuations in such a system would be quite high because of the time lag between real economic development and its impact on pension indexation. From the viewpoint of the NDC system's adequacy, despite the clearer indexation and better connection between contributions and benefits, it has no preference for countries facing demographic challenges since it does not help more than the other traditional systems (if well designed) to keep the replacement ratio on the same level. Also, from the perspective of a person, the pension point scheme gives equal value to each year of a career, but in the NDC scheme later years become more and more significant. It means people who lose their job in later years or have to retire because of health problems would be damaged much more. The pension points scheme distributes this risk across the whole career.

NOTES

1. Eurostat table [gov_10a_main], accessed 12 March 2020.
2. Calculated as the Lithuanian old-age pension expenditure per cent 5.6 divided by 34.9 and multiplied by 49.3.
3. https://ec.europa.eu/eurostat/tgm/web/table/description.jsp, accessed 12 March 2020.
4. The threshold of the risk of poverty is set at 60 per cent of the national median equivalised disposable income (after social transfers).

REFERENCES

Ahuja, A. (2011), 'Effects of life courses on women's pensions in Sweden', peer review comment paper, accessed 12 March 2020 at http://ec.europa.eu/social/main.jsp?catId=1024&langId=en&newsId=1409&moreDocuments=yes&tableName=news.

Anderson, K., and Backhan, M. (2013), *ASISP Annual National Report 2014: Sweden*. Brussels: European Commission.

Barr, N. (2013), 'The pension system in Sweden'. Report to the Expert Group on Public Economics. Stockholm: Ministry of Finance.

Bitinas, A., and Maccioni, F.A. (2014), 'Lithuanian pension system's reforms transformations and forecasts', *Universal Journal of Industrial and Business Management*, 2(1), 13–23.

Cichon, M. (1999), 'Notional defined contribution schemes: Old wine in new bottles?', *International Social Security Review*, 52, 87–105.

Fritzell, J., Heap, J., Nelson, K., Palme, J., and Schon, P. (2018), *ESPN Country Profile: Sweden 2017–2018*. Brussels: European Commission.

Gudaitis, T. (2009), 'Research of Lithuanian pension system reform: From conception to first annuities', *Management of Organizations: Systematic Research*, 49, 37–56.

Kridahl, L. (2018), Interview. Carried out under the project Challenges to Welfare State Systems in Lithuania and Sweden, financed by the Research Council of Lithuania.

Lazutka, R. (2008), 'Pensijų privatizavimo Lietuvoje tikslai ir rezultatai', *Ekonomika (mokslo darbai)*. Vilnius: VU, 2008, Nr.1.

Lazutka, R. (ed.) (2013), *Socialinis draudimas Lietuvoje: kontekstas, raida, rezultatai*. Vilnius: Lietuvos socialinių tyrimų centras.

Lis, M. (2018), 'Lithuania's pension system in the international perspective', paper presented at the Bank of Lithuania conference Lithuania's Pension System: How to Ensure Socially Just and Sustainable Pensions?, accessed 12 March 2020 at www.lb.lt/lt/renginiai/ekonomikos-konferencija-lietuvos-pensiju-sistema-kaip-uztikrinti-socialiai-teisinga-ir-tvaria-pensija.

Medaiskis, T. (2001), 'Changing the financing of Lithuanian pensions system', *International Social Security Review*, 54(2–3), accessed 12 March 2020 at http:// onlinelibrary.wiley.com/doi/10.1111/issr.2001.54.issue-2-3/issuetoc.

Medaiskis, T. (2011), 'Pensions at the time of recession: The case of Lithuania', *Zeitschrift fur Socialreform (Journal of Social Policy Research)*, 57, Heft 3, 251–266.

Medaiskis, T., and Eirošius, Š. (2019), 'A comparison of Lithuanian and Swedish old age pension systems', *Ekonomika*, 98(1), 38–59. doi: 10.15388/Ekon.2019.1.3.

Medaiskis, T., and Gudaitis, T. (2013), 'Assessing the impact of second pillar component on old age pension in Lithuania', *Ekonomika*, 92(4), accessed 12 March 2020 at www.zurnalai.vu.lt/ekonomika/article/view/2344.

Ministry of Health and Social Affairs (2016), *Swedish Old-Age Pension System*, Stockholm.

OECD (2018), *OECD Reviews of Labour Market and Social Policies: Lithuania*. Paris: OECD Publishing.

OECD Statistics Database (2020), 'Net pension replacement rates'. Data extracted 11 March 2020 from OECD.Stat.

Palme, J. (2018), Interview. Carried out under the project Challenges to Welfare State Systems in Lithuania and Sweden, financed by the Research Council of Lithuania.

Palmer, E. (2014), 'Financial sustainability of Swedish welfare commitments', *Public Policy Review*, Policy Research Institute, Ministry of Finance, Japan, 10(2), 253–276.

Palmer, E. (2018), Interview. Carried out under the project Challenges to Welfare State Systems in Lithuania and Sweden, financed by the Research Council of Lithuania.

Pensions Myndigheten (2020), Statisticdatabas, accessed 8 March 2020 at www .pensionsmyndigheten.se/statistik/pensionsstatistik/.

Scherman, K.G. (2007), 'The Swedish NDC system: A critical assessment', presented at the 2nd Colloquium of the Pension, Benefits and Social Security Section of the Actuarial Association, Helsinki, May 2007.

Scherman, K.G. (2018), Interview. Carried out under the project Challenges to Welfare State Systems in Lithuania and Sweden, financed by the Research Council of Lithuania.

SEB tyrimas: gyventojai mažiau tiki pensijų sistema ir pensija ima rūpintis patys (2017), accessed 12 March 2020 at www.seb.lt/naujienos/2017-02-07/seb-tyrimas -gyventojai-maziau-tiki-pensiju-sistema-ir-pensija-ima-rupintis.

SEB tyrimas: lietuvių pasiruošimas pensijai augo rekordiškai, bet džiaugtis dar anksti (2019), accessed 10 August 2020 at www.seb.lt/naujienos/2020-03-03/seb-tyrimas -lietuviu-pasiruosimas-pensijai-augo-rekordiskai-bet-dziaugtis-dar.

Swedish Pensions Agency (2019), *Orange Report 2018*, Stockholm.

Whitehouse, E. (2010), 'Decomposing notional defined contribution pensions: Experience of OECD countries' reforms', *OECD Social, Employment and Migration Working Papers*, No. 109, Paris: OECD Publishing, accessed 12 March 2020 at http://dx.doi.org/10.1787/5km68fw0t60w-en.

13. The inequality of public pension benefits for the elderly using Estonian data

Magnus Piirits

INTRODUCTION

Many developed countries have reformed their pension systems in one way or another to cope with their ageing populations. In addition to demographic developments, the changing world of work[1] is motivating further reforms in the pension world (OECD 2017, p. 155). In general, the retirement age is raised and some of the risks of the state are transferred to the person. Such reforms will have different effects, including on income distribution, either increasing or decreasing inequalities in the pension system. Thus, people's responsibility in the future will increase, and therefore the income and health of the individual and other factors become important elements in the collection of savings or pension rights for future income at retirement age. Since pensions are linked more to working-time income, this gives rise to the inequality of the income and the pension. Generally, the pension system reduces some part of the inequality of the income, which is a relevant function of the system (European Commission 2018, p. 52; Frick and Grabka 2010, p. 64; Immervoll and Richardson 2011, p. 62), and high redistributive effects are found in Europe (Wang and Caminada 2011, p. 2).

Pension systems cannot be directly compared with each other because the different national systems of the country are closely linked, such as the income tax system or health insurance, which may varyingly affect the welfare of the retirees. The pension system also depends on the country's historical background, and therefore, the system simply cannot be transferred to another country on the assumption that if it functions in one country it will certainly also be operational in another country (Holzmann et al. 2008, p. 5). The multi-pillar pension system proposed by the World Bank is in use in a number of countries.[2] Thus, the countries with the three-pillar system are similar in one way, but on the other hand, each country's system is still unique. This description corresponds to Estonia's pension system, which is representative of the World Bank's three-pillar pension system, but already the first pillar – that is, the state old-age pay-as-you-go (PAYG) system – is different. In addition, the second pillar – that is, the mandatory funded pension – has also increased the person's own contribution to the funded pension (Holzmann et al. 2005, p. 46; Schwarz and Arias 2014, p. 128).

The inequality of Estonia's old-age pensions has been one of Europe's lowest. The income quintile share ratio[3] for people aged 65 and older was 2.9 in 2010, but 3.6 in 2018. The average of the 27 member states of the European Union (EU) was 4.0 in 2010 based on Eurostat SILC data (Statistics on Income and Living Conditions) and increased by 0.1 points in 2018 (Eurostat 2019). Although the ratio is low in Estonia compared to other European countries, the quintile share ratio has risen by 0.7 points between 2010–2018. European countries have the future pension related to salary to a greater or lesser extent, and approximately 70 per cent of future pensions in Estonia depend on the wage of the person who earns an average wage their whole life (Piirits and Võrk 2019, p. 40). Therefore, income inequality in people younger than 65 years old can be used as an indicator for the future pension inequality. If the Nordic and Baltic countries are compared, then the largest absolute difference of the income quintile share ratio between two age groups (up to 65 years of age and age 65 and older) is 2.5 in Lithuania, followed by Latvia (1.6) and Estonia (1.3) (see Figure 13.1). In addition, Lithuania has the highest inequality (7.4) of people up to age 65, but Latvia has the highest inequality (5.1) of people over 65. While the inequalities in Lithuania and Latvia are larger than those of the EU-27, the inequalities of Estonia and the Nordic countries are lower.

Previous studies on the Estonian pension system have mainly been based on either the assessment of the situation of a typical person (for example, an average wage earner) or the aggregate national level. Intra- and intergenerational effects have not been well studied in Estonia. The first article about intragenerational effects of the Estonian pension system reforms was published by Piirits and Võrk (2019). Studies based on an intergenerational perspective have been conducted abroad, but similar studies on Estonia are non-existent.

The aim of this chapter is to assess the effects of pension reforms on income inequality in retirement age during 2017 to 2100 for the entire population. The chapter answers the following three research questions:

1. How much will inequality change in the three-pillar pension system until 2100?
2. How do reforms affect inequalities in pensions in the first pillar?
3. Is the income inequality in pensions less than in the labour market income inequalities, and if so, by how much?

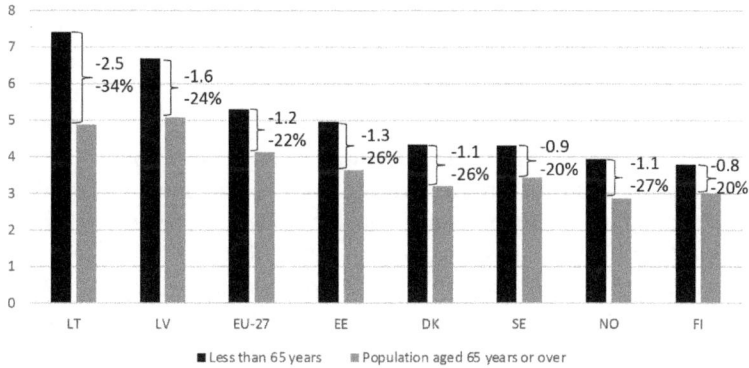

Source: Eurostat (2019).

Figure 13.1   Income quintile share ratio by two age groups in 2018 based on EU-SILC survey

Some reforms have tied the future pension tightly to the salary. For example, the PAYG scheme pension depends on the size of the salary and the introduction of mandatory and voluntary funded schemes. But some reforms decrease the link between salaries and future pensions. The reforms that are analysed in this chapter are:

1. PAYG scheme with service years;
2. PAYG scheme with insurance years;
3. PAYG + mandatory fully funded scheme (Pillar II);
4. PAYG + Pillar II + voluntary fully funded scheme (Pillar III);
5. PAYG + Pillars II and III + PAYG scheme with service years again;
6. PAYG + Pillars II and III + link retirement age to life expectancy.

Theoretically, pension systems may be categorised in several ways: based on financing, actuarial principles, benefit determination principles (whether a contribution or benefit is defined) or other. In general, different aspects of pension systems have been used to cover the widest possible range of interests. In more practical terms, the pension system is often divided into so-called pillars, where each pillar has its own purpose and mechanism of action. They differ from country to country in real systems, but in a larger picture, different goals are covered. It can be said that each system differs in some respects and there is not a single best pension system for all countries (Piirits n.d., p. 19).

The main social goals of the pension system are to prevent people from falling into poverty, and ensure benefit adequacy in terms of a reasonable replacement rate. From the perspective of public financing, the system should be sustainable, entailing a balance of long-term costs and revenues. In addition, the pension system should also consider other aspects, such as the impact on the labour market and the tax burden, and so on.

Many developed countries increase the individual contribution in preparation for retirement. As a result, pension systems lean more toward defined contributions (DC) than the defined benefits (DB) schemes. One example is the mandatory funded pension, as in the second pillar in Estonia. This should help to alleviate the problems of an ageing population and reduce budgetary pressure in the future. Goudswaard and Caminada (2010, p. 1) have found a strong positive relationship between public social expenditures and income distribution across Organisation for Economic Co-operation and Development (OECD) countries and negative relationships with private social expenditures.

Orenstein (2011) wrote a comprehensive article showing how more than 30 countries partially or fully transferred to the financed system, where every person had their own personal pension savings account, from the PAYG system in the period from 1981–2007. He adds that the financial crisis has slowed down this tendency, but it has not disappeared (Orenstein 2011, p. 65). The government cannot provide a more generous pension in the PAYG scheme in respect of one employee in the situation where there are more and more retirees, and therefore the importance of a DC scheme also increases (OECD 2014, p. 11; van Vliet et al. 2012, p. 13).

The European Commission has estimated that in many European countries between 2006 and 2046 the share of occupational and compulsory funded pensions will increase significantly (European Commission 2010, p. 77). It is found that the increase in private pensions (like occupational and compulsory funded pensions) increases the income inequality of retirees (Been et al. 2017, p. 1079; Goudswaard and Caminada 2010, p. 17; Schirle 2009, p. 32). Similar results are found by Bönke et al. but for different aspects – they found that the Gini coefficient elasticity is negative in PAYG pensions and positive toward income and investments; that is, funded DC schemes (Bönke et al. 2010, p. 508). Therefore, it is important to analyse inequality in such conditions as Europe has, and countries that have a similar system like the World Bank has recommended.

PAYG and DB systems are usually redistributive inside a generation, but when moving to a DC system where the size of a pension depends on the pension contributions, the distributional opportunity inside a cohort disappears. This might not be a concern, because higher-income groups have more savings opportunities, and they also have the opportunity to use the base amount of a PAYG scheme or guaranteed pension (Lindbeck and Persson

2003, p. 109). How reducing inequality affects economic growth is the question to which Garrec (2012) answered: 'greater progressivity results in less lifetime inequality but also less growth' (p. 55). Some public pension systems also have inequality-intensifying effects (Hwang 2016, p. 93).

Intrageneration equality can be divided between two axes. 'Horizontal equality' means that all people have the same internal rate of return if a pension is taken as an investment. 'Vertical equality' shows that people with different needs and characteristics have to be treated according to their needs. This also means that old-age pensioners who have worked for a low wage should not fall into poverty (Clements et al. 2014, pp. 8–10). Several studies have analysed the intragenerational potential effects and focus on just the inequalities and the effect of pension reforms (Aubert et al. 2013; Bonenkamp 2009; Klazar and Slintáková 2012; Lefèbvre 2007; van Vliet et al. 2012). There are simpler and more complex indicators for assessing inequalities – each indicator has its own advantages and disadvantages. In this chapter, the Gini coefficient was used as one of the indicators for assessing inequality, although it does not reveal exactly how incomes in the pension system are redistributed.

The rest of the chapter is organised as follows. In the next section the Estonian pension system is described by pillars: the PAYG scheme, the mandatory prefunded scheme and the voluntary prefunded scheme. In the third section the assumptions, scenarios, data used and data sources are presented. The fourth section shows how in the future inequality in scenarios will have begun to change. In the last section, a brief conclusion is presented.

THE ESTONIAN PENSION SYSTEM

The Estonian pension system consists of three pillars: the first – a state pension insurance scheme (a PAYG system with a point scheme); the second – a compulsory funded pension scheme (a DC scheme); and the third – a voluntary funded pension scheme (DC scheme). The following pension system description is mostly based on law (Riigi Teataja 2019b; 2019a).

State Pension: First Pillar

The state pension insurance scheme provides protection against the risks of old age, invalidity and survivorship using mainly employment-based old-age, work incapacity and survivors' pensions. In addition to common old-age pensions, there are rules for special pensions and pensions under favourable conditions (for example, pensions for the police, military, judges, artists and miners), which allow retirement under special conditions (Võrk et al. 2016, p. 8).

The coverage of the state pension insurance system (first pillar) is practically universal. Old-age pensions are comprised of three components: (1) the flat-rate base amount; (2) the pensionable length-of-service component, covering periods up to 1998; and (3) the insurance component, which is based on individual social tax payments to the state pension scheme, covering periods from 1999 onwards. Each year, individual social tax payments are converted into points using comparison with the average payment of the pension insurance part of the social tax. Both the length-of-service component and points are multiplied by the cash value (the monetary value of pension rights).

The old-age pension is redistributive through the flat-rate base amount, which in the second quarter of 2019 comprised 40 per cent of the average old-age pension. In addition, the length-of-service component is strongly redistributive, but as this considers only employment periods up to 1998, its role is gradually diminishing for new pensioners. However, it will start to grow again from 2021, as 50 per cent will be earned on the basis of service. Redistribution is also achieved through crediting pension rights for some non-active periods (including caring for children and military service).

Both the base amount and the cash value of one year of pensionable service and the pension insurance coefficient are indexed annually. The pension index is a weighted average of past consumer price indices and past growth of social tax revenues to the pension insurance system (in a 20/80 proportion since 2008). The index is 10 per cent higher for the base component and 10 per cent lower for the cash value of one year of pensionable service and the pension insurance coefficient.

Pensions are funded from the pension insurance part of the social tax (20 per cent), a payroll tax and additional contributions by employees. Part of the social tax (4 per cent) is transferred to the compulsory funded scheme if the person has joined the scheme, and every person adds an additional 2 per cent from their gross wage. Additional contributions to the voluntary pension scheme (third pillar) are possible.

Mandatory Fully Funded Scheme: Second Pillar

The mandatory funded pension scheme was set up in July 2002.[4] The PAYG system was partially replaced by a fully funded DC scheme by this decision. As a result of the amendment, 4 percentage points of social contributions were referred to the second pillar, to which a person additionally adds 2 per cent from their gross wage. Therefore, the individually accounted contribution to the first pillar is 16 per cent, and 6 per cent to the second pillar for a person who has joined the second pillar.

Citizens born in 1983 and later must join the second pillar. The preceding cohorts also had the opportunity, but they cannot reconsider their decision.

The last year to join was 2010, and this depended on the birth year. The second pillar covers 52 per cent of people born in 1942–1982 and 65 per cent of people born in 1956–1982. In 2020, there was also an opportunity to join for those born in 1970–1982.

It is possible to choose among four strategies that have different levels of risk. There are conservative funds (0 per cent of shares), balanced funds (up to 25 per cent of shares), progressive funds (up to 50 per cent of shares) and aggressive funds (up to 75 per cent of shares).[5] There are two possibilities for changing the fund: (1) directing contributions to a new fund, or (2) changing the pension fund units. These amendments can be made several times a year.

A person can start to receive payments only after retirement age; in 2016 the retirement age was 63. There are three payment options: a lump sum (if the value of Pillar II assets is under 10 times the national pension value, or NP),[6] a fund pension (with a value between 10 and 50 times the NP) and an annuity (with a value over 50 times the NP). In principle, people do not have freedom of choice because the choice depends on the value of the assets collected.

Voluntary Fully Funded Scheme: Third Pillar

The voluntary fully funded DC pension scheme was established in 1998. As it is a DC and voluntary scheme, people can decide their own contribution and, if necessary, modify it as appropriate. At the same time, the providers of the third pillar have appointed a minimum contribution in some cases. It is possible to temporarily suspend the contributions. The difference between the collection phase of the third pillar in normal investment is the income tax incentives. An investor in a third pillar can choose between the funds and the insurance.

Until the economic crisis, the number of investors in the third pillar increased, reaching 80,000 people in 2009; that is, 15 per cent of employed persons. From 2013–2017, the decline in the number of contributors stabilised and began to quietly rise. In 2017, 64,000 people – that is, 10 per cent of employed persons – made contributions to the third pillar. The average percentage of contributions from wages varied between 3 per cent and 5 per cent (Ministry of Finance 2018, p. 9).

The employer may also make contributions to the third pillar of the employee. Since 2012 contributions can be made at no additional taxation. However, there have been maximum limits set up for tax incentives (15 per cent of a person's gross income or 6,000 euros).

The possibilities for disbursements have not been put in place, but tax advantages have been created for those who start to have pay-outs after the age of 55 and use the annuity.

METHODOLOGY AND DATA

To achieve this chapter's aim, a population microsimulation model was developed. The model is named ESTPEN_MICRO and was built using the data analysis and statistical software Stata. The use of microsimulation means involving people with different backgrounds, which in turn affects the aggregated outcome of the pension reform. In addition, the people's future actions should be simulated in the microsimulation, which also adds the dispersion to the results of the pension-reform effects. The use of microsimulation of the entire population in order to assess inequality gives more stable results for several reasons: (1) the involvement of different cohorts who bear the effects of pension reforms in various scales, and (2) life-cycle simulation is not based on the typical person; that is, one person can obtain a higher wage in the first period and a lower wage in the second period.

Data

The microsimulation model requires individual-level data. First, long-term macroeconomic forecasts and Eurostat population forecasts are needed. The Ministry of Finance's (MoF) long-term macroeconomic forecast was originally drawn up until 2070. In this chapter, the same assumptions as used by the MoF for the last years leading up to 2070 have been used in order to extend the forecast and simulate pensions until 2100.

The macroeconomic data consists of five parts: (1) historic data (2000–2018); (2) the MoF short-term forecast (2019–2023); (3) a transition from the MoF short-term forecast to an ageing report projection (2024–2040); (4) an ageing report projection (2041–2070); (5) my own extension (2071–2100) based on 2061–2070 projections (Ministry of Finance 2019).

The growth of the Estonian economy was one of the fastest among European countries, but during the economic crisis the economic downturn was also one of the greatest. The consumer price index (CPI) is projected to be at a 2 per cent level. The growth of gross domestic product (GDP) (real) is projected to be between 1 per cent and 2 per cent in the long run. The average wage growth (nominal) is projected to be around the 4 per cent level. As the population decreases, especially the working-age population, the number of persons employed decreases and the rate of decline is estimated at 0.5 per cent on average.

The scenarios are based on the relevant retirement-age law. The statutory pension age (SPA) will reach 65 in 2026, according to the law. The SPA will stay at 65 in scenarios where it is not linked to life expectancy. The SPA will depend on the life expectancy from 2027 according to the law adopted at the

Table 13.1   Additional data used in the microsimulation model

Data description	Data period	Type	Source
Pension rights data: Micro-level data about earned entitlements, wages, pensions, type of pension	1999–2015	Micro-level	SIB
Demographic assumptions: Fertility and mortality rates	2018–2100	By age, gender and year	Eurostat long-term population projection
Education data for around 300,000 people	End of 2015	Micro-level	Estonian Education Information Board
Second-pillar data: value, strategy	End of 2015	Micro-level	Estonian Central Register of Securities (CSD)
Third-pillar data: Value, contribution	End of 2015	Micro-level	CSD
Overall background statistics	As available	Aggregated	Statistics Estonia, Eurostat

Source: Author.

end of 2018. The retirement age will reach 67 in the middle of the 2040s and will reach 70 by 2074 using the last-known population projections.

The literature shows that the difference in life expectancy is one of the factors in the redistribution (Bonenkamp 2009, p. 73). The difference in life expectancy for men and women aged 65 was 5.1 years in 2016, but the difference is decreasing, and it has been estimated that it will be 3.4 years by 2100.

The microsimulation model uses the Estonian population data (1.3 million people in 2016 and 1 million in 2100) on the basis of three registries. The model uses information that is described below (see Table 13.1) in addition to the above-described data. Social Insurance Board (SIB) data is the basis of the entire simulation as it includes current pensioners and all people who have ever paid social tax over the period 1999–2015. In addition to SIB data, new cohorts that follow Eurostat's population forecast (through birth rates and mortality rates) have also been simulated. Second- and third-pillar information is also added.

Scenarios

Seven scenarios were established to meet the aim of this chapter (see Table 13.2). Three of these are scenarios that have been in place for some time in the past, and one scenario is in force in the pension system. Another three scenarios involve legislated changes of the pension system at the end of 2018. Until the fourth scenario, the scenarios were built on top of each other, or it can be said that they are cumulative. New pension-reform scenarios are built on the existing system, and the last scenario takes all the new reform ideas together and is also built on the current pension system.

The pension system that was in force before 1999 had only the first pillar. The size of the pension depended on the service years (length of employment). This is scenario 1, and is used as the base scenario. At first, the way first-pillar entitlements are earned was reformed in 1999; that is, the entitlements are earned based on the size of the wage, not by employment. At this stage there was no indexation, but in the scenarios the same indexation is used for comparison reasons. In addition, the retirement age is the same for scenarios from before the 2018 legislation; that is, the retirement age will rise to 65 in 2026. The voluntary fully funded scheme introduced in 1998 is also included in the second scenario.

The mandatory fully funded scheme started in the middle of 2002, and this reform is used as scenario 3.

The change of the indexation is scenario 4. The index was made more dependent on social tax revenues. Indexation was changed to a 20/80 proportion instead of 50 per cent of CPI and 50 per cent of social tax revenues growth. It also increased the growth of the base amount of the first pillar. The base part exists in all scenarios. The pension system consists of three pillars where half of the first pillar depends on the size of the wage and the second and third pillars are fully dependent on the size of the wage.

Due to the financial sustainability and the solidarity aspects, the government proposed a number of amendments at the beginning of 2017 that should increase financial sustainability and solidarity (Piirits and Masso 2017, p. 1–2), and adopted them with some changes at the end of 2018. This study does not deal with financial sustainability and focuses only on how the pension reforms affect the distribution and solidarity of the pensions.

A majority of the reforms have been simulated, but flexible retirement is excluded because there is no data to simulate flexible retiring. This needs further investigation. Previous reforms have been built on top of each other, but the new reforms will be built on an existing system. All new reforms will be put together in the last scenario.

The first amendment would change the logic on how the first-pillar entitlements will be earned; that is, from 2021 50 per cent is earned from service years and 50 per cent from insurance years. Meanwhile, earned entitlements would remain as they were. In addition, it has been stated that the second-pillar contribution decreases the first-pillar service years' entitlements.

From 2027 the retirement age will be linked to life expectancy (a year after reaching the retirement age of 65). The life expectancy anchor point will be age 65. For example, if the life expectancy at the age of 65 rises by one month compared to the previous cohort, then the retirement age also increases by one

Table 13.2   Simulated reforms

Description	Actual years	Length of service	Insurance	Indexation	Pillar II	Pillar III
1. PAYG + service component	To 1998	Yes	No	50/50	No	No
2. PAYG + insurance component	1999–2002	No	Yes	50/50	No	Yes
3. Introduction of Pillar II	2002–2008	No	Yes	50/50	Yes	Yes
4. Indexation change in the PAYG	2008 to …	No	Yes	Quicker indexation of the base; 20/80	Yes	Yes
5. PAYG + new service component	2021	2021 to …: 50 per cent	2021 to …: 50 per cent	20/80	Yes	Yes
6. Linking pensionable age to life expectancy	2027	No	Yes	20/80	Yes	Yes
7. New reforms together	2021	2021 to …: 50 per cent	2021 to …: 50 per cent	20/80	Yes	Yes

Source: Author.

month. The change of life expectancy in five-year intervals is used as in the following equation (Riigi Teataja 2019c):

$$SPA_\tau = 65 + \frac{\sum_{\tau-8}^{\tau-4} LE_{65}}{5} - \frac{\sum_{2018}^{2022} LE_{65}}{5} \qquad (1)$$

Where

SPA_τ – Statutory pension age at year τ ;

LE_{65} – Life expectancy of 65-year-old people.

The SPA will not be changed if the change of life expectancy is less than one month; that is, the retirement age is determined by the accuracy of the month.

In addition, the maximum increase of the SPA could be three months in one year.

Finally, there is a scenario where the SPA is linked with life expectancy and combined with the new service component.

The old-age pensions, old-age pensions under favourable conditions and old-age pensions following early retirement have been calculated in the model as retirement income. Since the objective is to assess the distribution of pensions after retirement, the following pension types are, therefore, excluded: (1) the deferred old-age pension, because only a fraction of people use this – most superannuated and disability pensioners are moving to an old-age pension at retirement age; and (2) the survivor's pension, because the children are mostly the ones who receive it.

Only annuities have been used for comparison purposes in the mandatory and voluntary funded scheme pay-outs. Thus, all payments of the second pillar are calculated as an annuity. Insurance companies have to use unisex life tables to calculate the annuities.

RESULTS

All three pillars are assessed separately, then the results are presented together and by different characteristics. Since the pension reforms are mostly related to the first pillar, the second part of this subsection compares the first pillar and all pillars together. However, all indicators have been calculated only for those people who are entitled to a pension in a particular pillar. For example, the average of the third-pillar annuity is 200 euros, but there are only 50,000 people. At the same time, the first-pillar pension is 1,000 euros and the pension from all three pillars is 1,100 euros.

As, at one point, reform might generate a surplus in the pension system, it is likely to be distributed among retirees because the share of retirees in the population is increasing and the replacement rates are rather modest. Thus, in the following paragraphs, the size of the first pillar and the total pension have already been corrected by a surplus by increasing the flat-rate base amount.[7]

The pension system (from scenario 3) consists of three pillars: (1) mandatory PAYG point scheme, (2) mandatory fully funded DC scheme and (3) voluntary fully funded DC scheme. Although the roles of the second and third pillars are increasing, the first pillar will still play a key role in the future (around 70 per cent of the future average yearly pension of all retirees). People with second or third pillars will receive similar payments in those pillars in the future. If initially the size of the pension depends entirely on the first pillar, then the share of the second and third pillars will be higher in the future. Of course, it must be considered that the results represent all people who are retirees in a particular year. For example, people who receive a second-pillar annuity until 2050 are people whose birth year is from 1951–1985. So, the maximum contribution period is 11–43 years for them. Payment of an annuity has its own effect because an annuity is nominally the same amount for all retirement time; as it was at retirement it will be at age 80 as well.

Analysis of the results of the second and third pillars must also take into account that they have not been cut off (an annuity is also paid if a person has some euros in the second pillar). But the first-pillar benefits have been cut off; the minimum amount of the public pension is the NP, and the minimum amount for the old-age pension is the base amount. Although the second pillar has the minimum amount when the annuity is calculated, for comparison reasons an annuity for all is used.

The following paragraphs first describe the pension system replacement rates in certain years for all retirees. Here one replacement rate is represented: GRPL (gross relative pension level), the pension relative to the economy-wide average wage.

The first-pillar (PAYG scheme) results of the GRPL depend heavily on the number of people who are employed, because in both cases the second component of the GRPL (salary) is the same. Like most developed countries, Estonia also has an ageing population and low birth rate and, therefore, needs more employees. Thus, it can be assumed that the value of the first pillar in comparison with average wages is constantly decreasing. The results show that the gross pension proportion of the economy-wide average wage was on average 34 per cent in 2016, falling to around 18–25 per cent by 2050, and rising to 21–30 per cent by 2100 (see Figure 13.2). The importance of the second and third pillars is also increasing in comparison with the average wage developments, but this result reflects the longer contribution periods of fully funded schemes.

The situation in 2016 does not differ by the scenarios, because the first four scenarios have a slight impact and scenarios 5 to 7 have an impact later. The introduction of the insurance component slightly increases (1–2 percentage points) the average replacement rate compared to the first scenario. The difference comes from investments in the third pillar. The introduction of a mandatory funded scheme (scenario 3) increases the average replacement rate gradually, reaching a rate 4 percentage points higher in the 2050s and 6 percentage points in 2100. The change in indexation mechanism (scenario 4) increases the average replacement rate until the 2060s, because the change of indexation will affect the future pension more quickly than the funded scheme. The average replacement rate is a maximum 4 percentage points higher in scenario 4 than in scenario 3. Scenario 5 (return of the service component in PAYG scheme from 2021) and scenario 4 do not differ from one another in terms of the average replacement rate, because they have the same number of total retirees and amount of total money and differ in the PAYG scheme distri-

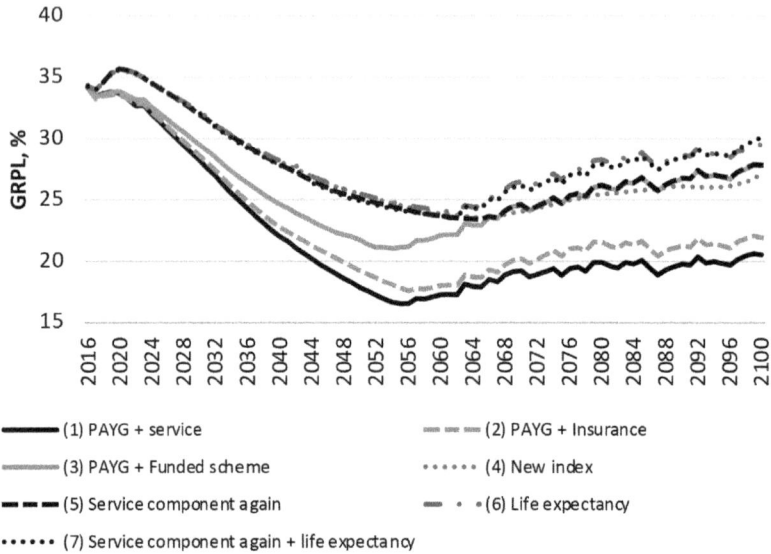

Note: Scenario (1) Base scenario; (2) PAYG + Insurance; (3) PAYG + Funded scheme; (4) New index; (5) Service component again; (6) SPA linked to life expectancy; (7) Service component again and SPA linked to life expectancy.
Source: Author's calculation.

Figure 13.2   All retirees' gross relative pension levels (GRPL) from the first, second and third pillars together by scenarios

bution. The SPA linked to life expectancy increases the average replacement rate by 2 percentage points compared to scenario 5 from the 2060s.

A previous study (Piirits and Võrk 2019, p. 54) examined the men born in 1980 who will retire in 2045 according to the SPA, and found that the Gini coefficient increased to 0.2 in the first pillar, 0.39 in the second pillar and 0.27 in the first and second pillars.

The base scenario (scenario 1) has the lowest Gini coefficient because in this scenario the amount of pension is not dependent on wages (see Figure 13.3). Inequality still changes because the employment varies. The introduction of the insurance component and third pillar will greatly increase the inequality of pensions. The introduction of the second pillar does not increase inequality in the first pillar; rather, it decreases it a little because people do not earn so many entitlements from the first pillar, but total inequality increases to the highest point compared to the other scenarios. Scenario 4 (new index) decreases overall inequality because the flat-rate base amount increases faster than the insurance part (linked to wages). The Gini coefficient increases by half to 70 per cent by 2050 in all scenarios since the baseline value of the coefficient is low (0.1). Although the service component will be partially returned in 2021, the inequality figure will start to change at the beginning of the 2060s. Linking the retirement age to the life expectancy has the opposite effect: increasing inequality in future pensions, because the working life is longer and wage inequality has a longer impact. All in all, there would be no effect on inequality if scenarios 5 and 6 are taken together in scenario 7.

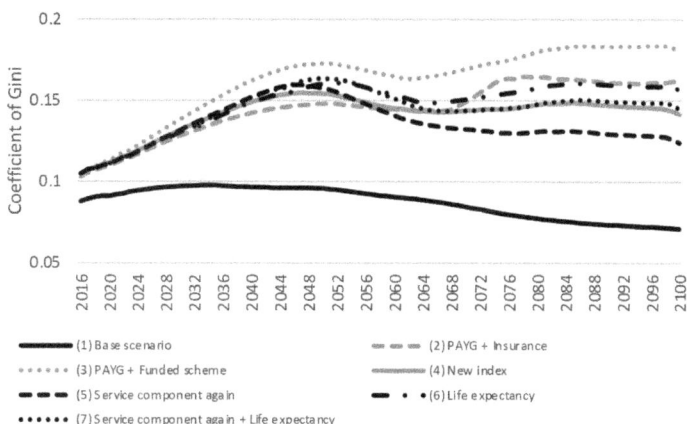

Source: Author's calculations.

Figure 13.3   All retirees' Gini coefficient of total pension from the first, second and third pillars by scenarios

Overall, the analysis revealed that future pensions are not as high as the result of the typical agent model, and the second- and third-pillar proportions are lower than in the typical agent model. The inequality from life-cycle wages is transferred to the retirement but the first pillar diminishes a great part of this. The positive effect of the scenarios is sustainability of the first-pillar system since those lead the first pillar from deficit to surplus at the end of the 2060s. The first-pillar deficit[8] would be around 1.1 per cent of GDP by 2050 if there was not an increase in retirement age. Since there have been no major changes in the population since 2060, the first pillar is also moving toward a surplus.

CONCLUSIONS

Estonia is an example of a country with the three-pillar pension system but with its own characteristics and peculiar history. At the end of the 1990s, the Estonian pension system consisted of a PAYG scheme that depended on length of service, where the pension entitlements were earned based on the length of activity (learning, military service, childcare and working). Therefore, the inequality of pensions has been relatively low. Although the discussions on reforming the pension system started in the early 1990s, the first major step was the replacement of length of service with an insurance component; that is, a wage-related share since 1999. At the same time, a voluntary prefunded scheme was also created. The link between earnings and future benefits was strengthened by the introduction of the second pillar – the compulsory funded pension scheme – in 2002. It takes many years until full maturation. The following two major reforms are linked to the first pillar – first, the pension index was changed to be more dependent on the growth of social tax receipts, and the flat-rate base part of the PAYG scheme was made to grow faster. The latest change was made at the end of 2018, when it was decided to bring back the length-of-service component to a 50 per cent proportion from 2021 and link the future retirement age to life expectancy at 65 years old. Those changes are not reflected in pensions so quickly, as those who have earned the service component live longer and new generations will retire later because of the increase of the retirement age.

The inequalities in pensions of the first pillar after the last (2018) pension reform will increase to 0.118 by 2050 from 0.102 in 2016. Although at first the inequality increases by 1.6 percentage points compared to the initial level, inequalities in recent years are stabilising and decreasing. The 2018 reforms aimed to improve the financial sustainability and to raise the future pensions of low-wage-earners. Accordingly, the future inequality should decrease. However, as the impact of these reforms is long-term, the effects only appear toward the end of this century. Therefore, inequality will decrease to the 0.068 level by 2100. The three-pillar system of total inequality increases by over 50 per cent by 2050 (from 0.105 to 0.163 in 2050) but half of the increase comes from the first pillar and another half from the funded schemes. As the inequality of the first and second pillars begins to decrease after 2050, the income inequality of the entire pension system declines to 0.144 by 2100. The pension system attains a higher sustainability with the 2018 legislated pension reforms. To sum up and answer research question 1 (how much does inequality change in the three-pillar pension system until 2100), the total inequality has a non-monotonic (inverted U-shape) trend of the Gini coefficient. The total inequality in 2100 would be higher than in 2016 but lower than in 2050, while the inequality of first-pillar old-age pensions will be lower than 2016 by 30 per cent (research question 2 – how do reforms affect inequalities in pensions in the first pillar).

While in wage simulation inequality is higher than 2015 real data (0.53 versus 0.47), all pillars are able to reduce inequality in wages because the Gini coefficient is lower. Total inequality would be 0.145 compared to 0.53 of wages' inequality. The second-pillar inequality will be half of it (0.267). The reasons for this are different. The first pillar substantially redistributes pensions, and even more after the last reform (scenarios 5 to 7). The second and third pillars are affected by two aspects: (1) wage inequality is expressed using one-year data and a person can be in different places in different years, but the pension is the cumulative result of all years; and (2) the choice of funds affects future pensions. To summarise and answer research question 3 (is the income inequality in pensions less than in labour market income inequalities, and if so, by how much), as the first-pillar pension also accounts for a large proportion of pensions in the future (70 per cent to 80 per cent), the future inequality of all pensions will also be largely affected by the inequalities of the first pillar, in which inequality will decrease in time.

NOTES

1. Especially working part-time and using different contracts for which pension rights are not earned.
2. For example, Latin America – Chile, Peru, Colombia, Argentina, Uruguay, Mexico, Bolivia, El Salvador, Costa Rica, Nicaragua, Ecuador, Dominican Republic – and Central and Eastern Europe and Central Asia – Hungary, Kazakhstan, Latvia, Croatia, Bulgaria, Slovakia, Estonia, Lithuania, Romania, Macedonia, Russia, Ukraine, Kosovo – and countries from East Asia, the Middle East and North Africa, sub-Saharan Africa and South Asia, but in each country it has been implemented differently (Holzmann et al. 2005).
3. Twenty per cent of the total income of the largest-income people is divided by 20 per cent of the total income of the lowest-income people.
4. Estonia's mandatory funded scheme has been voluntary since 2021; read more in Piirits and Laurimäe (2020).
5. Those levels changed during 2019. Aggressive funds can invest 100 per cent in shares.
6. The national pension was 205.2 euros per month in 2019.
7. Meaning that all retirees receive the same amount from the surplus.
8. It should be considered that only the share of the first-pillar contributions is taken into account, which is generally 16 per cent of the salary, and only those types of pension that have been used in the model are calculated as expenses.

REFERENCES

Aubert, P., C. Duc and B. Ducoudré (2013), 'French Retirement Reforms and Intragenerational Equity in Retirement Duration', *Economist (Netherlands)*, **161** (3), 277–305.

Been, J., K. Caminada, K. Goudswaard and O. van Vliet (2017), 'Public/Private Pension Mix, Income Inequality and Poverty among the Elderly in Europe: An Empirical Analysis Using New and Revised OECD Data', *Social Policy & Administration*, **51** (7), 1079–1100.

Bonenkamp, J. (2009), 'Measuring Lifetime Redistribution in Dutch Occupational Pensions', *De Economist*, **157** (1), 49–77.

Bönke, T., C. Schröder and K. Schulte (2010), 'Incomes and Inequality in the Long Run: The Case of German Elderly', *German Economic Review*, **11** (4), 487–510.

Clements, B. J., F. Eich and S. Gupta (2014), 'Equitable and Sustainable Pension Systems', in B. Clements, F. Eich and S. Gupta (eds), *Equitable and Sustainable Pensions: Challenges and Experience*, Washington, DC: International Monetary Fund, pp. 3–29.

European Commission (2010), 'Joint Report on Pensions: Progress and Key Challenges in the Delivery of Adequate and Sustainable Pensions in Europe – Country Profiles', Brussels: European Commission.

European Commission (2018), 'The 2018 Pension Adequacy Report: Current and Future Income Adequacy in Old Age in the EU; Joint Report. Volume I', Brussels: European Commission.

Eurostat (2019), 'S80/S20 Income Quintile Share Ratio by Sex and Selected Age Group: EU-SILC Survey [Ilc_di11]', accessed 9 March 2020 at https://ec.europa.eu/eurostat/databrowser/view/ilc_pns4/default/table?lang=en.

Frick, J. R., and M. M. Grabka (2010), 'Old-Age Pension Entitlements Mitigate Inequality: But Concentration of Wealth Remains High', *Weekly Report*, **6** (8), 55–64.

Garrec, G. L. (2012), 'Social Security, Income Inequality and Growth', *Journal of Pension Economics & Finance*, **11** (1), 53–70.

Goudswaard, K., and K. Caminada (2010), 'The Redistributive Effect of Public and Private Social Programmes: A Cross-Country Empirical Analysis', *International Social Security Review*, **63** (1), 1–19.

Holzmann, R., R. P. Hinz and H. von Gersdorff (2005), 'Old-Age Income Support in the 21st Century: An International Perspective on Pension Systems and Reform', Washington, DC: World Bank.

Holzmann, R., R. P. Hinz and M. Dorfman (2008), 'Pension Systems and Reform Conceptual Framework', World Bank Discussion Paper 824.

Hwang, S. (2016), 'Public Pensions as the Great Equalizer? Decomposition of Old-Age Income Inequality in South Korea, 1998–2010', *Journal of Aging & Social Policy*, **28** (2), 81–97.

Immervoll, H., and L. Richardson (2011), 'Redistribution Policy and Inequality Reduction in OECD Countries: What Has Changed in Two Decades?', *SSRN Scholarly Paper*, ID 1948026, Rochester, NY: Social Science Research Network.

Klazar, S., and B. Slintáková (2012), 'How Progressive Is the Czech Pension Security?', *Prague Economic Papers*, **3**, 309–27.

Lefèbvre, M. (2007), 'The Redistributive Effects of Pension Systems in Europe: A Survey of Evidence', LIS Working Paper Series 457.

Lindbeck, A., and M. Persson (2003), 'The Gains from Pension Reform', *Journal of Economic Literature*, **41** (1), 74–112.

Ministry of Finance (2018), 'Riikliku vanaduspensioni, kohustusliku kogumispensioni ja vabatahtliku kogumispensioni statistika [Statistics of state old-age pension, mandatory funded pension and voluntary funded pension]', accessed 10 March 2020 at www.pensionikeskus.ee/wp-content/uploads/rahandusministeeriumi-statistika/Pensioni-statistika%C3%BClevaade-2018-1.pdf.

Ministry of Finance (2019), 'Macroeconomic Long-Term Forecast until 2070', accessed 20 January 2020 at www.rahandusministeerium.ee/system/files_force/document_files/prognoos-kuni-2070-28-10-2019.xlsx?download=1.

OECD (2014), 'OECD Pensions Outlook 2014', Paris: OECD Publishing.

OECD (2017), 'Preventing Ageing Unequally', Paris: OECD Publishing.

Orenstein, M. A. (2011), 'Pension Privatization in Crisis: Death or Rebirth of a Global Policy Trend?', *International Social Security Review*, **64** (3), 65–80.

Piirits, M. (n.d.), 'The Impact of Pension Reforms on Pension Inequality in Estonia: An Analysis with Microsimulation and Typical Agent Models', dissertation, University of Tartu.

Piirits, M., and M. Laurimäe (2020), 'Estonia's Statutory Funded Pension Scheme on the Way to Being Made Voluntary', Brussels: European Commission.

Piirits, M., and M. Masso (2017), 'The Government of Estonia Proposes to Tie the Pension Age to Life Expectancy and Increase Solidarity in the State Old-Age Pension', Brussels: European Commission.

Piirits, M., and A. Võrk (2019), 'The Impact of Introduction of Funded Pension Scheme on Intragenerational Inequality in Case of Estonia: A Microsimulation Analysis', *International Social Security Review*, **72** (1), 33–57.

Riigi Teataja (2019a), 'Funded Pensions Act', accessed 1 March 2020 at www.riigiteataja.ee/en/eli/521012019010/consolide.

Riigi Teataja (2019b), 'State Pension Insurance Act', accessed 1 March 2020 at www.riigiteataja.ee/en/eli/504022019001/consolide.

Riigi Teataja (2019c), 'State Pension Insurance Act, since 2027', accessed 1 March 2020 at www.riigiteataja.ee/akt/103012019003.

Schirle, T. (2009), 'Income Inequality among Seniors in Canada: The Role of Women's Labour Market Experience', Canadian Labour Market and Skills Researcher Network Working Paper 51.

Schwarz, A. M., and O. S. Arias (2014), 'The Inverting Pyramid: Pension Systems Facing Demographic Challenges in Europe and Central Asia. Europe and Central Asia Reports', Washington, DC: World Bank.

van Vliet, O., J. Been, K. Caminada and K. Goudswaard (2012), 'Pension Reform and Income Inequality among Older People in 15 European Countries', *International Journal of Social Welfare*, **21**, 8–29.

Võrk, A., M. Piirits and M. Masso (2016), 'ESPN Thematic Report on Retirement Regimes for Workers in Arduous or Hazardous Jobs: Estonia', Brussels: European Commission.

Wang, C., and K. Caminada (2011), 'Disentangling Income Inequality and the Redistributive Effect of Social Transfers and Taxes in 36 LIS Countries', *SSRN Scholarly Paper*, ID 1909941, Rochester, NY: Social Science Research Network.

14. Stretching the canvas: beyond welfare state typologies to capability and agency

Barbara Hobson

Stretching the canvas is a metaphor that captures the conceptual and theoretical challenges that emerge from this book. Do typologies and models of family policy provide leverage for analysing welfare state change? How do the various policies (some contradictory and working at cross purposes) reflect competing currents in institutional, societal and cultural contexts, both in comparisons of Nordic and Baltic countries and within them? How do these cross-currents affect diverse groups? I address these questions using examples from the rich, contextualized analysis of sets of countries that are not often compared by welfare state researchers. All of these questions give rise to stretching the canvas in welfare state research. Stretching the canvas even wider, I provide a framework that encompasses the complex inequalities in these challenges, which derived from Amartya Sen's dynamic and multi-dimensional capability approach.

At the outset, I want to emphasize that I provide neither a summary nor synthesis here, since I could not do justice to the rich analysis and range of policy areas covered in this volume. My purpose in this exploratory chapter is to take the conversation on comparative welfare states further.

This chapter has four sections: the first engages with regimes and typologies with a critical lens, the second focuses on forms of hybridization and commonalities in Nordic and Baltic states, the third addresses diversity and its challenges, and the fourth applies the capability framework to one empirical example, followed by concluding remarks.

STRETCHING THE WELFARE REGIME PARADIGM

I begin this section with the welfare regime paradigm, which has been dominant in comparative welfare state research and has undergone numerous revisions and been challenged on many fronts (Orloff 2009). Esping-Andersen's three worlds of welfare capitalism (1990) became four worlds (adding a Latin

Rim cluster) and then five worlds (constructing the post-socialist cluster). Challenging the absence of gender dimensions in the Three Worlds, a burgeoning of gender regimes in typologies emerged, revolving around the degree to which gendered policy logics and discourse could weaken or strengthen the male breadwinner (Lewis 1992) or how care was organized (Anttonen and Sipilä 1996). These were followed by other typologies concerning how policy frameworks mitigate or sustain the poverty of lone mothers (Hobson 2004; Kilkey and Bradshaw 1999). In *Making Men into Fathers* (2002), David Morgan and I introduced a fatherhood regime that dealt with how states construct men's rights and responsibilities for fatherhood and fathering. Korpi (2000) incorporated a gender/class perspective embracing how institutional configurations in welfare states shape the capabilities of women for employment and economic independence.

Beyond the lack of fit of welfare states within country clusters and the critique of missing dimensions, the fundamental value of the welfare regime paradigm for comparative research has been questioned. Viewed as a static model, this paradigm does not provide analytical space for understanding changes over time or the processes driving cross-national differences in the transformation of welfare systems (Orloff 2009; Korpi et al. 2013; Hobson 2018). Two typologies, relevant to analyses of family policy and applied in various studies described in this book, seek to overcome these limitations: (1) Korpi's approach to different family support systems – dual-earner, dual-carer, market and traditional, and (2) another constructed around systems of support that promote a familialist (traditional family model) or defamilialist earner-carer model.

Defamilialization, a concept first coined by Ruth Lister, has gained traction in studies of comparative family policy with a gender perspective for several reasons. It encompasses not only families with children (work reconciliation policies), but also care of the elderly and other vulnerable groups (Lister 1994). Recent typologies have unpacked the dichotomy of familialism and defamilialism. Leitner (2003) identifies four dimensions in the varieties of implicit/ explicit familialism and defamilialism. Saraceno and Keck's (2010) typology is similar, with five dimensions: direct and indirect kinds of supports for defamilialism through public policies and through the market, direct supports for familialism (through specific policies) and familialism by default (little or no support). Rather than fixed categories of ideal types, Saraceno views them as a continuum, recognizing that some forms of familialism, by default or supported familialism as well as different forms of defamilialization, may be found in all countries. Similarly, Korpi et al. (2013) acknowledge that countries may not fit neatly into their typology of market, dual-earner and traditional family policy orientations.

Alternative Strategies

In response to the cross-currents in the various dimensions of welfare state typologies and the increasing complexity in policies frameworks, scholars have advocated disaggregated policy-centred approaches, unconvinced that typologies which reflect coherent welfare arrangements can be developed, or typologies of single policies even devised. Instead they advocate disaggregated policy-centred approaches (Kasza 2002; Gornick and Meyers 2003; Bannink and Hoogenboom 2007). Heterogeneity in welfare state regime clusters and incongruity within policy domains in welfare states reflect their hybrid natures and the difficulty of assigning them to ideal types (Ciccia 2017). Korpi et al. (2013) classify such hybrid welfare states as contradictory and Saraceno (2016) acknowledges them in her overlapping forms of familialism and defamilialism. Indeed, there is growing recognition that hybrid forms of welfare call for alternative strategies to capture the complexities in policy configurations. Ciccia (2017) argues for fuzzy-set analysis with ideal types that can reveal welfare state complexities and contradictory policy directions.

The fuzzy-set approach is essentially heuristic, with ideal types derived from existing typologies, revealing continuities and discontinuities in policy trajectories.[1] Ciccia's (2017) analysis begins with ideal types based on Nancy Fraser's Universal Male Breadwinner, Universal Caregiver and Caregiver Parity. She then introduces familialist/defamilialist classifications into the analysis. Cases considered to be pure are those that fit into a classification scheme with respect to many dimensions, whereas hybrid cases deviate with regard to one or several of these. This methodological strategy makes us aware that policies can have contradictory goals, and welfare state change may move in different directions across policy domains (Kvist 2007; Da Roit and Weicht 2013; Ciccia 2017). Although this approach seeks to resolve the weakness in assumptions of stability and continuity in regime topologies, it does not provider a dynamic model for analysis of the potential for change, nor does it address shifts in policy frameworks that can exert diverse effects on inequalities between different individuals and groups.

The capability approach provides a conceptual space for assessing both inequalities in agency between individuals and between groups within different policy contexts and the processes shaping the potential for change. In the last section of this chapter, I will elaborate on the capability approach and give examples of how it offers a conceptual framework with which to confront the policy challenges addressed in this book. I present a multi-dimensional model that reveals multiple interactions in capabilities (individual, institutional, organizational, societal and cultural) and opportunities for achievements in wellbeing and gender equality.

In the following section, I focus on the hybrid features of the Baltic and Nordic welfare states, exploring both their cross-currents and commonalities.

THE BALTIC AND NORDIC WELFARE STATES

In focusing on the two sets of Baltic and Nordic welfare states, the editors of this book are stretching the canvas of welfare state research in several ways. These are clusters of states that have not previously been compared by welfare state researchers. The book aims not merely to highlight the differences between these countries, but also to reveal common threads, shaped by trans-national actors (the European Union, or EU, in particular, with its directives, guidelines and discourses). The chapters in the book also show the divergencies within the two clusters. As in much of comparative research on welfare states, typologies are most often used here as heuristic devices to assess the extent to which welfare state policies fit the ideal types in the model, as well as to highlight the lack of coherence within country clusters. For this purpose, Korpi's configurative model (Korpi 2000; Korpi et al. 2013) and the defamilialist/familialist framework (Leitner 2003; Saraceno and Keck 2010) are applied in several studies (see Chapters 2, 5 and 6). This allows for a nuanced analysis of similarities and differences across a broad range of family policies, including benefits and transfers, care services (elderly and childcare) and pension systems.

Unsurprisingly, in comparisons with the Baltic states, the Nordic country cluster is at the far end of the defamilialist continuum, exemplifying the dual-earner/carer model, especially as it comes to the father's involvement in childcare (see Aidukaite and Telisauskaite-Cekanavice 2020, and Chapter 2). From a capability perspective, what I find most intriguing in the comparative and single-case studies are the cross-currents in policy domains and policy aims, as well as the contradictory cases and overlapping tendencies within typologies. I focus on how these are mirrored in complex inequalities through the interactions in class, gender, ethnicities/race and age embedded in different institutional/societal contexts.

Finland is presented as the outlier contradictory case among the Nordic states, providing familialist and supported defamilialist policies existing side by side. The Finnish welfare state exhibits many aspects of the Nordic gender-equality model: a high proportion of women in the labour force, and more working in full-time paid work compared with other Nordic countries; generous parental leaves; involvement of fathers in care; and extensive childcare services. Alongside such defamilialist support, there is familialist support in the form of a flat-rate care allowance of €342.95 per month for one child up to 3 years of age, and a means-tested care supplement up to €183.53 per month. Women overwhelmingly use the long leaves (52 percent after the first year of parental leave), and those with low education and few formal skills are more likely to take the longest leave, for three years (see Chapter 9). As Kuitto and Kuivalainen's (Chapter 9) analysis explains, the Finnish care allowance can not only hinder women's labour force attachment, but also affect wellbeing in later life. A three-year leave reduces the pension accrual rate by approximately one-half, which is reflected in the higher levels of poverty among elderly women. Compared with the other Nordic countries, the Finnish care allowance policy has had an impact on gender equality,[2] impeding men's claims for parental leave. The care allowance delineates Finland as a contradictory case in the Nordic context as well as an exemplar of how family policies have been undergoing hybridization (Duvander and Ellingsæter 2016). The policy remains contested in Finland, within political parties and gender discourse.

Although the geographically connected Baltic countries share historical legacies from the socialist regime era, their family policies nonetheless vary with respect to different combinations of explicit and implicit familialism and supported and default defamilialism. Although immediately after Soviet rule Baltic states proclaimed a 'get women back to families' policy, this was short-lived. By the mid-1990s, both the necessity for two-earner families and the EU recommendations for gender equality guided policy choices. The chapters in this book (Chapters 2 and 6) describe the numerous reforms and counter reforms in Baltic states with respect to policies that lay emphasis on support for a familialist traditional family model or a defamilialist dual-earner model in the following decades.

For example, Aidukaite's comprehensive overview of Baltic states places their various policies and outcomes in the familialist/defamilialist continuum (Chapter 2; see also Javornik 2014). Estonia is categorized as supporting childcare policies associated with the traditional family model, whereas Latvia is an example of default familialism (limited or in direct support of a traditional family model). Since joining the EU, all three countries have adopted relatively generous compensation for parental leave for both men and women, as well as specified paternity leave.

Lithuania is hardest to fit into a specific typology. On the one hand, its familialist policy supports one of the longest paid parental leaves: up to 12 or 24 months, and it can be shared by both parents or even used by grandparents. However, women are the users of the long leaves, given the lack of available childcare services for under-3s. At the same time, discourse and policies encourage gender equality and fathers' involvement through a generous replacement rate of paternity leave during the first year, at 100 percent if the leave is for only a year, but reduced to 70 percent if parents use more than one year and 30 percent in subsequent years. Only a very small proportion of fathers take advantage of their parental leave right to be caregivers.

Understanding these hybrid forms and differences within the Baltic states requires a broader multi-level lens looking beneath the state to regional differences in care services (see Chapter 7), as well as beyond the welfare state and to the impact of European institutions and global forces.

COMMONALITIES AND CONVERGENCES

The growing hybridization of family policy within the Baltic and Nordic clusters not only involves differences, but also commonalities and convergences that have shaped the contours of family policy across European countries (Chapter 1). Some obvious points of convergence have emerged from welfare state retrenchment and the impact of globalizing markets (Bonoli and Natali 2012), as reflected in the increasing levels of insecure and precarious jobs in countries where jobs had previously been protected and secure. The gendered pension gap addressed in several chapters (Chapters 5 and 9) is not only due to the career breaks women take for caregiving, but also to the increasing numbers of women in low-wage, poor-quality service sector jobs, with spells of unemployment and underemployment (Morel 2015; Shire 2015), exacerbated by the economic crisis of 2008 (Hellgren and Serrano 2019).

Undeniably, the EU has played a crucial role in creating common family policy goals among its member states with respect to activating women's labour force, promoting the involvement of fathers in care, and setting targets for childcare services. In the Baltic states, many of these reforms in family policies supporting a dual-earner model were enacted after these countries became members of the EU. Nevertheless, alongside these policies for social investment, the EU has advocated fiscal policies that seek to reduce public spending, and has promoted the marketization of care services for children and the elderly.

In the Baltic states, neither public provision nor markets fill the care deficit for elderly people, who rely on their children and/or other relatives (Chapter 8). In the Nordic countries, private markets for home help for the elderly have increased (Meagher and Szebehely 2013); the main users are middle- and upper-income groups (Hellgren and Hobson 2021). This shift reflects another aspect of greater hybridity in these welfare states. Sweden offers generous tax subsidies (50 percent of the cost), and the numbers of the elderly purchasing these services have risen exponentially (Fahlén et al. 2015). Although basic elderly care is covered (Chapter 10), budget cuts in municipalities based on more limited assessment of their needs for household services have placed a greater burden on working-class families to pick up the slack (Nyberg 2015; Hellgren and Hobson 2021).

Stretching the canvas of welfare state comparison entails engaging with the re-configurations in states, markets and families. The blurring of boundaries between state and market is apparent in various care policy schemes: payments that can be made to relatives who provide care, vouchers that can be used to purchase private services, and private markets subsidized.

Recalling Esping-Andersen's original framework of social politics *against* markets (Esping-Andersen 1985), researchers now refer instead to (social) politics and states *with* markets (Leibfried and Obinger 2000), encapsulated in the concept of welfare markets (Ledoux et al. 2021). Although this concept would appear to be an oxymoron, welfare markets offer an interpretative lens on the penetration of market mechanisms into various policy domains (Bode 2008; Gingrich 2011). Changes in pensions and care services are primary examples of salient challenges in family policy. In the Nordic states, although outsourcing and subsidies for services have not yet displaced existing forms of welfare, these nevertheless signal institutional change that generates inequalities in capability, wellbeing and agency for choice (Hellgren and Hobson 2021).

Pension reform across Europe has been driven by pressures on systems for sustainability, including aging populations and birth rates below replacement levels (Oláh 2015). Baltic and Nordic welfare states show how these forces have resulted in some systemic changes in pensions. Marketization schemes exist in all countries in these clusters, alongside occupational (earnings-related) and basic pensions. There is greater emphasis in the Baltic states on private schemes (Chapter 8) where market mechanisms were introduced in all facets of welfare in the post-socialist period. The Baltic states show the highest risks of relative poverty in old age among EU countries, according to Eurostat (2017)[3] (Chapter 13). In the Nordic states, welfare state change is discernible in growing inequalities that reflect inroads of market schemes, greater emphasis on earning-related pensions and, most importantly, reductions in basic minimum pensions. This process is most pronounced in Sweden, which shows the steepest decline in the minimum pension compared to other Nordic countries (Chapter 10), with higher rates of poverty among the elderly (the risk of relative poverty currently is above the EU average; Eurostat 2017).

Pension reforms also highlight the hybrid nature of welfare state clusters and reflect a more general pattern among European welfare states involving expansion of policies that promote reconciliation of employment and family, alongside retrenchment in unemployment insurance and the state-funded basic pension (Ferragina et al. 2012). In Nordic countries policies for combatting poverty and inequality have shifted emphasis from transfer- to service-based strategies aimed at increasing women's activity in the labour market (Chapter 4). This is less pronounced in the Baltic states, where family support in the form of means-tested benefits for families remains a core component in family policy. However, as Aidukaite and Senkuviene (Chapter 6) maintain, policy experts who compare Sweden and Lithuania agree that the best way to alleviate poverty, and in particular child poverty, is by providing jobs for both parents. The hegemony of the social investment paradigm is manifest across the Baltic and Nordic states.

DIVERSITY: EMPIRICAL AND THEORETICAL CHALLENGES

How are these currents in welfare state change and their intersections shaping complex inequalities in gender, age, class, race and ethnicity? Incorporating such diversity into the analysis of comparative frameworks for welfare state research poses both empirical and conceptual challenges. In their chapter comparing how men and women organize employment and care in the Nordic and Baltic states, Weselowski, Billingsley and Neyer (Chapter 5) under-line the limitations in the Statistics on Income and Living Conditions data, high-quality harmonized data over time, based upon one or two production workers in a family with two children. Since most women work in the service sector, gender bias in this data is unavoidable. More generally, this data does not allow analysis of the effects of various policies on different groups – for example, how ceilings on wage compensation during parental leave can prevent immigrants who lack work experience from taking parental leave, and how the lack of supports for single parents hampers the reconciliation of employment with care (ibid.).

Although single parents are delineated as a vulnerable group with a higher risk of poverty than coupled families (Chapter 4), they are given little attention in the chapters on policy challenges, gender inequality and wellbeing. For the most part, single parents are women, and in the Nordic dual-earner/carer model, which assumes a family with two earners who share care responsibili-ties in an individualized tax and pension system, these women are often poor in both money and time.

At the same time, single mothers are a diverse group and some have good jobs, and through the purchase of tax-subsidized domestic/care services of private markets can gain more time with children and leisure for themselves. However, a recent project in which I have been involved revealed that in Sweden, very few single-mother families took advantage of the tax subsidy (Fahlén et al. 2015). In research on policy studies, single mothers with little education are singled out as a group with weak capabilities (Jaehrling et al. 2015). They tend to have a greater risk of unemployment and often encounter statistical discrimination by employers who assume that they are burdened with care responsibilities (Hobson et al. 2011). An intersectional analysis should encompass consideration of single parents in the development of family support policies in the Baltic and Nordic welfare states, as well as addressing how the shifts in policy orientation toward social investment affect the wellbe-ing of single parents and their capabilities for making changes.

A central question posed in this book concerns which measures actually promote gender equality. From a capability perspective, we need to consider which policy measures and which institutional contexts help ensure inclusive gender equality. Using an intersectional approach, gender scholars have sought to address diversity within gender inequalities (McCall 2005; Choo and Ferree 2010; Collins and Bilge 2016). To advance the conversation on family policy and diversity further, we are obliged to ask: Which policies and which women? (Lister 2009; Hobson 2018).

With respect to migration flows, the Baltic countries are sending countries, and hence their main concern is with out-migration related to sustainability of the welfare state. In Norway and Sweden, immigrants now comprise a significant share of the population, a dramatic increase since 2013 reaching 50,000 and 100,000 asylum seekers, respectively (Chapter 4). Whereas immigrant families were previously conspicuously absent from studies on family policies in the Nordic countries, in recent decades they have become a salient dimension in research on unemployment, fertility and parental leave. They are a heterogeneous group, identified as European and non-European and differentiated into regions in official statistics. Such categorization masks racial/ethnic hierarchies and ignores variations in education, income and wealth. Among the Nordic country cluster, all require forty years of residence in order to receive a full pension, which discriminates against immigrants who arrive at a later age. This requirement calls into question the signature 'universalist' paradigm of the Nordic model.

Immigrant families are noted as a vulnerable group in Hakovirta and Nygård (Chapter 4), as made visible by the surge of migration over the last years, driving the poverty rates up to 19 percent in Sweden and 13 percent in Norway. In the Swedish political discourse, immigrant families are viewed as problematic, failing to adhere to norms of gender equality. Moreover, immigrant women are singled out as taking long parental leaves, which weakens their possibility of integrating into the labour market. The Swedish experts interviewed by Aidukaite and Sevkuviene (Chapter 6) mirror these attitudes, attributing the lower levels of employment of immigrant women to patriarchal familial worldviews. This essentialist (static) view of the influence of cultural differences within the context of parental leave lacks nuance, however, and fails to address the complex inequalities in immigrant women's experience.

In addition to the double burden of combining employment with family faced by women in general, many immigrant women are also often competing for jobs in the care service sector, which is highly gender-segregated and where language skills are essential. In addition, the educational credentials and skills as teachers and nurses, for example, acquired by immigrant women in countries outside the EU are often not recognized (Fahlén and Sánchez-Domínguez 2018). In this context, our own research derived from interviews with domestic workers in Sweden revealed that the National Employment Agency directed immigrant women even with high-level education to jobs in the low-wage service sector.

APPLYING THE CAPABILITY FRAMEWORK

Rather than a specific theory, the capability approach provides a general conceptual framework, an evaluative space, in which agency lies at the core: Sen (1992) asks us to consider not only what persons do but their possibilities for living a life that they see as intrinsically valuable.

The capability approach has been used in assessment or evaluation of policies; for example, as a basis for the United Nations Gender Empowerment Measure (GEM).[4] With respect to family policy, the capability framework has been applied to a range of research on work–life balance (Hobson 2014; Koslowski and Kadar-Satat 2019), childcare services (Yerkes and Javornik 2018) and fertility (Fahlén 2013). In all these studies, agency is intertwined with capability and the opportunities to achieve goals: how policies are implemented and the opportunities they afford for 'real' choice. For example, in their assessment of the potential for policy instruments to facilitate the capability of parents to organize childcare, Yerkes and Javornik (2018) argue that accessibility, affordability, quality and flexibility should all be incorporated, as well as their legal underpinnings, whether they are mandated as a right or not. All of these aspects influence the ability of parents to utilize these policies.

Although policy design clearly matters, as underscored by the chapters in this book, the capability perspective compels us to identify the constraints and opportunities for agency to gain access to benefits and claim rights, as well as the potential for making change. In connection with the aims of this book, addressing the challenges in designing family policies that reduce poverty and promote gender equality, the capability framework stretches the canvas in yet another direction, extending analysis of welfare state research. Its dynamic, multi-dimensional concept of agency, embedded in layers of institutional, cultural and societal context and their interactions, allows for analysis of how individuals and groups situated differently in welfare state policy frameworks influence their possibilities to access policies, as well as their sense of entitlement to claim these.

Policy for parental leave, which has now been the subject of massive research, provides an example of how policy design matters, at least partially, for explaining differences in fathers' use of parental leave. In my own work, I have examined the capability of fathers to exercise their right to parental leave (Hobson and Morgan 2002; Hobson and Fahlén 2009) by employing a multi-dimensional and multi-level framework (Hobson 2018).

We know from previous research (Ferrarini and Duvander 2010) that policy design matters for men's use of parental leave; that is, that low compensation for wage loss and inflexibility constitute barriers. Alternatively, there is general agreement that apportioning some weeks of paternal leave specifically to fathers has increased men's caregiving time with their children (Ray et al. 2010). However, the mandated non-transferable daddy month(s), the 'use it or lose it' policy and the 'daddy quota' (first introduced in the Nordic countries) have exerted the most pronounced impact on the number of men taking parental leave, as well as on the share of the total parental leave. In Sweden and Norway, the pioneers of the daddy quota, men's proportion of the leave has reached 27 percent (Sweden) and 21 percent (Norway)[5] of the total parental leave. Denmark is the counterfactual; fathers' share of the leave declined (Eydal et al. 2015).[6] In Finland, the father's share is only slightly higher than in Denmark (11 percent versus 10 percent), far below those in Sweden and Norway (Nordic Council of Ministers 2018).

In both Norway and Sweden, the daddy quota was introduced as the result of an orchestrated state campaign that was supported by the trade unions (Hobson 2018). The policy discourse framed as 'use it or lose it' was not just an economic incentive for men to claim their right to be caregiving parents, but also bolstered agency and the sense of entitlement to negotiate with recalcitrant employers (Hobson 2014; Brandth and Kvande 2015). Of course, not all fathers are in this enviable position, particularly those without fixed contracts or with precarious jobs. Fathers with the least capability for taking parental leave belong, in general, to vulnerable families, where the father is unemployed and the mother works in a low-wage sector (Hobson et al. 2006). As illustrated in Figure 14.1, the factors that influence the capability for exercising the right to parental leave are multi-dimensional and multi-level, encompassing the individual/family, institutions, policies and the workplace (Haas and Hwang 2009; Den Dulk et al. 2014). Societal dimensions (discourse and the support of unions) are also part of the conversion processes that shape men's agency for caregiving rights and for greater gender equality in the workplace and society. In the Nordic countries, immigrant fathers from countries outside Europe are least likely to take any parental leave at all (Tervola et al. 2017). Potential explanations for this situation include a patriarchal cultural background, maintained in culturally segregated communities. These fathers often experience their masculinity being threatened and a loss of authority in the family when their wives are working outside the home, and where gender equality is the norm and celebrated (Tervola et al. 2017).

Mussino et al. (2019) utilized Swedish register data to reveal a more complex set of interactions associated with why fathers do not claim their entitlement to parental leave. Although cultural norms do play a role, these researchers found that half of the difference in the use of parental leave by native-born

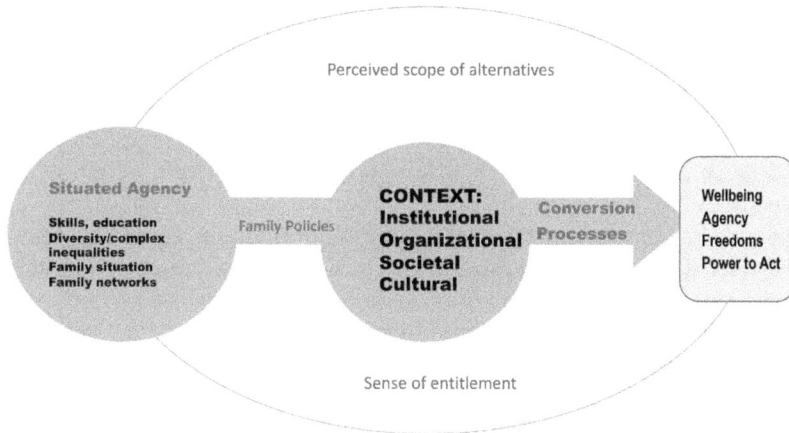

Figure 14.1   Family policies, capabilities and agency: a multi-dimensional model

inhabitants and immigrants could be explained by their employment situation. Moreover, over time this gap narrowed as immigrant fathers gained a more secure position in the labour market. Overall, immigrants in Sweden have constituted a disproportionately high number of those holding precarious jobs (Eurostat 2013), which disadvantages them in the context of parental leave, since the policy requires that access to the higher leave benefit requires consecutive employment to be eligible and compensation is earnings-related (see Chapter 5). This example brings into focus the difficulties in disentangling the complex interactions in capability and agency underlying choices. Are these influences cultural or structural? Other aspects of situated agency can have an effect: lack of family networks, or partner's employability (Hobson 2014). Clearly, the conversion of entitlements into capability and agency (freedoms) is multi-factorial, encompassing the cognitive and experiential, a father's perception of his scope of alternatives and sense of entitlement to claim rights, which are embedded in layers of situated agency, institutional, societal and cultural resources (see Figure 14.1).

The contradictions within the father's leave policy in Lithuania are spelled out by Aidukaite and Senkuviene (Chapter 6). They reveal how complex inequalities within policy design can lead to confounding practices. Since most mothers take more than one year of leave, the second year is reduced to 30 percent. However, the policy allows the parent using the leave to work full-time while receiving 30 percent of their salary. As a consequence, in most cases it is the father who formally takes the leave in the second year of the child's life, while in practice the mother remains at home as the caregiver

(Aidukaite and Telisauskaite-Cekanavice 2020). For low-income households, the parental leave is converted into a family support benefit. This situation, which undercuts the aim of promoting men's caregiving and gender equality, can be explained by gendered norms in both the workplace and larger society. At the same time, this practice also mirrors structural inequalities, the wide gender gap in pay and the high risk of poverty even after social transfers (Eurostat 2020).[7]

In many countries, the effects of a policy reform are subjected to scrutiny only years after the reform was enacted. The model I have developed for this chapter (see Figure 14.1), built upon earlier models in my scholarship, provides leverage for assessing the multi-dimensional aspects and the potential for change. Here, I will describe a recent policy change in the parental leave system in Finland to be put into effect in 2021. Put forward by the new Social Democratic Finnish prime minster, this Finnish policy, which mandates 6.6 months of parental leave each for the mother and father, has been hailed by international media as pathbreaking (Magra 2020). However, the care allowance remains intact, which supports a traditional family model. In fact, this inconsistency is built into the policy framework, which allows fathers to transfer 69 days of their leave to their partner and is approximately the same number of weeks as in the pre-existing paternity leave. Therefore, the question becomes to what extent this policy and associated discourse will activate men's sense of entitlement to claim what is mandated. Although this reform has been championed by the media (societal resources), unions and employers (organizational resources) are lukewarm and have expressed scepticism. Multi-dimensional aspects of situated agency and in the resources available to families will surely come into play, shaping a father's perceptions of his scope of alternatives and sense of entitlement to claim his share of parental leave (see Figure 14.1). The dynamic features of the capability approach (conversion processes) allow for analysis of new actors who enter the scene, as well as of contingencies and changes in political coalitions.

CONCLUSION: TAKING THE CONVERSATION FURTHER

In engaging with the chapters in this book, I have argued for alternative strategies and dynamic frameworks to capture the mutability and variability of welfare state change, as well as the complex inequalities that emerge from these processes.

The comparisons between the Nordic and Baltic countries make visible the hybrid features of welfare states. These reveal the shortcomings of typologies that assume coherence in policy frameworks and path dependencies and a residue of contradictory cases. Other typologies leave us with an infinite number of combinations of implicit, limited and explicit familialism and defamilialism in different policy areas, including childcare, elderly care, parental leaves and old-age pensions. Neither of these approaches provides conceptual space for assessing the dynamics of welfare state change, which can be driven by different processes and contingencies, such as the global economic crisis or a pandemic. More common and less dramatic are changes in policy that result from a shift in political parties in government. Frequent changes in government and reversals of previous policies can affect the seeding of new norms and long-term investment in institutional resources for implementing change, and weaken the sense of entitlement to claim rights.

Stretching the canvas in comparative welfare state research involves conceptual and empirical challenges. At the conceptual level, such expansion requires a focus on both processes and outcomes, on both policy design and the capability to convert policies into agency and change. With respect to the general aims of this book – that is, to address the challenges encountered by welfare states as they attempt to reduce poverty and enhance gender equality – the capability approach is germane. Both gender equality and poverty reduction are values to be achieved in Sen's writing and focal points in the scholarship (Sen 1999; Hobson 2018). In the capability framework, reduction of poverty is operationalized as wellbeing (freedom) (Sen 1992, 1999) and often intertwined with agency (freedom), as is apparent from the discussion above of parental leave and the lack of agency experienced by families with precarious work situations and low wages. More generally, such inequalities are reflected in the low expectations the poor have with regard to the future, and their inability to imagine alternative ways of living (Hobson 2018). Assessment of how effectively welfare states alleviate poverty through social benefits, school lunch vouchers and housing allowances does not reach inequalities in capability and opportunities for agency and choices and the power to act on them.

Inclusivity is a key dimension for assessing how policies work in practice, and social justice is fundamental to the capability approach (Sen 2009). With respect to gender equality, this entails an intersectional perspective, which assumes that gender is a complex variable in policy analysis. This implies examining how policies affect women and men from diverse backgrounds at different stages in life, as well as the diversity in family forms. In a previous study of care/domestic work, I shed light on the widening gap in capability between women that has resulted from the expansion of private markets for services, many of which receive governmental subsidies (Morel 2015; Shire 2015; Hobson 2018). Although such measures increase the capability of some women to reconcile work and family and pursue careers, they are dependent upon other women's labour in a precarious low-waged domestic work sector, mainly migrant women, many of whom are undocumented (Hobson 2018).

Social justice is foundational to the capability approach. Accordingly, the aim, design and implementation of policies should improve the capability of all, and especially those whose capability is weakest. The criteria for assessment are embodied in research questions that scholars applying a capability framework need to address: Which welfare states promote the capability for wellbeing and agency freedoms most effectively? Which specific policies are most inclusive and provide the most opportunity and potential for change? These conceptual tools undergird the multi-dimensional and dynamic capability framework. This approach does not exclude the creation of clusters of countries or paradigmatic examples, but requires their continuous updating and re-assessment in light of welfare state change.

NOTES

1. Fuzzy-set analyses categorize cases on the basis of theoretical concepts, aggregating them into sets that fit into various configurations (or ideal types) of social policy (Kvist 2007; Ciccia 2017).
2. Sweden discontinued the care allowance after a few years, after a change in government. In Norway, the benefit is much lower than in Finland, with fewer women using it, and with numbers decreasing over time (Duvander and Ellingsæter 2016).
3. Estonia shows the highest risk of poverty for pensioners, reaching 46 percent (Eurostat Statistics 2020).
4. https://archive.unescwa.org/gender-empowerment-measure.
5. Statistics are from Nordic Council of Ministers (2018). In Iceland fathers take 30 percent of the leave, but the overall length of leave is shorter, so this translates into fewer days of leave.
6. The new policy design in the Finnish parental leave system, passed in December 2020 to take effect in 2021, aims to increase men's use of the leave.
7. Eurostat (2020) shows that the Baltic countries have some of the highest risks for poverty, even when social transfers are taken into account.

REFERENCES

Aidukaite, J., and D. Telisauskaite-Cekanavice (2020), 'The Father's Role in Child Care: Parental Leave Policies in Lithuania and Sweden', *Social Inclusion*, 8 (4), 81–91.

Anttonen, A., and J. Sipilä (1996), 'European Social Care Services: Is it Possible to Identify Models?', *Journal of European Social Policy*, 6 (2), 87–100.

Bannink, D., and M. Hoogenboom (2007), 'Hidden Change: Disaggregation of Welfare State Regimes for Greater Insight into Welfare State Change', *Journal of European Social Policy*, 17 (1), 19–32.

Bode, I. (2008), *The Culture of Welfare Markets*, New York, NY: Routledge.

Bonoli, G., and D. Natali (eds) (2012), *The Politics of the New Welfare State*, Oxford: Oxford University Press.

Brandth, B., and E. Kvande (2015), 'Fathers and Flexible Leave', *Community, Work and Family*, 30 (2), 275–290.

Choo, H. W., and M. M. Ferree (2010), 'Practicing Intersectionality in Sociological Research: A Critical Analysis of Inclusions, Interactions, and Institutions in the Study of Inequalities', *Sociological Theory*, 8 (2), 129–149.

Ciccia, R. (2017), 'A Two-Step Approach for the Analysis of Hybrids in Comparative Social Policy Analysis: A Nuanced Typology of Childcare between Policies and Regimes', *Qual Quant*, 51 (8), 2761–2780.

Collins, P. H., and S. Bilge (2016), *Intersectionality*, Cambridge: Polity.

Da Roit, B., and B. Weicht (2013), 'Migrant Care Work and Care, Migration and Employment Regimes: A Fuzzy-Set Analysis', *Journal of European Social Policy*, 23 (5), 469–486.

Den Dulk, L., S. Groenverld and B. Peper (2014), 'Workplace, Work–Life Balance Support from a Capabilities Perspective', in B. Hobson (ed.), *Worklife Balance: The Agency and Capabilities Gap*, Oxford: Oxford University Press, pp. 153–173.

Duvander, A.-Z., and A. L. Ellingsæter (2016), 'Cash for Childcare Schemes in the Nordic Welfare States: Diverse Paths, Diverse Outcomes', *European Societies*, 18 (1), 70–90.

Esping-Andersen, G. (1985), *Politics against Markets: The Social Democratic Road to Power*, Princeton, NJ: Princeton University Press.

Esping-Andersen, G. (1990), *The Three Worlds of Welfare Capitalism*, Cambridge: Polity Press.

Eurostat (2013), 'Data Explorer, Temporary Employees as Percentage of the Total Number of Employees, by Sex, Age and Country of Birth', accessed November 2013 at http://appsso.eurostat.ec.europa.eu/nui/show.do?dataset=yth_empl_050& lang=en.

Eurostat (2017), 'At Risk of Poverty Rate for Pensioners', accessed 15 January 2021 at https://europa.eu/eurostat/web/products-eurostat-news/-/DDN-20190115-1.

Eurostat (2020), 'Income Poverty Statistics Explained', accessed 8 January 2021 at https://ec.europa.eu/eurostat/statistics-explained/pdfscache/1156.pdf).

Eydal, G. B., I. V. Gíslason, T. Rostgaard, T., B. Brandth, A.-Z. Duvander and J. Lammi-Taskula (2015), 'Trends in Parental Leave in the Nordic Countries: Has the Forward March of Gender Equality Halted?', *Community, Work & Family*, 18 (2), 167–181.

Fahlén, S. (2013), 'Capabilities and Childbearing Intentions in Europe: The Association between Work–Family Reconciliation Policies, Economic Uncertainties and Women's Fertility', *European Societies*, 15 (5), 639–662.

Fahlén, S., B. Hobson and M. Sánchez-Domínguez (2015), 'Outsourcing the Domestic: How Private Care/Domestic Workers Are Widening the Gap in Inequalities among Households', paper presented at the RC 19 Conference, 25–27 August, Bath.

Fahlén, S., and M. Sánchez-Domínguez (2018), 'Changing Sector? Social Mobility among Female Migrants in Care and Cleaning Sector in Spain and Sweden', *Migration Studies*, 6 (3), 367–399.

Ferragina, E., M. Seeleib-Kaiser and M. Tomlinson (2012), 'Unemployment Protection and Family Policy at the Turn of the 21st Century: A Dynamic Approach to Welfare Regime Theory', *Social Policy Administration*, 47 (2), 783–805.

Ferrarini, T., and A.-Z. Duvander (2010), 'Earner-Carer Model at the Crossroads: Reforms and Outcomes of Sweden's Family Policy in Comparative Perspective', *International Journal of Health Services*, 40 (3), 373–398.

Gingrich, J. (2011), *Making Markets in the Welfare State: The Politics of Varying Market Reforms*, Cambridge: Cambridge University Press.

Gornick, J., and M. Meyers (2003), *Families that Work: Policies for Reconciling Parenthood and Employment*, New York, NY: Russell Sage Foundation.

Haas, L., and P. Hwang (2009), 'Is Fatherhood Becoming More Visible at Work? Trends in Corporate Support for Fathers Taking Parental Leave in Sweden', *Fathering*, 7 (3), 303–321.

Hellgren, Z., and B. Hobson (2021), 'Welfare Markets and Household Services: Market Dynamics and Mechanisms in Two Different Institutional Contexts – Spain and Sweden', in C. Ledoux, K. Shire and F. van Hooren (eds), *The Dynamics of Welfare Markets: Private Pensions and Domestic/Care Services in Europe*, London: Palgrave Macmillan, pp. 103–129.

Hellgren, Z., and I. Serrano (2019), 'Financial Crisis and Migrant Domestic Workers in Spain: Employment Opportunities and Conditions during the Great Recession', *International Migration Review*, 53 (4), 1209–1229.

Hobson, B. (2004), 'Solo Mothers, Policy Regimes, and the Logics of Gender', in D. Sainsbury (ed.), *Gendering Welfare States*, London: SAGE, pp. 170–187.

Hobson, B. (ed.) (2014), *Worklife Balance: The Agency and Capabilities Gap*, Oxford: Oxford University Press.

Hobson, B. (2018), 'Gendered Dimensions and Capabilities: Opportunities, Dilemmas and Challenges', *Critical Sociology*, 44 (6), 883–898.

Hobson, B., L. Carlsson, S. Fahlén and E. Anderberg (2011), 'Country Report on Labour Market Participation and Socio-Economic Situation of Lone Parents in Sweden', report commissioned by Institut Arbeit und Qualifikation, University of Duisburg-Essen, accessed October 2020 at www.iaq.uni-due.de/aktuell/veroeff/2011/alleinerziehende01.pdf.

Hobson, B., A.-Z. Duvander and K. Halldén (2006), 'Men and Women's Agency and Capabilities to Create a Worklife Balance in Diverse and Changing Institutional Contexts', in J. Lewis (ed.), *Children, Changing Families and Welfare States*, Cheltenham, UK and Northampton, MA, USA: Edward Elgar Publishing, pp. 267–297.

Hobson, B., and S. Fahlén (2009), 'Two Scenarios for European Fathers: Adversity and Risk? Opportunities and Agency for a Work Family Balance', *Annals of the American Academy of Political and Social Science*, 624 (1), 214–233.

Hobson, B., and D. Morgan (2002), 'Introduction: Making Men into Fathers', in B. Hobson (ed.), *Making Men into Fathers*, Cambridge: Cambridge University Press, pp. 1–24.

Jaehrling, K., T. Kalina and L. Mesaros (2015), 'A Paradox of Activation Strategies: Why Increasing Labour Market Participation among Single Mothers Failed to Bring Down Poverty Rates', *Social Politics*, 22 (1), 86–110.

Javornik, J. (2014), 'Measuring State De-Familialism: Contesting Post-Socialist Exceptionalism', *Journal of European Social Policy*, 24 (3), 240–257.

Kasza, G. J. (2002), 'The Illusion of Welfare Regimes', *Journal of Social Policy*, 31 (2), 271–287.

Kilkey, M., and J. Bradshaw (1999), 'Lone Mothers, Economic Well-Being and Policies', in D. Sainsbury (ed.), *Gender and Welfare State Regimes*, New York, NY: Oxford University Press, pp. 147–184.

Korpi, W. (2000), 'Faces of Inequality: Gender, Class, and Patterns of Inequalities in Different Types of Welfare States', *Social Politics: International Studies in Gender, State and Society*, 7 (2), 127–191.

Koslowski, A., and G. Kadar-Satat (2019), 'Fathers at Work: Explaining the Gaps between Entitlement to Leave Policies and Uptake', *Community, Work & Family*, 22 (2), 129–145.

Korpi, W., T. Ferrarini and S. England (2013), 'Women's Opportunities under Different Policy Constellations: Gender, Class and Inequality Trade-Offs in Western Societies Re-Examined', *Social Politics*, 20 (1), 1–40.

Kvist, J. (2007), 'Fuzzy Set Ideal Type Analysis', *Journal of Business Research*, 60 (5), 474–481.

Ledoux, C., K. Shire and F. van Horeen (2021), *The Dynamics of Welfare Markets: Private Pensions and Domestic/Care Services in Europe*, London: Palgrave Macmillan.

Leibfried, S., and H. Obinger (2000), 'Welfare State Futures: An Introduction', *European Review*, 8 (3), 277–289.

Leitner, S. (2003), 'Varieties of Familialism: The Caring Function of the Family in Comparative Perspective', *European Societies*, 5 (4), 353–375.

Lewis, J. (1992), 'Gender and the Development of Welfare Regimes', *Journal of European Social Policy*, 2 (3), 159–173.

Lister, R. (1994), '"She Has Other Duties": Women, Citizenship and Social Security', in S. Baldwin and J. Falkingham (eds), *Social Security and Social Change: New Challenges to the Beveridge Model*, London: Harvester Wheatsheaf, pp. 31–44.

Lister, R. (2009), 'A Nordic Nirvana? Gender, Citizenship, and Social Justice in the Nordic Welfare States', *Social Politics: International Studies in Gender, State & Society*, 16 (2), 242–227.

Magra, I. (2020), 'Finland Plans to Give Dads Same Parental Leave as Moms', *New York Times*, 6 February, accessed 8 February 2021 at www.nytimes.com/2020/02/06/world/europe/finland-parental-leave-equality.html.

McCall, L. (2005), 'The Complexity of Intersectionality,' *Signs*, 30 (3), 1771–1800.

Meagher, G., and M. Szebehely (2013), *Marketization in Nordic Eldercare: A Research Report on Legislation, Oversight and Consequences*, Stockholm Studies of Social Work, 30, accessed 12 February 2021 at www.diva-portal.org/smash/get/diva2:667185/FULLTEXT01.pdf.

Morel, N. (2015), 'Servants for the Knowledge-Based Economy? The Political Economy of Domestic Services in Europe', *Social Politics*, 22 (2), 170–192.

Mussino, E., J. Tervola and A.-Z. Duvander (2019), 'Decomposing the Determinants of Fathers' Parental Leave Use: Evidence from Migration between Finland and Sweden', *Journal of European Social Policy*, 29 (2), 197–212.

Nordic Council of Ministers (2018), *Shared and Paid Parental Leave: The Nordic Gender Effect at Work*, accessed 9 February 2021 at https://nikk.no/wp-content/uploads/2019/11/2018-Shared-and-paid-parental-leave.pdf.

Nyberg, A. (2015), 'The Swedish RUT Reduction: Subsidy of Formal Employment or High-Income Earner's Leisure Time', in C. Carbonnier and N. Morel (eds), *The Political Economy of Household Services*, Basingstoke: Palgrave Macmillan, pp. 221–241.

Oláh, L. Sz. (2015), 'Changing Families in the European Union: Trends and Policy Implications', Families and Societies, Working Paper 44, accessed October 2020 at www.familiesandsocieties.eu/wp-content/uploads/2015/09/WP44Olah2015.pdf.

Orloff, A. S. (2009), 'Gendering the Comparative Analysis of Welfare States: An Unfinished Agenda', *Sociological Theory*, 27 (3), 317–343.

Ray, R., J. C. Gornick and J. Schmitt (2010), 'Who Cares? Assessing Generosity and Gender Equality in Parental Leave Policy Designs in 21 Countries', *Journal of European Social Policy*, 20 (3), 196–216.

Saraceno, C. (2016), 'Varieties of Familialism: Comparing Four Southern European and East Asian Welfare Regimes', *Journal of European Social Policy*, 26 (4), 314–326.

Saraceno, C., and W. Keck (2010), 'Can We Identify Intergenerational Policy Regimes in Europe?', *Journal of European Societies*, 12 (5), 675–696.

Sen, A. (1992), *Inequality Reexamined*, Cambridge, MA: Harvard University Press.

Sen, A. (1999), *Development as Freedom*, Oxford: Oxford University Press.

Sen, A. (2009), *The Idea of Justice*, London: Penguin.

Shire, K. (2015), 'Family Supports and Insecure Work: The Politics of Household Service Employment in Conservative Welfare Regimes', *Social Politics*, 22 (2), 193–219.

Tervola, J., A.-Z. Duvander and E. Mussino (2017), 'Promoting Parental Leave for Immigrant Fathers: What Role Does Policy Play?', *Social Politics*, 24 (3), 269–297.

Yerkes, A. M., and J. Javornik (2018), 'Creating Capabilities: Childcare Policies in Comparative Perspective', *Journal of European Social Policy*, 29 (4), 529–544.

Index